MODERN C++ AND WINDOWS STORE APPS

Sridhar Poduri

Dedicated to my grandfather

Late SriRama Murthy Poduri

CONTENTS AT A GLANCE

PROLOGUE

THE NEW WINDOWS 8 APPS.. 1

THE NEW NATIVE API 1

WHAT IS A WINDOWS 8 APP? 2

Fast and Fluid 2

Touch first experience 2

A new Application Model 2

Native XAML framework 5

Declarative Application Capabilities... 8

App Acquisition Process.. 9

Installation and Uninstallation Process 9

Sandboxed AppContainer 10

AppState.. 11

Process Lifecycle Management 12

Integration points with the Operating System 12

QUICK WALKTHROUGH OF A WINDOWS 8 APP 19

A Windows programming digest 19

Anatomy of our application... 20

WHERE ARE WE AND WHAT'S NEXT? 23

INTRODUCTION TO MODERN C++ 24

HELLO MODERN C++ 24

Auto type inference 25

Lambdas 26

Range 'for' 32

The new smart pointers.. 33

MOVE SEMANTICS 35

Rvalue references 36

WELCOME TO THE COMPONENT EXTENSIONS 39

C++ /CX, WINDOWS RUNTIME AND ISO-C++ 39

Hello World in C++ /CX 41

The /ZW compiler option.. 42

THE C++ /CX TYPE SYSTEM 43

String Conversions 81

ASYNCHRONOUS PROGRAMMING IN C++ /CX 83

CONCEPTS TO REMEMBER WHILE BUILDING WINRT COMPONENTS 85

BUILDING A WINRT COMPONENT USING C++ /CX 87

Create the C++ /CX component Project 87

Adding an activatable class to the component *87*

Create a JavaScript client app *88*

Adding async operations in C++ components *88*

BUILDING A WINRT COMPONENT USING C++ /CX AND ISO-C++ **99**

Walkthrough re-factoring a standard collection *99*

A PEEK INSIDE THE MAGIC OF C++ /CX **104**

GUIDANCE ON THE USE OF C++ /CX **110**

WHERE ARE WE AND WHAT'S NEXT? **111**

XAML IN WINDOWS 8 AND C++ /CX **112**

INTRODUCTION TO XAML **112**

HELLO WORLD WITH XAML AND C++ /CX **113**

Compiling XAML and generating C++ code *116*

BASIC XAML SYNTAX **119**

Elements and Attributes *119*

USING PANELS TO LAYOUT UX **126**

Canvas *126*

StackPanel *128*

Grid *129*

BASIC XAML CONTROLS **130**

Transformations *134*

Styling XAML controls *135*

WINDOWS 8 SIGNATURE XAML CONTROLS **140**

Virtualization Support in ListView and GridView controls *141*

HANDLING EVENTS **150**

Click Events *150*

Tapped Events *150*

Pointer Events *151*

Manipulation Events *151*

MARKUP EXTENSIONS **151**

StaticResource Markup Extension *152*

TemplateBinding Markup Extension *153*

DATA BINDING **153**

How to implement Binding in C++ /CX *153*

Binding Modes *154*

Data Templates *154*

Data Binding in C++ /CX *155*

Data Binding with existing C++ code *159*

BINDING TO A DATA MODEL **160**

BUILDING A XAML CUSTOM CONTROL **160**

Creating a User Control *161*

Creating a Basic Custom Control *163*

Customizing the control templates..*166*

USING ANIMATIONS IN XAML CONTROLS **168**

Transition animations..*168*

Theme animations...*169*

WHERE ARE WE AND WHAT'S NEXT **170**

C++ /CX, XAML AND DIRECTX – BETTER TOGETHER **171**

INTRODUCTION TO XAML + DIRECTX **171**

SURFACEIMAGESOURCE **173**

Creating a XAML + DX App to display images using Windows Imaging Component (WIC) *174*

VIRTUALSURFACEIMAGESOURCE **178**

XAML + DX Apps using VSiS – The Magazine App *179*

DESIGN CONSIDERATIONS WHEN USING SIS AND VSIS **191**

SWAPCHAINBACKGROUNDPANEL..**192**

THE DRAWIT APPLICATION – C++, XAML AND DIRECTX **192**

Creating the Basic Application *193*

Adding DirectX support *204*

Adding Input events..*212*

Adding Ink support *213*

Supporting Save..*216*

Integration with the Share charm *218*

WHERE ARE WE AND WHAT'S NEXT **219**

ADVANCED GPGPU PROGRAMMING **221**

INTRODUCTION **221**

Changes in GPU architectures *222*

Programming the GPU *223*

THE C++ AMP LIBRARY...**225**

C++ AMP Concepts *225*

COPYING DATA BETWEEN CPU AND GPU **233**

USING TILES IN C++ AMP **233**

The tiled_extent and the tiled_index classes..*234*

The tile_static and the tile_barrier classes...*236*

Tile Synchronization *236*

DEBUGGING C++ AMP APPLICATIONS..**238**

Debugging the GPU code *238*

DEVELOPING WINDOWS STORE APPS USING C++ AMP AND XAML **244**

Bitonic Sort case study *244*

Sample 2D Triangle Rotation as a XAML App...*248*

THE IMAGEEFFECTS APPLICATION **252**

Prerequisites...*252*

Running the sample *253*

Load image to a texture 255
Creating an accelerator_view from an ID3D11Device object 255
The C++AMP Compute Engine class 256
Interop between C++AMP and DirectX textures 262
The Output 265
WHERE ARE WE AND WHAT'S NEXT 265

UNDER THE COVERS 267

PLAYING BY THE RULES OF THE WINDOWS RUNTIME 267
Versioning Support in the Windows Runtime 268
Type System Overview 268
Some Standard Patterns in WinRT 278
INTRODUCTION TO THE WINDOWS RUNTIME LIBRARY 280
Exploring the Windows Runtime Library 281
HELLO WORLD XAML APP USING WINDOWS RUNTIME LIBRARY 283
Creating the XAML UI 283
Creating the Application class 287
Building the package 295
Creating a signing certificate 297
USING THE WINDOWS RUNTIME LIBRARY IN WINDOWS STORE APPS 300
Authoring a Simple WinRT component using WRL 300
Creating a C# client application to call into the WRL component 303
WHERE ARE WE AND WHAT'S NEXT 305

UNIT TESTING WINDOWS 8 C++ APPS 307

INTRODUCTION 307
UNIT TESTING NATIVE CODE 307
Create a Win32 DLL 307
Adding unit tests for a Win32 DLL 309
Test driven development with Test Explorer 310
ADDING UNIT TESTS FOR EXISTING C++ APPLICATIONS 319
Testing a static library 320
Refer exported functions from test project 320
Linking tests to object files 320
Add unit tests to an existing project 321
UNIT TESTS FOR WINDOWS STORE APPS 322
Developing a WinRT component using WRL 322
Unit testing the WinRT component 326
Developing a WinRT component using C++ /CX 331
Unit testing the C++ /CX based WinRT component 332
WHERE ARE WE AND WHAT'S NEXT 336

DEBUGGING WINDOWS STORE APPS 337

INTRODUCTION 337
LOCAL DEBUGGING 337
   Launch the debugger on the local machine.. 338
DEBUGGING IN THE SIMULATOR 339
   Launch the Simulator... 339
REMOTE DEBUGGING WINDOWS STORE APPS 341
DEBUGGING PLM EVENTS 343
   Test Suspend and Resume events.. 343
   Debugging background tasks 344
WHERE ARE WE AND WHAT'S NEXT 345

PERFORMANCE TIPS FOR XAML APPS 346

INTRODUCTION 346
REMAINING RESPONSIVE 347
   Never block the UI thread.. 347
   Async, async and async 347
   Do not invalidate UI... 348
   Checking the Frame rate counter 348
ENSURING FLUID ANIMATIONS 348
FAST APP ACTIVATION... 348
   Improving an app's startup performance... 349
APPLICATION LIFETIMES 350
OPTIMIZING DATA 351
   UI Virtualization 351
   Data Virtualization 352
   Item templates 352
   Item template Selectors 352
MEDIA PACKAGING INTO RESOURCES 353
WHERE ARE WE AND WHAT'S NEXT 353

INTRODUCTION TO WINDOWS AZURE MOBILE SERVICES 355

INTRODUCTION 355
GETTING STARTED WITH WINDOWS STORE APPS AND WINDOWS AZURE MOBILE SERVICES 355
   Before you begin 355
CREATING A SIMPLE WINDOWS STORE APP WITH WINDOWS AZURE MOBILE SERVICES 356
SUPPORTING PUSH NOTIFICATIONS USING WINDOWS AZURE MOBILE SERVICES 365
   Register your app 365
   Add push notifications... 370
   Update the insert script... 372
   Testing your app 373
WHERE ARE WE AND WHAT'S NEXT 374

A SNEAK PREVIEW OF WINDOWS PHONE 8.0 SHARED CODE 375

INTRODUCTION 375

THE VARIOUS API SETS IN WINDOWS PHONE 8 375

The .Net API for Windows Phone 8 376

The Windows Phone Runtime API 376

Win32 and COM API...376

MODIFYING THE TRIANGLERENDERER APP FOR WINDOWS PHONE 8 377

Before you begin 377

Creating the Windows Phone 8.0 app using Direct3D and C++.................................377

Creating the Windows Phone 8 app using C# and C++ component 387

WHERE ARE WE AND WHAT'S NEXT...389

EPILOGUE..390

Prologue

Something interesting happened on a cold and rainy day in Redmond. I was having lunch with two dear colleagues and friends, Ale Contenti and Vikas Bhatia, both of whom were working on the Visual C++ team. The lunch discussions were around a range of topics: the new C++11 standard, the C++ renaissance in the industry and more importantly the elephant in the room: Windows 8. Windows 8 is a once in a generational shift in terms of both the user interface and the developer platform that powers the UX and the application development story.

I was thinking of beginning to blog about the Windows Runtime and the C++ "projections" that Visual C++ was building. These "projections" would later come to be known as the "Component Extensions" or simply "/CX" which is what this book is all about. These extensions to the ISO-C++ programming language allow you, as a developer, to write clean and efficient code for the Windows Runtime, using the C++ programming language. Both Vikas and Ale suggested that I should contribute to the C++ community by writing a book, especially focused on areas where a developer could mix DirectX code along with the XAML framework that was to debut in Windows 8. Their strong opinion stemmed from the fact that I was a program manager on the Reader team. The Reader app was amongst the first C++/XAML app to be built on the Windows Runtime platform and we were working very closely with the Windows Runtime and XAML teams. I agreed to think up the suggestion to contribute to a book. Although I was excited about the idea, I was also very apprehensive about undertaking the endeavor. Like all normal humans, I delayed taking a decision before deciding to take the plunge and said yes.

Windows 8 is a generational shift in computing. It also comes at a time when a renaissance of sorts is sweeping across the industry and C++ is being used more than ever before. True to the times of change, Windows 8 is brimming with amazing technology for the native C++ developer. You need to look no further than the entire re-imagination of Windows 8. Windows 8 contains native code all the way from the chipset to the user experience layer. And the time was right to begin narrating our story.

It is the story of an amazing set of people coming together to design and build what I passionately believe is a very advanced and beautiful piece of software. While the book contains my name as an author, it is the designers, developers, testers and program managers across different feature teams in Windows and other divisions of Microsoft who made this software possible. I cannot name each and every one of them but thank them for creating Windows 8.

This book is all about the new set of technologies that make up the dizzying cocktail that is Windows 8. This book is not an encyclopedia of all these technologies that make up Windows 8. Instead, I have chosen to focus on a small set of topics to discuss. Mastering these topics will help you build apps for the Windows Runtime and upload them to the Windows Store. Learning the fundamentals also helps you build apps using WinRT APIs that were not discussed in this book. The WinRT APIs are very similar, not just in naming convention, but how they behave too. Learn to use a few WinRT APIs and you can easily translate those skills to consuming the other WinRT APIs.

Who Should Read This Book

This book is targeted for the C++ developer who wants to learn about the internals of the new platform. C++ developers who intend to bring forth their existing code base to the Windows Runtime platform will benefit from this book too. I have consciously avoided discussing patterns like the Model-View-ViewModel (MVVM) and the like in the book as patterns can be learnt and customized for specific needs of each application. Developers using languages such as Javascript or C# would benefit from the material presented in this book too as it will help them when building WinRT components using C++.

Assumptions

This book expects that you have at least a good understanding of application development using the C++ programming language and object-oriented programming concepts. Although the primary focus of this book is to explain the concepts of Windows 8 Application development using C++, this book includes a small set of examples in C# and Javascript. The majority of included samples are in C++.   In addition, I would recommend *C++AMP* by Ade Miller and Kate Gregory (Microsoft Press, 2012) as an excellent in-depth book for the C++AMP library.

With a heavy focus on developing Windows 8 applications using XAML, you should be fairly conversant with XAML. Programming Windows 6th Ed by Charles Petzold (Microsoft Press, 2013) is a great book to bootstrap you with XAML concepts.

Who Should Not Read This Book

If you are looking at step-by-step tutorials or walkthroughs to begin developing Windows 8 Apps using C++, then this book is not for you. The book is targeted at intermediate to advanced C++ developers who can easily benefit from the wide range of native technologies being discussed and incorporate them into their own apps. In addition, you should atleast be familiar with DirectX or related graphics technology concepts to obtain the full benefit out of the book. I do not cover DirectX API basics in the book.

Organization of This Book

This book is divided into eleven chapters, each of which focuses on a different technology that ship with Windows 8. Chapter 1 begins with an Introduction to Windows 8 Apps. It contains a high level introduction to the new application model and the native API. The chapter ends by building a simple DirectX app that demonstrates how easy it is to build Windows Store apps using modern C++.

Chapter 2 introduces you to some of the prominent C++11 concepts, such as lambdas, auto type deduction and shared_ptrs. The next section of the chapter introduces C++ /CX and discusses the type system in C++ /CX and how you can use the extensions to develop apps. It also discusses how to build components that can be shared across other WinRT languages like Javascript, C# or VB.net.

Chapter 3 introduces the XAML framework explaining the core concepts and illustrating how to develop XAML applications using C++ /CX.

Chapter 4 introduces the seamless integration story of XAML and DirectX. The excellent integration points are explained via an application walkthrough that allows you to draw on screen, using either touch or mouse.

Chapter 5 introduces the C++AMP library for advanced GPGPU programming. Integration of C++AMP is demonstrated by developing an image effects sample application.

Chapter 6 provides a deep dive into the Windows Runtime and its type system. We begin with a walkthrough on building a "Hello World" XAML application using Windows Runtime Library (WRL). While there is a segment of developers who prefer to use WRL for building Windows Store apps, this tutorial also serves as an excellent reminder as to what awaits those intending to use WRL for such purpose. This tutorial demonstrates the entire gamut of low-level COM programming, using a makefile for building the code and packaging the binaries and assets into the appx package.

Chapter 7 introduces "Unit testing native apps". The native unit testing framework is new to Visual Studio 2012 and allows you to write unit tests in C++ for your C++ code.

Chapter 8 contains useful information on debugging Windows Store apps using Visual Studio 2012.

Chapter 9 contains Performance tips for developing XAML applications using C++.

Chapter 10 contains an introduction to enabling support for Windows Azure Mobile Services in your C++ apps. In a cloud connected world of applications, the appendix focuses on how to consume Azure Services in C++ apps.

Chapter 11 contains information on sharing code between Windows 8 and Windows Phone 8. Sharing code between the two platforms enables you to take advantage of having common code and port your applications between the two platforms.

Finding Your Best Starting Point in This Book

The different sections of *Modern C++ and Windows Store apps* cover a wide range of technologies debuting with Windows 8. Depending on your needs and your existing understanding of the Windows Runtime platform, you may wish to focus on specific areas of the book. Use the following table to determine how best to proceed through the book.

If you are	Follow these steps
New to Windows and an existing C++ developer looking to learn about developing Windows Store apps	Begin with Chapter 1 and proceed to 2 and 3.
Want to familiarize yourself with modern C++11 concepts	Begin with Chapter 2

and understand C++ /CX	
Familiar with Windows Runtime and C++ but looking to learn about XAML	Briefly skim Chapters 1 and 2 if you need a refresh on the core concepts. Focus on Chapter 3 where XAML is introduced and learn to build apps using XAML and C++.
Familiar with DirectX technologies and want to build Windows Store apps	Begin with Chapter 3 where XAML is introduced and then move to Chapter 4
Familiar with C++ and XAML and want to add DirectX support in Windows Store apps	Begin with Chapter 4
Interested in the C++AMP library and GPGPU programming	Read chapter 5 for a brief introduction of C++AMP and how to integrate C++AMP in your Windows 8 app.
Interested in re-using existing C++ code and building Windows Runtime Components	Read the chapters 2, 3 and 4.
Interested in understanding the internals of the Windows Runtime and develop apps using WRL	Read chapter 1 and then proceed directly to chapter 6.
Interesting in learning about the unit testing capabilities in Visual Studio 2012	Read the Chapter 7
Want help with Debugging Windows Store apps	Read the Chapter 8
Want performance tips developing XAML apps using C++	Read the Chapter 9
Want to add Windows Azure Mobile Services support in C++ apps	Read the Chapter 10
Interesting in sharing code between Windows 8 and Windows Pone 8	Read the Chapter 11
Want to understand the C++ renaissance on the Microsoft platform?	Read the entire book ☺

Most of the book's chapters include hands-on samples that let you try out the concepts just learned. No matter which sections you choose to focus on, be sure to download and install the sample applications on your system.

Conventions and Features in This Book

This book presents information using conventions designed to make the information readable and easy to follow.

- In most cases, the book includes code snippets for C++ programmers.

- Boxed elements with labels such as "Note" provide additional information or alternative methods for completing a step successfully.

System Requirements

You will need the following hardware and software to complete the practice exercises in this book:

- A computer with Windows 8 installed.

- Visual Studio 2012 Express Edition or higher

- Computer that has a 1.6GHz or faster processor (2GHz recommended)

- 3.5GB of available hard disk space

- DirectX 11 capable video card running at 1366 x 768 or higher-resolution display. This is especially needed for the chapter discussing the C++AMP library.

- DVD-ROM drive (if installing Visual Studio from DVD)

- Internet connection to download software or chapter examples.

- A computer with Windows 8 RT installed, preferably the Microsoft Surface RT to test the ARM version of your apps.

Code Samples

Most of the chapters in this book include exercises that let you interactively try out new material learned in the main text. All sample projects can be downloaded from the following page:

http://sridharpoduri.com/downloads/

Installing the Code Samples

Follow these steps to install the code samples on your computer so that you can use them with the exercises in this book.

- Unzip the 9780989020800.zip file that you downloaded from the book's website (name a specific directory along with directions to create it, if necessary).

- You are free to use the samples as you wish. I do not, however, provide any warranty nor should you hold me responsible for any loss or damage arising from improper usage of the samples or accompanying code. The code is provided "as-is" and provides no warranties or rights.

Using the Code Samples

To walkthrough a sample, access the appropriate chapter folder in the samples folder, and open the project file. If your system is configured to display file extensions, Visual C++ project files use a .vcxproj extension; C# project files use .csproj as the file extension.

Acknowledgments

The immense dedication and passion of the entire Windows team has simply been amazing. This was my first Windows release and I was fortunate to witness from close quarters the entire action of researching competitive platforms, writing functional specifications, developing code, testing, managing the daily builds of Windows, and documenting the APIs with all the details that go along with the design philosophy behind the APIs themselves. I consider myself extremely lucky to be in the think of action as the XAML platform was being developed and to be part of a team that was writing the first Windows Store app on top of XAML. It was a first class experience that I could not trade for anything else.

A lot of folks contributed towards the making of this book. Thanks then to the following folks, in no particular order. If I have missed anyone it is entirely my mistake and I apologize for the same. To Mahesh Prakriya, Martyn Lovell and their respective teams for building the Windows Runtime, to Ashish Shetty, Sujal Parekh, Eduardo Leal-Tostado and their teams for bringing XAML into the native world and Herb Sutter and the entire Visual C++ team for building the awesome set of native technologies that ship along with Windows 8. Thanks to Alessandro Contenti and Vikas Bhatia for prodding me to get started with the book and my blog. I would like to thank my manager, Suryanarayana Shastri for encouraging me to undertake this endeavor. Thanks also go out to the following folks who took time out to review the content, answer questions and also provide critical commentary on the content thereby helping me learn the concepts myself and also help make the content better: Harry Pierson, Artur Laksberg, John Cuyle, Sean Barnes, Jaime Rodriguez, Chuck England, Kraig Brockschmidt, Kanna Ramasubramaniam, Saji Abraham, Daniel Moth, Paul Maybee, Pooja Nagpal, Amit Agrawal, David Fergusson, Terry Adams, Alessandro Contenti, Marian Luparu, Sriram Srinivasan, Julien Dollon, Aaron Saikovski and the others who silently lurked on the internal book reviewers list as well as the folks I have forgotten to add. Thanks also due to my direct team-mates in the Reader team, especially Francis Abraham, Lakshmi Narayana Mummidi, Subramanian Iyer and Mahesh Jha, who have been extremely helpful in sharing valuable insights learnt from building the Reader App using C++ and XAML. Nithin Ismail from my team built the AppBar template example that can be used in XAML apps. Thanks to Raghuram Lanka, Nitin Madnikar and Shiv Prashant Sood from the Windows Phone tools team for reviewing the Windows Phone 8.0 section in the appendix. Thanks also to folks who patiently answered the questions I raised and provided insightful answers. Thanks also due to Puneet Singh and David Jairaj, two wonderful colleagues who helped in the making of the book cover page.

Some of the icons for the Windows Store sample applications in the book were downloaded from the xaml project (www.thexamlproject.com) and SyncFusion Metro Studio (www.syncfusion.com). I have asked them for permission to use the same for my book and they have graciously granted me permission to use the icons. Thank you folks for all your help and support!

I am also extremely thankful to Tom Kirby-Green (twitter handle @tomkirbygreen, website: http://tomkirbygreen.com) who read through the draft manuscripts and provided great feedback on the content and the samples. The book is in such a polished shape thanks to Tom's untiring efforts.

I could not have completed this huge endeavor without the support of my wife, Priya. After I committed myself to authoring this book, we also found out that we were about to have our first child thereby doubling our joy as well. All of this was made extremely simple with the help and support of our gynecologists, Dr. Kalpana Alexander and Dr. Shobha of Matrika Hospital, Hyderabad, India and Dr. RaghavRam. The book was in development during the arrival of our bundle of joy, baby Aarush. I cannot thank enough my mother, Rajyalakshmi and my siblings Lavanya, Satish and Deepak who built an amazing support system at my house allowing me to focus completely on the book.

Finally, to all the C++ developers who migrated to greener pastures on the other competing platforms, welcome back!

Trademarks

Microsoft, DirectX, Visual Studio, Visual C++, Visual C#, Visual Basic .NET, Win32, Windows, Windows 8 are either registered trademarks of Microsoft Corporation in the United States and/or other countries. Other Product and Company names mentioned herein maybe trademarks of their respective owners. Use of a term in this book should not be regarded as affecting the validity of any trademark or service mark.

The book expresses the author's views and opinions. The information in this book is provided without any express, statutory or implied warranties. Neither the autor, nor resellers or distributors will be held liable for any damages caused or alleged to be caused either directly or indirectly by this book.

Errata & Book Support

I've made every effort to ensure the accuracy of this book and its companion content. Any errors that have been reported since the publication of this book will be listed on my website at http://sridharpoduri.com. If you find an error that is not already listed, you can report it to me through the same site or drop a mail to Win8book@sridharpoduri.com

You can also find me on Twitter @sridharpoduri

Chapter 1
The new Windows 8 Apps

In this chapter:

The new native API
What is a Windows 8 App
Quick walkthrough of a Windows 8 App
Where are we and What's Next

The new native API

Windows Runtime, or WinRT, is Microsoft's programming model that enables developers to write graphically rich, full screen, sandboxed, immersive apps for Windows 8. These Windows 8 apps are known as "Windows Store" apps as their only acquisition mechanism is via the Windows Store that launched simultaneously along with Windows 8.

Windows Programming has not changed much since Windows 1.0 was introduced in 1985. The basic model has remained the same up until Windows 7. Developers wrote C or C++ code that called traditional 'C style', non-object-orientated, flat, Windows APIs. To be fair Win16, as it back then, was fairly easy to use when it was first introduced; however with the passage of time and subsequent versions of Windows it grew to encompass 32 and 64 bit architectures as well as the Component Object Model (COM) and its numerous uses.

With Windows 8, Microsoft decided to reboot native development on Windows. The Windows Runtime is not a separate layer on Windows in the way that the Microsoft Foundation Classes (MFC) are, rather just like traditional Win32, it is part and parcel of Windows and is entirely built-in. It is new to Windows 8 and is built using an evolved form of the tried and trusted COM technologies. The new Windows Runtime or **WinRT** as it is referred to, and not to be confused with "Windows RT", is the primary Application Programming Interface (API) set that is provided to developers to develop Windows Store apps running on Windows 8.

Placed side by side, WinRT is much smaller than today's Win32. Win32 has more than 650,000 functions and types whereas WinRT includes about 1800 classes and methods. Moreover, once you learn a new WinRT API, for example the new Storage API, it is very easy to use the API across any language since the WinRT Projections present the API in your language of choice using idioms that are common to that language and its associated development culture.

At the most fundamental level, all Windows Runtime classes are COM co-classes implementing the new **IInspectable** interface rather than **IUnknown**. It is worth mentioning at this point that these WinRT classes cannot be instantiated using the regular COM functions, like CoCreateInstance. A more in-depth analysis of the Windows Runtime is provided in Chapter 6.

What is a Windows 8 App?

So what *is* a Windows 8 App? How does a Windows 8 App differ from a more traditional desktop application? The answer can be succinctly stated as: A Windows 8 App is built to conform to a well-defined application model, optimized for a touch-first experience and is acquired through the Windows Store. We will now focus on the aspects of the Windows Runtime that allows you to write Windows 8 Apps.

Fast and Fluid

Windows 8 Apps are designed to be fast and fluid. The entire platform has been reimagined and reengineered to provide the best experience to users. The key change in the platform that enables this fast and fluid experience is the pervasive use of asynchronous APIs. Any operation that can consume more than 50 milliseconds is now an asynchronous operation, furthermore no synchronous, or blocking, alternative is provided. We will explore async programming in more detail in chapter 2. Having async at the core of the system helps ensure that the UI thread is never blocked waiting for some I/O to complete or for a web service request to return etc thus resulting in a very responsive user experience.

Touch first experience

If you have developed Win32 apps in any form (using plain Win32 or MFC etc), you probably have run into the various WM_MOUSE messages, WM_KEY* messages etc. How do you design an app that should respond to touch as well as mouse inputs? The answer lies in a new abstraction introduced into WinRT.

For Windows 8 Apps, you do not respond to individual mouse/touch events. You always handle events of a new type called Pointer. A Pointer is an abstract representation of an input type that can be a touch input, stylus/Pen input or a mouse input. Handling Pointer events removes the burden of handling device specific events of various input types and creates a unified model that works irrespective of input device type or modality.

A new Application Model

The Windows::ApplicationModel namespace provides a Windows Store Application access to core system functionality. This namespace contains classes that provide information about the current Application Package, the PackageId, SuspendingOperation and the eventing mechanism associated with Application Suspension.

Windows::ApplicationModel::Activation

A Windows Store application can be "activated" in one of many ways. These include, but are not limited to,

- Launch - such as when the user tapped on a tile

- Search - the user wants to search within this app.

- Share Target - the user wants to share content and has activated this app.

- File - the app is registered to handle this file type.

- Protocol - the app is registered to handle this protocol.

- FileOpenPicker - the user wants to select files or folders that are provided by this app. For more information on Pickers, see the section on the Integration points with the Operating System below.

- FileSavePicker - the user wants to save a file and selected the app as a location. For more information on Pickers, see the section on the Integration points with the Operating System below.

For each of the activation mechanisms listed above, as well as the ones that are not listed, WinRT provides facility for setting up event handlers. When such activation occurs, the runtime calls back into your application code and provides rich information on the type of activation along with relevant arguments. For example, if I have written an application that intends to participate in the Share contract, upon Share Target activation, I would expect my app to receive a callback from WinRT along with special arguments for activation, namely ShareTargetActivatedEventArgs. The following table summarizes the special arguments for activation for each kind of activation.

TABLE 1-1   Table listing Activation Kinds and Activation Arguments

Activation Kind	Activation Arguments
Launch	LaunchActivatedEventArgs
Search	SearchActivatedEventArgs
ShareTarget	ShareTargetActivatedEventArgs
File	FileActivatedEventArgs
Protocol	ProtocolActivatedEventArgs
FileOpenPicker	FileOpenPickerActivatedEventArgs
FileSavePicker	FileSavePickerActivatedEventArgs
CachedFileUpdater	CachedFileUpdaterActivatedEventArgs
ContactPicker	ContactPickerActivatedEventArgs
Device	DeviceActivatedEventArgs
PrintTaskSettings	PrintTaskSettingsActivatedEventArgs
CameraSettings	CameraSettingsActivatedEventArgs

The Windows::ApplicationModel::Background namespace contains classes and methods that enable background and long running tasks in Windows Store applications. Background and long running tasks are special in the sense, they will continue running until they signal completion. This means that the Operating System does not "Suspend" or "Terminate" the app until it signals it has completed running and is in a ready state for Suspension.

Windows::ApplicationModel::Background

A Windows Store app can specify one or more Background Access states. These states are defined in the BackgroundAccessStatus enum, and can contain the following values.

- Unspecified: This enum value means that the user has not specified that the app can use background activity or update its badge status on the lock screen. The App cannot perform any background activity in this state. The App can, however, request access through the RequestAccessAsync API.

- AllowedWithAlwaysOnRealTimeConnectivity: This enum value means that the user has specified that the app can use background activity and/or update its badge status on the lock screen. The App will always be running and can use the Real Time Connectivity (RTC) broker. This should only be used for specialized application categories like IM, mail etc.

- AllowedMayUseActiveRealTimeConnectivity: This enum value means that the user has specified that the app can use background activity and/or update its badge status on the lock screen. The App might not function when the device is in a connected standby state.

- Denied: This enum value indicates that the user has chosen that the app cannot perform background activity and cannot update its badge on the lock screen.When an app is in this state, a call to the RequestAccessAsync method will not present the user with UI asking permission to do otherwise.

Windows::ApplicationModel::Core

The Windows::ApplicationModel::Core namespace contains classes and interfaces that provide fundamental application-level functionality for Windows Store Applications. This namespace contains two classes: CoreApplication and CoreApplicationView.

The CoreApplication object enables apps to handle state changes, manage windows and integrate with a variety of UI frameworks. In our case, we will be paying particular attention to XAML and CoreApplication integration. The CoreApplication object can subscribe to a variety of events pertaining to Application Lifecycle, like Exiting, Suspending and Resuming. While the CoreApplication class is an important one, developers building applications will probably encounter one of the related classes from the UI frameworks they are using.

The CoreApplicationView class represents an app window and its thread. This class contains 3 properties: CoreWindow, IsHosted and IsMain. CoreWindow gets the app window associated with the view, IsHosted returns a bool value whether the app is hosted or not and IsMain returns a bool whether the app view is the main app view or not.

Native XAML framework

For a very long time, C++ developers were stuck with using MFC or the plain old Win32 for GUI programming. However, with Windows 8, C++ developers now have their very own XAML framework, built natively into Windows. The framework is located under the Windows::UI::Xaml namespace in the Windows Runtime.

Chapter 3 and 4 focus on XAML and C++ /CX programming to create Windows Store apps.

At the root of the Windows::UI::Xaml namespace are a few important classes.

1. Application: Encapsulates the application and its available application services.

2. FrameworkElement: This class provides a framework of common APIs for objects that participate in UI and programmatic layout. The FrameworkElement also defines APIs relating to data binding, object tree and lifetime.

3. UIElement: The UIElement is a base class for most of the objects that have visual appearance and can process basic input in a user interface.

4. Window: The Window class represents an application Window.

5. Various event handlers: Handlers for various events such as WindowActivated, WindowClosed, VisualStateChange, RoutedEvents, SuspendingEvent, UnhandledException etc.

Windows::UI::Xaml::Controls provides UI controls and classes that support existing and custom controls. The XAML framework has built-in support for most common controls, such as,

1. AppBar: This object represents the container control that holds application UI components for commanding and experiences.

2. Button: This object represents a templated button control that interprets a Click or Tap user interaction.

3. Border: This object draws a border, background or both around another object.

4. Canvas: This object defines an area within which you can explicitly position child objects, using coordinates that are relative to the Canvas area.

5. CaptureElement: This object represents a media capture from a capture device, for example recorded video content.

6. CheckBox: This object represents a control that a user can select (check) or clear (uncheck). A CheckBox can also report its value mode as indeterminate.

7. ComboBox: This object represents a selection control that combines a non-editable text box and

a drop-down containing a list box that allows users to select an item from a list.

8. FlipView: The FlipView is a showcase control in Windows 8. The FlipView object represents an items control that displays one item at a time, and which enables "flip" behavior for traversing its collection of items.

9. Frame: This object represents a content control that supports navigation.

10. Grid: A Grid defines a flexible grid area that consists of columns and rows. Child elements of the Grid are laid out according to their row/column assignments and internal class logic.

11. HyperlinkButton: This is a button control that displays a hyperlink.

12. Image: This is a control that displays an image in the JPEG or PNG formats.

13. ListBox: A ListBox contains a list of selectable items.

14. ListView: This object represents a control that displays a list of data items.

15. MediaElement: This object represents a control that contains audio, video or both.

16. Page: The Page control encapsulates a page of content that can be navigated to.

17. Panel: The Panel object provides a base class for all Panel elements. Use Panel elements to position and arrange child objects in a UI page.

18. PasswordBox: This object represents a control for entering passwords.

19. ProgressRing: This object represents a control that indicates an ongoing operation. The typical visual appearance is a ring-shaped "spinner" that cycles an animation as progress continues.

20. ProgressBar: This object represents a control that indicates the progress of an operation, where the typical visual appearance is a bar that animates a filled area as progress continues.

21. RadioButton: This object represents a button that allows a user to select a single option from a group of options.

22. RichEditBox: This object represents a rich text editing control that supports formatted text, hyperlinks, inline images, and other rich content.

23. RichTextBlock: This object represents a rich text display container that supports formatted text, hyperlinks, inline images, and other rich content. Also, RichTextBlock supports a built-in overflow model.

24. ScrollViewer: This object represents a scrollable area that can contain other visible elements.

25. SemanticZoom: Another showcase control introduced in Windows 8. This object represents a scrollable control that incorporates two views that have a semantic relationship. For example, the ZoomedOutView might be an index of titles, and the ZoomedInView might include details and summaries for each of the title entries. Views can be changed using zoom or other interac-

tions.

26. Slider: This object represents a control that lets the user select from a range of values by moving a Thumb control along a track.

27. TextBox: This object represents a control that can be used to display single-format, multi-line text.

28. TextBlock: This object provides a lightweight control for displaying small amounts of text.

29. ToggleSwitch: This object represents a switch that can be toggled between two states.

30. Tooltip: This object represents a control that creates a pop-up window that displays information for an element in the UI.

31. UserControl: This object provides the base class for defining a new control that encapsulates related existing controls and provides its own logic.

The Windows::UI::Xaml::Media namespace provides basic media support, graphics primitives and a brush drawing API. The APIs include, but are not limited to, ArcSegment, BitmapCache, Brush, EllipseGeometry, FillRule, GradientBrush, ImageSource, ImageBrush, LineGeometry, PathGeometry, ScaleTransform, TileBrush etc.

The Windows::UI::Xaml::Media::Animation namespace contains classes and other objects that provide animation and storyboard API for transition animations, visual states or animated UI components.

- o Animations: The list of animations provided includes ColorAnimation, DoubleAnimation, DoubleAnimationUsingKeyFrames, DragItemThemeAnimation, DragOverThemeAnimation, DropTargetItemThemeAnimation, FadeInThemeAnimation, FadeOutThemeAnimation, PointAnimation, PointAnimationUsingKeyFrames, PointerDownThemeAnimation, PointerUpThemeAnimation, PopInThemeAnimation, PopOutThemeAnimation, PopupThemeAnimation, RepositionThemeAnimation, SplitCloseThemeAnimation, SplitOpenThemeAnimation, SwipeBackThemeAnimation and SwipeHintThemeAnimation.

- o Transitions: The list of transitions provided includes AddDeleteThemeTransition, ContentThemeTransition, EdgeUIThemeTransition, EntranceThemeTransition, PaneThemeTransition, PopupThemeTransition, ReorderThemeTransition and RepositionThemeTransition.

The Windows::UI::Xaml::Media::Imaging namespace provides types related to imaging and obtaining resources for bitmap images. From a C++ developer perspective, the two important classes in this namespace are SurfaceImageSource (SiS) and VirtualSurfaceImageSource (VSiS).

SurfaceImageSource provides DirectX shared surfaces to draw into and then composes the bits into app content. VirtualSurfaceImageSource extends the SurfaceImageSource to support scenarios when the content is potentially larger than what can fit on screen and the content must be virtualized in order to render optimally.

Finally, we have the Windows::UI::Xaml::Shapes namespace which defines basic shapes that are intended for decorative rendering or for compositing non-interactive parts of controls. The shapes included are Ellipse, Line, Path, Polygon, Polyline, Rectangle and Shape. Shape is the base class for all shape elements such as Ellipse, Polygon and Rectangle.

Declarative Application Capabilities

A package bundles together code as well as any file based resources that an app might need, these subcomponents of the app package are described by the package manifest. The package manifest is an XML document that contains the info the system needs to deploy, display, or update a Windows Store app. This info includes package identity, package dependencies, required capabilities, visual elements, and extensibility points. Every app package must include one package manifest. The package manifest is digitally signed as part of signing the app package. After signing, you can't modify the manifest without invalidating the package signature. After the package has been installed, the package manifest file appears in the directory for the installed package.

When you submit your app to the Windows Store, it is checked to ensure that the declared capabilities match the description of the app. Declaring a large number of capabilities or declaring certain capabilities that users may be sensitive about may increase the level of scrutiny of your app when you submit it to the Windows Store. When customers get your app from the Windows Store, they are notified of all the capabilities that the app declares. In other words, if you want users to download your app it pays to be frugal, only declare the minimum of capabilities you need.

The following table summarizes the various capability values you can declare in the Application manifest.

TABLE 1-2 Windows Store App Capabilities

Capability	Description
internetClient	Your Internet connection for outgoing connections to the Internet.
internetClientServer	Your Internet connection, including incoming unsolicited connections from the Internet – the app can send information to or from your computer through a firewall. You do not need to declare **internetClient** if this capability is declared.
privateNetworkClientServer	A home or work network – the app can send information to or from your computer and other computers on the same network.
documentsLibrary	Your documents library, including the capability to add, change, or delete files. The package can only access file types that it has declared in the manifest. The app cannot access document libraries on HomeGroup computers.
picturesLibrary	Your pictures library, including the capability to add, change, or delete files. This capability also includes pictures libraries on HomeGroup computers, along with picture file types on locally connected media servers.
videosLibrary	Your videos library, including the capability to add, change, or delete files. This capability also includes videos libraries on HomeGroup computers, along with video file types on locally connected media servers.
musicLibrary	Your music library and playlists, including the capability to

	add, change, or delete files. This capability also includes music libraries and playlists in the music library on HomeGroup computers, plus music file types on locally connected media servers.
enterpriseAuthentication	Your Windows credentials, for access to a corporate intranet. This application can impersonate you on the network.
sharedUserCertificates	Software and hardware certificates or a smart card – used to identify you in the app. This capability may be used by your employer, bank, or government services to identify you.
removableStorage	Removable storage, such as an external hard drive or USB flash drive, or MTP portable device, including the capability to add, change, or delete specific files. This package can only access file types that it has declared in the manifest.

App Acquisition Process

For Windows 8 Apps, there is just one place to acquire apps from and that is the Windows Store. Every Windows 8 PC will have a Store application that connects to the Windows Store and allows users to browse the app catalog, read reviews, look at screenshots of the apps and install the apps with a one click operation.

Each app is provided a product landing page which describes what functionality the app provides, whether the app is free or paid and also the capabilities it needs. These capabilities are declared in the application manifest (described above) and are meant to help the user understand what device or system capabilities are requested by the app. Some capabilities are prompted explicitly at first launch, such as access to the camera, while other capabilities are not explicitly prompted for.

Apps can also choose to have a trial offer and users can opt to try the app before purchasing. Whether a user installs a trial version of an app, the complete version or a free version, Windows downloads the application package and installs the app.

Installation and Uninstallation Process

The installation process has been streamlined so much that the process is almost silent with no custom installers, annoying license agreements or unwanted dialogs popping up demanding interaction from the user. When a user chooses to install an app from the Store, Windows begins a download operation that fetches the application package from the Store, unpacks the package, reads the application manifest and then proceeds to create application specific folders as needed. It also installs the App specific tile on the Start screen, adds registry entries in case of file association mapping etc. All of this is done without any manual intervention needed by the user or is user monitoring necessary.

In keeping with the Windows 8 promise of providing a hassle free experience for end users when they acquire apps, Windows Store apps do not and cannot have their own installers as noted above. Instead, application files are packaged with the manifest that describes its capabilities and requirements, and also serves as the declarative instructions for a standard installer, so it can create the necessary registry settings and so forth—and remove those settings during uninstallation.

In addition to keeping the system clean, such declarative installation is a great boon to developers as there is no need to write an installer at all! It's also a great boon to the user because installation happens much more quickly and without the usual series of dialog boxes asking you to make decisions users really don't care about. The new installation is driven by the application manifest, which is created by the app developer to specify all of the relevant details about the entire application. The application manifest is an xml file, as we have seen above, and follows a pre-defined schema. This architecture allows the system to 'reflect' over, infer and understand the impact of installing or uninstalling the application prior to beginning the installation process itself. It's no longer possible for the act of installing an application to just randomly splatter DLLs all over the system, possibly updating existing ones that might be used by other apps and then only revert some of its changes on uninstall. The App Package model, combined with the new single system-provided, data driven, installer architecture helps provide a semi transactional installer experience, giving end users the confidence that they can at last speculatively install something from the Windows App Store, and remove it again if it's not to their liking, without possibly wrecking their system as is the case with 'home grown' installers. Increased user confidence around installation, combined with the seamless, zero popup dialog experience, and removes much of the fear of installing apps and results in increased app sales for developers.

Sandboxed AppContainer

Most users today have learnt the hard way that they cannot in general trust software downloaded from the internet. As an application developer just knocking up an ad-hoc website for users to download your app from may be easy, but it's not as secure a delivery mechanism as the Windows Store and you will have to do all the extra work to build up user confidence regarding trust. Most users have no way of knowing whether it is reasonable safe to download apps and install them from the internet. If your company is well known, then users rely on your company reputation to keep their systems' safe and free from malware. A lot of apps look perfectly legitimate and might be extremely useful to its users. However the users do not know what exactly the app is doing. Is it transferring some data to a web service or compromising the user's privacy by sharing the user's location?

To address these concerns, Windows Store applications written for Windows 8 are acquired and installed through the Windows app store exclusively as previously noted. This means that every app must pass a certification process that includes both automatic and manual tests before it's made available. This provides validation services that the open web cannot. For one, automatic testing subjects the app to a host of virus and malware scanners, which will provide a higher level of detection than any single scanner on a user's machine, and not be subject to malware attacks that might turn a user's scanning off entirely. Manual testing for its part means that a human being works with the program to evaluate whether it does what it says it does, and nothing more.

A further safeguard is that applications must explicitly declare their intent to access sensitive resources through the Capabilities section of their manifest. Those capabilities are as follows:

- Internet access (as client, server, or both)

- Access to data libraries (documents, pictures, videos, music; in the case of documents, access is limited to specific file types associated with the application and those files the application creates)

- User credentials and certificates

- Removable storage

- Devices: identified by GUID or by friendly names. These names cover microphone (audio in), portable devices (including mobile phone, camera, and portable media players), geolocation, SMS, and sensors.

Windows strongly enforces these declared capabilities at runtime, which means that if the application didn't declare them up front then any subsequent attempt to access those resources (through the Windows Runtime APIs) will simply fail. A common error first time WinRT developers encounter is to forget to include the appropriate capability declaration in the manifest, in which case your code is technically correct but won't work because of this enforcement!

Even so, just declaring a capability isn't the end of the story, because the user can still disallow those capabilities. That is, they can tell Windows to disallow the camera, the microphone, and so on.

Beyond capabilities, all modern Windows applications, regardless of which language or UI framework they use, run within a special sandboxed environment, called the "app container". This is what limits the API surface area accessible by the application, thereby disallowing many kinds of activities that would compromise privacy, security, and data.

AppState

While a Windows Store applications cannot simply litter the user's system with 'random files', the app is given unlimited access to a special folder created specifically the app. This special folder, in the user's AppData folder, is where the application manages its state between sessions. When an application is uninstalled, this entire folder is removed, thereby removing all traces of the application footprint. Note that any files that an application created in shared libraries are retained though.

An application gets to its AppData folder through a specific object class (from the Windows::Storage::ApplicationData) rather than by means of a direct pathname. This AppData object then provides objects for Local, Roaming, and Temporary folders, as well as objects to work with individual Local and Roaming settings. Applications thus have everything they need to manage both structured and unstructured state, that is, through individual settings or through files of the app's own design.

What's most interesting about the Roaming data in particular is that Windows 8 will automatically synchronize any such data across a user's devices. This is so a user can work with an app on one device, then later open that app on another device and have the same state. This Roaming only works if the user has signed in using a Microsoft Account and has enabled his apps and data to roam.

Process Lifecycle Management

Windows 8 includes improved support for enabling better battery live on computers that are not always plugged in and charging. This in part is via the support for automatic Process Lifecycle Management. A user cannot interact and give input to Windows Store apps unless they are in the foreground; Windows suspends such apps that are not in the foreground.

The bottom line is this: Whether an app is being suspended or terminated, the app does get a chance to save its state. This saving operation should complete within 5 seconds. When the app is resumed or restarted, it gets a chance to restore state, if it had saved state successfully earlier. The following figure best illustrates the App Lifecycle.

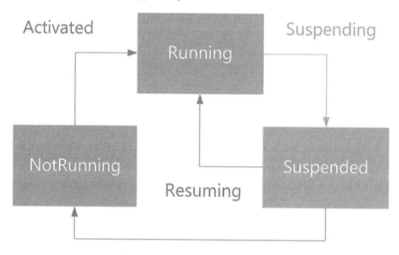

FIGURE 1-1 App Lifecycle

Integration points with the Operating System

Contracts are new to Windows 8. Contracts are the mechanism via which Windows Store apps declare how they support other apps and Windows 8. These mechanisms are declared via the Application manifest and are required to call the supported WinRT APIs to communicate with Windows and other Windows Store apps.

App to App Picking Contract

As a developer, you can help your users pick files from another app directly from within your app. This means users are free to choose files that are stored and presented by the apps they install on their computers. A Windows Store app can launch the file picker window to let the user browse their system and pick files or folders for the app to operate on. Your app can also use the interface to provide other apps with files, folders etc. See Figure 1-2 and 1-3 below for a screenshot of the File Picker.

FIGURE 1-2 A cropped view of the file picker

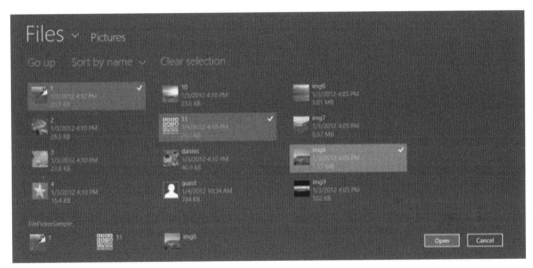

FIGURE 1-3 A view of the file picker showing the pictures library.

All File Picker windows have common UI Elements at the top and bottom of the Window that display important information to the user. This includes information such as the Folder Name, Sort by criteria, a list of locations that the user can browse for files, and the current selected items. The Window also has an Open and Cancel buttons at the bottom right corner of the Window. Users can choose a list of locations from the list in the upper left of the file picker letterbox. See Figure 1-2 above.

The locations listed in the drop down list of the file picker letterbox can be file system locations, like the Documents library or the Pictures library or they can also be apps that provide files and/or save locations. As such apps appear as locations, the file picker acts as the interface that allows the user pick a file that is provided by one app to open using another app. The following figure, 1-4 illustrates the control flow during this operation.

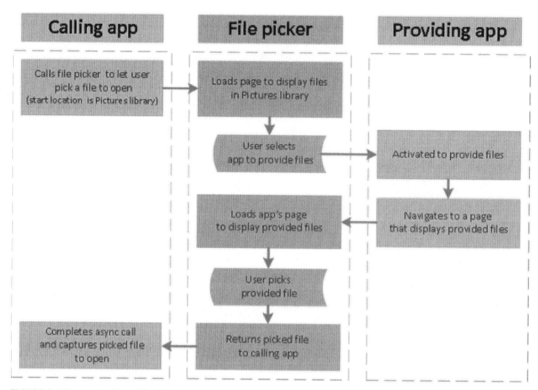

FIGURE 1-4 Demonstration of the file picker app to app workflow

Calling a file picker lets the user give pick files and folders for your app to work with. And when the user gives your app access to a folder, the app also gets access to its subfolders. File pickers give users explicit control over which files and folders your app can access. And if your app works with individual files or small lists of files, like most apps, you might be able to use the file pickers as the primary way your app accesses files and folders, letting you avoid declaring capabilities in your app manifest and possibly simplifying the review process for your app when you submit it to the Windows Store.

The following figure 1-5 illustrates this process.

FIGURE 1-5 File picker allowing user to choose picture from pictures library.

When your app gets files or a folder from a file picker, you should add the items to your futureAc-cessList (in the Windows::Storage::AccessCache namespace) so that your app can easily access the items again later.

Calling a file picker to save a file using a new name, file type, or location

Calling a file picker to save a file lets users specify the name, file type (or extension), and location of the file. Add a "save as" feature to your app by adding a UI control that calls a file picker that lets the user save a file using a new name, file type, or location. The following screen shot shows a file picker that was called to let the user specify the name, and file type of a file to save in the current location, the Documents library.

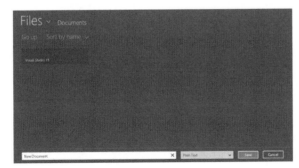

FIGURE 1-6 The save as file picker

Providing services using File Pickers

Your app can use file pickers as an interface to provide three services to other apps: access to files, a save location, and/or updates for particular files. To provide one (or more) of these services, you must participate in the associated app contract, which includes declaring the contract in your app manifest, responding to the corresponding activated event, and, in some cases, creating a page that will be loaded in the center area of a file picker window.

The Share Contract

Users often come across information they are excited to share with their friends or use in another app. The Share contract provides a lightweight and easy experience to accomplish this. Share is always universally accessible, via the Share charm. This can be accessed with a single swipe.

As a developer, you can make your app support the Share contract. Implementing the Share contract means that users can share content from your app with another app, and vice versa. Participating in this contract means you don't have to write too much extra code or provide a custom implementation for other apps to plug into. Any app that implements the Share contract can share content to and from any other app implementing the Share contract.

Apps that need to support the Share contract do so in two ways. There is the Source app, which contains the content that the user wants to share. Then there is the target app which receives the shared content. You can develop apps that are both share sources as well as destinations. The next step involves deciding what type of content to share or receive. Once this is finalized, you use the methods from the Windows::ApplicationModel::DataTransfer namespace to package the data.

In order to support the contract, you also need to declare the capability in the application manifest. If you are using Visual Studio, it provides a quick way to do so. As part of this process, you need to choose what data formats and file types your app can accept. The figures below, show how the property can be set using the Manifest Editor.

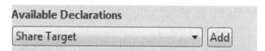

FIGURE 1-7 Choosing the share target in the manifest editor.

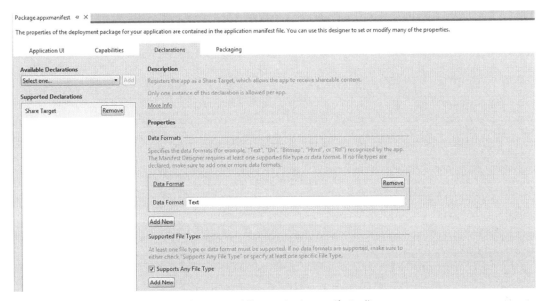

FIGURE 1-8 Setting the data format and supported file type in the manifest editor

When the user selects the Share charm, Windows automatically limits the number of apps it presents to those that support the data being shared.

The following figure shows the workflow for the Share contract.

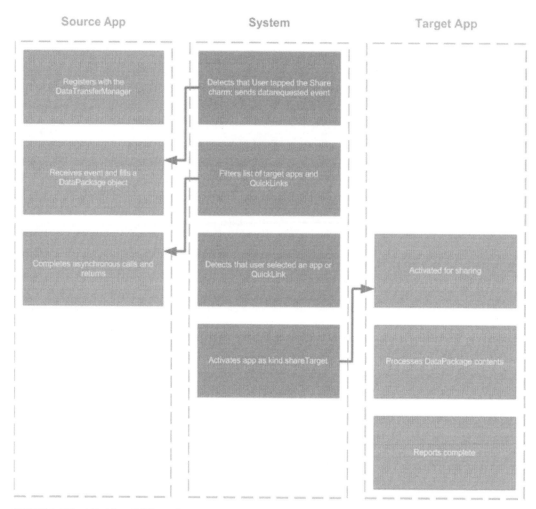

FIGURE 1-9 The Workflow Of Share Contract

As a target app, there are a couple of things you should consider. First, when the user selects your app, Windows will display it using the Snap view. This view is one of four ways that a Windows Store app can be displayed on the screen. Make sure your app supports this mode, and that it presents a clean, uncluttered interface for sharing content. You can also specify a specific form or XAML-backed UI that opens when the app is activated through the Share charm. That way, you can create a customized experience specifically for sharing.

Quick walkthrough of a Windows 8 App

Now that we know what makes for a Windows 8 App, let us learn how to build a quick and easy Windows 8 App using C++, XAML and DirectX. Do not worry about new syntax or semantics as we will explore them in greater detail in the subsequent chapters. For now, all you need to know is this:

- C++ has a set of extensions, named Component Extensions or CX to create Windows Runtime apps.

- You instantiate a Windows Runtime class by using the special syntax "ref new".

- You use the "^" (the hat operator) to disambiguate between WinRT objects and classic C++ objects.

- The component extensions produce 100% native code with no dependency of managed code whatsoever.

A Windows programming digest

Broadly speaking within the Microsoft Windows ecosystem, every C or C++ program starts its life by the OS either calling its *main* function if it's a console application or its *WinMain* function it it's a Windows application with a message pump etc.

This has not changed in the Windows 8. All Windows Store apps, especially the C++ apps, continue to start execution with a main/WinMain function. For Windows Store applications you are unlikely to ever write the main* function yourself, in general developers will use the relevant project template in Visual Studio 2012 to generate a basic Windows Store App.

What has definitely changed though is this: In Win32 developers coded a huge message loop and handled Window messages that were of interest to the application experience. This message loop no longer needs to be explicitly coded in Windows Store apps. Instead, you decide which messages to handle declaratively in XAML and the system calls your code when the corresponding message arrives and needs to be handled.

Another change that Windows 8 brings is that there are no explicit WM_PAINT type messages to be handled. Since Windows 8 Graphics is based on DirectX and is hardware accelerated, the frameworks take the burden of drawing UI controls on screen. Although most XAML controls contain an Invalidate method, you should not rely on calling them frequently. Instead, you should let the XAML framework handle the re-painting requirements.

The details of how all of this happens is very interesting but beyond the scope of this book. However we will take a brief look at how XAML handles drawing requests. When your XAML app begins execution, a visual tree is built. You can think of the visual tree as a tree-based hierarchy of all the XAML UI elements you have laid on screen, say for example, in MainPage.xaml. Once the visual tree is built, the rendering takes over to render the UI elements that are in the visual tree.

If you've used older UI frameworks you might well ask: what happens if you add a UI element through code at runtime rather than declaratively in XAML markup at design time? You might be tempted to call Invalidate to force a re-render. You should not do that. When the next refresh pass of the XAML framework occurs, it will automatically render all of the newly added elements in the visual tree.

With this information, let us get started!

Anatomy of our application

Our application is a bouncing ball animation. We will create a C++ XAML app that animates a bouncing ball on screen. As the ball touches the edges of the screen, it bounces in the opposite direction. In addition, the user can swipe from the bottom of the screen to bring up an ApplicationBar and change the ball color on the fly without re-setting the animation.

Our main UI is a XAML Page which contains a SwapChainBackgroundPanel. A SwapChainBackgroundPanel allows you to directly render content onto the swapchain and present it. We will explore the SwapChainBackgroundPanel in more detail in Chapter 4. For now, let us focus on getting things to work. After the SwapChainBackgroundPanel, we will define an application bar containing two buttons for changing colors: Previous Color and Next Color. The complete UI declared in XAML markup is as follows:

LISTING 1-1 XAML markup for the bouncing ball animation

```
<Page
    x:Class="DXBouncingBall.DirectXPage"
    xmlns="http://schemas.microsoft.com/winfx/2006/xaml/presentation"
    xmlns:x="http://schemas.microsoft.com/winfx/2006/xaml"
    xmlns:local="using:DXBouncingBall"
    xmlns:d="http://schemas.microsoft.com/expression/blend/2008"
    xmlns:mc="http://schemas.openxmlformats.org/markup-compatibility/2006"
    mc:Ignorable="d">
    <SwapChainBackgroundPanel x:Name="SwapChainPanel">
    </SwapChainBackgroundPanel>
    <Page.BottomAppBar>
        <AppBar Padding="10,0,10,0">
            <Grid>
                <StackPanel Orientation="Horizontal" HorizontalAlignment="Left">
                    <Button Style="{StaticResource AppBarButtonStyle}"
                            Tag="Previous"
                            AutomationProperties.AutomationId="PreviousAppBarButton" Content="&#xE112;"
                            AutomationProperties.Name="Previous Color"
                            Click="OnPreviousColorPressed"/>
                </StackPanel>
                <StackPanel Orientation="Horizontal" HorizontalAlignment="Right">
                    <Button Style="{StaticResource AppBarButtonStyle}"
                            Tag="Next"
                            AutomationProperties.AutomationId="NextAppBarButton" Content="&#xE111;"
                            AutomationProperties.Name="Next Color"
                            Click="OnNextColorPressed"/>
```

```
        </StackPanel>
      </Grid>
    </AppBar>
  </Page.BottomAppBar>
</Page>
```

Onto actual code. Before we can begin animating and bouncing the ball, we need to set up a structure to store the position of the ball between updates. This structure will store the current position and size of the ball, as well as the delta values, how much we want it to move each frame.

```
typedef struct _BALLINFO
    {
            int width;
            int height;
            int X;
            int Y;

            int dX;
            int dY;
}BALLINFO;
```

We also have a struct containing a range of colors what can be applied to the ball.

```
static const std::array<ColorF, 7> BallColors =
{
    ColorF::Orchid,
    ColorF::DeepPink,
    ColorF::Red,
    ColorF::DarkOrange,
    ColorF::Gold,
    ColorF::GreenYellow,
    ColorF::Aqua
};
```

After our application is initialized and resources are loaded, we will begin the process of rendering the ball and animating it. In order to animate the ball with smooth fluidity, we define two helper methods: Update and Render. Update is called every time a render needs to occur and Render redraws the ball at the new position computed in Update. In the Update method, we compute the ball position and store the values in the BALLINFO structure.

LISTING 1-2 Updating time dependent objects in the Update method of the Renderer

```
// Add code to update time dependent objects here.
const auto windowWidth = m_d3dRenderTargetSize.Width;
const auto windowHeight = m_d3dRenderTargetSize.Height;

m_ballPosition.X += m_ballPosition.dX;
m_ballPosition.Y += m_ballPosition.dY;

if (m_ballPosition.X < m_ballPosition.width)
    {
            m_ballPosition.X = m_ballPosition.width;
            m_ballPosition.dX = BALL_DELTA;
```

```
            }
            else if (m_ballPosition.X + m_ballPosition.width > static_cast<int>(windowWidth))
            {
                    m_ballPosition.X = static_cast<int>(windowWidth) - m_ballPosition.width;
                    m_ballPosition.dX = -BALL_DELTA;
            }

            if (m_ballPosition.Y < m_ballPosition.height)
            {
                    m_ballPosition.Y = m_ballPosition.height;
                    m_ballPosition.dY = BALL_DELTA;
            }
            else if (m_ballPosition.Y + m_ballPosition.height > static_cast<int>(windowHeight))
            {
                    m_ballPosition.Y = static_cast<int>(windowHeight) - m_ballPosition.height;
                    m_ballPosition.dY = -BALL_DELTA;
            }
```

Once we have the updated positions, we need to render the ball at the new positions. We do precisely that in the Render helper method.

```
m_d2dContext->BeginDraw();

m_d2dContext->Clear(ColorF(ColorF::CornflowerBlue));

m_d2dContext->FillEllipse(
    Ellipse(Point2F(static_cast<float>( m_ballPosition.X ),
                    static_cast<float>( m_ballPosition.Y)),
                    static_cast<float>( m_ballPosition.width),
                    static_cast<float>( m_ballPosition.height)),
                    m_blackBrush.Get());

// Ignore D2DERR_RECREATE_TARGET. This error indicates that the device
// is lost. It will be handled during the next call to Present.
const auto hr = m_d2dContext->EndDraw();
if (hr != D2DERR_RECREATE_TARGET)
{
    DX::ThrowIfFailed(hr);
}

m_renderNeeded = false;
```

When the user chooses to bring up the application bar and change the ball color, we simply lookup the Color table and set the ball color to the next/previous color index in the table.

```
m_ballColorIndex++;
if (m_ballColorIndex >= static_vast<int>(BallColors.size()))
{
    m_ballColorIndex = 0;
}
```

Finally, we will have to setup an eventing mechanism between XAML and the SwapChain to coordinate rendering synchronization. Fortunately, XAML exposes an event called CompositionTarget::Rendering that enables us to setup an event callback that fires every time a refresh is needed.

We subscribe to this event in the constructor of our Page class and add the OnRendering method that calls into our Update and Render helper methods.

```
m_timer->Update();

m_renderer->Update(m_timer->Total, m_timer->Delta);

m_renderer->Render();

m_renderer->Present();
```

That is it. Our app is now ready. If you build and deploy the app on a Windows 8 device, including Surface RT, you should see a ball animating smoothly on screen and bouncing off the edges. You can download the complete sample, DXBouncingBall, from the book samples download location.

FIGURE 1-10 Bouncing Ball sample

Where are we and what's Next?

Now that we have dipped our toes into understanding what makes a Windows 8 app and how easy it is to build one, we will turn our attention to C++11 and C++ /CX.

Chapter 2
Introduction to Modern C++

In this chapter:

Hello Modern C++
Welcome to the Component Extensions
C++ /CX, Windows Runtime and ISO C++
The C++ /CX Type System
Asynchronous Programming in C++ /CX
Concepts to remember while building C++ /CX components
Building a WinRT component using C++ /CX
Building a WinRT component using C++ /CX and ISO-C++
A peek inside the magic of C++ /CX
Guidance on the use of C++ /CX
Where are we and What's Next

Hello Modern C++

C++ has undergone a revolutionary change since it was standardized in the late 90's. As Herb Sutter famously paraphrased, "It is not your daddy's C++". The new, recently revised standard, C++11 introduces facilities into the language that enhance developer productivity, promotes type safety, enable higher levels of abstraction all all without sacrificing the efficiency and performance of the generated code which has always been C++'s raison d'etre.

Modern C++ emphasizes the following principles:

- Auto type inference instead of explicit type names.

- Smart pointers instead of raw pointers.

- std::string and std::wstring types instead of raw char[] arrays.

- Standard template library (STL) containers like vector, list, and map instead of raw arrays or custom containers.

- STL algorithms instead of manually coded ones.

- Exceptions, to report and handle error conditions.

- Inline lambda functions instead of small functions implemented separately.

In this brief introduction to Modern C++, we will visit the following C++11 facilities that will come handy as we move along to writing Windows 8 Apps later on. For a more in-depth reference on C++11, bookmark the ISO C++ Committee website http://www.isocpp.org. The site contains a wealth of information on C++11, in-depth articles, tutorials, videos etc demonstrating the use of modern C++ programming paradigms. Another source of great information/code samples etc is the Visual C++ team blog, which at the time of this writing is at http://blogs.msdn.com/b/vcblog. Here are the C++ 11 features we'll be covering in this book:

- Auto type inference instead of explicit type names.

- Lambdas

- Range 'for'

- The new smart pointers: unique_ptr, shared_ptr and weak_ptr

- Move semantics and perfect forwarding

Auto type inference

In Modern C++, if the compiler is able to determine the type of a variable from its initialization, you need not provide the type explicitly. This, in short, is the idea behind the 'auto' keyword. Consider the following code snippet:

int x = 10;

int y = x;

The code snippet initializing the variable 'y' can be more compactly written as:

auto y = x;

Although this is a somewhat contrived example of using the auto keyword, the motivation behind introducing the type inference facility was to save the programmer from having to type lengthy type names such as those found within the Standard Library. In addition to this some types are, in compiler-speak, 'unutterable' such types include the function-objects generated on your behalf from the new lambda syntax, auto lets you create a corresponding local variable for such lambda instances without having to know the type. Consider the following std::map definition:

std::map<int, std::wstring> myMap;

Now if you want to declare an iterator to iterate over this collection, you would have to write code similar to the following:

std::map<int, std::wstring>::iterator itBegin = myMap.begin();

With C++11, the above line can be compactly re-written as:

auto itBegin = myMap.begin();

The code is now much cleaner and shorter too!

Lambdas

C++ has always been able to call itself a multiparadigm language, one of these being functional programming. One of the key concepts in functional languages is the ability to treat code and data interchangeably and this often takes the form of being able to pass functions to other functions, or in turn have functions return functions as values. Before C++ 11 programming in such a style necessitated labouriously hand crafting so-called 'function objects', these where little classes (or sometimes structs) what would overload the function-call operator and being structs or classes could even package data (state) in with the logic. C++ 11 takes this to the next level by introducing a compact and elegent syntax that enables such function objects to be written inline at their point of use as lambda expressions. Just like regular functions lambdas can have any number of parameters, however in addition to this they can 'capture' variables from the scope in which they are declared. Some care has to be taken with such captured variables to ensure that if the lambda is invoked after the enclosing scope has been left any captured variables are still valid. In every day use you will find that the new lambda syntax is far more appropriate and elegant than the corresponding explicit function-object form, or for that matter, function-pointers, which are an even older technology for passing functions to other functions. That said lambdas are not universally superior to these predating techniques. One thing is sure; lambda functions reenergize the practical effectiveness and applicability of the C++ Standard Library. Such C++ luminaries as Scott Meyers have long estolled the value of the C++ Standard Library and its various containers and algorithms; however until now many developers have shied away from using it because it required fragmenting ones algorithms into spacially disperate function-objects. The C++ 11 lambda syntax makes using the Standard Library elegant, productive and far, far more readable.

Let us take a quick look at a basic lambda

```
auto func = [] () { cout << "Can you spot the lambda function here?" ; } ;
func();
```

The [] is the lambda introducer, also known as the capture specification, which informs the compiler that a lambda function is being created. Every function needs an argument list. In case of the simple lambda defined above, the empty parenthesis () indicates we are not passing in any arguments to the lambda. You can also choose to pass arguments to lambdas that you create. We will see a lot of such instances when writing async tasks for Windows 8 apps.

Again we're using the new type inference support that auto enables to declare the func variable. A current limitation of auto is that it can only be used to declare local variables, if we wanted to store the lambda in a class, or pass is it to another bit of code we'd need to write:

```
std::function<void()> func = [] () { cout << "Can you spot the lambda function here?" ; } ;
```

The auto keyword makes it easy by inferring the type of a function pointer and saves you, the developer, from having to muck around with knowing the function pointer syntax. The actual call to the lambda is made when we call the function named func().

Your lambda need not return a value. In our example above, we do not return a value. If however, you write code that returns a value, you have two choices: You can let the compiler automatically deduce the return type or you can explicitly inform the type being returned.

For example: [] () { return 42; } informs the compiler that your return type is an integer.

Similarly: [] () -> int { return 42; } informs the compiler explicitly that the return type is an integer.

C++ allows you to write highly performant code and lambdas provide a great flexibility in allowing you to choose a capture syntax that meets your needs.

Let us now explore how to code lambda functions along with the capture options.

The "Hello World" lambda

The following code prints the numbers beginning with 0 to 9. We will use a simple lambda function to print the numbers stored in a vector.

LISTING 2-1 Lambda printing numbers 0 to 9

```
#include <algorithm>
#include <iostream>
#include <vector>
using namespace std;

void main() {
    vector<int> v;

    for (int i = 0; i < 10; ++i) {
        v.push_back(i);
    }

    for_each(v.begin(), v.end(), [](int n) { cout << n << " "; });
    cout << endl;
}
```

Lambdas with implicit return type deduction

If a lambda contains only a return expression, then the type is deduced automatically as the example below illustrates.

LISTING 2-2 Lambda with implicit return type deduction

```
#include <algorithm>
#include <deque>
#include <iostream>
#include <iterator>
#include <vector>
using namespace std;

void main() {
    vector<int> v;

    for (int i = 0; i < 10; ++i) {
```

```
        v.push_back(i);
    }

    deque<int> d;

    transform(v.begin(), v.end(), front_inserter(d), [](int n) { return n * n * n; });

    for_each(d.begin(), d.end(), [](int n) { cout << n << " "; });
    cout << endl;
}
```

Lambdas with explicit return types

Lambdas containing multiple statements and control flow do not have their return types automatically deduced. In such a case, you must explicitly specify the return type. The -> <type> is the return type clause. In the example below, the -> double is the optional lambda return type clause.

LISTING 2-3 Lambda specifying explicit return type

```
#include <algorithm>
#include <deque>
#include <iostream>
#include <iterator>
#include <vector>
using namespace std;

void main() {
    vector<int> v;

    for (int i = 0; i < 10; ++i) {
        v.push_back(i);
    }

    deque<double> d;

    transform(v.begin(), v.end(), front_inserter(d), [](int n) -> double {
        if (n % 2 == 0) {
            return n * n * n;
        } else {
            return n / 2.0;
        }
    });

    for_each(d.begin(), d.end(), [](double x) { cout << x << " "; });
    cout << endl;
}
```

Lambdas with a capture list

All of the previous code examples have demonstrated what are known as stateless lambdas. Lambdas, however, are not condemned to live without a state. You can create stateful lambdas too, by specifying a capture list. The lambda introducer, [ ], if left empty, is a stateless lambda. Within the lambda introducer, you can specify a capture list.

LISTING 2-4 Lambda specifying a capture list

```cpp
#include <algorithm>
#include <iostream>
#include <vector>
using namespace std;

void main() {
    vector<int> v;

    for (int i = 0; i < 10; ++i) {
        v.push_back(i);
    }

    int x = 0;
    int y = 0;

    cout << "Input: ";
    cin >> x >> y;

    v.erase(remove_if(v.begin(), v.end(), [x, y](int n) { return x < n && n < y; }), v.end());

    for_each(v.begin(), v.end(), [](int n) { cout << n << " "; });
    cout << endl;
}
```

Capturing everything by value

In order to capture all the variables by value, you need not specify each individual variable within the lambda introducer. You can use the = operator within a lambda introducer to specify that everything should be captured by value.

LISTING 2-5 Lambda variable capture by value

```cpp
#include <algorithm>
#include <iostream>
#include <vector>
using namespace std;

void main() {
    vector<int> v;

    for (int i = 0; i < 10; ++i) {
        v.push_back(i);
    }

    int x = 0;
    int y = 0;

    cout << "Input: ";
    cin >> x >> y;

    v.erase(remove_if(v.begin(), v.end(), [=](int n) { return x < n && n < y; }), v.end());
```

```
    for_each(v.begin(), v.end(), [](int n) { cout << n << " "; });
    cout << endl;
}
```

Modifying captured copies within a lambda

If you want to modify the captured copies inside a lambda, you should use the mutable keyword. By default, a lambda's function call operator is const and using mutable makes it non-const.

LISTING 2-6 capture value modification within a lambda

```
#include <algorithm>
#include <iostream>
#include <vector>
using namespace std;

void main() {
    vector<int> v;

    for (int i = 0; i < 10; ++i) {
        v.push_back(i);
    }

    int x = 1;
    int y = 1;

    for_each(v.begin(), v.end(), [=](int& r) mutable {
        const int old = r;

        r *= x * y;

        x = y;
        y = old;
    });

    for_each(v.begin(), v.end(), [](int n) { cout << n << " "; });
    cout << endl;

    cout << x << ", " << y << endl;
}
```

Capturing by reference

If you want to avoid copies, observe updates to the local variables within the lambda and modify the values in the local variables, then you should capture by reference. The syntax to capture by reference is to use & before each of the capture variable in the lambda introducer. You can also use default captures by just specifying & within the lambda introducer and not have to specify each capture variable.

LISTING 2-7 Lambda capture specifying capture by reference

```
#include <algorithm>
#include <iostream>
#include <vector>
```

```
using namespace std;

void main() {
    vector<int> v;

    for (int i = 0; i < 10; ++i) {
        v.push_back(i);
    }

    int x = 1;
    int y = 1;

    for_each(v.begin(), v.end(), [&x, &y](int& r) {
        const int old = r;

        r *= x * y;

        x = y;
        y = old;
    });

    for_each(v.begin(), v.end(), [](int n) { cout << n << " "; });
    cout << endl;

    cout << x << ", " << y << endl;
}
```

Mixing value captures and reference captures

You can specify some variables to be captured by value and others by reference and have all of them within a single lambda introducer. However, it is easier to specify a default capture and override capture behavior of specific local variables.

LISTING 2-8 Mixing by value and by reference captures

```
#include <algorithm>
#include <iostream>
#include <vector>
using namespace std;

void main() {
    vector<int> v;

    for (int i = 0; i < 10; ++i) {
        v.push_back(i);
    }

    int sum = 0;
    int product = 1;

    int x = 1;
    int y = 1;

    for_each(v.begin(), v.end(), [=, &sum, &product](int& r) mutable {
```

```
        sum += r;

        if (r != 0) {
            product *= r;
        }

        const int old = r;

        r *= x * y;

        x = y;
        y = old;
    });

    for_each(v.begin(), v.end(), [](int n) { cout << n << " "; });
    cout << endl;

    cout << "sum: " << sum << ", product: " << product << endl;
    cout << "x: " << x << ", y: " << y << endl;
}
```

Capturing the this pointer

Capturing the **this** pointer is no different. You just mention this in the lambda introducer and within the lambda body access all data members of the class.

Range 'for'

C++ finally has a convenient syntax to iterate over a range of values. In simple terms, you can provide a container to your for loop and it will iterate over the container. A range based for loop looks like this:

```
vector<int> vec;
vec.push_back(1);
vec.push_back(2);
vec.push_back(3);
for (int i: vec)
{
        std::cout << i;
}
```

This simple example uses a vector of type integer to iterate over the contents of the vector and print its contents. For a more complex collection like a map, you can use the auto keyword to deduce the iterator type and then choose to print the map data.

```
map<int, std::wstring> myMap;
myMap[1] = L"First";
myMap[2] = L"Second";

for (auto x : myMap)
{
        std::wcout<< x.first << L"<" << x.second.c_str()  << L">" << endl;
}
```

The new smart pointers

Smart pointers are defined in the *std* namespace in the <memory> header file. They are crucial to the RAII or Resource Acquisition Is Initialization programming idiom. The main goal of this idiom is to ensure that resource acquisition occurs at the same time that the object is initialized, so that all resources for the object are created and made ready in one line of code. In practical terms, the main principle of RAII when applied to memory management is to give ownership of any heap-allocated resource to a stack-allocated object whose destructor contains the code to delete or free the resource and also any associated cleanup code. When you initialize a raw pointer or resource handle to point to an actual resource, pass the pointer to a smart pointer immediately.

Access the encapsulated pointer by using the familiar pointer operators, -> and *, which the smart pointer class overloads to return the encapsulated raw pointer. Please note, however, that no separate garbage collector runs in the background; memory is managed through the standard C++ scoping rules so that the runtime environment is faster, more efficient and deterministic.

> Always create smart pointers on a separate line of code, never in a parameter list, so that a subtle resource leak won't occur due to certain parameter list allocation rules.

Smart pointers are designed to be as efficient as possible both in terms of memory and performance. For example, the only data member in **unique_ptr** is the encapsulated pointer. This means that **unique_ptr** is exactly the same size as that pointer, either four bytes or eight bytes. Accessing the encapsulated pointer by using the smart pointer overloaded * and -> operators is not significantly slower than accessing the raw pointers directly.

Smart pointers have their own member functions, which are accessed by using "dot" notation. For example, some STL smart pointers have a reset member function that releases ownership of the pointer. This is useful when you want to free the memory owned by the smart pointer before the smart pointer goes out of scope.

The following are the new smart pointers available with C++11.

std::unique_ptr

A unique_ptr allows exactly one owner of the underlying pointer. A unique_ptr should be your default choice for a plain old C++ object, unless you know for certain that you require a **shared_ptr**. A unique_ptr can be moved to a new owner, but not copied or shared. The unique_ptr replaces **auto_ptr**, which is deprecated.

```
std::unique_ptr<int> p1(new int(42));
std::unique_ptr<int> p2 = p1; //Compile error.
std::unique_ptr<int> p3 = std::move(p1); //Transfers ownership. p3 now owns the memory and p1 is rendered invalid.
p3.reset(); //Deletes the memory.
p1.reset(); //Does nothing.
```

std::shared_ptr

A shared_ptr is a reference-counted smart pointer. Use when you want to assign one raw pointer to multiple owners, for example, when you return a copy of a pointer from a container but want to keep the original. The raw pointer is not deleted until all **shared_ptr** owners have gone out of scope or have otherwise given up ownership. The size is two pointers; one for the object and one for the shared control block that contains the reference count.

```
std::shared_ptr<int> p1(new int(42));
std::shared_ptr<int> p2 = p1; //Both now own the memory.

p1.reset(); //Memory still exists, due to p2.
p2.reset(); //Deletes the memory, since no one else owns the memory.
```

shared_ptr plays very nicely with the auto keyword we saw earlier. Take a look at the first line above, note that we need to repeat the type 'int' twice. The Standard Library contains the make_shared template function that avoids this.

```
#include <iostream>
#include <memory>
#include <string>

using namespace std;

class Thing
{
public:
    Thing(const char* name): m_name(name) {}
    ~Thing() { cout << m_name << endl; }

private:
    string m_name;
};

void _tmain()
{
    auto t = make_shared<Thing>("Luna");
}
```

Using make_shared in conjunction with auto not only avoids repeating the name of the type being allocated, it is also more robust in the presence of any exceptions thrown during the construction of the shared_ptr instance.

std::weak_ptr

The weak_ptr is a special-case smart pointer for use in conjunction with **shared_ptr**. A **weak_ptr** provides access to an object that is owned by one or more **shared_ptr** instances, but does not participate in reference counting. Use when you want to observe an object, but do not require it to remain alive. Required in some cases to break circular references between **shared_ptr** instances.

```
std::shared_ptr<int> p1(new int(42));
std::weak_ptr<int> wp1 = p1; //p1 owns the memory.
```

```
k(); //Now p1 and p2 own the memory.
he memory still exists
```

ed by p1.

---

geared towards providing maximum performance benefits for
ıum performance overhead, there are still some cases where
ne such case is copying of large objects.

ments into STL collections would result in the creation of tem-
ɔied over into the collection and the temporary objects being
e of temporary object, the compiler would sometimes optimize
:imization).

string concatenation. It is normal to have code such as this:

create and construct a temporary object which would then be
;tr and the temporary would then be discarded.

. collections from functions. Consider the following example:

```
:int>& v)
```

A function such as CreateVector shown above, would probably get called in code as follows:

```
vector<int> v1 = CreateVector(vec);
```

There are quite a few temporary objects being constructed and thrown away during the entire call
sequence of calling the CreateVector and then returning the newly constructed vector. When the
CreateVector is called, it constructs a new vector vec and then proceeds to fill it up. When code
comes up to the return statement, the entire contents of the vector vec must be copied back. Technically, there could be two copies: one to copy into a temporary object and another when the object
is to be assigned back to the vector instance v1. The first temporary object might be optimized away

as part of the return value optimization but the second cannot be avoided. This might be a very simple example but it conveys the point: too many unnecessary copies which result in a performance hit!

C++11 introduces move constructors and move assignment operators to solve this issue. Move constructors avoid the performance hit by performing a shallow copy and "swap" a few pointers to change ownership of the underlying object. The move concepts are very useful to where deep copying is usually involved. In such cases, a move operation will only copy the object's memory (changing the pointer) as that is all that is necessary.

So how does move semantics work? Rvalues are the answer!

Rvalue references

Expressions in C++ fall into two categories: lvalues and rvalues. If you can obtain the address of an expression, it is an lvalue else it is an rvalue. When you call functions, the return values usually indicate whether an lvalue or an rvalue is involved. If the return type is a reference, the C++ standard says it is an lvalue else it is an rvalue.

Rvalue references are defined with the double ampersand &&. T&& refers to an rvalue reference of type T. The regular T& references are now called as lvalue references. Similar to lvalue references, rvalue references must be initialized and cannot be re-assigned. So, where does all of this come into play?

Move constructor and move assignment operator

When working with rvalue references, a common occurrence is to create a move constructor and move assignment operator. Like a plain old copy constructor, a move constructor takes an object instance as its argument and proceeds to create a new instance of an object with one major difference. Instead of performing a deep copy, we will simply move the objects around!

Moving object pointers is not simple as it sounds. If the underlying type is an int, we just copy it. If the type, however, is a pointer, then things get interesting. In such a case, rather than allocate a new object, initialize memory, we will simply swap the pointer and nullptr the temporary object. Let us see how this works with an example.

```
class A
{
public:
    A()
    {
            cout << "normal constructor" <<endl;
    }

    A(const A& rhs)
    {
            cout << "copy constructor" <<endl;
    }
```

```
};
vector<A> v1;
v1.push_back( A() );
```

If we were to construct a collection of object type A using a vector as shown above, the normal constructor as well as the copy constructor will be invoked. If, we were to add a move constructor to the class A, then things change.

```
A(A&& rhs)
    {
            cout << "move constructor" <<endl;
    }
```

Now, if we invoke the code, we will see that the move constructor will be invoked instead of the copy constructor. This provides performance benefits when used in real world code. You should implement move constructors and move assignment operators wherever possible in your code. A notable difference with normal constructors is that the compiler does not generate a move constructor or a move assignment operator for your code automatically as it does for normal constructors.

Moving class members

This is all hunky dory but how does one move data members? The short answer is by copying each member manually. Let us add two data members to the class A: a type int and a pointer to an integer type.

We introduce two private data members to class A as shown below.

```
int _x;
int* _y;
```

Let us now add a move copy constructor to copy data members manually.

```
A(A&& rhs) : _x(rhs._x), _y(rhs._y)
    {
            cout << "move constructor" <<endl;
            rhs._y = nullptr;
    }
```

Finally, we will add a move assignment operator.

```
A& operator=(A&& rhs)
    {
            delete _y;
            _x = rhs._x;
            _y = rhs._y;

            rhs._y = nullptr;

            return *this;
    }
```

Adding a move constructor and move assignment operator brings in performance benefits by doing away with expensive copy operations. So where are all the modern C++ semantics used? The STL has been thoroughly revised to use move semantics wherever possible, so performance benefits are provided to all user applications. In addition, Visual C++ 2012 introduces extensions to the C++ programming to make Windows 8 Store app development easier. Modern C++ facilities such as auto and lambdas can be extensively used to write Windows Store apps using C++. But before diving into how to develop Windows Store apps using C++, let us now turn our attention to C++ Component Extensions.

Welcome to the Component Extensions

Visual C++ 2012 introduces a new native programming model for creating Windows Store Applications and Windows Runtime components. The new model makes it possible for native code to interop with managed or Javascript code without the need for wrappers, shims or translation layers. Using the new model also help you create:

- Windows Store Applications using C++ and XAML as User interface.

- Windows Runtime components authored in C++ but consumed in other languages.

- Windows Store DirectX games and graphics intensive applications.

No matter what category your applications falls into, you can be completely sure that the C++ code you write is 100% native with no dependency on managed or Javascript code!

This section introduces C++ /CX, a set of extensions to the ISO-C++ programming language. These extensions, represented by /CX, for component extensions, are designed to simplify the creation and consumption of Windows 8 Windows Store applications and Windows Runtime components. The extensions are designed to program using idioms that are much simpler and more natural than traditional COM programming. In addition, using the extensions enables you to interact easily with Visual Basic, C# or JavaScript and other languages that support the Windows Runtime.

In the second half of the chapter, we take a quick look at how the Parallel Patterns Library enables developers to write "async" code using tasks and explore how to build reusable WinRT components using C++ /CX. We conclude this chapter with a recommendation on how to consume C++ /CX in your C++ applications.

C++ /CX, Windows Runtime and ISO-C++

C++ is a very powerful programming language with a vast feature set that is a natural choice for professional software development. The Windows Runtime is a new programming model and API, introduced with Windows 8 that enables developers to create Windows Store applications. C++ /CX is a binding between ISO-C++ programming language and the new Windows Runtime. Figure 2-1 shows the symbiotic relationship between ISO-C++, C++ /CX and WinRT.

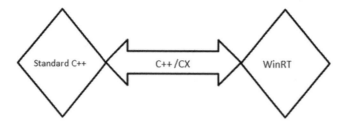

FIGURE 2-1 How C++ /CX connects ISO-C++ and WinRT

C++ /CX enables you to develop native applications faster and enables you, as a developer, to focus on your application's features and business logic. C++ /CX is used in the following scenarios:

1. Windows Runtime components that are consumed by Javascript or C# or Visual Basic. We discuss the creation of Windows Runtime components in the latter part of this chapter.

2. Windows Store Applications with XAML as User Interface. We will discuss XAML for C++ in Chapter 3.

3. Windows Store DirectX games and graphics intensive applications. We will discuss the mixing of XAML and DirectX in Chapter 4.

Microsoft has extended Standard C++ via language extensions earlier too. The earlier experiments resulted in the now infamous Managed Extensions for C++ and later in C++/CLI. The pairing of C++/CLI was the first genuine effort to unify a statically typed language (C++) with a framework that supported a garbage-collected, language-independent programming model. This pairing, as we shall see, is what enabled the Visual C++ team at Microsoft to produce the C++ component extensions for Windows Runtime, C++ /CX.

At this point, we should note the following pertinent issues, relevant to our understanding of these component extensions as well as the Windows Runtime.

1. The new component extensions produce 100% native code with no dependency on any managed framework whatsoever.

2. Using the new **/ZW** compiler directive generates native code whereas using the **/clr** compiler directive generates managed code. We will be using the **/ZW** compiler directive throughout the book to produce 100% native code. You cannot use the **/clr** option when targeting WinRT. The **/clr** option is still supported by the compiler when targeting the CLR specifically.

3. Targeting the Windows Runtime by just using standard C++ code is possible. However, the resultant code tends to be verbose, and results in repetitive code and takes programmer focus away from application logic to hand crafting the boiler plate code needed to get an app

running on the Windows Runtime. Hand written C++ code works well for small samples, but breaks down spectacularly when creating XAML applications.

Using C++ /CX, you can easily leverage your existing knowledge and skills to build Windows Store applications for Windows 8. In addition, you can also reuse existing code written using standard C++ while developing Windows 8 applications.

With this background, let us now turn our attention to writing our first application using C++ /CX.

Hello World in C++ /CX

As is customary for all programming languages, let us create a simple "Hello World" application using C++ /CX. Open Notepad and enter the following code. Save it to disk with a name, such as "First.cpp"

LISTING 2-9 Hello World in C++ /CX

```cpp
#include <iostream>
using namespace std;
using namespace Platform;

int main(Array< String^>^ args)
{
    String^ str = "Hello World!";
    wcout<<str->Data()<<endl; // accessing the content of the String^
    return 0;
}
```

1. In order to compile this, open the Visual Studio 2012 x86 Native tools command prompt.

2. Navigate to the folder where you saved "First.cpp".

3. Type the following command and hit "ENTER"

    a. Cl.exe /c /ZW /EHsc first.cpp

4. The above command compiles the code and generates first.obj.

5. Type the following command and hit "ENTER"

    a. Link.exe first.obj vccorlib.lib runtimeobject.lib /SUBSYSTEM:CONSOLE

6. You now have an executable named "first.exe" in your project path.

7. Executing first.exe outputs the string "Hello World" at the console window.

8. Congratulations, you have successfully written your first C++ /CX program

A few things to note here: aside from the Platform namespace, the String class and the signature of the program entry point *main*, the program looks like a normal C++ program. What this means is you can write Windows Store applications using the familiar C++ syntax plus a few platform specific extensions without the need to learn C# or VB.net. In addition to using the C++ /CX signature for the program entry point *main*, you can also use one of the following standard-compliant entry points for *main*:

- int main(void)

- int main()

- int main(int argc, char** argv)

- int main(int argc, char* argv[])

It is not mandatory to use the C++ /CX signature entry point for *main*; using this special signature initializes the WinRT on the main thread automatically for you.

The /ZW compiler option

In order to use the component extensions, you should enable the **/ZW** compiler directive. This directive creates a Windows Runtime application that is capable of consuming the new Windows Runtime framework types such as XAML, the pickers etc.

Table 2-1 lists all the applicable compiler options to enable component extensions

TABLE 2-1   Compiler options to enable C++ component extensions

Compiler Option	Description
/ZW	Enables Windows Runtime language extensions.
/ZW:nostdlib	The nostdlib parameter prevents the compiler from using the standard, predefined search path to find assembly and .winmd files. The /ZW compiler option implicitly specifies the following compiler options: /FI vccorlib.h, which forces inclusion of the vccorlib.h header file that defines many types that are required by the compiler. /FU Windows.winmd, which forces inclusion of the Windows.winmd metadata file that's provided by the operating system and defines many types in the Windows Runtime. /FU Platform.winmd, which forces inclusion of the Platform.winmd metadata file that's provided by the compiler and defines most types in the Platform family of namespaces.
/AI dir	Adds a directory, which is specified by the dir parameter, to the search path that the compiler uses to find assembly and .winmd files.
/FU file	Forces the inclusion of the specified assembly, module, or .winmd file. That is, you don't have to specify #using file in your source code. The compiler automatically forces the inclusion of its own Windows metadata file, Platform.winmd.
/D "WINAPI_FAMILY=2"	Creates a definition that enables the use of a subset of the Win32 SDK that's compatible with the Windows Runtime.

Tip As a best practice, do NOT use #using file in source code to add references to WinRT components. Use the VS way of adding project references. This is achieved by right clicking on Project file and choosing References option.

Table 2-2 lists the linker options to build applications with component extensions.

TABLE 2-2   Linker options to build apps with component extensions

Linker option	Description
/APPCONTAINER[:NO]	Marks the executable as runnable in the appcontainer (only).
/WINMD[:{NO|ONLY}]	Emits a .winmd file and an associated binary file. This option must be passed to the linker for a .winmd to be emitted. NO—Doesn't emit a .winmd file, but does emit a binary file. ONLY—Emits a .winmd file, but doesn't emit a binary file.
/WINMDFILE:filename	The name of the .winmd file to emit, instead of the default .winmd file name. If multiple file names are specified on the command line, the last name is used.
/WINMDDELAYSIGN[:NO]	Partially signs the .winmd file and places the public key in the binary. NO—(Default) Doesn't sign the .winmd file. /WINMDDELAYSIGN has no effect unless /WINMDKEYFILE or /WINMDKEYCONTAINER is also specified
/WINMDKEYCONTAINER:name	Specifies a key container to sign an assembly. The name parameter corresponds to the key container that's used to sign the metadata file.
/WINMDKEYFILE:filename	Specifies a key or a key pair to sign the assembly. The filename parameter corresponds to the key that's used to sign the metadata file.

The C++ /CX Type System

The Visual C++ component extensions (C++/CX) support the type system that's defined by the Windows Runtime architecture. The type system defined by the Windows Runtime architecture enables data types and functions to be shared between applications and components written in any language with support for the Windows Runtime. Today, this list of languages includes C++/CX, Visual Basic, Visual C#, and JavaScript.

C++/CX provides built-in base types and implementations of fundamental Windows Runtime types. The base types are provided in the Platform::default namespace and are included in the platform.winmd file. The Platform namespace is implicitly added to every C++ /CX project you create with Visual Studio. In addition, you can consume any Windows Runtime type, or create classes, structs, interfaces, and other user-defined types that can be consumed by other components and applications.

Reference types **are instantiated only via** reference-counted pointers (also known as handles) to Windows Runtime objects. These reference-counted pointers are represented in code using the ^ or 'hat' symbol. C++/CX automatically modifies the reference count (ref count) of an object when it is instantiated, copied, set to null, or goes out of scope. When the reference count becomes zero, the object's destructor is immediately invoked just as in any C++ program. There is no separate garbage collection mechanism in C++/CX.

The following constructs are valid for instantiating C++ objects and Windows Runtime objects:

- **MyWinRTType^**

- **MyNativeType***

- MyWinRTType*

- MyNativeType^

Here MyWinRTType is a Windows Runtime class whereas MyNativeType is a standard C++ class. For this release of Visual C++, instantiation of Windows Runtime objects and C++ objects are only supported via the first two mechanisms listed above. All Windows Runtime objects use the ^ whereas the standard C++ types use the *. The compiler does not support using a ^ for standard C++ type and a * for the Windows Runtime types imported via metadata.

Classes and Structs

C++ /CX support user-defined reference classes and structs, and user-defined value classes and structs. Public forms of these types can be passed between Windows Runtime components and apps, whereas standard C++ classes and structs cannot.

> **Note** All Windows Runtime types should be declared within a namespace and cannot be declared at the global namespace level. All examples used in the discussion assume that the types are declared within a namespace. The complete examples provided along with the book follow this pattern.

Runtime classes and Structs

A Windows runtimeclass definition has two parts, just like in standard C++: the class head, composed of the keywords *ref class* and the class body, enclosed by a pair of curly braces. For example,

```
public ref class MyButton sealed
{
// my button types and functions
};
```

Within the body of a runtume class, the class data members, member functions and properties are declared. As with standard C++, the access levels of the data members, member functions and properties are also specified.

To declare a runtume class, use the *ref class* contextual keyword. A runtime class can contain public, protected, and private function members, data members, and nested classes. By default, the accessibility is private.

Once a class is declared, the type can be referred to by specifying the class name, as follows:

```
MyButton objButton; or
MyButton^ objButton = ref new MyButton();
```

A 'ref struct' is also a Windows runtime class (same as a 'ref class'), except that a ref struct declares a runtime class that by default has public accessibility.

You can instantiate a runtime class if has at least one implicit or explicit public constructor. In these cases, the compiler applies the required attributes to the class and stores that information in the .winmd file of the app. A runtime class also needs a public destructor to be declared if you want to create instances of runtime classes using stack-based semantics.

> **Tip** You can freely mix standard C++ types and functions in a Windows Runtime class. However you can pass only public WinRT classes, intrinsic types, value structs, and value classes between Windows Runtime components.

The following code is valid to pass across the Windows Runtime ABI boundary

LISTING 2-10 Passing C++ /CX code across the ABI

```
public ref class ValidClass sealed
{
public:
   ValidClass();
   ~ValidClass();

public:
   String^ DisplayMessage();
}
```

The following code is not valid to be passed across the Windows Runtime ABI boundary

LISTING 2-11 Failing C++ /CX code across the ABI

```
public ref class ValidClass sealed
{
public:
   ValidClass();
   ~ValidClass();

public:
   std::wstring DisplayMessage();
}
```

Table 2-3 shows the declaration of various types in C++ /CX.

TABLE 2-3 Declaration of various types in C++ /CX

WinRT Type	Declaration syntax

Reference types	ref class MyRefClass
	{
	    void Func() {.....};
	};
	ref struct MyRefStruct
	{
	    void Func() {...};
	};

Value types	value class MyValueClass
	{
	    //only basic types and String^ types allowed.
	};
	value struct MyValueClass
	{
	    //only basic types and String^ types allowed.
	};

Interfaces	interface class IMyInterface
	{
	    void Func();
	};
	interface struct IMyInterface
	{
	    Void Func();
	};

Just as in Standard C++, struct and class can be used interchangeably in C++ /CX too. They follow the visibility rules set out in Standard C++ as well. In a class, methods are *private* by default whereas in a struct methods are *public* by default. In the above table, MyRefClass::Func and MyValue-Class::Func are both *private* whereas MyRefStruct::Func and MyValueStruct::Func are both *public*. Interface methods are always *public*; declaring an interface as a struct is equivalent to declaring it as a class.

You define a Windows runtime class by using the ref class keyword. When you define a runtime class variable, you must append the handle-to-object modifier (^, pronounced "hat") to the type name. The hat modifier is used instead of the pointer modifier (*). This is because a runtime class is aware of the WinRT rules such as Activation and the IInspectable interface. This in turn, allows the compiler to internally manage reference counts of the said object. Use the arrow (->) class-member-access operator to access the members of the declared object.

If you instantiate a runtime class on the heap, use the **ref new** keyword instead of the **new** keyword on the right side of the assignment. On the left side of the assignment, append the hat modifier to the type that you declare. Alternatively, use the auto keyword instead of specifying a type; the compiler will deduce the type from the type of the assignment. For example, the following two declarations are legal:

```
A^ one = ref new A();
auto one = ref new A();
```

You can also use stack based semantics to instantiate runtime classes. Listing 2-4 declares a runtime class named "A". You can instantiate an instance of class A by simply declaring

```
A objA;
// make method calls on objA
```

The lifetime of objA is limited to the scope in which it has been declared. This is similar to standard C++ and the destructor of class A would get automatically invoked when the object goes out of scope even if the re-count of the instance did not reach 0. Calling any methods on the instance after that (in case you kept alive another reference to that stack allocated object) would result in a platform exception being thrown. C++ /CX maps the destructor of the class to the **IClosable** WinRT interface which is projected in C++ /CX as Platform::IDisposable interface. You can also declare a reference to WinRT types by appending the tracking reference modifier (%) to the type name. A reference holds the address of an object, but behaves syntactically like an object. Assigning an object to a tracking reference increments the reference count on the object. Use the dot (.) class-member-access operator to access the members of the declared object.

The following code samples demonstrate how to declare runtime classes and copy constructors.

LISTING 2-12 Declaring runtime classes and copy constructors

```
ref class A sealed
{
internal:
    A(A% other)
    {
        Platform::Details::Console::WriteLine(__FUNCTION__ "(A%);");
        Value = other.Value;
    }
public:
    A(A^ other)
    {
        Platform::Details::Console::WriteLine(__FUNCTION__ "(A^);");
        Value = other->Value;
    }
    A()
    {
        Platform::Details::Console::WriteLine(__FUNCTION__ "();");
    }
    void Print()
    {
        Platform::Details::Console::WriteLine(Value);
    }
    property int Value;
};
[Platform::MTAThread]
int main()
{
    Platform::Details::Console::WriteLine("One");
    A^ one = ref new A();
    one->Value = 42;
```

```
    Platform::Details::Console::WriteLine("two");
    A^ two = ref new A(one);

    Platform::Details::Console::WriteLine("three");
    A^ three = ref new A();
    three = one;

    Platform::Details::Console::WriteLine("four");
    A four(one);

  A five(*one);

    one->Print();
    two->Print();
    three->Print();
    four.Print();
    five.Print();
}
```

The output of the above code is as shown in Figure 2-2. We can thus conclude:

- Using the internal access modifier masks the function from being called outside of the module in which it is defined.

- Object one is constructed by calling the public constructor of class A.

- Object two is constructed by calling the public copy constructor of class A.

- Object three is constructed by calling the public constructor of class A. Assigning three = one, only copies the handle (i.e. addrefs 'one' variable and releases 'three' variable) thus deleting the just created instance ('three').

- Object four is constructed by calling the public copy constructor of class A. However in this case, object four is created on the stack versus the heap.

- Object five is constructed by calling the internal copy constructor of class A.

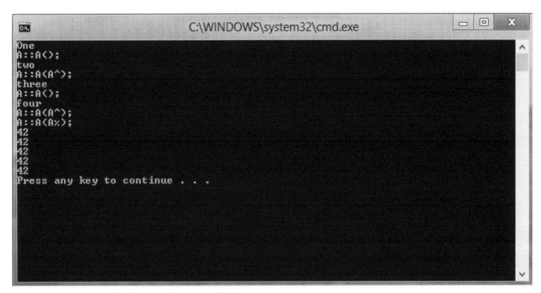

FIGURE 2-2 Output of code from the listing 2-4 above

Class Modifiers

Using the sealed modifier prevents further derivation of a ref class. A sealed class cannot be used as a base class for any other class. Trying to do so results in a compiler error.

```
ref class SealedClass sealed
{
};
ref class Test : SealedClass    // This generates a compiler error
{
};
```

Using the *internal* modifier indicates that the given element is available to only other code within the same compilation unit but private to the metadata generated. So in other words, the code is *private* outside the compilation unit but *public* within the same compilation unit. Combination of access modifiers is also allowed. The order of the keywords does not matter. However, the less restrictive access is always applicable to the compilation unit and the more restrictive access to the metadata. Thus you can specify *private private, protected private, public protected* etc for access control. Table 2-4 summarizes the access modifiers and their impact.

TABLE 2-4   Access modifiers and their visibility impact

Modifiers Used	Visible within same compilation unit	Visible outside to the class
Public	Yes	Yes
Private	No	No
Protected	To derived classes	To derived classes
Internal	Yes	No

Data Members

Class data members are declared in a similar way as one declares variables. For example, the MyButton class may have the following members:

```
public ref class MyButton sealed
{
internal:
String^     Caption; // string for the Button Name
int         Width;   // Width of the Button
int         Height;  // Height of the Button
};
```

Any standard type can be used to declare a data member including pointers to functions.

Member functions

The member functions of a runtime class are declared inside the class body. For example:

```
public ref class MyButton sealed
{
internal:
String^     Caption; // string for the Button Name
int         Width;   // Width of the Button
int         Height;  // Height of the Button
public:
intGetWidth();           // returns the Width of the Button
intGetHeight();          // returns the Height of the Button
};
```

And just like in standard C++, the function definitions can be placed inside the body. For example:

```
public ref class MyButton
{
public:
String^     Caption; // string for the Button Name
int         Width;   // Width of the Button
int         Height;  // Height of the Button
public:
intGetWidth() { return Width; }       // returns the Width of the Button
intGetHeight() { return Height; }     // returns the Height of the Button
};
```

Runtime Class objects

The definition of a runtime class does not cause any storage to be allocated. Storage is only allocated when an object of the class type is defined. For example, based on the MyButton class declared above,

```
MyButton objButton or
MyButton^ objButton = ref new MyButton();
```

reserves the necessary storage to store the handle to the new instance. The call "ref new MyButton" dynamically allocates the necessary storage to instantiate the object. As discussed in the first chapter, "Introduction to the Windows 8 Apps", the Windows Runtime components are COM objects implementing the **IInspectable** interface and adhering to the rules laid down by the WinRT Abstract Binary Interface (ABI). The **IInspectable** interface inherits from the classic COM interface, **IUnknown** and also contains three new members. These are:

- Getlids : fetches the interfaces implemented by the current Windows Runtime component

- GetRuntimeClassName: returns the fully qualified name of the current Windows Runtime object.

- GetTrustLevel: returns the trust level of the current Windows Runtime object.

It is important to note here that no Windows Runtime component has a dual interface. In other words, WinRT components do not implement the **IDispatch** interface. As discussed earlier, the C++ component extensions, map WinRT concepts to standard C++ concepts. For example, activation of a WinRT component done at the ABI level via the **_RoActivateInstance_** function, is mapped to the constructor of the runtime class. No parameters are passed to the constructor when activation happens. Similarly, reference counting implementation for IUnknown::AddRef and IUnknown::Release are similar to the usage of a shared_ptr, which is a standard C++ smart pointer class for managing object lifetimes.

> **Tip** IDispatch was originally designed to support automation. Like all COM interfaces, IDispatch also derives from IUnknown and exposes objects, methods, and properties to Automation programming tools and other applications. For more information, see "Inside COM" by Dale Rogerson and published by Microsoft Press.

Instantiating WinRT classes using C++ /CX

The **ref new** keyword is used to instantiate WinRT classes using C++ /CX. This returns a pointer to a pointer to a vtable. It is similar to the **new** operator from Standard C++, it does have a few differences. There is no equivalent to the placement new or an array form of new. Although Standard C++ allows global overload of the new operator (which is a bad thing to do), you cannot overload **ref new** globally or in any translation unit. The compiler also generates a default copy-assignment operator for your ref class in case you have not written one.

As we shall discuss later in the chapter, using the **ref new** operator produces an object that implements the **IUnknown interface**, the **IInspectable interface** and the **IWeakReferenceSource** interface. ref new is strongly typed and returns an object of the type requested. This is a pointer to an object that as a first member has a pointer to a vtable.. The vtable is laid out exactly as follows:

FIGURE 2-3 vtable layout of a ref class in C++ /CX

Boxing and unboxing

C++/CX supports boxing, which is a process that converts a value type and its value to a reference type, and unboxing, which converts a boxed type back to its unboxed form. Unary reference types, and collective types such as arrays, can boxed and unboxed.

You can perform boxing by one of the following means:

- Assign a value type to a reference type; for example, Object^.

- Use the safe_cast<T>() function to cast the type. An exception is thrown if the cast fails.

- Use the dynamic_cast<T> function to cast the type. The function yields nullptr if the cast fails.

- Use the **Platform::IBox<T>** or **Platform:IBoxArray<T>** template type to declare a boxed type that's based on a value type. If the boxing operation fails, **Platform::InvalidCastException** is thrown.

The following code sample shows how to Box and unbox different types.

LISTING 2-13 Box and unbox different types

```
value class Vxx
{
public:
    int Number;
};
int main(Platform::Array<Platform::String^>^ args)
{
    Vxx vobject;
    vobject.Number = 5;

    //let us now create a box value
    IBox<Vxx>^ boxobj = vobject;
```

```
auto vb2 = ref new Box<Vxx>(vobject);

Object^ obj = vobject;
Vxx vobj2 = boxobj->Value;
Vxx vobj4 = (Vxx)vb2;
Vxx vobj6 = (Vxx)obj;

// use a cast
Vxx vobj3 = *(Box<Vxx>^)obj;

// Non-throwing ways of getting the value from an untyped box.
auto b = dynamic_cast<Box<Vxx>^>(obj);

// Erroneous operations
Vxx vobj7 = (Vxx)*obj;
// Pass a default value if o is not a box<V>^.
Vxx vobj8 = (b == nullptr) ? Vxx() : *b;

return 0;

}
```

Standard C++ types and C++ /CX classes

Until now, we have taken a look at ref classes and how to construct them. In this section, we will look at how to mix standard C++ types (built-in as well as user defined) and C++ /CX ref classes.

> **Note** You can mix Standard C++ types in C++ /CX classes without any restrictions. However, between Windows Runtime components, you can only pass public WinRT classes, WinRT structs, value structs and value classes.

The following code sample shows how to mix Standard C++ types and C++ /CX classes. The full code is available in the **CxxCpp** sample. Our example uses a canonical Person class declared under a namespace 'x'. This Person class is an ISO-C++ class devoid of any platform specific code. In the runtime class Person, we will have an instance of x::Person as a private member. All calls to the methods of the runtime class Person will be delegated down to the corresponding methods of the x::Person instance.

LISTING 2-14 Mixing Standard C++ types and C++ /CX reference types

```
ref class Person sealed
{
    public:
            Person();
            virtual ~Person();

    private:
            x::Person _person;
...
}
int main()
```

```
{
    // create person attributes using standard C++ strings
    std::wstring fName = L"John";
    std::wstring lName = L"Doe";
    std::wstring email = L"John.Doe@somewhere.com";

    //create the Cpp Cx Person object and set attributes
    //These attributes are set on the embedded native stdPerson object
    Person^ p = ref new Person();
    p->FirstName = ref new String(fName.c_str());
    p->LastName = ref new String(lName.c_str());
    p->EmailAddress = ref new String(email.c_str());

    //let us output the data to the command line
    using namespace Platform::Details;
    Console::WriteLine(p->FirstName);
    Console::WriteLine(p->LastName);
    Console::WriteLine(p->FullName);
    Console::WriteLine(p->EmailAddress);
    return 0;
}
```

Class Inheritance

C++ /CX support for inheritance is not the same as Standard C++. Multiple inheritance of classes is not supported. However, your ref class can inherit publicly from one concrete class and implement multiple interfaces. The idea behind this restriction is to prevent some of the problems with the Standard C++ style multiple inheritance (such as the diamond inheritance problem). Multiple inheritance has its merits. The *iostreams* library in C++ is a perfect example of such an inheritance model. However, for each good usage of multiple inheritance there are countless examples of misuse. Hence the restriction on the usage of multiple inheritance in C++ /CX.

A private base ref class is not required to derive from an existing unsealed class. If you require an object hierarchy to model your own program structure or to enable code reuse, then use private or internal ref classes, or better yet, standard C++ classes. You can expose the functionality of the private object hierarchy through a public sealed ref class wrapper.

Consider the following class hierarchy. The compiler generates an error when we attempt to compile this code.

LISTING 2-15 Inheritance hierarchy in C++ /CX

```
ref class B
{
};

ref class C
{
};

ref class D : B, C
{
```

```
};
```

It emits the following error message

```
error C2890: 'D' : a ref class can only have one non-interface base class
the ref class 'B' is a base class of 'D'
the ref class 'C' is a base class of 'D'
```

What is even more interesting is the diagnostic message that is generated:

```
error C2385: ambiguous access of '__abi_reference_count'
could be the '__abi_reference_count' in base 'B'
or could be the '__abi_reference_count' in base 'C'
This diagnostic occurred in the compiler generated function 'long D::__abi_QueryInterface(Platform::Guid
&,void **)'
```

The compiler is complaining about the presence of multiple instance of some field __abi_reference_count. As we shall see later in the section on "A peek inside the magic of C++ /CX", each runtime class has a generated field __abi_reference_count that is needed to implement the well-known COM reference counting. This reference counting mechanism is used to properly destruct runtime class objects without the usage of an explicit *delete* call on runtime class objects. Usage of *delete* is only even needed when

- Your ref class is storing costly or exclusive resources that require deterministic cleanup and don't subscribe/play well with reference counted schemes e.g. database connections, file handles, etc.

- Your runtime class is part of a circular dependency of WinRT objects. In this case, the circle needs to be explicitly broken (via a delete in C++ /CX or other means in other languages) to ever release any of the objects.

Note The inheritance model for public ref classes is specifically designed for support of the XAML object hierarchy; it is not intended as a general inheritance model.

Class inheritance requires that a class is accessible; that is, that it is declared public or protected. Metadata about the class is injected into the corresponding Windows metadata file (.winmd). A ref class that has a public or protected constructor in C++/CX must be declared as sealed. This restriction means that there is no way for classes that are written in other languages such as C# or Visual Basic to inherit from types that you declare in a Windows Runtime component that's written in C++/CX.

Virtual methods can be superseded by more derived classes in an inheritance chain. With the accessibility principle and virtual methods in mind, here are the basic rules of inheritance in C++ /CX:

- Runtime classes can inherit directly from at most one base runtime class, but can implement any number of interfaces.

- If a class has a public constructor, it must be declared as sealed to prevent further derivation.

- You can create public unsealed base classes that have internal or protected private constructors, provided that the base class derives directly or indirectly from an existing unsealed base class such as **Windows::UI::Xaml::DependencyObject**. Inheritance of user-defined ref classes across .winmd files is not supported; however, a ref class can inherit from an interface that's defined in another .winmd file. You can create derived classes from a user-defined base ref class only within the same Windows Runtime component or Windows Store app.

- For ref classes, only public inheritance is supported..

- A base class can define protected non-virtual methods.

- Declare virtual methods as protected or public, and don't specify a private modifier (this includes protected private). Otherwise, an error is emitted.

- In constructors and destructors, virtual calls invoke the most derived override. Unless you are certain which override will be called, we recommend that you not make virtual calls in a constructor or destructor.

The contextual keyword *override* is used to indicate an explicit intention to override a virtual function.

The following code sample shows how to use the *override* keyword to override the base class implementation of a virtual function.

LISTING 2-16 Using the override keyword to override base class implementation of virtual functions

```
ref class B
{
public:
    B() {};

    virtual void DoSomething() { wcout << __FUNCTION__  <<endl; }
};

ref class C : B
{
public:
    virtual void DoSomething() override
    {
            wcout << __FUNCTION__  <<endl;
    }
};
[Platform::MTAThread]
int main()
{
    C c;
    c.DoSomething();
    return 0;
```

```
}
```

If you execute this code, you will see that the call to DoSomething on object c, does indeed call the implementation in class C. If you ignore the *override* keyword, the compiler emits an error.

Inheritance and Special functions

Special member functions such as constructors and destructors are not inherited. It is important to note here that inheritance of runtime classes within the same translation unit is different when compared to the cross ABI runtime inheritance of WinRT classes.

Constructors

Just like in Standard C++, constructors are not inherited. Each derived class must define appropriate constructors. The base class constructor may be called using the initializer list from the derived class constructor, as shown below.

LISTING 2-17 Inheritance and constructors

```
ref class B
{
internal:
    B() { wcout << __FUNCTION__  <<endl; }
    int data;

    B(int number) : data(number)
    {
            wcout << "B::B(int)"  <<endl;
    }
};

ref class C sealed : B
{
public:
    C(int x) : B(x)
    {
            wcout << "C::C(int)"  <<endl;
    }


};
[Platform::MTAThread]
int main()
{
    B b;
    C c(100);
    return 0;
}
```

Running this code prints the following output:

```
B::B
```

```
B::B(int)
C::C(int)
```

Destructors

There is a subtle difference in the way destructors behave in C++ /CX when compared to Standard C++. In Standard C++, the destructor of the base class is recommended to be *virtual* since this ensures that all destructors in the inheritance hierarchy get called. If you have a non-*virtual* destructor in your base class, it prevents this chaining happening.

In C++ /CX, destructors are always called up the inheritance hierarchy. This is irrespective of the base class destructor being declared *virtual* or not. However, this functionality will not be accessible for developers in this release of C++ /CX. You cannot author base classes in C++ /CX.

LISTING 2-18 Default chaining of destructors from derived to base classes

```
ref class Base
{
internal:
   Base() {}
   ~Base()
   {
           wcout << __FUNCTION__ <<endl;
   }
};

ref class Derived sealed : Base
{
public:
   Derived () {}
   ~Derived()
   {
           wcout << __FUNCTION__ <<endl;
   }
};

[Platform::MTAThread]
int main()
{
   Derived d;
}
```

Running this code outputs the following since the base class destructor is automatically invoked. As with Standard C++, the most derived class destructor executes first.

```
Derived::~Derived
Base::~Base
```

Upcasting and DownCasting

In Standard C++, Upcasting does not require any explicit or special cast. The same holds true for C++ /CX too.

```
Derived^ d = ref new Derived();
Base^ b = d;
```

When performing a safe_cast or a dynamic_cast, the types (to and from) don't need to be related. Only a static_cast will check that the types are related and issue a compile-time error if they are not.

```
Base^ b = ref new Derived();
Derived^ d = safe_cast<Derived^>(b);
d = dynamic_cast<Derived^>(b);
```

Both will work, but the behavior is different in the case that the cast fails. dynamic_cast will return nullptr when the cast fails, requiring a null handle check after the cast statement. safe_cast will throw an InvalidCastException instead.

The following example demonstrates casting with Windows Runtime types. safe_cast<T> throws if the cast fails, and dynamic_cast<T> returns nullptr if the cast fails.

LISTING 2-19 Casting in C++ /CX

```
using namespace Platform;
using namespace Windows::Storage;
using namespace Windows::Storage::Search;

auto options = ref new QueryOptions(CommonFileQuery::DefaultQuery, nullptr);
auto query = KnownFolders::PicturesLibrary->CreateFileQueryWithOptions(options);

Object^ opt = options;
Object^ q = query;

// Throws if the cast fails.
auto opt1 = safe_cast<QueryOptions>(options);

// Returns nullptr if the cast fails.
auto q1 = dynamic_cast<QueryOptions>(query);
```

Interfaces

A Windows Runtime class—that is, a ref class—can implement interfaces just like a regular C++ class does. An interface can inherit one or more interfaces, and the interface can overload its member functions.

An interface has the following characteristics.

- The members of an interface can include properties, methods, and events.
- Fields and static members are not permitted.
- All members are public.

- Types that are used as parameters can only be Windows Runtime types.

The following example shows how to declare and implement interfaces for a ref class.

LISTING 2-20 Declaring and implementing interfaces in C++ /CX

```cpp
ref class B
{
   public:
      virtual void f() { Console::WriteLine("B::f"); }
      virtual void g() { Console::WriteLine("B::g"); }
};
interface class I
{
   void f();
   void g();
};

ref class C : B, I
{
   public:

   // f overrides B::f and implements I::f
   virtual void f() override
   {
      Console::WriteLine("C::f");
   }
   // g overrides B::g AND implements I::g
   virtual void g() override
   {
      Console::WriteLine("C::g");
   }
};

[Platform::MTAThread]
int main()
{
   B^ b = ref new B();
   C^ c = ref new C();
   I^ i = c;

   b->f(); // calls B::f
   c->f(); // calls C::f
   i->f(); // calls C::f since C::f implements I::f
   B^ bc = c;  // b pointing to instance of C
   bc->f(); // calls C::f since C::f is unrelated
   // behavior with the override specifier
   b->g();  // calls B::g
   c->g();  // calls C::g
   i->g();  // calls C::g since C::g implements I::g
   bc->g(); // calls C::g since C::g overrides B::g
}
```

The output of the above code is as follows:

```
B::f
C::f
C::f
C::f
B::g
C::g
C::g
C::g
```

Preventing Interface Name Collisions

The language construct used by C++ /CX, to allow support for interfaces that have name conflicts is called explicit interface implementation. You create one method definition for each interface that has the method and provide a hint to the compiler. The compiler uses this hint to generate code that knows what version of the method to use when called through a particular interface. If the method call is made via an object, the calling code must resolve the ambiguity. The following code sample shows how to prevent name collisions in interfaces.

LISTING 2-21 Preventing interface name collisions

```
interface class IA { void f(); };
interface class IB { void f(); };

ref class R : IA, IB
{
   public:
   virtual void f1() = IA::f
   {
      Console::WriteLine("R::f1 == IA::f");
   }
   virtual void f2() = IB::f
   {
      Console::WriteLine("R::f2 == I2::f");
   }
};

[Platform::MTAThread]
int main()
{
   R^ r = ref new R();
   IA^ i1 = r;
   IB^ i2 = r;
   r->f1();        // OK -- call through the object.
   r->f2();        // OK -- call through the object.

   i1->f();        // OK -- call f1.
   i2->f();        // OK -- call f2.
}
```

Interfaces and Access Control

You can use the *private* access modifier on a method from an interface being implemented in a runtime class. This means that the method can only be called via the interface object and not the class object. Attempting to make the method call using the class object results in a compiler error. The following code sample demonstrates how to use access control on an interface method.

LISTING 2-22 Interfaces and access control

```
interface class IInterface
{
    void PrintFunc();
    int PrintNumber();
};
ref class R : IInterface
{
        // The virtual keyword is required to implement the interface.
        virtual void PrintFunc() sealed = IInterface::PrintFunc
        {
                wcout << __FUNCTION__ <<endl;
        }
    public:
        virtual int PrintNumber() { return 42 ; }
};

[Platform::MTAThread]
int main()
{
    R^ r = ref new R();
    IInterface^ ir = r;
    ir->PrintFunc();  // PrintFunc may be called through the interface.
    r->PrintFunc();  // Error: PrintFunc is private.
    wcout << r->PrintNumber() <<endl;      // OK
}
```

Partial Classes

A partial class supports scenarios in which you, as a developer, are modifying one part of a class definition and the XAML designer is also modifying code in the same class. Using partial classes prevent code from being overwritten mistakenly.

To define a partial class, use the *partial* keyword immediately before the class-keyword of a normal class definition. Partial definitions are supported only in the following constructs.

- ref class or ref struct

This example demonstrates a partial ref class:

```
partial ref class MyClass {/* ... */};
```

A partial class can contain member functions, variables etc that are available to normal classes.

At the point of the full definition of the class X, the behavior is the same as if the definition of X had declared all base classes, members, and so on, in the order in which they were encountered and defined in the partial classes. That is, the contents of the partial classes are treated as though they were written at the point of full definition of the class, and name lookup and other language rules are applied at the point of the full definition of the class as if the contents of the partial classes were written in place

The following two code examples have identical meaning and effect. The first example uses a partial class and the second example doesn't.

Restrictions on Partial classes

- A partial class can't be a template.

- A partial class cannot span beyond one translation unit.

- The partial keyword is supported only in combination with the ref class keyword or the value class keyword.

The following code shows two partial class headers generated from a default XAML application in Visual Studio. Please note this is a Blank Application and hence the classes look nearly empty.

LISTING 2-23 Generated Code for App.xaml. File listing for App.g.h

```
#pragma once
//----------------------------------------------------------------------------
//      This code was generated by a tool.
//
//      Changes to this file may cause incorrect behavior and will be lost if
//      the code is regenerated.
//----------------------------------------------------------------------------
#include "XamlTypeInfo.g.h"

namespace PartialClass_App
{
    partial ref class App :  public ::Windows::UI::Xaml::Application,
        public ::Windows::UI::Xaml::Markup::IXamlMetadataProvider,
        public ::Windows::UI::Xaml::Markup::IComponentConnector
    {
    public:
        void InitializeComponent();
        virtual void Connect(int connectionId, ::Platform::Object^ target);

        [Windows::Foundation::Metadata::DefaultOverload]
        virtual ::Windows::UI::Xaml::Markup::IXamlType^ GetXam-
lType(::Windows::UI::Xaml::Interop::TypeName type);
        virtual ::Windows::UI::Xaml::Markup::IXamlType^ GetXamlType(::Platform::String^ fullName);
        virtual ::Platform::Array<::Windows::UI::Xaml::Markup::XmlnsDefinition>^ GetXmlnsDefinitions();
    private:
        ::XamlTypeInfo::InfoProvider::XamlTypeInfoProvider^ _provider;
```

```
        bool _contentLoaded;


    };
}
```

LISTING 2-24 Generated Code for MainPage.xaml. File listing for MainPage.g.h

```
#pragma once
//-----------------------------------------------------------------------------
//      This code was generated by a tool.
//
//      Changes to this file may cause incorrect behavior and will be lost if
//      the code is regenerated.
//-----------------------------------------------------------------------------
namespace PartialClass_App
{
    partial ref class MainPage : public ::Windows::UI::Xaml::Controls::Page,
        public ::Windows::UI::Xaml::Markup::IComponentConnector
    {
    public:
        void InitializeComponent();
        virtual void Connect(int connectionId, ::Platform::Object^ target);

    private:
        bool _contentLoaded;


    };
}
```

Properties

As per the rules of the Windows Runtime, all Windows Runtime types expose public data as properties. These properties are accessed just like accessing a public data member of an ordinary C++ class. As you author a WinRT type, you can implement properties within blocks that contain a get/set accessor methods or both. Using the accessor methods allows you to perform validations on the parameters being passed or throw exceptions for invalid arguments.

A property can contain both a set accessor, which assigns a value to the property, and a get accessor that retrieves the value of the proprty. The property is read-only if it provides only a get accessor, write-only if it provides only a set accessor, and read/write (modifiable) if it provides both accessors.

LISTING 2-25 using Properties in C++ /CX classes

```
public ref class Employee sealed
{
```

```
private:
   Platform::String^ Name;
   int EmpID;
public:
  // Trivial property
  property Platform::String^ Name;
  // Read-only property
  property Platform::String^ EmployeeName
  {
     Platform::String^ get() { return Name; }
  }

  // Read-write property
  property int EmpID
  {
     int get() { return EmpID; }
     void set(int value)
     {
        if (value <= 0) { throw ref new Platform::InvalidArgumentException(); }
        EmpID = value;
     }
  }
}
```

A trivial property is a read/write property for which the compiler automatically implements the accessors and backing store. You don't have access to the compiler's implementation. However, you can declare a custom property and explicitly declare its accessors and backing store. Within an accessor, you can perform any logic that you require, such as validating the input to the set accessor, calculating a value from the property value, accessing a database, or firing an event when the property changes.

The above code example shows how to declare and access a property. The first property, Name, is known as a trivial property because the compiler automatically generates a set accessor, get accessor, and a backing store.

The second property, EmployeeName, is a read-only property because it specifies a property block that explicitly declares only a get accessor. Because the property block is declared, you must explicitly declare a backing store; that is, the private String^ variable, Name. Typically, a read-only property just returns the value of the backing store.

The third property, EmpID, is a read-write property because it declares a property block that declares both a set accessor and a get accessor.

The set accessor performs a user-defined validity test on the assigned value. And unlike C#, here the name value is just the identifier for the parameter in the set accessor; it's not a keyword. If value isn't greater than zero, Platform::InvalidArgumentException is thrown. Otherwise, the backing store, quantity_, is updated with the assigned value.Collections

As discussed earlier, the Windows Runtime defines interfaces for collection of supported types. These interfaces are defined in the Windows::Foundation::Collection (WFC) namespace. C++ /CX provides the actual implementation of these interfaces in the collections.h header file. The implementations are placed under the Platform::Collections (PC) namespace.

> **Tip** Within C++ /CX code, you can make free use of Standard Template Library (STL) collections, or any other collection type. However, if your app needs to pass collections back and forth across the Windows Runtime abstract binary interface (ABI) you must use Windows Runtime collection types.

The C++ team went to great length to support semantics similar to the standard collections on the WinRT collections. This means that using a WinRT collection type should feel very similar to using an equivalent standard collection type. Table 2-6 shows the resemblance between WinRT collections and standard C++ collections.

TABLE 2-5   Resemblance between WinRT collections and standard C++ collections

WinRT collection interface	Platform::Collections implementation	Standard C++ collection resemblance
WFC::IVector	PC::Vector	std::vector
WFC::IMap	PC::Map	std::map
WFC::IVectorView	PC::VectorView	Use a const vector
WFC::IMapView	PC::MapView	Use a const map
WFC::IObservableCollection	PC::Vector and PC::Map	N/A

If you need to pass an instance of an IVector to another WinRT component, use an instance of Vector from the Platform::Collections namespace. Similar to the standard C++ vector, the PC::Vector enables you to add, remove and access items in the collection using Iterators. A PC::Vector is also implicitly convertible to an IVector. One of the additional benefits of the PC::Vector is the ability to use the standard C++ STL algorithms on instances of PC::Vector.

> **Tip** You can use a std::vector in your C++ /CX code as much as you want to. But remember to pass only Vector when code crosses the WinRT ABI boundary. This means you should construct a PC::Vector from a std::vector and pass the instance of PC::Vector. The PC::Vector constructor allows you to pass a std::vector and creates the PC::Vector instance. It is really that easy!

Listing 2-26 shows a basic example of usng a PC::Vector.

LISTING 2-26 using collections in C++ /CX

```
Vector<int>^ vec = ref new Vector<int>();
vec->Append(1);
vec->Append(2);
vec->Append(3);
```

```
vec->Append(4);
vec->Append(5);

namespace WFC = Windows::Foundation::Collections;
Platform::Collections::VectorIterator<int> it =
        std::find(WFC::begin(vec), WFC::end(vec), 3);

int j = *it; //j = 3
int k = *(it + 1); //k = 4
unsigned int n;
bool found = vec->IndexOf(4, &n); //n = 3
n = vec->GetAt(4); // Alternate way to get at fourth item
```

LISTING 2-27 Mixing STL collections and C++ /CX collections

```
IVector<int>^ Class1::GetInts()
{
std::vector<int> vec;
for(int i = 0; i < 10; i++)
{
vec.push_back(i);
}

auto beg = std::begin(vec);
auto end = std::end(vec);

return ref new Vector<int>(vec);
}
```

C++/CX supports events that occur when a collection object is changed or reset, or when any element of a collection is inserted, removed, or changed.

The **VectorChangedEventHandler** and **MapChangedEventHandler** delegates are provided so that you can specify event handlers for collections. The **CollectionChange** enumeration is provided so that you use the event arguments to determine what caused the event. This code lists the collection delegates and enumeration:

```
// Vector
delegate VectorChangedEventHandler(IObservableVector* sender, IVectorChangedEventArgs* eventArgs);


// Map
delegate MapChangedEventHandler(IObservableMap* sender, IMapChangedEventArgs* eventArgs);

// Event arg values
enum class CollectionChange { Reset, ItemInserted, ItemRemoved, ItemChanged };
```

> **Note** Always prefer to use the standard collection types in your code. Convert them to the WinRT types only when interfacing with WinRT APIs or when crossing the ABI boundary.

Templates in C++ /CX

WinRT does not allow parameterized types other than the ones discussed earlier. This means that C++ templates are not published to metadata and therefore cannot have public or protected accessibility in your app. You can use standard C++ templates internally in your app. You can, however, define a private ref class as a template and you can declare an explicitly specialized template ref class as a private member in a public ref class.

The following code example demonstrates how to use a fully instantiated template to define My-Class.

LISTING 2-28 Consumption of templates in C++ /CX

```
namespace Other
{
template<typename T, class I>
ref class MyClass
{
public:
    MyClass(T s) {}
};



template<> private ref class  MyClass<Platform::String^, int> sealed
    {
    public:
        MyClass(Platform::String^ s) {}
        void DoSomething(int i){}
    };
}
```

You can consume the instantiated template as shown in the following example:

```
MyClass<String^, int>^ mt = ref new MyClass<String^, int>(ref new String(L"test"));
mt->DoSomething(108);
```

Enums

C++/CX supports the enum class keyword, which is the new Standard C++ variation of the classic enum keyword.

Omitting an access specifier on an enum defaults the enum to a standard C++ enum.

WinRT only allows a unit32 or in32 as an underlying enum type. Confirming with this rule, C++ /CX enum class or enum struct declaration can also specify an underlying numeric type which can either be a uint32 or int32 type. If the underlying type is a uint32, the enum must also have the [Flags] attribute set.

LISTING 2-29 using enums in C++ /CX

```
public:
[FlagsAttribute]
    enum class SeasonWithFlags
    {
            Summer,
            Fall,
            Winter,
            Autumn,
            All = Summer | Fall | Winter | Autumn
    };
public:
    enum class SeasonNoFlags
    {
            Summer,
            Fall,
            Winter,
            Autumn
    };
```

Delegates

WinRT supports delegates and C++ /CX enables you to declare and consume delegates. Delegates are type-safe function pointers and have public visibility. Invoking a delegate executes the method it references.

Delegates are named types and define a method signature. Delegates are most commonly used in conjunction with events with the exception of the WinRT async pattern.

The declaration of a delegate resembles a function declaration except that the delegate is a type. You typically declare a delegate at namespace scope.

After you declare a delegate type, you can declare class members of that type, or methods that take objects of that type as parameters. A method or function can also return a delegate type.

LISTING 2-30 Using delegates in C++ /CX

```
namespace CxxDelegates
{
    ref class Person;
    public delegate Platform::String^ GetNameDelegate(Person^ p);

    public ref class Person sealed
    {
            public:
                    Person() {}
                    Person(String^ firstName, String^ lastName, String^ email)
                    {
                            fName = firstName;
                            lName = lastName;
                            emailAddress = email;
                    }
```

```
            virtual ~Person() {}

private:
            String^ fName;
            String^ lName;
            String^ emailAddress;

public:

            property String^ FirstName
            {
                    String^ get()
                    {
                            return fName;
                    }

                    void set(String^ firstName)
                    {
                            if (firstName->IsEmpty())
                            {
                                    throw ref new Platform::InvalidArgumentException();
                            }
                            fName = firstName;
                    }
            }

            property String^ LastName
            {
                    String^ get()
                    {
                            return lName;
                    }

                    void set(String^ lastName)
                    {
                            if (lastName->IsEmpty())
                            {
                                    throw ref new Platform::InvalidArgumentException();
                            }
                            lName = lastName;
                    }
            }

            property String^ EmailAddress
            {
                    String^ get()
                    {
                            return emailAddress;
                    }

                    void set(String^ emailID)
                    {
                            if (emailID->IsEmpty())
                            {
```

```
                                        throw ref new Platform::InvalidArgumentException();
                        }
                        emailAddress = emailID;
                }
        }


        String^ GetFullName(GetNameDelegate^ func )
        {
                return func(this);
        }
    };
}

int main(Platform::Array<Platform::String^>^ args)
{
    //Simple delegate
    Person^ pLambda = ref new Person("John", "Doe", "John.Doe@usinglambdas.com");

    //Delegate using a lambda
    auto lambdaDelegate = ref new GetNameDelegate([] (Person^ p)
    {
            return p->FirstName + L" " + p->LastName;
    });
    //the delegate can then be called as follows
    String^ strLambdaOutput = lambdaDelegate(pLambda);
    wcout<< strLambdaOutput->Data()<<endl;
    return 0;
}
```

Tip Note that you use the "^" symbol when you refer to the delegate type, just as with any Windows Runtime reference type.

Client code first constructs the delegate instance by using ref new and providing a lambda that is compatible with the delegate signature and defines the custom behavior.

```
//Delegate using a lambda
auto lambdaDelegate = ref new GetNameDelegate([] (Person^ p)
{
        return p->FirstName + L" " + p->LastName;
});
```

You can construct a delegate from any of the following objects:

- lambda

- static function

- pointer-to-member

- std::function

Delegates and Threading

Since a delegate is just a type-safe function pointer, it executes code when invoked. This means you should pay particular attention to invoking delegates within a multi-threaded application. Here are some guidelines to follow.

- If your code and the delegate invoking the function are running on the same thread, the delegate can safely access all objects on that thread. For example, if the thread is the UI thread then the delegate can directly access and manipulate all the user interface objects without the need for any additional synchronization options or context switching facilities.

- Most WinRT components can run either in a Single threaded apartment (STA) or Multi-threaded Apartment (MTA). If your app runs in a single threaded apartment, you should pay attention when calling WinRT components. In such a case, the delegate will be invoked on the STA thread.

- If your delegate calling code and the function invoked by the delegate are on different threads, then you are responsible for synchronizing access to shared resources. This is most often encountered when using concurrency::task objects. You should place any shared resources under synchronization primitives and avoid race conditions or deadlocks that surface in code at inappropriate times!

- You should not capture local variables by reference within a delegate. These local variables might no longer be valid and have gone out of scope when the delegate is invoked. This has nothing to do with WinRT or delegates: rather, this is how life time of local variables is in standard C++!

- There are times when you want your delegate to be executed on the thread it was created. In this case you should always use the CallbackContext parameter. Every WinRT delegate has an overloaded constructor which accepts a CallbackContext parameter.

Exceptions

WinRT does not report errors as exceptions. Rather it uses standard HRESULT values to report errors and exceptions. C++ /CX however, throws exceptions when errors are encountered. All standard Windows Runtime error values are converted to equivalent strongly typed exceptions and are thrown.

Standard C++ has a std::exception class that serves as a base class for all standard C++ library exceptions. Similarly, C++ /CX defines a base exception class, Platform::Exception which is a ref class. All exceptions are implemented as ref classes derived from Platform::Exception. For common Windows Runtime HRESULT values that represent error conditions, C++ /CX contains distinct exception classes in the Platform namespace. Exceptions that are not part of this common set are reported as Platform::COMException class and you can use the HResult field of the exception class to determine the actual HRESULT. Each exception class also has a Message property that contains the system-supplied string that describes the exception. This property is a read-only property, which means you cannot change it when you re-throw the exception.

The following types of exceptions are permitted to be caught and to throw.

- You can throw and catch exceptions from a WinRT API

- You can throw and catch exceptions derived from std::exception, that is, standard C++ exceptions.

- You can also define your own exception type and throw/catch the same. In order to create a custom exception, do not derive from Platform::Exception. Create a custom HRESULT value and create an instance of a COMException and use it instead.

- You have to pay particular attention to your exception reaching the WinRT ABI boundary. If your component will be used by clients written in other languages supporting the Windows Runtime, you should throw only a Windows Runtime exception.

- If an exception that is not a Windows Runtime, such as a user defined custom exception or a C++ exception reaches the WinRT ABI boundary, the process is terminated. This is known as "Failfast termination".

So how do you create an instance of a Platform::Exception? Turns out there are two ways to construct a Platform::Exception instance. You can instantiate a Platform::Exception by using one of two constructors that take either an HRESULT parameter, or an HRESULT parameter and a Platform::String^ parameter that can be used for debug purposes.

The preferred way though, is to declare an exception by using one of two Platform::Exception::CreateException() method overloads that take either an HRESULT parameter, or an HRESULT parameter and a Platform::String^ parameter. Using the CreateException static function has the added advantage that creates the most derived type in the Exception hierarchy (e.g. call CreateException(E_FAIL) will create a FailureException class. Calling ref new COMException(E_FAIL) will just create a COMException with an hr member value of E_FAIL and it will not be caught by a catch(FailureException^ex) in all cases. Table 2-6 lists the standard exception classes and their descriptions.

TABLE 2-6 Table of standard exceptions in the Windows Runtime

Name	Underlying HRESULT	Description of Exception
COMException	User-defined hresult	Thrown when an unrecognized HRESULT is returned from a COM method call.
AccessDeniedException	E_ACCESSDENIED	Thrown when access is denied to a resource or feature.
ChangedStateException	E_CHANGED_STATE	Thrown when methods of a collection iterator or a collection view are called after the parent collection has changed, thereby invalidating the

		results of the method.
ClassNotRegisteredException	REGDB_E_CLASSNOTREG	Thrown when a COM class has not been registered.
DisconnectedException	RPC_E_DISCONNECTED	Thrown when an object is disconnected from its clients.
FailureException	E_FAIL	Thrown when an operation fails.
InvalidArgumentException	E_INVALIDARG	Thrown when one of the arguments that are provided to a method is not valid.
InvalidCastException	E_NOINTERFACE	Thrown when a type can't be cast to another type.
NotImplementedException	E_NOTIMPL	Thrown if an interface method hasn't been implemented on a class.
NullReferenceException	E_POINTER	Thrown when there is an attempt to de-reference a null object reference.
OperationCanceledException	E_ABORT	Thrown when an operation is aborted.
OutOfBoundsException	E_BOUNDS	Thrown when an operation attempts to access data outside the valid range.
OutOfMemoryException	E_OUTOFMEMORY	Thrown when there's insufficient memory to complete the operation.

All exceptions have a HResult property and a Message property. The HResult property gets the exception's underlying numeric HRESULT value. The Message property gets the system-supplied string that describes the exception. Because this property is read-only, you cannot change it when you re-throw the exception.

This example shows how to throw a Windows Runtime exception for synchronous operations:

LISTING 2-31 creating a custom Windows Runtime exceptions

```
//create a custom exception type
COMException^ CreateCustomException(unsigned short errorCode)
{
    // we will throw if errorCode == 0 just for illustration
    if (errorCode == 0)
    {
        throw ref new InvalidArgumentException();
    }
    HRESULT customhr = MAKE_HRESULT(SEVERITY_ERROR, FACILITY_ITF, errorCode);

    return ref new COMException(customhr);
}
```

The following code shows how to catch the exception.

```
try
    {
        auto exception = CreateCustomException(-1);
    }
    catch (InvalidArgumentException^ ex)
    {
        //log exception data
        wcout<< ex->HResult.ToString()->Data() <<endl;
        wcout<< ex->Message->Data() <<endl;
```

```
    }
```

Events in C++ /CX

WinRT supports events and WinRT components can publish events in its public interface. This allows consumers of such components to subscribe to the events and perform appropriate actions when said events occur.

You can declare an event in a ref class or an interface, and you can declare it as public, internal (public/private), public protected, protected, private protected, or private. A trivial event, just like trivial properties, has an implicit backing store, and add and remove accessor methods. You can also specify your own accessors, in the same way that you can specify custom get and set accessors on a property. The implementing class cannot manually cycle through the event subscriber list in a trivial event.

The following example shows how to declare an event. Notice that the event has a delegate type and is declared by using the "^" symbol.

LISTING 2-32 using events in C++ /CX

```cpp
ref class ReminderInfo
{ /* ... */ };
ref class Appointment;
delegate void ReminderEventHandler(Appointment^ source, ReminderInfo^ info);
ref class Appointment
{
public:
  Appointment(Platform::String^ title, Platform::String^ location, Windows::Foundation::DateTime time);
  event ReminderEventHandler^ Reminder;
};
```

The following example shows how client code can use the += operator to subscribe to the event, and can provide a delegate event handler to be invoked when the event is fired. The event handler is implemented here as a lambda expression, but you could also use a named function.

LISTING 2-33 using the += operator to subscribe to events

```cpp
void ReminderPopUp(Appointment^ source, ReminderInfo^ info);
void Beep();
auto appt = ref new Appointment("Drinks", "Sambar, Ballard", Windows::Foundation::DateTime());
appt->Reminder += ref new ReminderEventHandler([](Appointment ^source, ReminderInfo ^info) {
  ReminderPopUp(source, info);
});
auto cookie = appt->Reminder::add(
  ref new ReminderEventHandler([](Appointment ^source, ReminderInfo ^info) {
    Beep();
}));
/* ... */
appt->Reminder::remove(cookie);
```

> **Warning** Do not block within the event handler method. Doing so blocks the event source from in-

voking other event handlers for the subscribed event. This is because the event source sequentially calls into all the event handlers from the same thread.

The order in which the event source invokes event handlers on event receivers is not guaranteed and may differ from call to call.

Arrays in C++ /CX

WinRT supports the following Array types

- PassArray - Used when the caller passes an array to a method.

- FillArray - Used when the caller passes an array for the method to fill.

- ReceiveArray - Used when the caller receives an array that the method allocates.

C++ /CX provides input parameter types to support the WinRT Array types. For the WinRT PassArray, you should use const Platform::Array<T> as the input parameter. For the WinRT FillArray, you should use Platform::WriteOnlyArray<T>. Finally, for the WinRT ReceiveArray, you can either return the array as a return value as an Array^ or return it as an out parameter as type Array^*.

As a general guideline, you should use std::vector as much as possible within your code and only construct a Platform::Array or Platform::WriteOnlyArray type when your code crosses the WinRT ABI boundary.

The PassArray

When your C++ code receives an array from a Windows Runtime component and if your code does not modify the received array, it is known as a PassArray. Since your code does not modify the array, it receives it as a const Array^.

```
int ComputeSum(const Array<int>^ list)
{
    int sum = 0;
    auto size = list->Length;
    for(unsigned int x = 0; x < size; ++x)
    {
            sum += list[x];
    }
    return sum;
}
```

The ReceiveArray

When your C++ code needs to allocate memory and initialize an array, it is known as a ReceiveArray.

```
void CreateRecvArray(Array<int>^* list)
{
    auto temp = ref new Array<int>(100);
```

```
    for(unsigned int i = 0; i < temp->Length; i++)
    {
        temp[i] = i;
    }
    *list = temp;
}
Array<int>^ CreateRecvArray2()
{
    auto temp = ref new Array<int>(10);
    for(unsigned int i = 0; i < temp->Length; i++)
    {
        temp[i] = i;
    }
    return temp;
}
```

The FillArray

When you want to allocate an array in the caller, and initialize or modify it in the callee, use WriteOnlyArray.

```
void CreateList(WriteOnlyArray<int>^ list)

{

    // You can write to the elements directly.

    for(unsigned int i = 0; i < list->Length; i++)

    {

        list[i] = i;

    }

}
```

You can also convert an Array to instances of supported collections like a Platform::Collections::Vector or std::vector.

> **Warning** When passing data across the WinRT ABI boundary, use the Platform::ArrayReference to avoid unnecessary data copies. When you pass an ArrayReference as an argument to a parameter that takes a Platform::Array, the ArrayReference will store the data directly into a C-style array that you specify. You should be careful, however, to synchronize data access to this C-style array since ArrayReference has no lock on the data.

Threading and Marshaling

When authoring ref classes, you can apply attributes that specify the threading model and marshaling behavior of instance of that class. You can specify the threading model that Windows will use when the class or entry point is activated. The threading model can be specified by using the **ThreadingModelValue** attribute defined in the **Windows::Foundation::Metadata** namespace to the class or entry point. The **ThreadingModelValue** can take one of the following values from the

ThreadingModel enum class.

TABLE 2-7 ThreadingModel enumeration values

ThreadingModel Enumerator	Description
STA	Single-threaded apartment
MTA	Multithreaded apartment
Both	Both single-threaded and multithreaded apartments

We know that a ref class is activatable if it contains at least one public constructor. The C++ compiler automatically generates a **[Activable]** attribute in the corresponding metadata file (.winmd file). The following code sample shows how to specify threading models on ref classes.

```
[Threading(ThreadingModel=ThreadingModel::STA)]
public ref class MyClass
{
};
```

Similarly, the threading model for an entry point can be specified as follows:

```
using namespace Platform;
[MTAThread]
int main(Array<String^>^ args)
{
}
```

Similarly, you can specify the Marshaling behavior that Windows will use while marshaling your component across to other interfaces/components. In order to do so, you need to apply the **Windows::Foundation::Metadata::MarshalingBehaviorAttribute::MarshalingAttributeValue** to the component. The **MarshalingAttributeValue** can take one of the following values from the **MarshalingType**

TABLE 2-8 MarshalingType enumeration values

MarshalingType Enumerator	Description
None	The class prevents marshaling on all interfaces. That is, IMarshal::MarshalInterface will fail with E_NOINTERFACE for all interfaces of the class.
Agile	The class marshals and unmarshals to the same pointer value on all interfaces. That is, the class aggregates the free-threaded marshaler (FTM), or provides similar behavior.
Standard	The class does not implement IMarshal or forwards to Co-GetStandardMarshal, on all interfaces.

The following code sample shows how to specify MarshalingType for a ref class.

```
[MarshalingBehavior(MarshalingType=MarshalingType::Agile)]
public ref class MyClass
{
};
```

Agile Pointers

While the Windows Runtime and the C++ component extensions hide all the gory details related to apartments, marshaling etc occasionally you might want to manually marshal **non-agile** objects across apartments. The C++ runtime provides a helper class, Agile<T>, to explicitly marshal a handle to a ref object (T^) to call an object member in another COM apartment. Agile<T> throws an exception if it is not able to obtain a proxy to the class. It maintains a handle to the object and a data structure called the *context* of the object. This data structure, *context*, is a set of runtime properties associated with the COM object and is used to service this COM object. An instance of *context* resides in exactly one COM apartment. Agile<T> supports the default, copy and move constructors. These constructors greatly help in associating an instance of the Agile<T> class with the handle and *context* of the specified object type and a destructor that disassociates the current handle and *context* from the Agile<T> object.

Weak References in C++ /CX

The component extensions track the creation and usage of ref classes through a reference counting mechanism. One of the issues with a type-system based on reference counting has got to do with detecting and collecting reference cycles. A reference cycle occurs, when a first object refers to a second one, the second refers to a third and so on such that the final object refers to the first. A common pattern when this occurs is when using lambda captures. These captures are strong references but they are a common source of cycles in COM. The recommendation is to minimize captures, use the delegate/event parameters to reach the other objects, or capture weak references and then resolve them in the lambda.

In order to solve the reference cycle problem, C++ /CX types implement the **IWeakReference-Source** interface.

All C++ ref classes implicitly implement the **IWeakReferenceSource** interface. This list also includes built in classes like array^, vector^ and String^. There is no way for the user to disable automatic implementation of the **IWeakReferenceSource** interface. This is because the semantics of a smart pointer are baked into the implementation of a handle (^) and as mentioned above, the implementation of the **IWeakReferenceSource** is the mechanism by which the C++ runtime offers users who want to solve the reference cycle problem.

The **IWeakReferenceSource** refers to an object for which a pointer to **IWeakReference** can be obtained. The **IWeakReference** object has a method named *Resolve*, which retrieves a strong reference to an object, if it exists or throws an exception otherwise.

In the case of inheritance, a ref class when instantiated alone, will support WeakReference. However, in the case of aggregated classes, it will not support WeakReference. In the case of aggregation, the most derived object controls whether WeakReference support is available or not. That is, a QueryInterface call for **IWeakReference** is not blindly forwarded to the base types.

Another interesting point to note is that **IWeakReferenceSource** and **IWeakReference** are declared as private interfaces. This declaration means they are not allowed to be specified as parameters in any Windows Runtime APIs.

The Platform::WeakReference allows a C++/CX developer to hold a weak reference which can be achieved with the following syntax

MyFoo^ f = ref new MyFoo();

Platform::WeakReference wf(f);

... use wf

try { auto f2 = wf.Resolve<MyFoo>(); }

catch() {...}

Namespaces in C++ /CX

For developers writing programs that target the Windows Runtime, the C++/CX compiler and its supporting header files provide namespaces that define a wide range of WinRT supported types. The namespaces define the built-in numeric types; strings, arrays, and collections; Visual C++ exceptions that represent Windows Runtime errors; and language-specific enhancements to standard Windows Runtime types. The built-in namespaces are the default namespace, Platform namespace and Windows::Foundations::Collections namespace.

The following types are declared in the default namespace

TABLE 2-9   Table showing the types declared in the::default namespace

Name	Description
char16	A 16-bit nonnumeric value that represents a Unicode (UTF-16) code point.
float32	A 32-bit IEEE 754 floating-point number.
float64	A 64-bit IEEE 754 floating-point number.
int16	A 16-bit signed integer.
int32	A 32-bit signed integer.
int8	An 8-bit signed numeric value.
uint16	A 16-bit unsigned integer.
uint32	A 32-bit unsigned integer.
uint64	A 64-bit unsigned integer.
uint8	An 8-bit unsigned numeric value.

The Object and String types are declared under the Platform namespace. The ::default namespace is a double-lookup namespace (just like ::cli:: in C++/CLI). This means that the following is legal (without having a using namespace default anywhere):

float32 f = 0.1f;

If however there is a user defined type with the same name (in the example float32), then the user would disambiguate the default::float32 by explicitly writing the namespace:

default::float32 f = 0.1f;

float32 fx; // this is the user type.

In addition, all built-in types also support four default methods. They are:

- Equals method: determines whether the specified object is equal to the current object.

- GetHashCode method: returns the hash code for this instance

- GetType method: returns a string that represents the current type.

- ToString method: returns a String that represents the current type.

String Conversions

C++ supports different types of strings like char, std::string etc and conversions between one form to the other has always been a favorite topic of discussion. C++ /CX introduces the Platform::String type because WinRT strings have characteristics that didn't map to any of the existing ones. More notably WinRT strings are immutable.

The Platform::String class is authored to seamlessly mix and convert from one string type to another. You should be careful to use the Platform::String class only when you are interfacing with the Windows Runtime types or when authoring a component that will be used across the Windows Runtime ABI boundary (component used from C# or JavaScript). It is important to note that the Platform::String class was not designed to be a full-fledged String class. The class provides just enough support to convert from String to standard C++ string types and these standard C++ strings can then be used for regular string manipulation operations.

This code sample shows how to convert between Platform::String^ and standard C++ string type.

LISTING 2-34 String conversions between String and standard string types

```
// Initializing a String^ by using string literals
String^ str1 = "Test"; // ok for ANSI text. uses current code page
String^ str2("Test");
String^ str3 = L"Test";
String^ str4(L"Test");
//Initialize a String^ by using another String^
String^ str6(str1);
auto str7 = str2;
// Initialize a String from wchar_t* and wstring
wchar_t msg[] = L"Test";
String^ str8 = ref new String(msg);
std::wstring wstr1(L"Test");
String^ str9 = ref new String(wstr1.c_str());
String^ str10 = ref new String(wstr1.c_str(), wstr1.length());

// Concatenation
auto str1 = "Hello" + " World";
```

```
auto str2 = str1 + " from C++/CX!";
auto str3 = String::Concat(str2, " and the String class");

// Comparison
if (str1 == str2) { /* ... */ }
if (str1->Equals(str2)) { /* ... */ }
if (str1 != str2) { /* ... */ }
if (str1 < str2 || str1 > str2) { /* ... */};
int result = String::CompareOrdinal(str1, str2);

if(str1 == nullptr) { /* ...*/};
if(str1->IsEmpty()) { /* ...*/};
// Accessing individual characters in a String^
auto it = str1->Begin();
char16 ch = it[0];
// Create a String^ variable statically or dynamically from a literal string.
String^ str1 = "AAAAAAAA";
// Use the value of str1 to create the ws1 wstring variable.
wstring ws1( str1->Data() );
// The value of ws1 is L"AAAAAAAA".
// Manipulate the wstring value.
wstring replacement( L"BBB" );
ws1 = ws1.replace ( 1, 3, replacement );
// The value of ws1 is L"ABBBAAAA".
// Assign the modified wstring back to str1.
str1 = ref new String( ws1.c_str() );
```

C++ /CX also allows global initialization of String^ types. The following string initialization is perfectly legal.

```
using namespace Platform;
String^ str = L"hello world";
void main(){}
```

Asynchronous Programming in C++ /CX

As discussed earlier, async APIs are present all over WinRT. Although C++ /CX provides support for handling async events, hooking up to the async status handlers etc; it is verbose and cumbersome when compared to the abstractions available to JavaScript and C# developers. What C++ developers do have, however, is a very powerful task based asynchronous programming model made available through the Parallel Patterns Library (PPL). Before jumping into the task based asynchronous programming, let us take a look at how a C++ developer would code for async without PPL for WinRT.

In the example below, we create an instance of a FileOpenPicker and set the Start location of the Picker to the DocumentsLibrary. We also set options in order to display only file types docx and pdf. We then make a call to the **PickSingleFileAsync** method on the picker. **PickSingleFileAsync**, as the name suggests is an async API. The asynchronous object has a **Completed** event handler, which we setup via the call to the "ref new AsyncOperationCompletedHandler". When the PickSingleFileAsync returns, it calls back into the BlankPage::FileSelectionDone function that is passed as a callback completion handler.

Of course, all of this is very simplified. Different async APIs result in different types of async handlers. Some of them are AsyncOperationCompleted, AsyncOperationWithProgress, AsyncAction, AsyncActionWithProgress etc. You can clearly see where this is heading: not only is it tedious to remember to setup the right kind of async handlers, you should also remember to dispatch messages if you want them to be accessed on the UI thread.

```
auto picker = ref new Windows::Storage::Pickers::FileOpenPicker();
picker->SuggestedStartLocation = Windows::Storage::Pickers::PickerLocationId::DocumentsLibrary;
picker->FileTypeFilter->Append(".docx");
picker->FileTypeFilter->Append(".pdf");
auto file = picker->PickSingleFileAsync();
file->Completed = ref new AsyncOperationCompletedHandler<StorageFile^>(this,
&BlankPage::FileSelectionDone);
```

Asynchronous programming using PPL tasks

The Parallel Patterns Library (PPL), included with Visual Studio 2012 provides first class support for higher level abstractions like tasks, parallel algorithms and containers such as concurrent_vector etc in order to make parallel and asynchronous programming in C++ easy and productive.

The task class in the PPL version that ships with Visual Studio 2012 allows you, as a developer, to represent a unit of work that can be executed asynchronously. You can write code as individual tasks or create a chain of dependent tasks and the runtime takes care of scheduling them optimally for you. You no longer have to worry about manual management of threads, thread pools etc.

If you have heard about "***promises***" in Javascript; then you should be familiar with the composability feature of task groups in PPL. A ***promise*** in Javascript represents the result of a potentially long running and not necessarily complete operation. Instead of blocking and waiting for the long-running computation to complete, the pattern returns an object which represents the promised result. A promise implements a method for registering callbacks for state change notifications, commonly named the *then* method.

Similarly, PPL tasks allow you to group tasks and declare one to be a continuation of the previous task. This allows you to build combine tasks in many different ways. Let us now visit a canonical example of opening a file from the Documents Library and then reading its contents.

```cpp
auto picker = ref new FileOpenPicker();
picker->FileTypeFilter->Append(".txt");
picker->SuggestedStartLocation = PickerLocationId::DocumentsLibrary;

create_task(picker->PickSingleFileAsync()).then([this](StorageFile^ file)
{
    if (file)
    {
        task<IRandomAccessStream^> openTask(file->OpenAsync(FileAccessMode::Read));
        openTask.then([this](IRandomAccessStream^ stream)
        {
            auto reader = ref new DataReader(stream);
            task<UINT> loadTask(reader->LoadAsync(stream->Size));
            loadTask.then([this, reader](UINT bytesRead)
            {
                this->FileContent->Text = reader->ReadString(bytesRead);
            });
        });
    }
});
```

In the example above, the parameter to the **.then** method is a lambda expression. It can be a function pointer, a function object or std::function but from here on out we will just call it a "lambda" because it is just a callback function. The return type of the **.then** method is also a task<T>. The type T is determined by the return type of the lambda passed to the **.then** method. A simple guide rule to remember the return type is this: if the lambda returns an expression of type T, the **.then** returns a task<T>.

Composability of tasks does not stop with creating nested task operations. PPL also includes powerful semantics to combine output from multiple tasks and then return the result. This **join** operation, for example, is implemented by the **when_all** method. The **when_all** method takes a sequence of tasks and returns the resulting task, which collects the output of all the constituent tasks into a std::vector. The operator && is a shortcut to represent a **join** operation.

A simple example of using task groups is to read contents of a file and update the UI. PPL handles automatic marshaling of data to the UI thread thus obviating the need to manually call the Dispatcher functions.

```cpp
auto package = Windows::ApplicationModel::Package::Current;
StorageFolder^ item = package->InstalledLocation;
task<StorageFile^> getFileOp(item->GetFileAsync(fileName));
getFileOp.then([this](StorageFile^ file)
{
```

```
    return FileIO::ReadTextAsync(file);
}).then([this](task<String^> content)
{
    this->FileContent->Text += content.get();
});
```

Authoring WinRT components with async support is a little more involved and we will discuss building WinRT components in the next section.

In WinRT all blocking operations are asynchronous, and PPL makes asynchronous programming easy and highly composable. For more information on the PPL, please refer to Ade Miller's book, Parallel Programming with Microsoft Visual C++, published by Microsoft Press.

We have covered a lot of ground so far; beginning with a discussion on C++ /CX and its features. We then moved on to the many String conversion routines that are supported between C++ /CX and standard C++ string types. We finally focused on the support for task based asynchronous programming that is enabled via the Parallel Patterns Library. Let us now turn our attention to building WinRT components using C++ /CX.

Concepts to remember while building WinRT components

As you begin contemplating coding your WinRT components using C++ /CX, it is important to remember a few, but important, WinRT concepts. Paying careful attention to these concepts will help you avoid costly development issues later on and will expose all the functionality of your component to consumers.

WinRT is the Windows Operating System defining a native Abstract Binary Interface (ABI). For far too long, Windows did not have an ABI. Win32 was predominantly 'C' based and languages like C# and JavaScript had to jump through multiple hoops like P/Invoke or custom marshallers to make use of Win32.

As you write code for your WinRT component using C++ /CX, use standard C++ types for all the internal component logic. Only use the C++ /CX or WinRT types when you need to pass data across the WinRT ABI. Your component will also use delegates and events that can be handled from WinRT-supported languages like JavaScript, C# and VB.net. All the components we develop in this chapter will follow this pattern.

As mentioned above, only WinRT types can be passed across the ABI boundary. If you attempt to pass a standard C++ type such as std::wstring, either as a return type or as a parameter to a public method of a runtime class, the compiler will flag it as an error. Table 2-10 lists some common types and how the compiler treats them when passing the types across the WinRT ABI boundary. All other types, like class instances, standard C++ collection types like std::vector, std::map etc should be converted into the WinRT equivalent types at the ABI boundary.

TABLE 2-10   Passing common C++ types across the WinRT ABI boundary

C++ type	Can be passed across WinRT ABI	Implicitly converted to WinRT equivalent
Int	Yes	Yes, converted to int32
Double	Yes	Yes, converted to float64
signed char	Yes	Yes, converted to int8
unsigned char	No	No, not converted and not supported in WinRT
short	Yes	Yes, converted to int16
unsigned short	Yes	Yes, converted to uint16
unsigned int	Yes	Yes, converted to uint32
long long -or- __int64	Yes	Yes, converted to int64
unsigned long long -or- unsigned __int64	Yes	Yes, converted to uint64
float	Yes	Yes, converted to float32
bool	Yes	Yes, converted to Platform::Boolean
wchar_t -or- L'c'	Yes	Yes, converted to char16
std::string or std::wstring	No	Not converted.

Building a WinRT component using C++ /CX

In this section, let us create a simple WinRT component that exports a method named Add. This method accepts two parameters of type integer and returns the computed sum as a result.

Create the C++ /CX component Project

Let us now create the component project using Visual Studio 2012.

- On the Visual Studio menu bar, choose File, New, Project.

- In the New Project dialog box, in the left pane, expand Visual C++ and then select the node for Windows Store apps.

- In the center pane, select Windows Runtime Component and then name the project CxxAddComponent.

- Choose the OK button.

Adding an activatable class to the component

Before our component can be consumed by clients, we need to add an activatable class. An activatable class allows the instantiation of the class from JavaScript or C# by using the "new" expression. Following the guidelines of the Windows Runtime, you should declare a runtime class as sealed to prevent further inheritance.

Open the Class1.h file from the CxxAddComponent project created above. You will notice that the Class1 is declared as public ref class and sealed. In fact, Class1 is the name of our activatable class and the basic infrastructure has already been setup for you.

You can now go ahead and add a public method to Class1 named Add. Add takes two parameters of type int and returns a value of type int.

```
int Add(int a, int b);
```

Open Class1.cpp and add the implementation for the Add method as follows:

```
int Class1::Add(int a, int b)
{
    return a + b;
}
```

Build the project and your component is now ready. No need of adding code to IDL, header and source files. In fact, you write code as if it is a regular C++ class, although such code needs to abide by the rules of the Windows Runtime, and voila your component is ready.

Create a JavaScript client app

Let us now create a client app written using JavaScript to call into the CxxAddComponent created above.

1. In Visual Studio, add a new JavaScript Blank App project to the CxxAddComponent solution. Name the project JSTestApp.

2. In the JSTestApp project, add a reference to the CxxAddComponent project by right clicking on the Reference Node and choosing Add Reference.

3. In default.html, replace the body section with these UX elements:

```
<div>
    <input id="a" />
    <input id="b" />
    <p id="result">Result:</p>
    <button onclick="Add()">Add</button>
</div>
```

4. In default.js, implement the OnClick function.

```
function Add() {
    "use strict";

    var addNumbers = new CxxAddComponent.Class1();

    var a = document.getElementById("a");
    var b = document.getElementById("b");

    document.getElementById("result").innerHTML = "Result: " + addNumbers.add(a.value, b.value);

}
```

5. Build the solution and launch the JSTestApp. Input two integers in the two text boxes and then click on the Add button. The result will be displayed on screen.

Adding async operations in C++ components

According to the Windows Runtime guidelines, any operation that can potentially take more than 50 ms (milliseconds) to complete should always be implemented as asynchronous methods. An asynchronous method always executes on the background thread and does not block the main thread or the UI thread.

You should use the task and continuation model of the Parallel Patterns Library (PPL) to define background tasks and all nested/chained continuation tasks. Since the task class is specific to C++, you should convert a task object into a WinRT interface that can be consumed by client apps. In order to facilitate such conversion, WinRT provides four interfaces that can be used to represent asynchronous operations. They are:

- IAsyncAction – An IAsyncAction interface represents an asynchronous action that neither returns any value nor provides any progress information.

- IAsyncActionWithProgress – An IAsyncActionWithProgress interface represents an asynchronous action that does not return any value but only provides progress information.

- IAsyncOperation<T> - An IAsyncOperation<T> interface represents an asynchronous operation that returns a value of T but does not provide any progress information.

- IAsyncOperationWithProgress<T> - An IAsyncOperationWithProgress<T> interface represents an asynchronous operation that returns a value of T and also provides progress information.

Tip It is important to note that an async action returns no value whereas an async operation returns a value.

PPL provides the create_async helper function that allows C++ components to create instances of the asynchronous interfaces mentioned above. The create_async function, present in the concurrency namespace, creates a Windows Runtime asynchronous action or operation that represents the completion of a task. It usually takes a function that represents some work to be done (usually as a lambda function) and creates a task object for the work to be done. It then wraps the task into one of the four async WinRT interfaces. How does the create_async method determine what async WinRT interface should the task object be mapped to? Table 2-11 shows how.

TABLE 2-11   create_async task mapping to WinRT async interfaces

Return value	Progress reported	WinRT async interface mapping
No	No	IAsyncAction
No	Yes	IAsyncActionWithProgress
Yes	No	IAsyncOperation<T>
Yes	Yes	IAsyncOperationWithProgress<T>

If the work function does not return a value and also does not report a progress, then create_async returns IAsyncAction. Similarly, if the work function returns a value T but does not report a progress, then create_async returns IAsyncOperation<T>.

All of the four WinRT async interfaces provide a Cancel method that can be used to cancel the asynchronous operation. PPL task objects however, do not provide a Cancel method. PPL tasks work with cancellation tokens. PPL task cancellation can be connected with WinRT cancel methods in two ways.

1. When you call create_async, pass a cancellation_token to the work function.

2. If create_async creates an asynchronous operation that runs another task, use an explicit cancellation_token for all the created tasks.

Armed with this information, let us now create a C++ component that exposes an async operation through a runtime class.

> **Tip** Use the task class directly when your C++ component will be used by a client app written in C++ code. Use create_async only when the C++ component will be used by another language or by another WinRT component!

Creating the C++ /CX component to read file contents

Our component contains one method to read a text file present in the Documents Library. You should also copy the file "127.txt" into your Documents Library. The "127.txt" is available along with the samples.

You will add support for all the four WinRT async interfaces which will help you understand the differences between each interface.

- On the Visual Studio menu bar, choose File, New, Project.

- In the New Project dialog box, in the left pane, expand Visual C++ and then select the node for Windows Store apps.

- In the center pane, select Windows Runtime Component and then name the project CxxReadFileComponent.

- Choose the OK button.

We will rename the name of the generated class from Class1 to ReadFile. Replace the code in class1.h with code from listing 2-35

LISTING 2-35 ReadFile class declaration

```
#pragma once

namespace CxxReadFileComponent
{
    public ref class ReadFile sealed
    {
    public:
        ReadFile();

            //reads the contents of the file but neither returns a value or the progress
            Windows::Foundation::IAsyncAction^ ReadTxtFileAsync(Platform::String^ fileName);

            //reads the contents of the file but returns only a progress
            Windows::Foundation::IAsyncActionWithProgress<double>^
                    ReadTxtFileWithProgressAsync(Platform::String^ fileName);

            //reads the contents of the file and returns the number of bytes read.
            //Does not return progress
            Windows::Foundation::IAsyncOperation<int>^ GetByteCountAsync(Platform::String^ fileName);

            //reads the contents of the file and returns the number of bytes read.
```

```
            //also provides progress information
            Windows::Foundation::IAsyncOperationWithProgress<int, double>^
                    GetByteCountWithProgressAsync(Platform::String^ fileName);

    private:
            int m_bytesRead;
    };
}
```

In our new runtime class, ReadFile, we have declared four public methods for each of the WinRT async methods. Now replace the contents from Class1.cpp with code from listing 2-36.

LISTING 2-36 ReadFile class implementation

```
// Class1.cpp
#include "pch.h"
#include "Class1.h"
#include <collection.h>
#include <ppltasks.h>

using namespace CxxReadFileComponent;
using namespace Platform;
using namespace Platform::Collections;
using namespace Windows::Foundation;
using namespace Windows::Foundation::Collections;
using namespace Windows::Storage;
using namespace Windows::Storage::Streams;
using namespace concurrency;


ReadFile::ReadFile()
{
}

IAsyncAction^ ReadFile::ReadTxtFileAsync(String^ fileName)
{
    return create_async([this, fileName]{
            StorageFolder^ item = KnownFolders::DocumentsLibrary;
            task<StorageFile^> getFileTask(item->GetFileAsync(fileName));
            getFileTask.then([](StorageFile^ storageFile){
                    task<IRandomAccessStream^>
streamTask(storageFile->OpenAsync(FileAccessMode::Read));
                    streamTask.then([](IRandomAccessStream^ istream){
                    auto Reader = ref new DataReader(istream);
                    task<UINT> bytesReadTask(Reader->LoadAsync(istream->Size));
                    try
                    {
                            UINT bytesRead = bytesReadTask.get();
                    }
                    catch(Exception^ ex)
                    {
                            String^ result = ex->Message;
                    }
            });
            });
    });
```

```
        }

//we will return a dummy progress on this operation for illustration purposes only
IAsyncActionWithProgress<double>^ ReadFile::ReadTxtFileWithProgressAsync(Platform::String^ fileName)
{
    return create_async([this, fileName](progress_reporter<double> reporter)
    {
            StorageFolder^ item = KnownFolders::DocumentsLibrary;
            task<StorageFile^> getFileTask(item->GetFileAsync(fileName));
            reporter.report(10.0);
            getFileTask.then([reporter](StorageFile^ storageFile)
            {
                    task<IRandomAccessStream^>
streamTask(storageFile->OpenAsync(FileAccessMode::Read));
                    reporter.report(25.0);
                    streamTask.then([reporter](IRandomAccessStream^ istream)
                    {
                            reporter.report(40.0);
                            auto Reader = ref new DataReader(istream);
                            task<UINT> bytesReadTask(Reader->LoadAsync(istream->Size));
                            reporter.report(60.0);
                            try
                            {
                                    UINT bytesRead = bytesReadTask.get();
                                    reporter.report(100.0);
                            }
                            catch(Exception^ ex)
                            {
                                    String^ result = ex->Message;
                            }
                    });
            });
            reporter.report(100.0);
    });
}


IAsyncOperation<int>^ ReadFile::GetByteCountAsync(Platform::String^ fileName)
{
    return create_async([this, fileName]() -> int
    {
            StorageFolder^ item = KnownFolders::DocumentsLibrary;
            task<StorageFile^> getFileTask(item->GetFileAsync(fileName));
            getFileTask.then([this](StorageFile^ storageFile)
            {
                    task<IRandomAccessStream^>
streamTask(storageFile->OpenAsync(FileAccessMode::Read));
                    streamTask.then([this](IRandomAccessStream^ istream)
                    {
                            auto Reader = ref new DataReader(istream);
                            task<UINT> bytesReadTask(Reader->LoadAsync(istream->Size));
                            try
                            {
                                    m_bytesRead = bytesReadTask.get();

                            }
```

```
                              catch(Exception^ ex)
                              {
                                      String^ result = ex->Message;
                              }
                        });
                });
                return m_bytesRead;
        });
}


IAsyncOperationWithProgress<int, double>^ ReadFile::GetByteCountWithProgressAsync(Platform::String^
fileName)
{
    return create_async([this, fileName](progress_reporter<double> reporter) -> int
    {
            StorageFolder^ item = KnownFolders::DocumentsLibrary;
            task<StorageFile^> getFileTask(item->GetFileAsync(fileName));
            reporter.report(10.0);
            getFileTask.then([this, reporter](StorageFile^ storageFile)
            {
                    reporter.report(25.0);
                    task<IRandomAccessStream^>
streamTask(storageFile->OpenAsync(FileAccessMode::Read));
                    streamTask.then([this, reporter](IRandomAccessStream^ istream)
                    {
                            reporter.report(40.0);
                            auto Reader = ref new DataReader(istream);
                            task<UINT> bytesReadTask(Reader->LoadAsync(istream->Size));
                            reporter.report(60.0);
                            try
                            {
                                    m_bytesRead = bytesReadTask.get();
                                    reporter.report(100.0);
                            }
                            catch(Exception^ ex)
                            {
                                    String^ result = ex->Message;
                            }
                    });
            });
            reporter.report(100.0);
            return m_bytesRead;
    });
}
```

Build the project and our component is now ready to be used in a WinRT app. Just for a change, let us now build a C# application to consume our component.

Create a C# client app for the ReadFile component

To consume the ReadFile component methods from a Windows Store app, use the Visual C# Blank App (XAML) template to add a second project to the Visual Studio solution, CxxReadFileComponent. This example names the project CSTestApp. Then, from the CSTestApp project, add a reference to the CxxReadFileComponent project.

Replace the markup in MainPage.xaml with the following. This markup defines the UI to enable you to call into the C++ component we created.

LISTING 2-37 MainPage XAML markup listing

```xml
<Page
    x:Class="CSTestApp.MainPage"
    xmlns="http://schemas.microsoft.com/winfx/2006/xaml/presentation"
    xmlns:x="http://schemas.microsoft.com/winfx/2006/xaml"
    xmlns:local="using:CSTestApp"
    xmlns:d="http://schemas.microsoft.com/expression/blend/2008"
    xmlns:mc="http://schemas.openxmlformats.org/markup-compatibility/2006"
    mc:Ignorable="d">

    <Grid Background="{StaticResource ApplicationPageBackgroundThemeBrush}">
        <Grid.ColumnDefinitions>
            <ColumnDefinition Width="300"/>
            <ColumnDefinition Width="300"/>
        </Grid.ColumnDefinitions>
        <Grid.RowDefinitions>
            <RowDefinition Height="125"/>
            <RowDefinition Height="125"/>
            <RowDefinition Height="125"/>
        </Grid.RowDefinitions>

        <StackPanel Grid.Column="0" Grid.Row="0">
            <Button Name="b1" Click="ReadTxtFileAsync">Read Text File</Button>
            <TextBlock Name="tb1"></TextBlock>
        </StackPanel>

        <StackPanel Grid.Column="1" Grid.Row="0">
            <Button Name="b2" Click="ReadTxtFileWithProgressAsync">Read Text File with Progress</Button>
            <ProgressBar Name="pb1" HorizontalAlignment="Left" Width="100"></ProgressBar>
            <TextBlock Name="tb2"></TextBlock>
        </StackPanel>

        <StackPanel Grid.Column="0" Grid.Row="1">
            <Button Name="b3" Click="GetByteCountAsync">Get Byte Count</Button>
            <TextBlock Name="tb3"></TextBlock>
        </StackPanel>

        <StackPanel Grid.Column="1" Grid.Row="1">
            <Button Name="b4" Click="GetByteCountWithProgressAsync">Get Byte Count with Progress</Button>
            <ProgressBar Name="pb4" HorizontalAlignment="Left" Width="100"></ProgressBar>
            <TextBlock Name="tb4"></TextBlock>
        </StackPanel>

        <StackPanel Grid.Column="0" Grid.Row="2">
            <Button Name="b5" Click="GetByteCountHandleErrors">Get Byte Count and Handle Errors</Button>
            <ProgressBar Name="pb5" HorizontalAlignment="Left" Width="100"></ProgressBar>
            <TextBlock Name="tb5"></TextBlock>
        </StackPanel>
```

```
            <StackPanel Grid.Column="1" Grid.Row="2">
                <Button Name="b6" Click="GetByteCountCancellation">Get Byte Count with Cancellation</Button>
                <Button Name="cancelButton" Click="cancelGetPrimes" IsEnabled="false">Cancel</Button>
                <ProgressBar Name="pb6"  HorizontalAlignment="Left" Width="100"></ProgressBar>
                <TextBlock Name="tb6"></TextBlock>
            </StackPanel>
        </Grid>
</Page>
```

Add the following code to MainPage.xaml.cs. This code defines a ReadFile object and handles all the button click event handlers we declared in MainPage.xaml

LISTING 2-38 MainPane.xaml.cs implementation of async methods from the ReadFile component

```csharp
private CxxReadFileComponent.ReadFile readFile = new CxxReadFileComponent.ReadFile();
private async void ReadTxtFileAsync(object sender, RoutedEventArgs e)
        {
            b1.IsEnabled = false;
            tb1.Text = "Working...";

            var asyncAction = readFile.ReadTxtFileAsync("127.txt");

            await asyncAction;
            b1.IsEnabled = true;
            tb1.Text = "Done.";
        }

        private async void ReadTxtFileWithProgressAsync(object sender, RoutedEventArgs e)
        {
            b2.IsEnabled = false;
            tb2.Text = "Working...";

            var asyncAction = readFile.ReadTxtFileWithProgressAsync("127.txt");
            asyncAction.Progress = new AsyncActionProgressHandler<double>((action, progress) =>
            {
                pb1.Value = progress;
            });

            await asyncAction;

            tb2.Text = "Done";
            b2.IsEnabled = true;
        }

        private async void GetByteCountAsync(object sender, RoutedEventArgs e)
        {
            b3.IsEnabled = false;
            tb3.Text = "Working...";

            var asyncOperation = readFile.GetByteCountAsync("127.txt");

            await asyncOperation;

            tb3.Text = "Read " + asyncOperation.GetResults().ToString() + " bytes of data";
```

```
            b3.IsEnabled = true;

        }

        private async void GetByteCountWithProgressAsync(object sender, RoutedEventArgs e)
        {
            b4.IsEnabled = false;
            tb4.Text = "Working...";

            var asyncOperation = readFile.GetByteCountWithProgressAsync("127.txt");
            asyncOperation.Progress = new AsyncOperationProgressHandler<int, double>((operation, progress)
=>
            {
                pb4.Value = progress;
            });

            await asyncOperation;

            tb4.Text = "Read " + asyncOperation.GetResults().ToString() + " bytes of data";
            b4.IsEnabled = true;
        }

        private async void GetByteCountHandleErrors(object sender, RoutedEventArgs e)
        {
            b5.IsEnabled = false;
            tb5.Text = "Working...";

            var asyncOperation = readFile.GetByteCountWithProgressAsync("127.txt");
            asyncOperation.Progress = new AsyncOperationProgressHandler<int, double>((operation, progress)
=>
            {
                pb5.Value = progress;
            });

            try
            {
                await asyncOperation;
                tb5.Text = "Read " + asyncOperation.GetResults().ToString() + " bytes of data";
            }
            catch (ArgumentException ex)
            {
                tb5.Text = "ERROR: " + ex.Message;
            }

            b5.IsEnabled = true;
        }


        private IAsyncOperationWithProgress<int, double> asyncCancelableOperation;

        private async void GetByteCountCancellation(object sender, RoutedEventArgs e)
        {
            b6.IsEnabled = false;
            cancelButton.IsEnabled = true;
            tb6.Text = "Working...";
```

```
        asyncCancelableOperation = readFile.GetByteCountWithProgressAsync("127.txt");
        asyncCancelableOperation.Progress = new AsyncOperationProgressHandler<int,
double>((operation, progress) =>
        {
            pb6.Value = progress;
        });

        try
        {
            await asyncCancelableOperation;
            tb6.Text = "Read " + asyncCancelableOperation.GetResults().ToString() + " bytes of data";
        }
        catch (System.Threading.Tasks.TaskCanceledException)
        {
            tb6.Text = "Operation canceled";
        }

        b6.IsEnabled = true;
        cancelButton.IsEnabled = false;
    }

    private void cancelGetPrimes(object sender, RoutedEventArgs e)
    {
        cancelButton.IsEnabled = false;
        asyncCancelableOperation.Cancel();
    }
```

One final change we need to make before building the project is to declare capability to the Documents Library in the AppxManifest. You should also declare a File Type Association declaration for the ".txt" extension in the AppxManifest under the Declarations tab. Setup these declarations, save the AppxManifest file and build the solution. Press F5 to launch the app. Clicking on the various buttons should call into the C++ /CX component and return the status of the async operations. You should see output as shown.

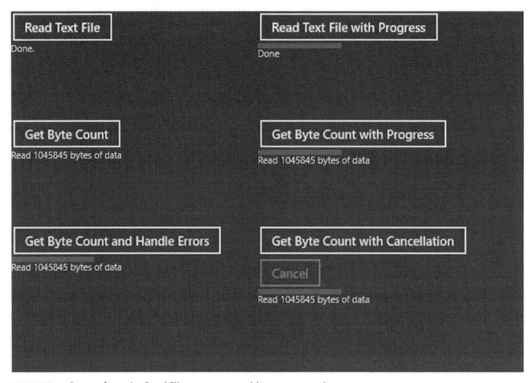

FIGURE 2-4 Output from the Read File component with async operations.

Building a WinRT component using C++ /CX and ISO-C++

Until now, we have explored how to create WinRT components using C++ /CX. Such components were heavily focused on explaining WinRT and building reusable components for WinRT supported languages such as JavaScript/C# or VB.net. We will now switch gears and focus on how we can reuse existing ISO-C++ code to build WinRT components.

Walkthrough re-factoring a standard collection

In this section, we will re-factor a standard collection such as a std::vector to be exposed by a WinRT component. We will add standard WinRT features as we progress through the process of building a WinRT compliant component.

In this walkthrough, we have existing code that reads a file located at the root of the user's C drive and builds a word list from the contents of the file. Once it has completed building the word list, it returns the list as a standard vector collection of strings. The file is named Odyssey.txt and picked up from Project Gutenberg.

LISTING 2-39 Simple C++ code to read a text file and return a list of words

```cpp
std::vector<std::wstring> BuildList(const std::wstring& fileName)
{
    std::vector<std::wstring> WordList;
    std::wifstream in_file(fileName.c_str());
    if (in_file.fail())
    {
        std::wcout<<" File not found "<<std::endl;
        return WordList;
    }
    std::wstring word;
    while (!in_file.eof())
    {
        in_file >> word;
        WordList.push_back(word);
    }
    return WordList;
}
```

In order to expose this functionality as a WinRT component, we need to make a few changes to the code itself. First, WinRT components do not have access to any folder on the file system. They need to declare their capabilities in the App Manifest. So, our first change to the component is more of a requirement: the file to read should be present in the user's Document Library. However, there is one limitation. The Documents Library is a virtual folder and does not have a fully qualified path. What you can choose to do is either launch the file picker and let the user choose the file or package the file along with your app. We will choose the latter option and package the app along with the appx package.

The next design goal is to minimize any code changes to our existing functionality. We do not want to re-write the portion of code that works perfectly fine (although it is desirable as we shall see a little later).

Once we build this component, we would want to verify that everything works by consuming it from a C# client app. We could do it in C++ /CX too but for this exercise, let us consume the component from a non-C++ language to highlight the diversity of languages in the WinRT world. So, let's get started.

Launch Visual Studio 2012 and create a new Project of type Windows Runtime Component under the Visual C++ -> Windows Store App node. Replace the name of the default generated class from Class1 to WordList. With the changes, our runtime class definition is as below

LISTING 2-40 WordList class definition

```
namespace CxxBuildWordList
{
    public ref class WordList sealed
    {
    public:
        WordList();
            Windows::Foundation::Collections::IVector<Platform::String^>^
BuildWordList(Platform::String^ fileName);
    };
}
```

The implementation of our runtime class is given below. We have chosen to implement the metho of building a word list in a very crude manner. It blocks the thread while building the word list, does not return until it is completed etc. In short, violates most of the tenets of WinRT apps. Our BuildWord-List method takes a String parameter (which we ignore) and calls our helper function BuildList. Build-List is the existing implementation of our earlier example using std::ifstream which reads the contents of a file and build a vector of strings. We do not change any code in the helper function.

LISTING 2-41 The BuildWordList method implementation

```
IVector<String^>^ WordList::BuildWordList(Platform::String^ fileName)
{
    Vector<String^>^ vec = ref new Vector<String^>();
    auto appLocation = Windows::ApplicationModel::Package::Current->InstalledLocation;
    auto itemPath = appLocation->Path;
    itemPath += "\\Assets\\Odyssey.txt";

    std::wstring s = itemPath->Data();
    std::string str;
    str.assign(s.begin(), s.end());
    std::vector<std::string> list = BuildList(str);

    auto it = list.begin();
    auto end = list.end();

    for (; it != end; ++it)
    {
            std::string str(*it);
```

```
            std::wstring s;
            s.assign(str.begin(), str.end());
            vec->Append(ref new String(s.c_str()));
    }
    return vec;

}
```

Finally, our helper function. That's it.

LISTING 2-42 Helper function reading file contents written in standard C++

```
std::vector<std::string> BuildList(const std::string& fileName)
{
    std::vector<std::string> WordList;
    std::ifstream in_file(fileName.c_str());
    if (in_file.fail())
    {
            std::wcout<<"File not found"<<std::endl;
            return WordList;
    }
    std::string word;
    while (!in_file.eof())
    {
            in_file >> word;
            WordList.push_back(word);
    }
    return WordList;
}
```

Once our helper function returns a std::vector containing std::string types, we need to populate a WinRT Vector type. As per the rules of WinRT, we can only pass standard WinRT types across the ABI boundary. In addition, we should also convert each and every string from std::string to Platform::String type and populate the Vector instance that we pass across the ABI boundary. Finally, it is important to note here that a Platform::Collections::Vector<T> instance is implicitly converted to a Windows::Foundation::Collections::IVector<T>.

Before we move on making any further changes, here are some good design guidelines.

- Use std::vector as much as possible with your C++ code.

- Change the std::vector to a Platform::Vector only when you are passing the vector to the WinRT ABI boundary.

- When you use string types with a vector, decide upfront whether to use std::string or Platform::String. If you use std::string, you will have to convert them to Platform::String later on instead of paying the cost of conversion upfront.

- As a good performance optimization, use the move constructor to efficiently initialize a Platform::Vector from a std::vector.

- Use std::map for all C++ code. Our example demonstrated using std::vector but the same rules and guidelines apply for a map type as well.

- Use std::map internally and convert it to Platform::Collections::Map when passing across the WinRT ABI boundary.

- Lookup and insert operations are costly to perform on a Map. Instead, perform all insert and lookup operations on the std::map.

- If you store value types in either a Vector or Map, such as Windows::Foundation::DateTime, you should also provide an custom function object that supports equality comparison.

We will now change the code to use WinRT thread pool and use a background thread to read the file contents into the vector. Windows Store apps and components can use the Operating System provided thread pool to complete work in parallel threads. Using the system provided thread pool frees you, as a developer, from having to create threads manually and keep track of their execution/cancellation states. The system provided thread pool manages a set of threads and assigns work for threads as they become available. The work to be performed is usually maintained in a queue. The thread pool is great for asynchronous programming because you can use the thread pool to perform additional work and not block the UI. If you want to use the system provided thread pool to offload your code into a background thread, you should follow these steps:

The RunAsync method in the Windows::System::Threading::ThreadPool class accepts a lambda function that represents the work to be completed. This lambda returns an IAsyncAction object which you should use to handle work completion. With this knowledge, we can now re-write our code as follows.

LISTING 2-43 Word List API using the WinRT thread pool API

```
//Word List building function using the system thread pool API
IAsyncAction^ WordList::BuildWordListTp(Platform::String^ fileName)
{
    auto workItemDelegate = [this](IAsyncAction^ workitem)
    {
            auto status = workitem->Status;
            if (AsyncStatus::Canceled == status)
            {
                    // handle cancellation here
            }

            //do the actual work here
            vec = ref new Vector<String^>();
            auto appLocation = Windows::ApplicationModel::Package::Current->InstalledLocation;
            auto itemPath = appLocation->Path;
            itemPath += "\\Assets\\Odyssey.txt";

            std::wstring s = itemPath->Data();
            std::string str;
            str.assign(s.begin(), s.end());
            std::vector<std::string> list = BuildList(str);
```

```
            auto it = list.begin();
            auto end = list.end();

            for (; it != end; ++it)
            {
                    std::string str(*it);
                    std::wstring s;
                    s.assign(str.begin(), str.end());
                    vec->Append(ref new String(s.c_str()));
            }
    };

    auto workItemHandler = ref new Windows::System::Threading::WorkItemHandler(workItemDelegate);

    IAsyncAction^ action = Windows::System::Threading::ThreadPool::RunAsync(workItemHandler,
Windows::System::Threading::WorkItemPriority::Normal);
    return action;
}
```

Since the thread pool RunAsync API returns only an IAsyncAction, we will define a property that re-turns the fully populated Vector collection after the async operation is completed.

```
    property Windows::Foundation::Collections::IVector<Platform::String^>^ GetWordList
    {
            Windows::Foundation::Collections::IVector<Platform::String^>^ get()
            {
                    return vec;
            }
    }
```

We will add a new button in our test application and in the button click handler call the thread pool version of our API.

LISTING 2-44 C# button click handler calling the component API using the thread pool

```
    private async void Button_Click_1(object sender, RoutedEventArgs e)
    {
        wordList.ItemsSource = null;
        var fileName = "Odyssey.txt";//just a dummy name here
        WordList list = new WordList();
        var asyncAction = list.BuildWordListTp(fileName);
        await asyncAction;
        wordList.ItemsSource = list.GetWordList;


    }
```

When you run the test application, you can see the UI not responding with our initial version of the API. When you use the thread pool API, you observe that the UI is not blocked and you can still per-form operations on the UI. Using the thread pool API is a good way to bring forth your existing code into the new asynchronous world of the Windows Runtime while not having to modify large amounts of existing code or writing everything from scratch!

A peek inside the magic of C++ /CX

So how does C++ /CX perform all the magic tricks associated with creating WinRT compliant classes and types? Let's take a sneek peek. A thorough discussion of WinRT follows in Chapter6 but for now, let us begin with a very simple example.

A WinRT class should implement the following interfaces:

1. IInspectable

2. IActivationFactory

3. IWeakReference

4. Any other needed interfaces

5. Derive your class from **FtmBase** in order to make your class Agile. Deriving from **FtmBase** aggregates the FreeThreadedMarshaller. You should also pay particular attention to ensuring thread safety in your classes.

While WRL does assist in implementing these interfaces by providing helper classes, it does get complicated as you begin to write components that need to communicate with more of WinRT APIs such as XAML. C++ /CX simplifies the process by automatically implementing the needed interfaces for your ref class by default, thus helping generate the boiler plate code efficiently behind the scenes. You are then left to focus on the part of consuming other WinRT APIs and the language does a great job at helping you consume WinRT APIs. So how does C++ /CX perform this magic of implementing the IInspectable and other interfaces?

Let us take a simple example to dig into the magic of C++ /CX.

> **Warning** Please note that this output format may change any time in future releases and is only meant to help in understanding how C++ /CX glues things together. You should not make any assumptions on the generated code nor take it as a binding guarantee that things will always work in this manner.

Consider the following ref class declaration:

LISTING 2-45 Simple ref class to demonstrate C++ /CX code generation and binding to WinRT types

```
public ref class WinRTExample sealed
{
public:
    WinRTExample() {};
    ~WinRTExample() {};
void DoSomething();
};
```

The **ref class** keyword before the class name, WinRTExample, defines a COM object implementing the **IInspectable** interface and in turn the **IUnknown** interface. The compiler generates the code automatically. The WinRT ABI mandates that any reference to a WinRT object is a pointer to a list of vtables. The compiler generates this list of vtables and makes the right "fixup" for each method call on the WinRT object.

When you use the handle to object modifier (or the '^', pronounced the hat), your code is now pointing to a pointer to an array of function pointers. In the sample class above, the array of function pointers consist of IUnknown methods, IInspectable methods, plus some other methods to handle reference counting and WinRT ABI semantics.

The compiler also implements the **IDisposable** interface. It is important to note here that the **IDisposable** is not the managed equivalent of an interface with the same name. The **IDisposable** is the projected name of the WinRT **IClosable** interface. The **IClosable** interface has a single method: **Close** whose sole motivation to exist is to release system resources that are exposed by a Windows Runtime object.

When you define a ref class in C++/CX it is agile by default; that is, it has a **ThreadingModel=Both** and **MarshallingType=Agile**. This means that the compiler is generating code to implement the FtmBase class needed to support Agility.

What is given below is the code that is generated for the simple class defined above. This is useful to understand how the compiler treats the C++ /CX code and how the layout of various structs/classes, properties and interface implementations are generated.

```
class __IWinRTExamplePublicNonVirtuals   size(4):

   +---

   | +--- (base class Object)

 0 | | {vfptr}

   | +---

   +---



__IWinRTExamplePublicNonVirtuals::$vftable@:

   | &__IWinRTExamplePublicNonVirtuals_meta

   | 0

 0 | &Object::__abi_QueryInterface

 1 | &Object::__abi_AddRef

 2 | &Object::__abi_Release

 3 | &Object::__abi_GetIids

 4 | &Object::__abi_GetRuntimeClassName
```

```
5 | &Object::__abi_GetTrustLevel

6 | &__IWinRTExamplePublicNonVirtuals::__abi_DoSomething

7 | &__IWinRTExamplePublicNonVirtuals::DoSomething


__IWinRTExamplePublicNonVirtuals::DoSomething this adjustor: 0

__IWinRTExamplePublicNonVirtuals::__abi_DoSomething this adjustor: 0

class __WinRTExampleActivationFactory    size(16):

    +---

    | +--- (base class IActivationFactory)

    | | +--- (base class Object)

0 | | | {vfptr}

    | | +---

    | +---

    | +--- (base class Object)

4 | | {vfptr}

    | +---

8 | __abi_FTMWeakRefData __abi_reference_count

    +---


__WinRTExampleActivationFactory::$vftable@IActivationFactory@:

    | &__WinRTExampleActivationFactory_meta

    | 0

0 | &__WinRTExampleActivationFactory::__abi_QueryInterface

1 | &__WinRTExampleActivationFactory::__abi_AddRef

2 | &__WinRTExampleActivationFactory::__abi_Release

3 | &__WinRTExampleActivationFactory::__abi_GetIids

4 | &__WinRTExampleActivationFactory::__abi_GetRuntimeClassName

5 | &__WinRTExampleActivationFactory::__abi_GetTrustLevel

6 | &__WinRTExampleActivationFactory::__abi_Platform_Details_IActivationFactory___abi_ActivateInstance

7 | &__WinRTExampleActivationFactory::ActivateInstance
```

```
__WinRTExampleActivationFactory::$vftable@Object@:

   | -4

 0 | &thunk: this-=4; goto __WinRTExampleActivationFactory::__abi_QueryInterface

 1 | &thunk: this-=4; goto __WinRTExampleActivationFactory::__abi_AddRef

 2 | &thunk: this-=4; goto __WinRTExampleActivationFactory::__abi_Release

 3 | &thunk: this-=4; goto __WinRTExampleActivationFactory::__abi_GetIids

 4 | &thunk: this-=4; goto __WinRTExampleActivationFactory::__abi_GetRuntimeClassName

 5 | &thunk: this-=4; goto __WinRTExampleActivationFactory::__abi_GetTrustLevel


__WinRTExampleActivationFactory::ActivateInstance this adjustor: 0

__WinRTExampleActivationFactory::__abi_QueryInterface this adjustor: 0

__WinRTExampleActivationFactory::__abi_AddRef this adjustor: 0

__WinRTExampleActivationFactory::__abi_Release this adjustor: 0

__WinRTExampleActivationFactory::__abi_GetIids this adjustor: 0

__WinRTExampleActivationFactory::__abi_GetRuntimeClassName this adjustor: 0

__WinRTExampleActivationFactory::__abi_GetTrustLevel this adjustor: 0

__WinRTExampleActivationFactory::__abi_Platform_Details_IActivationFactory____abi_ActivateInstance this
adjustor: 0

class WinRTExample    size(32):

   +---

   | +--- (base class __IWinRTExamplePublicNonVirtuals)

   | | +--- (base class Object)

 0 | | | {vfptr}

   | | +---

   | +---

   | +--- (base class IDisposable)

   | | +--- (base class Object)

 4 | | | {vfptr}

   | | +---

   | +---

   | +--- (base class Object)
```

```
 8 | | {vfptr}

   | +---

   | +--- (base class IWeakReferenceSource)

   | | +--- (base class __abi_IUnknown)

12 | | | {vfptr}

   | | +---

   | | +--- (base class Object)

16 | | | {vfptr}

   | | +---

   | +---

20 | __abi_FTMWeakRefData __abi_reference_count

28 | __abi_disposed

   | <alignment member> (size=3)

   +---
```

```
WinRTExample::$vftable@__IWinRTExamplePublicNonVirtuals@:

   | &WinRTExample_meta

   | 0

 0 | &WinRTExample::__abi_QueryInterface

 1 | &WinRTExample::__abi_AddRef

 2 | &WinRTExample::__abi_Release

 3 | &WinRTExample::__abi_GetIids

 4 | &WinRTExample::__abi_GetRuntimeClassName

 5 | &WinRTExample::__abi_GetTrustLevel

 6 | &WinRTExample::__abi_Sample___IWinRTExamplePublicNonVirtuals___abi_DoSomething

 7 | &WinRTExample::DoSomething
```

```
WinRTExample::$vftable@IDisposable@:

   | -4

 0 | &thunk: this-=4; goto WinRTExample::__abi_QueryInterface

 1 | &thunk: this-=4; goto WinRTExample::__abi_AddRef
```

```
2 | &thunk: this-=4; goto WinRTExample::__abi_Release

3 | &thunk: this-=4; goto WinRTExample::__abi_GetIids

4 | &thunk: this-=4; goto WinRTExample::__abi_GetRuntimeClassName

5 | &thunk: this-=4; goto WinRTExample::__abi_GetTrustLevel

6 | &thunk: this-=4; goto WinRTExample::__abi_Platform_IDisposable____abi_<Dispose>

7 | &thunk: this-=4; goto WinRTExample::<Dispose>


WinRTExample::$vftable@Object@:

   | -8

0 | &thunk: this-=8; goto WinRTExample::__abi_QueryInterface

1 | &thunk: this-=8; goto WinRTExample::__abi_AddRef

2 | &thunk: this-=8; goto WinRTExample::__abi_Release

3 | &thunk: this-=8; goto WinRTExample::__abi_GetIids

4 | &thunk: this-=8; goto WinRTExample::__abi_GetRuntimeClassName

5 | &thunk: this-=8; goto WinRTExample::__abi_GetTrustLevel


WinRTExample::$vftable@__abi_IUnknown@:

   | -12

0 | &thunk: this-=12; goto WinRTExample::__abi_QueryInterface

1 | &thunk: this-=12; goto WinRTExample::__abi_AddRef

2 | &thunk: this-=12; goto WinRTExample::__abi_Release

3 | &thunk: this-=12; goto
WinRTExample::__abi_Platform_Details_IWeakReferenceSource____abi_GetWeakReference

4 | &thunk: this-=12; goto WinRTExample::GetWeakReference


WinRTExample::$vftable@Object@IWeakReferenceSource@:

   | -16

0 | &thunk: this-=16; goto WinRTExample::__abi_QueryInterface

1 | &thunk: this-=16; goto WinRTExample::__abi_AddRef

2 | &thunk: this-=16; goto WinRTExample::__abi_Release

3 | &thunk: this-=16; goto WinRTExample::__abi_GetIids
```

```
4 | &thunk: this-=16; goto WinRTExample::__abi_GetRuntimeClassName

5 | &thunk: this-=16; goto WinRTExample::__abi_GetTrustLevel
```

```
WinRTExample::DoSomething this adjustor: 0

WinRTExample::<Dispose> this adjustor: 0

WinRTExample::__abi_QueryInterface this adjustor: 0

WinRTExample::__abi_AddRef this adjustor: 0

WinRTExample::__abi_Release this adjustor: 0

WinRTExample::__abi_GetIids this adjustor: 0

WinRTExample::__abi_GetRuntimeClassName this adjustor: 0

WinRTExample::__abi_GetTrustLevel this adjustor: 0

WinRTExample::GetWeakReference this adjustor: 0

WinRTExample::__abi_Platform_IDisposable____abi_<Dispose> this adjustor: 0

WinRTExample::__abi_Platform_Details_IWeakReferenceSource____abi_GetWeakReference this adjustor: 0

WinRTExample::__abi_Sample___IWinRTExamplePublicNonVirtuals____abi_DoSomething this adjustor: 0
```

The code generated by the compiler may look verbose but is every bit as performant as hand crafted code. For a component implementing multiple interfaces, a cast across multiple interfaces generates code equivalent to a dynamic_cast, only requiring an adjustment in the thunking code. If the component is behind the ABI boundaries, it generates into a QueryInterface call, just like in traditional COM.

Guidance on the use of C++ /CX

Consider the following guidance when using C++ /CX.

- Write as much Standard, portable C++ code as possible.

- Leverage the support for mixing Standard C++ types and the Windows Runtime type, as defined in the *Platform* namespace as much as possible.

- Only opt to use the component extensions when interacting with Windows Runtime APIs or at the ABI layer.

- Use the component extensions when your code needs to be accessed across the Windows Runtime boundary. For example, if you component would be accessed from JavaScript or C#.

- If your C++ /CX class uses standard C++ code, contain the same either as private or internal to the C++ /CX class.

Where are we and what's Next?

This chapter introduced Modern C++, C++ /CX and took you on a whirlwind tour of some of the features of the C++ language and the component extensions. We also looked at WinRT runtime classes, differentiate between Standard C++ and the extensions, while also focusing on how to create C++ /CX components. Before moving to C++11, we also looked at some advanced concepts in C++ /CX like Weak References and a discussion on how smart pointer semantics are baked into the ^ by looking at how the compiler generates code for a ref class. We also discussed how to build WinRT components using C++ /CX and how such components can be used from languages other than C++ (JS and C# usage).

We now turn our attention to developing Windows Store apps and begin with a discussion of the UI Framework for C++ developers in Windows 8, **XAML**.

Chapter 3
XAML in Windows 8 and C++ /CX

In this chapter:

Introduction

Hello World with XAML and C++ /CX

Basic XAML Syntax

Using Panels to Layout UX

Basic XAML Controls

Windows 8 Signature XAML Controls

Handling Events

Markup Extensions

DataBinding

Binding to a Data Model

Building a XAML custom control

Using Animations in XAML controls

Where are we and what's next

Introduction to XAML

XAML or e**X**tensible **A**pplication **M**arkup **L**anguage is the new native User Interface API stack for developing Windows Store applications in Windows 8. XAML is XML with a special schema, and is used to create a user interface in a declarative syntactic form. XAML is

- Declarative

- Hierarchical

- Supports de-coupling of UI from implementation through the use of dependency properties

- Supports type extension.

There are three main parts in XAML-based Windows Store apps.

1. XAML markup itself (.xaml extension)

2. The generated code for the XAML files

3. The code-behind files where you place your source code (.h and .cpp).

Because of this clear distinction between designer generated markup files, the corresponding generated code files and the code-behind source files written by the developer, C++ /CX supports partial classes to enable designers and developers to work independently of each other when working together on a XAML-based Windows Store app. Furthermore, support for partial classes ensures that any code that is generated by tools such as graphical XAML editors can be placed in a separate source file from that that either the human developer or designer edits.

Using XAML, you can associate a separate source file (both .h and .cpp) for a single XAML file containing a hierarchical description of various user interface elements. This source file can contain code that responds to events and manipulate objects that were declared in the markup. Visual Studio 2012 contains support to edit the markup files with designer tools such as Microsoft Expression Blend 2012 or the built-in Designer in Visual Studio 2012 without any loss of information. This support means that designers and developers can continue developing applications without loss of data. XAML files are XML files with the .xaml extension.

This chapter is a high level overview of XAML, focusing on topics of interest to C++ developers. For more in-depth coverage of XAML please refer to Programming Windows 6th Ed by Charles Petzold.

Hello World with XAML and C++ /CX

We begin our exploration of XAML with a simple, yet canonical example of "Hello World". Follow these steps and let us get cracking with code.

1. Launch Visual Studio 2012.

2. Click File->New Project.

3. In the New Project dialog, click Templates, choose Visual C++ and then click on Windows Store.

4. In the Middle Pane, select "Blank App (XAML)"

5. Type a name for the Project, say, "**HelloApp**" and click OK.

6. Visual Studio creates the solution and a project within the solution containing a number of automatically generated files.

7. In the Solution Explorer Pane, expand the Solution node and the Project Node. You will see the complete list of generated files.

8. Click on the arrow before the MainPage.xaml, you will see two files: MainPage.xaml.cpp and MainPage.xaml.h.

9. Double click on the MainPage.xaml.cpp/MainPage.xaml.h to open these files.

10. The 3 files MainPage.xaml, MainPage.xaml.cpp and MainPage.xaml.h constitute the class and UI definition of the MainPage class.

11. Double click on the MainPage.xaml file. This action opens the xaml file in the Visual Designer with split panes: The top pane shows how the UI looks and the bottom pane shows the corresponding XAML markup.

12. Let us add the following markup to the Grid definition in MainPage.xaml

```
<TextBlock Text="Hello World"
            FontSize="120"
            FontFamily="Segoe UI"
            FontStyle="Oblique"
            FontWeight="Bold"
            Foreground="White"
            HorizontalAlignment="Center"
            VerticalAlignment="Center"
    />
```

13. If you compile the app and launch it from Visual Studio using F5, you will notice the output similar to the following

FIGURE 3-1 Hello World output

Let us explore the MainPage.xaml.cpp file in more detail. For the **HelloApp** project we created, the MainPage.xaml.cpp listing is given below.

LISTING 3-1 MainPage.xaml.cpp for the HelloApp project

```cpp
//
// MainPage.xaml.cpp
// Implementation of the MainPage class.
//

#include "pch.h"
#include "MainPage.xaml.h"

using namespace HelloApp;

using namespace Platform;
using namespace Windows::Foundation;
using namespace Windows::Foundation::Collections;
using namespace Windows::UI::Xaml;
using namespace Windows::UI::Xaml::Controls;
using namespace Windows::UI::Xaml::Controls::Primitives;
using namespace Windows::UI::Xaml::Data;
using namespace Windows::UI::Xaml::Input;
using namespace Windows::UI::Xaml::Media;
using namespace Windows::UI::Xaml::Navigation;

// The Blank Page item template is documented at http://go.microsoft.com/fwlink/?LinkId=234238

MainPage::MainPage()
{
    InitializeComponent();
}

/// <summary>
/// Invoked when this page is about to be displayed in a Frame.
/// </summary>
/// <param name="e">Event data that describes how this page was reached.  The Parameter
/// property is typically used to configure the page.</param>
void MainPage::OnNavigatedTo(NavigationEventArgs^ e)
{
    (void) e; // Unused parameter
}
```

The MainPage.xaml.cpp file does not contain much code. It begins with a list of namespace references to various APIs in the Windows Runtime. The first namespace "Platform" is the C++ component extensions namespace, discussed in chapter 2. The others are the namespaces corresponding to various "XAML" and core Windows Runtime functionality. MainPage.xaml.h, the primary header for the MainPage class is listed below.

LISTING 3-2 Listing for the MainPage.xaml.h from the HelloApp project

```cpp
//
// MainPage.xaml.h
// Declaration of the MainPage class.
//

#pragma once
```

```
#include "MainPage.g.h"
namespace HelloApp
{
    /// <summary>
    /// An empty page that can be used on its own or navigated to within a Frame.
    /// </summary>
    public ref class MainPage sealed
    {
    public:
            MainPage();

    protected:
            virtual void OnNavigatedTo(Windows::UI::Xaml::Navigation::NavigationEventArgs^ e) override;
    };
}
```

The MainPage class declares a public constructor and an OnNavigatedTo event. Nothing fancy here. At this stage you might be wondering how the XAML markup maps to the corresponding code in the MainPage C++ class. The answer lies in "generated code".

Compiling XAML and generating C++ code

The process of compiling XAML and its corresponding C++ code occurs in two stages. During the initial build phase, the XAML compiler generates C++ code from the markup and places them in appropriately named <XAML file name>.g.h and <XAML file name>.g.hpp files. For example, consider a simple Button control defined in XAML as follows:

```
<Button x:Name="btnItemAdd" Content="Add"/>
```

As the XAML compiler generates code, it creates an instance of a Windows::UI::Xaml::Controls::Button in the MainPage class definition. At this point however, the MainPage class definition is still incomplete and hence it is called a partial class. The XAML compiler places the Button instance declaration in the MainPage.g.h file as a private member variable of the MainPage class as follows:

```
private: ::Windows::UI::Xaml::Controls::Button^ btnItemAdd;
```

The generated code in MainPage.g.hpp contains code to load the XAML file from the application resources and then bind the **btnItemAdd** variable to the actual Button control.

```
// Get the Button named 'btnItemAdd'
```

```
btnItemAdd                                                              =
safe_cast<Windows::UI::Xaml::Controls::Button^>(static_cast<Windows::UI::Xam
l::IFrameworkElement^>(this)->FindName(L"btnItemAdd"));
```

Because the class is a partial class and contains declarations for the UI elements in generated code, Intellisense in the code-behind class, where you place your source code, shows all the things you have defined as if you had code written for them. In fact, if you look at the declaration of the Button more closely, you would notice that the variable name the XAML compiler assigned to the Button instance, **btnItemAdd**, is actually taken from the Name attribute. The Name attribute itself is inside the **x:** namespace, which by the way, is the default namespace that XAML generates. The **x:** namespace itself has several attributes including **x:Uid**, **x:Name** and **x:FieldModifier**. Without specifying the x:Name attribute, there is no way for a named instance of a variable being generated by the XAML compiler. If however, you want dependency inversion, then there is no need to specify a name for the controls.

LISTING 3-3 Listing of MainPage.g.h and MainPage.g.hpp from the HelloApp project

```
#pragma once
//---------------------------------------------------------------------------
//     This code was generated by a tool.
//
//     Changes to this file may cause incorrect behavior and will be lost if
//     the code is regenerated.
//---------------------------------------------------------------------------
namespace HelloApp
{
    partial ref class MainPage : public Windows::UI::Xaml::Controls::Page,
        public Windows::UI::Xaml::Markup::IComponentConnector
    {
    public:
        void InitializeComponent();
        virtual void Connect(int connectionId, Platform::Object^ target);

    private:
        bool _contentLoaded;
    };
}
//---------------------------------------------------------------------------
//     This code was generated by a tool.
//
//     Changes to this file may cause incorrect behavior and will be lost if
//     the code is regenerated.
//---------------------------------------------------------------------------
#include "pch.h"
#include "MainPage.xaml.h"
using namespace Windows::Foundation;
using namespace Windows::UI::Xaml;
using namespace Windows::UI::Xaml::Controls;
using namespace Windows::UI::Xaml::Markup;
using namespace HelloApp;

void MainPage::InitializeComponent()
{
    if (_contentLoaded)
        return;

    _contentLoaded = true;

    // Call LoadComponent on ms-appx:///MainPage.xaml
    Windows::UI::Xaml::Application::LoadComponent(this, ref new
Windows::Foundation::Uri(L"ms-appx:///MainPage.xaml"),
```

```
Windows::UI::Xaml::Controls::Primitives::ComponentResourceLocation::Application);
}

void MainPage::Connect(int connectionId, Platform::Object^ target)
{
    (void)connectionId; // Unused parameter
    (void)target; // Unused parameter
    _contentLoaded = true;
}
```

MainPage is defined as a partial class in the generated code. You might recall from the Chapter on C++ /CX that a partial class is a declaration lets the compiler know that other files may contribute to the declaration of the class. The declaration in MainPage.h actually, completes the declaration of the **MainPage** class.

XAML lets you define UI *declaratively*, however you can still write code to imperatively add, remove, or interact with elements on your page. Let us now create a similar Hello World App, by generating the UI through C++ code, instead of through mark-up.

1. Launch Visual Studio 2012.

2. Click File->New Project.

3. In the New Project dialog, click Templates, choose Visual C++ and then click on Windows Store.

4. In the Middle Pane, select "Blank App (XAML)"

5. Type a name for the Project, say, "**HelloAppCode**" and click OK.

6. Visual Studio creates the solution and a project within the solution containing a number of automatically generated files.

7. In the Solution Explorer Pane, expand the Solution node and the Project Node. You will see the complete list of generated files.

8. Click on the arrow before the MainPage.xaml, you will see two files: MainPage.xaml.cpp and MainPage.xaml.h.

9. In the MainPage.xaml file, delete the section declaring the Grid element.

10. Add a private function to the MainPage class. Let us name this function, CreateText. The function returns void and does not accept any parameters.

11. The CreateText function is implemented below.

   LISTING 3-4 Listing for CreateText function

```
void MainPage::CreateText()
{
        auto grid = ref new Grid();
        auto gridBackground = ref new SolidColorBrush();
        gridBackground->Color = Windows::UI::Colors::Black;
```

```
    this->Content = grid;
    auto helloText = ref new TextBlock();
    helloText->Text = "Hello World";
    grid->Children->Append(helloText);
}
```

When you compile and run the **HelloAppCode**, you will see output exactly the same as the output for **HelloApp**. While this is a stripped down example of demonstrating how everything that is declared in XAML can be achieved through C++ code, you should not try to follow this approach. As a matter of fact, you should try to generate much of your user interface through XAML as much as possible and write very little C++ code. Very simply the more you build your UI imperatively through code rather than XAML the less advantage you'll be able to take of designer friendly tooling like Blend.

Now that you have seen how to generate a simple "Hello World" style application using XAML and C++, we now turn our attention to exploring the syntax.

Basic XAML Syntax

XAML is a dynamic set of runtime classes that are built hierarchically representing a User interface. In its serialized form, it is an xml markup represented as a .xaml file. You can easily translate from one form to another without any loss of information during the translation process. You can also edit the XAML in its XML form or programmatically at the API level to change your UI. This can be done either statically or dynamically.

A XAML file is a valid XML file. However, certain XAML concepts also have a very different meaning and interpretation when compared with XML. For example, XAML supports setting properties using elements rather than using simple strings. Visual Studio 2012 and Microsoft Blend 2012 can be used to produce correct XAML syntax. This is true whether you use the XAML text editor or the Visual Designer. In Visual Studio, the designer surface allows you to drop controls on the surface and drag them around for a RAD (rapid application development) experience. And, when you use the XAML editor, Intellisense auto-correct, and other language features help to make sure your XAML is XML compliant, and that it matches the XAML concepts.

Elements and Attributes

XAML is serialized from an object graph into XML as elements and attributes. For simple things, where an object property is a simple string value, the attribute syntax can be used. So, for example, the Content property of a button is what the button displays. If the content is simple text, then you can simply use the attribute syntax to describe it. But, if you want to make the content of the button to be something more complex, then you will need to use the element syntax to describe the contents. The basic element syntax looks like this:

```
<Button ...>
```

```
<Button.Content>

    <... elements like normal XAML describing the content of the button/>

</Button.Content>
```

```
</Button>
```

Note that the basic syntax is that within the element you define the name of the parent element, followed by a dot (".") and the object's property name. You can do this several levels deep if needed.

A good example is the <Grid/> control.

```
<Grid Background="{StaticResource ApplicationPageBackgroundThemeBrush}">

    <Grid.ColumnDefinitions>

        <ColumnDefinition/>

        <ColumnDefinition/>

    </Grid.ColumnDefinitions>

    <Grid.RowDefinitions>

        <RowDefinition/>

        <RowDefinition/>

    </Grid.RowDefinitions>

    <TextBlock x:Name="Foo" Grid.Column="0" Grid.Row="1" Text="Hello World" Font-Size="120"              FontFamily="Seqoe UI" FontStyle="Oblique" FontWeight="Bold" Fore-ground="Green" HorizontalAlignment="Center" VerticalAlignment="Center"/>

        </Grid>
```

Note that here on the <Text> element, the Grid.Column and Grid.Row are "attached properties" which are global properties that can be applied to any object described by a XAML element. At a basic level an element declared in XAML corresponds to an object in a backing runtime representation. Thus an element declaration in XAML equates to a declaration of an object.

The XAML specification defines rules that enable mapping WinRT namespaces, types, and properties into equivalent XML namespaces, types and properties. Consider the following code samples in XAML and C++ /CX

LISTING 3-5 XAML and C++ source to create a Button

XAML:

```
<Button xmlns="http://schemas.microsoft.com/winfx/2006/xaml/presentation"
Content = "Hello World" />
```

C++ /CX:

```
Windows::UI::Xaml::Controls::Button^ btn = ref new Windows::UI::Xaml::Controls::Button();
btn->Content = "Hello World";
```

The XAML code can be viewed in tools such as XAMLPadX or even Internet Explorer. When viewed via such tools, you would notice the Button fills up the entire screen with the caption displayed as "Hello World". The C++ /CX code would need to be compiled into an application and only then can the Button object viewed on screen.

Please note that while you can use XAMLPadX to view Windows 8 XAML code, the tool has been deprecated and no further versions of the tool are planned.

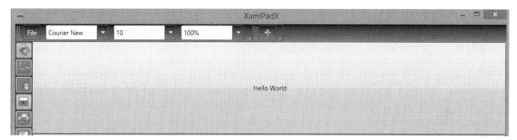

FIGURE 3-2 A XAML Button viewed in XamlPadX

Let us look at another code sample that hooks up events using XAML and the equivalent code using C++ /CX. For the XAML sample, modify the MainPage.xaml in the **HelloApp** and add a <Button> control. For the Button control, we set the Content property of the Button to "Hello World" and add a **Click** event handler, "Btn_Click". You might wonder how a string such as "Btn_Click" gets translated into a corresponding event handler. This is achieved via "Type converters" which allow you to easily move between string data in XML to the object graph. The **Click** event is a **RoutedEventHandler** and XAML's built-in type converters allow you to type in text for an attribute and convert it to the corresponding **RoutedEventHandler**. A **Routed Event** bubbles up through the UI element tree even if elements within the tree mark it as handled. Thus our Button control will receive the **Click** event even if an intermediary control marks it as handled.

LISTING 3-6 XAML and C++ code with event handlers

XAML:

```
<Button xmlns="http://schemas.microsoft.com/winfx/2006/xaml/presentation"
Content = "Hello World" Click="Btn_Click"/>
```

C++ /CX:

```
Windows::UI::Xaml::Controls::Button^ btn = ref new Windows::UI::Xaml::Controls::Button();
btn->Click += ref new Windows::UI::Xaml::RoutedEventHandler(&App1::MainPage::btn_Click);
btn->Content = "Hello World";
```

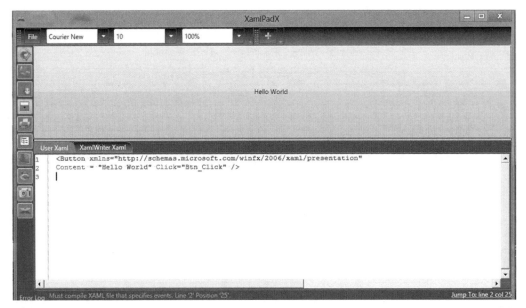

FIGURE 3-3 A XAML Button with added event handler viewed in XamlPadX. Note the error at the bottom of the image

These examples illustrate that XAML supports:

- Serialization of an in-memory object graph. The serialized object graph, especially for Windows Store apps, is native code running in WinRT close to the metal.

- Attached properties

- Dependency inversion (dependency properties and routed events)

- Type convertors

- Attaching event handlers in markup is equivalent to setting event handlers in code-behind.

We might pause to ask a simple question: how does the XML namespace defined in the examples above map to C++ /CX code? The answer lies in XAML namespaces.

Namespaces

In the example above, we have declared the Button class to refer to a namespace, such as, http://schemas.microsoft.com/winfx/2006/xaml/presentation, before adding the Content Property.

Namespaces are used in various programming languages to determine how identifiers are interpreted. Namespaces can greatly help in resolving ambiguities if identifiers are being reused. For example, identifiers and types used by the C++ Standard Template Library are found in the *std* namespace. In the C++ /CX world, the C++ types mapping to the Windows Runtime types can be found in the *Platform* namespace. Similarly, namespaces in XAML serve a similar purpose.

Consider the same XAML sample illustrated in Listing 3-1 above.

```
<Button xmlns="http://schemas.microsoft.com/winfx/2006/xaml/presentation"
Content = "Hello World" />
```

XAML uses namespaces and extends them as follows:

- The default namespace attribute, **xmlns**, is reserved for use by XAML. The value of the attribute is a URI usually, http://schemas.microsoft.com/winfx/2006/xaml/presentation.

- XAML uses prefix declarations to declare non-default namespaces, and prefix usages in elements and attributes to reference that namespace.

- XAML has a concept of default namespace, which by convention is the **x:** namespace as mentioned above.

- Namespace definitions inherit in an XML document from parent element to child element.

- Attributes of an element inherit the element's namespaces.

We know that XAML is used to declare objects and their properties, as well as establish visual tree hierarchies in Windows Store applications for Windows 8. The objects, thus declared in XAML, are actually backed by corresponding type libraries. These type libraries, can either be built in, such as Windows::UI::Xaml, or defined by other languages, frameworks and/or other developers. The following are valid examples of such type libraries.

- Core libraries that are part of the Windows Runtime.

- Distributed libraries, either provided by Microsoft or by third parties.

- Libraries that represent the definition of a third-party control that your app incorporates and your package redistributes.

- Your own library, as created by your project, which holds some or all of your user code.

A XAML file always declares a default XAML namespace in its root element. In our sample above, the XAML parser would expect that an element **Button** exists and is present in the default namespace. If, however, **Button** does not exist in the default namespace, you must explicitly qualify it with a prefix that represents the namespace where the **Button** element exists. This is similar to the usage of "std::cout" if one were to omit the "using namespace std" declaration in a source .cpp file using methods from the C++ Standard Library.

XAML namespaces apply to the specific element on which they are declared, and also to any element that is contained by that element in XAML structure. For this reason, XAML namespaces are almost always declared on root elements to take advantage of this inheritance.

For types that come from libraries other than the core libraries you must declare and map a XAML namespace with a prefix to reference the types from that library. You declare prefix mappings as attributes by first specifying the keyword **xmlns:**, then the prefix you want. The value of that attribute then must contain the keyword **using:**, then the specific code-backing namespace. The form of the namespace name always uses a dot as a separator between namespace hierarchies when you declare it in XAML. This is the case even if you write that component in C++ (C++ would normally have **::** as the separator between namespace hierarchy segments).

If you are referencing custom types from the primary app's application definition or page definitions, those types are available without further dependent assembly configuration, but you still must map the code namespace that contains those types. A common convention is to map the prefix "local" for the default code namespace of any given XAML page. This convention is often included in starting project templates for XAML projects.

The following example illustrates usage of namespaces in XAML.

LISTING 3-7 Namespace usage in default App.xaml

```
x:Class="App1.App"
xmlns="http://schemas.microsoft.com/winfx/2006/xaml/presentation"
xmlns:x="http://schemas.microsoft.com/winfx/2006/xaml"
xmlns:local="using:App1">
```

The "x" prefix/XAML language XAML namespace contains several programming constructs that you use often in your XAML. For example, the following code sample shows the usage of multiple prefixes for namespaces.

LISTING 3-8 Namespace usage in MainPage.xaml

```
<Page
    x:Class="App1.MainPage"
    IsTabStop="false"
    xmlns="http://schemas.microsoft.com/winfx/2006/xaml/presentation"
    xmlns:x="http://schemas.microsoft.com/winfx/2006/xaml"
    xmlns:local="using:App1"
    xmlns:d="http://schemas.microsoft.com/expression/blend/2008"
    xmlns:mc="http://schemas.openxmlformats.org/markup-compatibility/2006"
    mc:Ignorable="d">
...
/Page>
```

> **You often see XAML files that define the prefixes "d" (for designer namespace) and "mc" (for markup compatibility). Generally these are for infrastructure support that is related to exchanging the XAML between tools or processes, and you don't need to interact with elements in these namespaces in typical XAML UI definitions.**

The most common **x:** prefixes are:

Term	Description
x:Key	Sets a unique user-defined key for each resource in a ResourceDictionary. The key token string is the argument for the StaticResource markup extension to retrieve any such resource from another XAML usage.
x:Class	Specifies the code namespace and class name for the class that provides code-behind for a XAML page, and names the class that is created or joined by the build actions that support the XAML markup compiler when the app is compiled. You must have such a class to support code-behind, or to have your XAML content be initialized as Window.Content. For these reasons you almost always see "x" mapped, even if there are no resources and you never use x:Name.
x:Name	Specifies a run-time object name for the instance that exists in run-time code after an object element defined in XAML is processed. You use x:Name for element-naming when the more convenient FrameworkElement.Name property is not supported.

Property Elements

XAML in Windows 8 allows arbitrary content to be placed inside its controls. This composition is enabled via the **Content** property.

Here is the C++ code that embeds a simple rectangle to make a Button.

LISTING 3-9 Setting Content property via C++ code

```
Button^ btn  = ref new Button();
Windows::UI::Xaml::Shapes::Rectangle rect;
rect.Height = 60;
rect.Width = 40;
SolidColorBrush b(Windows::UI::Colors::Blue);
rect.Fill = %b;
btn->Content = rect;
```

XAML, however, does not have a string attribute that allows you to set a Rectangle as its Content. XAML supports Property Elements which allows a Rectangle to be set as Button Content. Property Elements are distinguished from normal elements by the way they are declared. Property Elements always follow the *TypeName.PropertyName* whereas normal properties are set as XML attributes in XAML. Property Elements are also always used inside the *TypeName* element and do not have attributes of their own (the lone exception being x:Uid for localization purposes).

LISTING 3-10 Setting Content property via XAML

```
<Button>
  <Button.Content>
    <Rectangle Height="60" Width="40" Fill="Blue"></Rectangle>
  </Button.Content>
</Button>
```

Using Panels to Layout UX

XAML contains many layout controls that enable you, as a developer, to layout your UX. Layout is critical to enabling your application UI to scale and adjust from an 8" slate to a 72" desktop monitor with HD resolution.

A XAML page begins with a panel element. The panel is a container for the page content and controls the positioning and rendering of the content. It is safe to say that if you display anything using XAML, you would be displaying using some sort of a panel element.

Panel elements can be nested; this allows you to divide the available display area into individual regions and each region is controlled by a panel element. Some of the panel elements supported by XAML are:

1. **Canvas**: A Canvas let you define an area within which you can explicitly position child objects, using coordinates that are relative to the Canvas area.

2. **StackPanel**: A StackPanel lets you arrange child elements into a single line that can be oriented horizontally or vertically.

3. **Grid**: A Grid lets you define a flexible grid area that consists of columns and rows. Child elements of the Grid are measured and arranged according to their row/column assignments and internal class logic.

Canvas

The Canvas is the most primitive panel element. It provides the most flexibility regarding positioning and arranging elements on screen. It allows you to specify the location for each child element as well as the order in which the Canvas draws the elements. You can specify the location for the child elements using its properties: *Left, Top, Right and Bottom*.

LISTING 3-11 Using a Canvas in XAML

```
<Canvas Background="Black">
        <Rectangle Fill="White" Height="435.82" Canvas.Left="84.419" Stroke="White" Canvas.Top="59.703"
Width="416.418"/>
        <TextBlock Height="41.403" Canvas.Left="158.224" TextWrapping="Wrap" Text="Hello to Canvas!"
Canvas.Top="86.761" Width="294.03" FontWeight="Bold" FontFamily="Arial" FontStyle="Normal" FontSize="25"
Foreground="#000000"/>
        <Ellipse Fill="White" Height="262.761" Canvas.Left="158.224" Stroke="Black" Canvas.Top="147.864"
Width="239.97"/>
</Canvas>
```

The above Canvas definition in markup generates the following user interface.

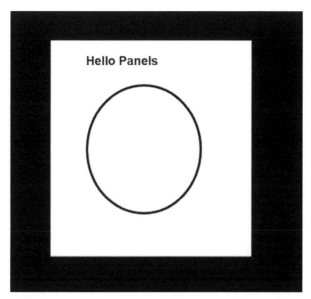

FIGURE 3-4 Canvas layout of elements based on XAML listing 3-11 above

The above XAML declarations can also be achieved using plain C++ /CX code. This is illustrated with the **CanvasApp** sample enclosed with the book.

The CanvasApp sample app renders our canvas and all its elements. The following screenshot shows how it renders on a PC running Windows 8.

FIGURE 3-5 Canvas layout of elements based on CanvasApp

128

StackPanel

One of the most frequently used panel elements is the StackPanel. As the name implies, the Stack-Panel arranges the child elements sequentially, as in a stack. It is important to note here that the StackPanel has no inherent properties to specify positioning: *Top, Left, Right and Bottom*. The only property you can set is the **Orientation** property. The **Orientation** property, of type, Windows::UI::Xaml::Controls::Orientation, can either be set to Horizontal or Vertical.

LISTING 3-12 Using a StackPanel to layout elements

```
<StackPanel x:Name="stack" Background="Black" Orientation="Horizontal" Margin="5">
        <Rectangle Fill="White" Height="435.82" Width="416.418" Margin="5"/>
        <TextBlock Height="41.403" TextWrapping="Wrap" Text="Hello to Canvas!" Width="257"
FontWeight="Bold" FontFamily="Arial" FontStyle="Normal" FontSize="25" Foreground="White"
Margin="0,364,0,363"/>
        <Ellipse Margin="5" Fill="White" Height="262.761" Width="239.97"/>
    </StackPanel>
```

The above markup generates a UI similar to this figure.

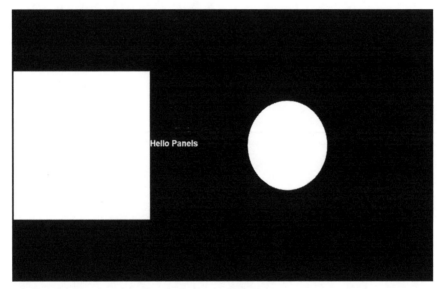

FIGURE 3-6 StackPanel with Horizontal Orientation

The sample **StackPanelApp** enclosed with the book demonstrates how similar results can be achieved through C++ code and the resulting UI is similar to the one generated using markup.

FIGURE 3-7 StackPanel layout of elements based on the StackPanelApp

Grid

The Grid panel is the most frequently used panel. Visual Studio and Blend, by default, use the Grid panel for the default layout panel for a page. This is because the Grid panel is by far, the most flexible panel. It allows you to position and arrange child elements in a multirow and multicolumn layout. The *RowDefinition* and *ColumnDefinition* properties allow you to define the number of rows and columns. Explicit positioning of child elements can then be specified using the *Row* and *Column* attached properties.

Child elements of a Grid are drawn in the order in which they appear in markup or code. The following XAML shows how to create a Grid with 3 rows and 3 columns. The height of the first and third rows is just large enough to hold the text while the second row fills up the available height. The "auto" value for the Height property for the first and third rows is what sets the height to be just large enough. Grid.Row always defaults to zero and hence everything will be displayed in Column 0 and Row 0 by default, unless rows and columns are not explicitly specified. The "*" value for the Width property in the Grid columns means that the column is assigned the width of its content.

LISTING 3-13 Using a Grid

```
<Grid x:Name="LayoutRoot" Background="{StaticResource ApplicationPageBackgroundThemeBrush}">
      <Grid.RowDefinitions>
          <RowDefinition Height="auto" />
          <RowDefinition />
          <RowDefinition Height="auto" />
      </Grid.RowDefinitions>
      <Grid.ColumnDefinitions>
          <ColumnDefinition Width="*" />
          <ColumnDefinition Width="*" />
```

```
        </Grid.ColumnDefinitions>

<Rectangle Fill="White" Height="45.82" Stroke="Black" Width="416.418" Margin="5" Grid.Column="0"
Grid.Row="0"/>
<Ellipse Margin="5" Fill="White" Height="162.761" Stroke="Black" Width="139.97" Grid.Column="0"
Grid.Row="2"/>
        <TextBox Text="This is a Rectangle" Height="40"  Grid.Column="1" Grid.Row="0" />
        <TextBox Text="This is an ellipse" Height="40"  Grid.Column="1" Grid.Row="2" />
    </Grid>
```

This markup produces output similar to the figure shown below.

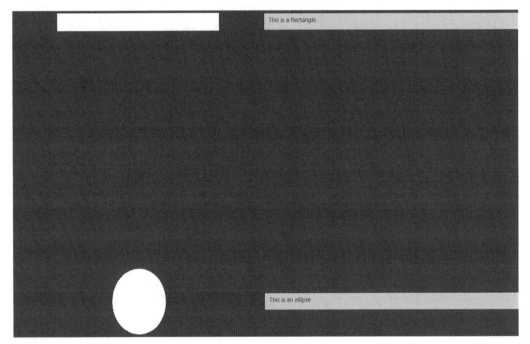

FIGURE 3-8 Output of the Grid declaration mentioned in listing 3-13 above

Basic XAML Controls

The XAML framework supports a wide variety of controls. These include various types of buttons, scroll bars, combo boxes, list boxes, listview controls etc. In addition, XAML also includes three new showcase controls for Windows 8: the AppBar, FlipView and the Semantic Control. We will discuss these three showcase controls in the next section.

The BasicControls sample included with the book demonstrates using the following XAML controls and concepts:

1.   Various Button controls like Button, RadioButton, HyperlinkButton etc.

2. ComboBox controls

3. Miscellaneous controls like the ImageControl, Tooltip and Popup controls.

4. Various types of progress controls like ProgressBar, ProgressRing etc.

5. Slider controls with different styles.

6. Text controls with different styles.

7. Changing the visual style of a control using the Button as an example.

8. Templating controls using the Button control as an example.

9. Using the Visual State Manager to add visual state behaviors to custom controls.

Let us take a quick look at how to use some of the Basic XAML Controls.

1. **Button**: A Button control is used to interpret a user initiated Click interaction.

```
<Button x:Name="myBtn" Content="Button" HorizontalAlignment="Left" Height="57" Margin="580,332,0,0"
VerticalAlignment="Top" Width="201"/>
```

2. **CheckBox**: This object represents a control that a user can select (check) or clear (uncheck) or indeterminate.

```
<CheckBox Content="CheckBox" HorizontalAlignment="Left" Height="36" Margin="563,315,0,0"
VerticalAlignment="Top" Width="120"/>
```

3. **ComboBox**: This object represents a selection control that combines a non-editable text box and a drop-down containing a list box that allows users to select an item from a list.

```
<ComboBox HorizontalAlignment="Left" Margin="715,273,0,0" VerticalAlignment="Top" Width="176">
    <ComboBoxItem Content="Item1"/>
    <ComboBoxItem Content="Item2"/>
    <ComboBoxItem Content="Item3"/>
</ComboBox>
```

4. **HyperlinkButton**: As the name implies, the HyperlinkButton is used to represent a hyperlink control. For example, clicking on the following HyperlinkButton, opens the Modern IE (or your default browser) and navigates to http://dev.windows.com

```
<HyperlinkButton NavigateUri="http://dev.windows.com" Content="HyperlinkButton"
HorizontalAlignment="Left" Height="51" Margin="546,372,0,0" VerticalAlignment="Top" Width="156"/>
```

5. **Image**: The Image control is used to represent images in the JPEG or PNG formats. The following markup, for example, uses the SplashScreen.jpg from the project assets and displays the image on screen.

```
<Image HorizontalAlignment="Left" Height="60" Margin="727,363,0,0" VerticalAlignment="Top"
Width="164" Source="Assets/SplashScreen.png"/>
```

You can also set the Source property of the Image control to a URI like this:

```
<Image HorizontalAlignment="Left" Height="60" Margin="727,363,0,0" VerticalAlignment="Top"
Width="164" Source="http://sridharpoduri.com/wp-content/uploads/2012/06/100_0456-700x525.jpg"/>
```

6. **ListBox**: A ListBox contains a list of items that can be selected.

```
<ListBox HorizontalAlignment="Left" Height="42" Margin="468,40,0,0" VerticalAlignment="Top"
Width="182">
    <ListBoxItem Content="ListItem1"/>
    <ListBoxItem Content="ListItem2"/>
    <ListBoxItem Content="ListItem3"/>
</ListBox>
```

A more convenient way of populating the ListBox is to use the **ItemSource** property to bind content. This is illustrated in the data binding section later on.

7. **ListView**: This object represents a control that displays a list of data items.

```
<ListView HorizontalAlignment="Left" Height="42" Margin="690,40,0,0" VerticalAlignment="Top" Width="269">
        <ListViewItem>
            <Image Source="http://sridharpoduri.com/wp-content/uploads/2012/06/100_0456-700x525.jpg"
/>
        </ListViewItem>
        <ListViewItem>
            <Image Source="http://sridharpoduri.com/wp-content/uploads/2012/06/100_0484.jpg" />
        </ListViewItem>
</ListView>
```

8. **PasswordBox**: This object represents a control for entering passwords.

```
<PasswordBox HorizontalAlignment="Left" Height="23" Margin="995,45,0,0" VerticalAlignment="Top"
Width="251" Password="Password"/>
```

9. **ProgressRing**: This object represents a control that indicates an ongoing operation. The typical visual appearance is a ring-shaped "spinner" that cycles an animation as progress continues.

```
<ProgressRing HorizontalAlignment="Left" Height="127" Margin="1044,142,0,0" VerticalAlignment="Top"
Width="173" IsActive="True"/>
```

10. **ProgressBar**: This control is used to represent the progress of an ongoing operation.

```
<ProgressBar HorizontalAlignment="Left" Height="34" Margin="690,291,0,0" VerticalAlignment="Top"
Width="249" Value="75" IsIndeterminate="True"/>
```

11. **RadioButton**: This object represents a button that allows a user to select a single option from a group of options.

```
<RadioButton Content="RadioButton" IsChecked="True" HorizontalAlignment="Left" Height="34"
Margin="468,291,0,0" VerticalAlignment="Top" Width="166"/>
```

12. **Slider**: This object represents a control that lets the user select from a range of values by moving a Thumb control, which is a primitive control, along a track.

```
<Slider Value="28" HorizontalAlignment="Left" Height="44" Margin="214,281,0,0"
VerticalAlignment="Top" Width="176"/>
```

13. **TextBox**: This object represents a control that can be used to display single-format, multi-line text.

```
<TextBox HorizontalAlignment="Left" Height="34" Margin="995,291,0,0" TextWrapping="Wrap" Text="This is
a TextBox" VerticalAlignment="Top" Width="222"/>
```

14. **TextBlock**: This object provides a lightweight control for displaying small amounts of text.

```
<TextBlock FontSize="18" FontFamily="Segoe UI" FontWeight="ExtraBold" HorizontalAlignment="Left"
Height="52" Margin="56,376,0,0" TextWrapping="Wrap" Text="TextBlock" VerticalAlignment="Top"
Width="334"/>
```

15. **ToggleSwitch**: This object represents a switch that can be toggled between two states.

```
<ToggleSwitch Header="ToggleSwitch" HorizontalAlignment="Left" Height="75" Margin="496,394,0,0"
VerticalAlignment="Top" Width="170"/>
```

The complete markup for all the above controls is listed below.

LISTING 3-14 XAML ControlsApp markup

```
<Grid Background="{StaticResource ApplicationPageBackgroundThemeBrush}">
    <CheckBox Content="CheckBox" HorizontalAlignment="Left" Height="36" Margin="31,106,0,0"
VerticalAlignment="Top" Width="120"/>
    <Button Content="Button" HorizontalAlignment="Left" Margin="31,34,0,0" VerticalAlignment="Top"
Width="120"/>
    <ComboBox HorizontalAlignment="Left" Margin="214,40,0,0" VerticalAlignment="Top" Width="176">
        <ComboBoxItem Content="Item1"/>
        <ComboBoxItem Content="Item2"/>
        <ComboBoxItem Content="Item3"/>
    </ComboBox>
    <HyperlinkButton NavigateUri="http://dev.windows.com" Content="HyperlinkButton"
HorizontalAlignment="Left" Height="51" Margin="31,182,0,0" VerticalAlignment="Top" Width="156"/>
    <Image HorizontalAlignment="Left" Height="60" Margin="214,106,0,0" VerticalAlignment="Top"
Width="164" Source="http://sridharpoduri.com/wp-content/uploads/2012/06/100_0456-700x525.jpg"/>
    <ListBox HorizontalAlignment="Left" Height="126" Margin="468,40,0,0" VerticalAlignment="Top"
Width="166" >
        <ListBoxItem Content="ListItem1"/>
        <ListBoxItem Content="ListItem2"/>
        <ListBoxItem Content="ListItem3"/>
        <ListBoxItem Content="ListItem4"/>
        <ListBoxItem Content="ListItem5"/>
    </ListBox>
    <ListView HorizontalAlignment="Left" Height="182" Margin="690,40,0,0" VerticalAlignment="Top"
Width="253" ScrollViewer.VerticalScrollBarVisibility="Auto">
        <ListViewItem>
            <Image Source="http://sridharpoduri.com/wp-content/uploads/2012/06/100_0456-700x525.jpg"
/>
        </ListViewItem>
        <ListViewItem>
            <Image Source="http://sridharpoduri.com/wp-content/uploads/2012/06/100_0484.jpg" />
        </ListViewItem>
    </ListView>
    <PasswordBox HorizontalAlignment="Left" Height="23" Margin="995,45,0,0" VerticalAlignment="Top"
Width="251" Password="Password"/>
```

```
        <ProgressRing HorizontalAlignment="Left" Height="127" Margin="1044,142,0,0"
VerticalAlignment="Top" Width="173" IsActive="True"/>
        <ProgressBar HorizontalAlignment="Left" Height="34" Margin="690,291,0,0" VerticalAlignment="Top"
Width="249" Value="75" IsIndeterminate="True"/>
        <RadioButton Content="RadioButton" IsChecked="True" HorizontalAlignment="Left" Height="34"
Margin="468,291,0,0" VerticalAlignment="Top" Width="166"/>
        <Slider Value="28" HorizontalAlignment="Left" Height="44" Margin="214,281,0,0"
VerticalAlignment="Top" Width="176"/>
        <TextBox HorizontalAlignment="Left" Height="34" Margin="995,291,0,0" TextWrapping="Wrap"
Text="This is a TextBox" VerticalAlignment="Top" Width="222"/>
        <TextBlock FontSize="18" FontFamily="Segoe UI" FontWeight="ExtraBold" HorizontalAlignment="Left"
Height="52" Margin="56,376,0,0" TextWrapping="Wrap" Text="TextBlock" VerticalAlignment="Top" Width="334"/>
        <ToggleSwitch Header="ToggleSwitch" HorizontalAlignment="Left" Height="75" Margin="496,394,0,0"
VerticalAlignment="Top" Width="170"/>
    </Grid>
```

Transformations

XAML supports a wide variety of **Transforms**. Consider the following supported transform operations:

1. **RotateTransform**: Applying this transform causes the object to rotate by the amount specified in the Angle property.

2. **MatrixTransform**: This arbitrary affine transform is used to manipulate objects in a two-dimensional plane.

3. **TranslateTransform**: Applying this transform causes the object to move according to the X and Y properties.

4. **ScaleTransform**: Applying this transform will shrink or stretch the object according to the ScaleX and ScaleY properties.

5. **SkewTransform**: Applying this transform slants the object, using the AngleX, AngleY, and Center properties.

6. **CompositeTransform**: A combination of Rotate, Translate, Scale and Skew Transforms.

A simple example showing how to use transforms is listed below. In this example, we have two shapes (Ellipse and Rectangle) and a ListBox. We apply various transforms on the shapes and the controls.

LISTING 3-15 Applying transforms on Shapes and Controls

```
    <Grid Background="{StaticResource ApplicationPageBackgroundThemeBrush}">
        <Canvas Height="400" Width="600">
            <Ellipse Width="100" Height="100" Fill="Aqua" Stroke="Black" StrokeThickness="8">
                <Ellipse.RenderTransform>
                    <RotateTransform Angle="-17" />
                </Ellipse.RenderTransform>
            </Ellipse>
            <Rectangle Width="200" Height="100" Fill="Yellow" Stroke="Black" StrokeThickness="15"
```

```
Canvas.Top="200" Canvas.Left="100">
            <Rectangle.RenderTransform>
                <CompositeTransform TranslateX="40" TranslateY="40"  ScaleX="2" ScaleY="1.3"
Rotation="45"/>
            </Rectangle.RenderTransform>
        </Rectangle>

        <ListBox Canvas.Top="37" Canvas.Left="364" >
            <ListBox.RenderTransform>
                <CompositeTransform ScaleX="3" ScaleY="1" Rotation="15" SkewX="7" SkewY="14"
TranslateX="10" TranslateY="25" />
            </ListBox.RenderTransform>
            <ListBoxItem>ListItem 1</ListBoxItem>
            <ListBoxItem>ListItem 2</ListBoxItem>
            <ListBoxItem>ListItem 3</ListBoxItem>
        </ListBox>
    </Canvas>
  </Grid>
```

Styling XAML controls

Control Templates

The **ControlTemplate** defines how a control appears on screen. A XAML control is usually a composition of multiple UI elements and using a **ControlTemplate** you can modify the appearance and behavior of a control.

You can customize the visual appearance, behavior and structure of any built-in control by giving the control a **ControlTemplate**. Creating a **ControlTemplate** allows you to replace the appearance of a control without changing its functionality. For example, you can make the buttons in your application round rather than the default square shape, but the button will still raise the Click event. If you're familiar with traditional Win32 development then whereas you might have once coded a WM_PAINT handler to customize the drawing of some aspect of the UI, with XAML you use a control template to declaratively achieve the same result.

As a best practice, if you are completely redefining the control template you should base it on the current template. If you don't base your control template on the current template, you are likely to lose functionality. Defining your control template using Microsoft Blend 2012 or Visual Studio 2012 is the best way to minimize errors/lost functionality. Another important point to note is your control template may not work without setting all the template parts.

> **Creating a ControlTemplate is completely achieved thorough XAML without writing any source code.**

Defining Control Templates in XAML

The Template property specifies the **ControlTemplate** of a control. Like many properties, the Template property can be set in the following ways:

- Locally set Template to a ControlTemplate that is defined inline.

- Locally set Template to a reference to a ControlTemplate that is defined as a resource.

- Set Template and define a ControlTemplate in a Style.

The following example demonstrates setting the Template property locally and defining the **ControlTemplate** inline.

```
<Button Content="Button1">
  <Button.Template>
    <ControlTemplate TargetType="Button">
      <!-- ControlTemplate goes here.-->
    </ControlTemplate>
  </Button.Template>
</Button>
```

The following example demonstrates defining the **ControlTemplate** as a resource and setting the Template to a reference to the resource.

```
<StackPanel>
  <StackPanel.Resources>
    <ControlTemplate TargetType="Button" x:Key="newTemplate">
      <!-- ControlTemplate goes here.-->
    </ControlTemplate>
  </StackPanel.Resources>
  <Button Template="{StaticResource newTemplate}" Content="Button1"/>
</StackPanel>
```

We will now define a control template for a normal Button control and change its appearance to a "Refresh" button. Our Refresh button should have the following characteristics:

- Button is round in shape

- Button has an arrow to indicate refresn v/s plain text.

We will add the control template for the Button to the Resources section of the Page where we would like our new Button to be displayed. Before we define the actual template, we need to define the Style. This is achieved by using the Style attribute and setting the TargetType to Button. The TargetType indicates the base control whose style we are overriding with the new style. We specify a value for the Key attribute and use this value later on when we create the actual Button control. Within the Style definition, we can also add various properties for the Refresh Button and set their values. For the purpose of our example, we will set the Background, Foreground, BackgroundBrush, FontFamily and FontSize properties.

```
<Style x:Key="RefreshButtonStyle" TargetType="Button">

    <Setter Property="Background" Value="Transparent"/>
    <Setter Property="Foreground" Value="Black"/>
    <Setter Property="BorderBrush" Value="Transparent"/>
```

```
<Setter Property="FontFamily" Value="Segoe UI"/>
<Setter Property="FontSize" Value="9"/>
```

You can now define the ControlTemplate property and customize the look of the Button.

```
<Setter Property="Template">
```

Within the Template property section, you can define the ControlTemplate Target property and set its value to Button as we will be completely redefining the control template of a normal Button control.

Since our original goal was to make a round button, you can define an Ellipse whose Width and Height properties are equal, say 40, to define a circular shape. You can then define a TextBlock whose Name property is set to "Glyph" and the Text is set to  which represents an arrow in the Segoe font family. Our complete control template looks as follows:

LISTING 3-16 Control template for a Button

```
<Style x:Key="RefreshButtonStyle" TargetType="Button">
        <Setter Property="Background" Value="Transparent"/>
        <Setter Property="Foreground" Value="Black"/>
        <Setter Property="BorderBrush" Value="Transparent"/>
        <Setter Property="FontFamily" Value="Segoe UI"/>
        <Setter Property="FontSize" Value="9"/>
        <Setter Property="Template">
            <Setter.Value>
                <ControlTemplate TargetType="Button">
                    <Grid>
                        <StackPanel Orientation="Vertical">
                            <Grid  Margin="0,14,0,5" >
                                <Ellipse x:Name="ButtonEllipse" Height="40" Width="40"
Fill="Transparent" HorizontalAlignment="Center"
                                    Stroke="Black" StrokeThickness="2" VerticalAlignment="Center"/>
                                <TextBlock x:Name="Glyph" Text="&#xE10E;" FontFamily="Segoe UI Symbol"
FontSize="24.777" HorizontalAlignment="Center"
                                    VerticalAlignment="Center"/>
                            </Grid>
                            <TextBlock Text="{TemplateBinding Content}" HorizontalAlignment="Center"
                                FontFamily="Segoe UI" FontSize="12"/>
                        </StackPanel>
                    </Grid>
                </ControlTemplate>
            </Setter.Value>
        </Setter>
    </Style>
```

Now wherever we declare a Button control and want to customize its appearance, we set the Style property of the Button to the Key value we provided to the Style property, which in our case is RefreshButtonStyle.

```
<Button x:Name="StyledButton" Content="Refresh" Visibility="Collapsed"
Style="{StaticResource RefreshButtonStyle}" VerticalAlignment="Center"/>
```

Our Normal button and the Refresh button appearance is as shown below

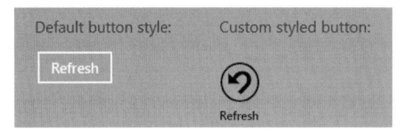

Defining Visual States for Controls

The Refresh button created above does not change visual behavior when a mouse hover action takes place over the button. It does not even change state when a Tap or Click action is initiated. In order to make a control change visual state when certain events occur, you can use the Visual State Manager to add visual state behaviors to your custom controls.

You can add VisualStateGroups within the ControlTemplate section in the markup. Each VisualStateGroup will contain behavior for the custom Button control that will define its appearance. For example, when the Button receives a Pressed event, it is desirable to change the state of the Glyph to White and the surrounding region of the Button to Black. Similarly, during a mouse hover, it is desirable to change animate and change the ellipse color to a lighter shade. Our now changed control template looks as follows:

LISTING 3-17 Control template for Button specifying Visual States

```
<Page.Resources>
        <Style x:Key="VSMRefreshButtonStyle" TargetType="Button">
            <Setter Property="Background" Value="Transparent"/>
            <Setter Property="Foreground" Value="Black"/>
            <Setter Property="BorderBrush" Value="Transparent"/>
            <Setter Property="FontFamily" Value="Segoe UI"/>
            <Setter Property="FontSize" Value="9"/>
            <Setter Property="Template">
                <Setter.Value>
                    <ControlTemplate TargetType="Button">
                        <Grid>
                            <VisualStateManager.VisualStateGroups>
                                <VisualStateGroup x:Name="CommonStates">
                                    <VisualState x:Name="Normal"/>
                                    <VisualState x:Name="PointerOver">
                                        <Storyboard>
                                            <ColorAnimation Duration="0" To="LightGray"
Storyboard.TargetProperty="(Ellipse.Fill).(SolidColorBrush.Color)" Storyboard.TargetName="ButtonEllipse"
/>
                                        </Storyboard>
```

```
                            </VisualState>
                            <VisualState x:Name="Pressed">
                                <Storyboard>
                                    <ColorAnimation Duration="0" To="Black"
Storyboard.TargetProperty="(Ellipse.Fill).(SolidColorBrush.Color)" Storyboard.TargetName="ButtonEllipse"
/>
                                    <ColorAnimation Duration="0" To="White"
Storyboard.TargetProperty="(TextBlock.Foreground).(SolidColorBrush.Color)" Storyboard.TargetName="Glyph"
/>
                                </Storyboard>
                            </VisualState>
                            <VisualState x:Name="Disabled">
                                <Storyboard>
                                    <ColorAnimation Duration="0" To="Gray"
Storyboard.TargetProperty="(Ellipse.Stroke).(SolidColorBrush.Color)"
Storyboard.TargetName="ButtonEllipse" />
                                    <ColorAnimation Duration="0" To="Gray"
Storyboard.TargetProperty="(TextBlock.Foreground).(SolidColorBrush.Color)" Storyboard.TargetName="Glyph"
/>
                                </Storyboard>
                            </VisualState>
                        </VisualStateGroup>
                    </VisualStateManager.VisualStateGroups>
                    <StackPanel Orientation="Vertical">
                        <Grid  Margin="0,14,0,5" >
                            <Ellipse x:Name="ButtonEllipse" Height="40" Width="40"
Fill="Transparent" HorizontalAlignment="Center"
        Stroke="Black" StrokeThickness="2" VerticalAlignment="Center"/>
                            <TextBlock x:Name="Glyph" Text="&#xE10E;" FontFamily="Segoe UI Symbol"
FontSize="24.777" HorizontalAlignment="Center"
        VerticalAlignment="Center"/>
                        </Grid>
                        <TextBlock Text="{TemplateBinding Content}" HorizontalAlignment="Center"
        FontFamily="Segoe UI" FontSize="12"/>
                    </StackPanel>
                </Grid>
            </ControlTemplate>
        </Setter.Value>
    </Setter>
</Style>
</Page.Resources>
```

Now when we use this Refresh button, we can see the Button change state whenever a mouse hover occurs or when it receives a Click or Tap event.

Windows 8 Signature XAML Controls

Windows 8 also includes new signature controls. These controls showcase the value proposition of the platform: "content over chrome".

1. **ListView**: The ListView is a control that is used often to display data pertaining to your app. The ListView enables data to be displayed in a vertical layout. It is derived from ItemsControl class and also implements the ISemanticZoomInformation interface.

   The ListView is often used to show an ordered list of items, such as results of a search request or a list of items to choose from. The Reader application from the Windows Store uses the ListView control to display Find results from a find operation. It also uses the ListView to display Bookmarks in the PDF/XPS document and allows the user to jump to the selected item.

   ```
   <ListView x:Name="listView1" SelectionChanged="ListView_SelectionChanged">
       <x:String>Item 1</x:String>
       <x:String>Item 2</x:String>
   </ListView>
   ```

2. **GridView**: The GridView is a control that is used often to display data pertaining to your app. The ListView enables data to be displayed in a horizontal layout. It is derived from ItemsControl class and also implements the ISemanticZoomInformation interface. The GridView is commonly used when you need to show a rich visualization of each item that takes up a lot of space otherwise.

   ```
   <GridView
               x:Name="itemGridView"
               AutomationProperties.AutomationId="ItemGridView"
               AutomationProperties.Name="Items In Group"
               TabIndex="1"
               Grid.Row="1"
               Margin="0,-14,0,0"
               Padding="120,0,120,50"
               ItemsSource="{Binding Source={StaticResource itemsViewSource}}"
               ItemTemplate="{StaticResource Standard500x130ItemTemplate}"
               SelectionMode="None"
               IsSwipeEnabled="false"
               IsItemClickEnabled="True"
               ItemClick="ItemView_ItemClick">

           <GridView.Header>
               <StackPanel Width="480" Margin="0,4,14,0">
                   <TextBlock Text="{Binding Subtitle}" Margin="0,0,18,20" Style="{StaticResource
   SubheaderTextStyle}" MaxHeight="60"/>
                   <Image Source="{Binding Image}" Height="400" Margin="0,0,18,20
   Stretch="UniformToFill" AutomationProperties.Name="{Binding Title}"/>
                   <TextBlock Text="{Binding Description}" Margin="0,0,18,0" Style="{StaticResource
   BodyTextStyle}"/>
               </StackPanel>
           </GridView.Header>
   ```

```
        <GridView.ItemContainerStyle>
            <Style TargetType="FrameworkElement">
                <Setter Property="Margin" Value="52,0,0,10"/>
            </Style>
        </GridView.ItemContainerStyle>
    </GridView>
```

Virtualization Support in ListView and GridView controls

In addition to facilitating the display of data either in vertical or horizontal orientations, both the ListView and GridView controls allow virtualization of data and UI. Virtualization is especially helpful when you have a large amount of data that needs to be displayed in your UI. Performance degradation is a serious concern when displaying such large data or providing for manipulation of such data. This virtualization support is actually enabled in the ItemsControl class and virtualization is supported on any XAML control that derives from the ItemsControl class.

When you add an item to an ItemsControl, the item is wrapped in an item container. For example, an item added to a GridView is wrapped in a GridViewItem. The problem with this is if your data set contains a few thousand items (which is not an uncommon scenario with connected apps today), then for each item in the data set, a corresponding item container is created and kept alive in memory.

One way to solve this problem is for apps to keep track of what should be in memory and remove the items not needed. This places an unwanted burden on developers. Luckily XAML provides a built-in solution for this problem. The solution is UI virtualization. XAML will continue to keep the data set in memory but will create an item container only when the item is almost ready to be displayed in the UI. This UI virtualization is turned ON by default for all the apps created with Visual Studio 2012 using the project templates. It is a good practice to have virtualization turned ON and let XAML handle all the minute details of the virtualization logic v/s turning it OFF and having to manage virtualization on your own when your apps needs it.

This is the approach used by the Reader App that ships with Windows 8. The Reader App was the first Windows Store app built with C++ and XAML. Within Reader each page in a document is actually a ListViewItem rendering the page data. With UI virtualization turned ON, only a few pages are bound to an actual ListViewItem and XAML re-uses the ListViewItems as needed when the user scrolls or pans through the pages in a document.

When using UI virtualization, the size of a control's viewport is impacted by the size of its parent container. For some apps, it might be desirable to restrict the size of each item within the parent container. In the XAML below, we place a GridView inside a Grid. The viewport of the GridView is restricted to the size of the parent Grid. The user can then scroll hidden items into view by using scroll bars or pan horizontally using touch to fetch hidden items into view.

```
<Grid Height="400" Width="600">
    <GridView Background="DarkGreen" ItemsSource="{Binding}"/>
</Grid>
```

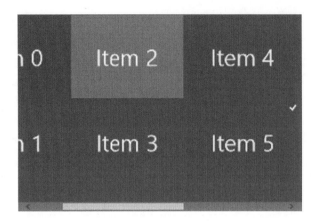

Some containers let their children use unlimited space to display their content, even if the space extends beyond the visible bounds of the container. In the XAML below, we place a GridView inside a Canvas. The viewport of the GridView expands to fit all its items and stretches beyond the visible bounds of the container. There are no scroll bars, so the user can't scroll hidden items into view.

```
<Canvas Height="400" Width="600">
    <GridView Background="DarkGreen" ItemsSource="{Binding}"/>
</Canvas>
```

Some containers do not perform virtualization when the ItemControl's viewport size isn't restricted. Good examples of containers that don't perform vistualization are Canvas, StackPanel and the ScrollViewer. These containers create an item container for each item in the collection. UI virtualization can be enabled by settings the size of the ItemControl directly. If you do not set this property, it will be sized by the parent container and virtualization disabled.

In the XAML below we set the Height and Width on the GridView. This restricts the size of the viewport, and items outside of the viewport are virtualized.

```
<Canvas>
    <GridView Background="DarkGreen" ItemsSource="{Binding}"
            Height="400" Width="600"/>
</Canvas>
```

If you change the default ItemsPanel, you should be pay attention to using a panel that supports virtualization as before. This is because an ItemsControl uses its corresponding ItemsPanel to determine how items are placed in the UI. If you swap the default panel with a replacement panel and the new panel supports UI virtualization, then your control will continue to perform virtualization as before. Else it will not. WrapGrid and VirtualizingStackPanel are examples of standard virtualizing panels.

We have previously mentioned that with UI virtualization, the entire data set is continued to be stored in memory and only the UI items are virtualized. While this solves the problem with creating hundreds and possibly thousands of item instances, it still does not solve the issue with very large data sets. To further optimize consuming resources, you should use data virtualization to fetch only a subset of the data. The virtualization logic built into XAML is smart enough to apply UI virtualization to the subset of data created by the data virtualization logic!

Data virtualization is categorized into two types.

- **Random access** – True to its name, this strategy allows you to fetch data within different ranges. For example, if your GridView is bound to a collection of 10,000 items and the user pans to the middle of the collection, your app can choose to download only items 4500 to 5000. If the user pans to the end of the list, your app can download only items 9500 – 10000. The scroll bar's scroll indicator or the pan indicator is always sized to represent its position in the complete 10,000 item set. For C++ /CX apps that use random access data virtualization, your data source should implement an IObservableVector.

- **Incremental** – The other contrasting approach to random access data virtualization is the incremental mode. In this mode, your app downloads data incrementally. For example, if your GridView is bound to a collection of 10,000 items, your app can choose to download only items 1-100. The scroll bar's thumb is sized to represent its position in the initial 100 item data set. When the user scrolls near the end of the list, items 101 – 200 are downloaded. The scroll bar's thumb is resized to represent its position in the updated 100 item data set. In order to use incremental data virtualization, you must use a data source that implements ISupportIncrementalLoading. When you use incremental data virtualization with a ListView or GridView, you can use DataFetchSize, IncrementalLoadingThreshold, IncrementalLoadingTrigger, LoadMoreItemsAsync to control how your app loads data.

3. **AppBar**: The AppBar is a simple UI construct that can display a menu or other controls at the top or bottom of the page. The AppBar is used for providing contextual commanding in the application. The AppBar can be placed either at the top or the bottom of the screen. Swiping up from the bottom of the screen brings up the AppBar. The equivalent keyboard shortcut is **Win + Z** and the equivalent shortcut for mouse is the right button click. The AppBar is programmed to be a light dismiss control: tapping/clicking anywhere outside the AppBar dismisses the AppBar.

It is important to note that the AppBar contains a property named **IsSticky**. IsSticky determines if the AppBar closes on light dismiss or not. While the facility to override light dismiss has been provided, you should stick to the principles of Windows Store apps as much as possible: Take the AppBar out of view for the users and instead let them focus on the content inside the application.

The AppBar does not have specific "AppBarItems" to append to the control. Instead, developers have to provide the items to be contained within the AppBar and provide the visual styling. The sample AppBarSample provided along with the book provides a template for the AppBar.

TheAppBarSample.xaml defines a simple AppBar that serves as a best practice while designing your own AppBar. It has support for both Portrait and Landscape modes and support for Visual State changes. It also uses the same template for supporting Snap mode as well. The AppBarSample.xaml is also included along with the book samples.

LISTING 3-18 AppBar sample

```
<!--
// Sample AppBar with button templates for Landscape and Portrait.
// Snap mode also use the same button template for Portrait.
-->

        <AppBar Background="#FF85CB01" BorderBrush="#FF85CB01">
        <AppBar.Resources>
                        <!-- AppBar button brush resources -->
            <SolidColorBrush x:Key="AppBarButtonBackgroundThemeBrush" Color="#FF85CB01" />
            <SolidColorBrush x:Key="AppBarButtonDisabledForegroundThemeBrush" Color="#66FFFFFF" />
            <SolidColorBrush x:Key="AppBarButtonForegroundThemeBrush" Color="#FFFFFFFF" />
            <SolidColorBrush x:Key="AppBarButtonPointerOverBackgroundThemeBrush" Color="#21FFFFFF" />

                        <!-- AppBar button template for use in Landscape mode -->
        <Style x:Key="AppBarButtonStyle" TargetType="Button">
            <Setter Property="Template">
                <Setter.Value>
                    <ControlTemplate TargetType="Button">
                        <Grid Width="100" Background="{StaticResource
AppBarButtonBackgroundThemeBrush}">
                            <VisualStateManager.VisualStateGroups>
                                <VisualStateGroup x:Name="CommonStates">
                                    <VisualState x:Name="Normal"/>
                                    <VisualState x:Name="PointerOver">
                                        <Storyboard>
                                            <ObjectAnimationUsingKeyFrames
Storyboard.TargetProperty="Fill" Storyboard.TargetName="IconBase">
                                                <DiscreteObjectKeyFrame KeyTime="0"
Value="{StaticResource AppBarButtonPointerOverBackgroundThemeBrush}"/>
                                            </ObjectAnimationUsingKeyFrames>
                                        </Storyboard>
                                    </VisualState>
                                    <VisualState x:Name="Pressed">
                                        <Storyboard>
                                            <ObjectAnimationUsingKeyFrames
Storyboard.TargetProperty="Fill" Storyboard.TargetName="IconBase">
                                                <DiscreteObjectKeyFrame KeyTime="0"
Value="{StaticResource AppBarButtonForegroundThemeBrush}"/>
                                            </ObjectAnimationUsingKeyFrames>
                                            <ObjectAnimationUsingKeyFrames
Storyboard.TargetProperty="Foreground" Storyboard.TargetName="IconGlyph">
                                                <DiscreteObjectKeyFrame KeyTime="0"
Value="{StaticResource AppBarButtonBackgroundThemeBrush}"/>
                                            </ObjectAnimationUsingKeyFrames>
                                        </Storyboard>
                                    </VisualState>
                                    <VisualState x:Name="Disabled">
```

```xml
                                    <Storyboard>
                                        <ObjectAnimationUsingKeyFrames
Storyboard.TargetProperty="Stroke" Storyboard.TargetName="IconBase">
                                            <DiscreteObjectKeyFrame KeyTime="0"
Value="{StaticResource AppBarButtonDisabledForegroundThemeBrush}"/>
                                        </ObjectAnimationUsingKeyFrames>
                                        <ObjectAnimationUsingKeyFrames
Storyboard.TargetProperty="Foreground" Storyboard.TargetName="IconGlyph">
                                            <DiscreteObjectKeyFrame KeyTime="0"
Value="{StaticResource AppBarButtonDisabledForegroundThemeBrush}"/>
                                        </ObjectAnimationUsingKeyFrames>
                                        <ObjectAnimationUsingKeyFrames
Storyboard.TargetProperty="Foreground" Storyboard.TargetName="ContentPresenter">
                                            <DiscreteObjectKeyFrame KeyTime="0"
Value="{StaticResource AppBarButtonDisabledForegroundThemeBrush}"/>
                                        </ObjectAnimationUsingKeyFrames>
                                    </Storyboard>
                                </VisualState>
                            </VisualStateGroup>
                            <VisualStateGroup x:Name="FocusStates">
                                <VisualState x:Name="Focused">
                                    <Storyboard>
                                        <DoubleAnimation Duration="0" To="1"
Storyboard.TargetProperty="Opacity" Storyboard.TargetName="FocusVisualWhite"/>
                                        <DoubleAnimation Duration="0" To="1"
Storyboard.TargetProperty="Opacity" Storyboard.TargetName="FocusVisualBlack"/>
                                    </Storyboard>
                                </VisualState>
                                <VisualState x:Name="Unfocused"/>
                                <VisualState x:Name="PointerFocused"/>
                            </VisualStateGroup>
                        </VisualStateManager.VisualStateGroups>
                        <Grid x:Name="IconPresenter" HorizontalAlignment="Center"
VerticalAlignment="Top" Margin="0,12,0,0">
                            <Ellipse x:Name="IconBase" HorizontalAlignment="Center"
Height="40" StrokeEndLineCap="Square" Stroke="White" VerticalAlignment="Top" Width="40"
StrokeThickness="2"/>
                            <TextBlock x:Name="IconGlyph" HorizontalAlignment="Center"
VerticalAlignment="Center" FontFamily="Segoe UI Symbol" Text="{TemplateBinding Tag}" FontSize="18.667"
TextAlignment="Center"/>
                        </Grid>
                        <ContentPresenter x:Name="ContentPresenter"
ContentTemplate="{TemplateBinding ContentTemplate}" ContentTransitions="{TemplateBinding
ContentTransitions}" Margin="6,57,6,11" VerticalAlignment="Top" HorizontalAlignment="Center">
                            <TextBlock TextWrapping="Wrap" Text="{TemplateBinding Content}"
FontSize="12"  FontWeight="Normal" TextAlignment="Center" MaxWidth="88"/>
                        </ContentPresenter>
                        <Rectangle x:Name="FocusVisualWhite" IsHitTestVisible="False"
Opacity="0" StrokeDashOffset="1.5" StrokeEndLineCap="Square" Stroke="{StaticResource
FocusVisualWhiteStrokeThemeBrush}" StrokeDashArray="1,1"/>
                        <Rectangle x:Name="FocusVisualBlack" IsHitTestVisible="False"
Opacity="0" StrokeDashOffset="0.5" StrokeEndLineCap="Square" Stroke="{StaticResource
FocusVisualBlackStrokeThemeBrush}" StrokeDashArray="1,1"/>
                    </Grid>
                </ControlTemplate>
```

```
                          </Setter.Value>
                      </Setter>
                  </Style>

                              <!-- AppBar button template for use in Portrait mode; where button label is
hidden -->
                  <Style x:Key="AppBarButtonPortraitStyle" TargetType="Button">
                      <Setter Property="Template">
                          <Setter.Value>
                              <ControlTemplate TargetType="Button">
                                  <Grid Width="60" Background="{StaticResource
AppBarButtonBackgroundThemeBrush}">
                                      <VisualStateManager.VisualStateGroups>
                                          <VisualStateGroup
x:Name="CommonStates">
                                              <VisualState
x:Name="Normal"/>
                                              <VisualState
x:Name="PointerOver">
                                                  <Storyboard>

    <ObjectAnimationUsingKeyFrames Storyboard.TargetProperty="Fill" Storyboard.TargetName="IconBase">

    <DiscreteObjectKeyFrame KeyTime="0" Value="{StaticResource
AppBarButtonPointerOverBackgroundThemeBrush}"/>

    </ObjectAnimationUsingKeyFrames>
                                                  </Storyboard>
                                              </VisualState>
                                              <VisualState
x:Name="Pressed">
                                                  <Storyboard>

    <ObjectAnimationUsingKeyFrames Storyboard.TargetProperty="Fill" Storyboard.TargetName="IconBase">

    <DiscreteObjectKeyFrame KeyTime="0" Value="{StaticResource AppBarButtonForegroundThemeBrush}"/>

    </ObjectAnimationUsingKeyFrames>

    <ObjectAnimationUsingKeyFrames Storyboard.TargetProperty="Foreground"
Storyboard.TargetName="IconGlyph">

    <DiscreteObjectKeyFrame KeyTime="0" Value="{StaticResource AppBarButtonBackgroundThemeBrush}"/>

    </ObjectAnimationUsingKeyFrames>
                                                  </Storyboard>
                                              </VisualState>
                                              <VisualState
x:Name="Disabled">
                                                  <Storyboard>

    <ObjectAnimationUsingKeyFrames Storyboard.TargetProperty="Stroke" Storyboard.TargetName="IconBase">

    <DiscreteObjectKeyFrame KeyTime="0" Value="{StaticResource
AppBarButtonDisabledForegroundThemeBrush}"/>
```

```
      </ObjectAnimationUsingKeyFrames>

   <ObjectAnimationUsingKeyFrames Storyboard.TargetProperty="Foreground"
Storyboard.TargetName="IconGlyph">

   <DiscreteObjectKeyFrame KeyTime="0" Value="{StaticResource
AppBarButtonDisabledForegroundThemeBrush}"/>

      </ObjectAnimationUsingKeyFrames>

                                                    </Storyboard>
                                                  </VisualState>
                                            </VisualStateGroup>
                                          <VisualStateGroup
x:Name="FocusStates">
                                                  <VisualState
x:Name="Focused">
                                                    <Storyboard>

   <DoubleAnimation Duration="0" To="1" Storyboard.TargetProperty="Opacity"
Storyboard.TargetName="FocusVisualWhite"/>

   <DoubleAnimation Duration="0" To="1" Storyboard.TargetProperty="Opacity"
Storyboard.TargetName="FocusVisualBlack"/>

                                                    </Storyboard>
                                                  </VisualState>
                                                  <VisualState
x:Name="Unfocused"/>

                                                  <VisualState
x:Name="PointerFocused"/>
                                            </VisualStateGroup>
                                       </VisualStateManager.VisualStateGroups>
                                       <Grid x:Name="IconPresenter"
HorizontalAlignment="Center" VerticalAlignment="Top" Margin="0,12">
                                                 <Ellipse x:Name="IconBase"
HorizontalAlignment="Center" Height="40" StrokeEndLineCap="Square" Stroke="White" VerticalAlignment="Top"
Width="40" StrokeThickness="2"/>
                                                 <TextBlock x:Name="IconGlyph"
HorizontalAlignment="Center" VerticalAlignment="Center" FontFamily="Segoe UI Symbol"
Text="{TemplateBinding Tag}" FontSize="18.667" TextAlignment="Center"/>
                                             </Grid>
                                             <Rectangle x:Name="FocusVisualWhite"
IsHitTestVisible="False" Opacity="0" StrokeDashOffset="1.5" StrokeEndLineCap="Square"
Stroke="{StaticResource FocusVisualWhiteStrokeThemeBrush}" StrokeDashArray="1,1"/>
                                             <Rectangle x:Name="FocusVisualBlack"
IsHitTestVisible="False" Opacity="0" StrokeDashOffset="0.5" StrokeEndLineCap="Square"
Stroke="{StaticResource FocusVisualBlackStrokeThemeBrush}" StrokeDashArray="1,1"/>
                                        </Grid>
                                   </ControlTemplate>
                              </Setter.Value>
                        </Setter>
                  </Style>
            </AppBar.Resources>

                  <!-- AppBar container to host buttons -->
```

```
            <StackPanel Orientation="Horizontal" HorizontalAlignment="Right" Margin="0,0,4,0">
                <Button x:Name="SampleButton1" Content="Capture" Tag="&#xE114;" Style="{StaticResource
AppBarButtonStyle}"/>
                <Button x:Name="SampleButton2" Content="Refresh" Tag="&#xE117;" Style="{StaticResource
AppBarButtonStyle}"/>
            </StackPanel>
        </AppBar>
```

4. **FlipView**: The FlipView control is an items control that enables placement of a collection of items. It displays one item at a time and provides "flipping" behavior to navigate between items. With the FlipView control, users have a predictable method of viewing one item at a time in an engaging and touchable fashion. The control supports navigation via touch, mouse and keyboard modalities. Unlike other flipping solutions, users interact with items via direct, touch-first, manipulations which are fluid and smooth. The control also responds to DirectManipulation and provides visible cues into the navigation of items as the users move from one item to another. With the FlipView control, application developers now have an easy way to create compelling flipping experiences for users. The FlipView control obviates the need for creating a custom control to support flipping, tracking items as the user flips, memory management, animations etc. The FlipView can be oriented either horizontally or vertically and provide flipping experience. A typical Horizontal FlipView is shown below.

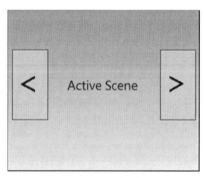

FIGURE 3-9 Horizontal FlipView

A typical Vertical FlipView is shown below.

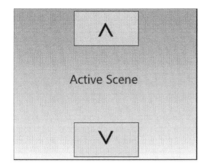

FIGURE 3-10 Vertical FlipView

SemanticZoom: The SemanticZoom control is a new control type introduced in Windows 8. The SemanticZoom control allows navigation between two different views. You can see an implementation of the SemanticZoom control on the Start screen. When you ZoomOut using either touch or using Ctrl + mouse scroll or Ctrl +/-, you can see the tiles zooming out into groups. A SemanticZoom control is a scrollable control that represents two views connected semantically.

For example, suppose you build a PhotoViewer application. In such an app, the ZoomOut view can include thumbnails of individual pictures and allow users to navigate across the entire picture Library. The ZoomedIn view can be used to render each picture at full screen size within a FlipView control to allow panning across pictures at full screen resolution.

ScrollViewer: The ScrollViewer is a control that can be used to display content larger than available viewing area. Users can scroll to the content beyond the viewport either by panning with touch or by clicking on the scroll thumb with a mouse or by using the arrow keys on the keyboard.

The ScrollViewer control encapsulates a ContentControl and can display two scrollbars: one each in Horizontal and Vertical directions. The HorizontalScrollBarVisibility and VerticalScrollBarVisibility properties control the conditions under which the vertical and horizontal ScrollBar controls appear.

Panning and zooming functionality is built into the ScrollViewer. The XAML ScrollViewer relies on the Windows 8 Direct Manipulation feature. Touch interaction in Windows 8 enables the use of physical gestures to manipulate "direct manipulation" of UI elements and thus provide a real-world experience when interacting with objects on screen. This is called Direct Manipulation or DM.

All the DM event processing is done on the render thread and not the UI thread. This aligns well with the Windows 8 motto of "fast and fluid" interactions. The UI is never in a busy state or hung state while events are processed.

Handling Events

Windows 8 provides a "no-compromise" approach towards computing using various input modalities. Application developers should provide a first class experience to their users whether their users interact with the system using touch, keyboard or mouse. In order to help developers build applications that can handle any input modality, XAML provides different types of events. These can be broadly classified as:

1. Click events

2. Tap events.

3. Pointer events.

4. Manipulation events.

Click Events

Click events are generated when the user clicks on a control using a mouse. For example, when a user clicks on a Button using the mouse, the button receives a Click event that needs to be handled. You can specify the click event handler in XAML by adding the "Click" property to your controls. Intellisense in Visual Studio does a great job of creating the function declaration in the corresponding header and source files (.h and .cpp files). The Click events are not bubbled up the visual tree unlike the Tapped and Pointer events which bubble all the way up. If you do not want events to bubble up the visual tree, you can set the "Handled" attached property to true. Setting the Handled property to true causes XAML not to bubble up the events.

```
<Button Content="Button" Height="96" Canvas.Left="45" Canvas.Top="27" Width="241" Click="Button_Click_1"
/>
```

The click event handler in this example, Button_Click_1, is a routed event and this handles the input arguments of type **RoutedEventArgs**. A routed event is a type of event that can invoke handlers on multiple listeners in an element tree, rather than just on the object that raised the event. A RoutedEventsArgs contains state information and event data associated with a routed event.

Tapped Events

Tap events are generated when the user taps on a control via touch.

```
<Button Content="Button" Height="96" Width="241" Tapped="Button_Tapped_1"/>
```

The Tapped event handler, Button_Tapped_1, is a Tapped event handler. The argument type **TappedRoutedEventArgs** is derived from **RoutedEventArgs** and provides event data for the Tapped event.

Pointer Events

In addition to Click and Tapped events, the framework also has the ability to supply what are called Pointer events. Pointer events can be thought of as the equivalent of WM_MOUSEMOVE, WM_MOUSEENTER etc messages from Win32. XAML supports various kinds of such pointer events, the most notable ones being, PointerCaptureLost, PointerMoved, PointerPressed and PointerReleased. For example, the example below shows the button subscribing to the PointerPressed event.

```
<Button Content="Button" Height="96" Canvas.Left="45" Canvas.Top="27" Width="241"
PointerPressed="Button_PointerPressed_1"/>
```

The pointer event handlers are of type **PointerEventHandler** and the arguments are of type **PointerRoutedEventArgs**, derived from RoutedEventArgs. The **PointerRoutedEventArgs** provides event data for pointer message events related to specific user interface elements, such as Pointer-Pressed.

Manipulation Events

XAML supports manipulation events on the ScrollViewer. These events are supported in coordination from the Direct Manipulation (DM) feature and are fired on the UI thread. You can subscribe to the *OnManipulationInertia*, *OnManipulationStarting*, *OnManipulationStarted*, *OnManipulationCompleted* and *OnManipulationDelta* events and respond accordingly to the amount of manipulation on the screen.

Markup Extensions

Markup extensions are a XAML language concept that is often used in the Windows Runtime XAML implementation. In XAML attribute syntax, curly braces "{" and "}" indicate a markup extension usage. This usage directs the XAML processing to escape from the general treatment of attribute values as either a literal string or a directly string-convertible value. Instead, a parser calls code that backs that particular markup extension, which constructs an object tree from the markup.

Windows Runtime XAML supports markup extensions that are defined under the default client XAML namespace and understood by its XAML parser:

- **Binding**: supports data binding, which defers a property value until it is interpreted under a data context.

- **StaticResource**: supports referencing resource values that are defined in a ResourceDictionary.

- **TemplateBinding**: supports control templates in XAML that can interact with the code properties of the templated object.

Windows Runtime also supports a very basic markup extension that is defined in the XAML language

XAML namespace, **x:Null**. You can use this to set nullable values in XAML, such as within a control template for a nullable CheckBox.

Properties that take a reference-type value (where the type has no converter) require property element syntax (which always creates a new instance) or an object reference through a markup extension. The markup extensions generally return an existing instance from some other part of the object graph for the app, or defer a value to run time. (x:Null is an exception because it just returns null, but Binding, StaticResource and most other markup extensions return object references.)

By using markup extensions, every property that is settable in XAML is potentially settable in attribute syntax, with the attribute value string referencing a markup extension usage. You can use attribute syntax to provide reference values for a property even if it doesn't support attribute syntax for direct object instantiation. Or you can enable specific behavior that defers the general requirement that XAML properties be filled by value types or just-in-time created reference types.

For example, the next XAML sets the value of the Style property of a Border by using attribute syntax. The Style property takes an instance of the Style class, a reference type that by default could not be created using an attribute syntax string. But in this case, the attribute references a particular markup extension, StaticResource. When that markup extension is processed, it returns a reference to a style that you defined earlier as a keyed resource in a resource dictionary.

StaticResource Markup Extension

The StaticResource markup extension is used for looking up for already defined resource references. The StaticResource evaluation is made at the time of loading the XAML files and hence care should be taken not to refer resources that will be defined at a later point of time. This is because when the evaluation is being performed, the XAML engine does not have access to the run time object graph, which actually makes perfect sense since the object graph would not be constructed yet.

XAML resources are defined in a ResourceDictionary and the StaticResource extension references the key of the referring resource in the dictionary. Defining resources in a dictionary is a god practice if they are intended to be used by multiple instances and it they contain properties that are needed for various UI elements in your application.

A typical example of the usage of the StaticResource extension is to refer to common theme brushes and styles. For example, a Grid view application generated by Visual Studio would have the following Grid definition in MainPage.xaml

```
<Grid Background="{StaticResource ApplicationPageBackgroundThemeBrush}">
```

The Grid declared above relies on the StaticResource extension to bind the Background property to a brush represented by the ApplicationPageBackgroundThemeBrush.

TemplateBinding Markup Extension

The TemplateBinding extension is used in conjunction with a **ControlTemplate** definition in XAML to link property values in the control template to an exposed property on the templated control. For example, a control that incorporates a TextBlock in its compositing, which is used to display the control's own Text property, might include this XAML as a part in the control template

```
<TextBlock Text="{TemplateBinding Text}" .... />
```

Data Binding

Data binding provides a simple way for Windows Store apps to display and interact with data. The primary motivation behind data binding is that how the data is displayed is separated from the management of that data. A connection, or binding, between the UI and a data object allows data to flow between the two. When a binding is established and the data changes, the UI elements that are bound to the data can display changes automatically. Similarly, changes made by the user in a UI element can be saved in the data object. For example, if the user edits the value in a control, the underlying data value is automatically updated to reflect that change.

How to implement Binding in C++ /CX

Every binding must specify a source and target. The source should be a Windows Runtime object with the **BindableAttribute** specified or an object that implements the **ICustomPropertyProvider**. The target can be any **DependencyProperty** of a FrameworkElement. Dependency properties are properties that provide support for value expressions, data binding, animation, and property change notification.

The binding engine in XAML gets information from the Binding object about the following:

1. The source and target objects.

2. The direction of the data flow. You specify the direction by setting the **Binding.Mode** property.

3. The value converter, if one is present. You specify a value converter by setting the Converter property to an instance of a class that implements the IValueConverter interface. For example, in order to specify a value converter for the Text property of a TextBox, you would set the binding Converter property and binding Mode properties as shown below.

    ```
    <TextBox x:Name="tbValueConverterDataBound" Text="{Binding Element-
    Name=sliderValueConverter, Path=Value, Mode=TwoWay, Converter={StaticResource
    GradeConverter}}"/>
    ```

The binding is created in XAML by using the {Binding ...} syntax. If you want to specify the binding in code, you can set the DataContext property in code to the corresponding binding.

Binding Modes

The Binding class has a Mode property that determines the flow of data. Windows Store apps can use three types for bindings.

1.   **OneTime** bindings update the target with the data from the source when the binding is created.

2.   **OneWay** bindings update the target with the data from the source when the binding is created and whenever the data changes. This is the default binding mode.

3.   **TwoWay** bindings update the target and source when either of them changes.

For changes to the source object to propagate to the target, the source must implement the **INotifyPropertyChanged**. **INotifyPropertyChanged** has the **PropertyChanged** event. This event tells the binding engine that the source has changed so that the binding engine can update the target value.

Data Templates

Data Templates are similar to Control templates. While control templates allow you to customize the appearance of controls, data templates allow you to customize the visualization of data bound to controls. **DataTemplate** objects are particularly useful when you are binding an ItemsControl such as a ListBox to an entire collection. By default, the ListBox uses the default representation to render data and the default happens to be a simple TextBlock. This is not a particularly helpful or interesting way to visualize data bound to a ListBox! In such cases, you can use a **DataTemplate** to define the appearance of data objects. The content of your **DataTemplate** becomes the visual structure of your data objects.

In our BasicControls sample, we have a ListBox that is bound to a list of Scenario objects. Each Scenario object has a Title (Platform::String) and ClassType (Windows::UI::Xaml::Interop::TypeName) fields. Our ListBox is defined in the MainPage.xaml as follows:

```
<TextBlock x:Name="ScenarioListLabel" Text="Select Scenario:" Grid.Row="1"  Style="{StaticResource
SubheaderTextStyle}" Margin="0,5,0,0" />
<ListBox x:Name="Scenarios" Margin="0,0,20,0" Grid.Row="2"
…..
</ListBox>
```

Without a data template, our ListBox would display items as BasicControls.Scenario rather than use the individual Title for each Scenario object. This would happen because, barring any special instruction to the ListBox, it uses the default way of calling the **ToString** function on the underlying object to display the objects in the collection. We should thus have an implementation of the **ToString** function in the Scenario class thus provides the **Title** value when the **ToString** method is called.

```
public ref class Scenario sealed

    {

    public:

            Scenario() {}

    public:

            Platform::String^ ToString()

            {

                    return Title->ToString();

            }

    .. more code

}
```

One way is to set the ItemTemplate property of the ListBox to a DataTemplate. Anything you specify in the DataTemplate becomes the visual structure of the underlying data object. In the case of the BasicControls sample, the data template is fairly simple. We specify that each item appears as a TextBlock element within a StackPanel. The TextBlock is bound to the **Name** property of the Scenario class.

Finally when we build the actual list of Scenario objects in code behind and before setting the Item-Source property to the ListBox, you should call the **ToString** on each Scenario object when creating the ListBoxItems.

```
auto item = ref new ListBoxItem();
```

```
item->Content = _scenario[x]->ToString();
```

The BasicControls sample contains the complete code for the data template and all other concepts introduced upto now. We will now turn our attention to actually implementing data binding using C++ /CX.

Data Binding in C++ /CX

All apps deal with some type of data in various forms. Whether this data is local to the app, or originates within the local system or from a remote source such as the cloud, there is a high probability that you will surface some part of this data in your application UI. Examples of such usage include photos downloaded from online repositories, contact data from online address books etc.

Data binding has been one of the strongest feature points of all XAML frameworks beginning with WPF. XAML in Windows 8 continues to provide data binding functionality. We will first explore a simple example to perform data binding in C++ /CX.

The data we'll be binding to in this section is a classic Person class. I have chosen a Person entity to keep the example simple and easy to explain. All the concepts we explore will translate to any C++ /CX application that relies on data binding.

We will now create a "Person" class that will then be used to bind to XAML elements in the Main-Page.xaml. Our Person class has four properties: FirstName, LastName, EmailAddress and FullName. Of these, the first three are read-write properties meaning they have public get/set methods whereas the FullName property is only a get property.

For the XAML framework to bind with C++ /CX types, you should use the [BindableAttribute] metadata attribute for the C++ /CX type.

Our Person class looks like the listing below.

LISTING 3-19 Person class listing for the data binding sample

```cpp
#include "pch.h"

namespace DataBindingApp
{
    [BindableAttribute]
    public ref class Person sealed
    {
    public:
            Person();
            virtual ~Person();

    private:
            String^ m_firstName;
            String^ m_lastName;
            String^ m_emailAddress;
            String^ m_fullName;

    public:
            property String^ FirstName
            {
                    String^ get()
                    {
                            return m_firstName;
                    }

                    void set(String^ value)
                    {
                            if (value->IsEmpty())
                            {
                                    throw ref new Platform::InvalidArgumentException();
                            }
                            m_firstName = value;
                    }
            }
    }
```

```
property String^ LastName
{
        String^ get()
        {
                return m_lastName;
        }

        void set(String^ value)
        {
                if (value->IsEmpty())
                {
                        throw ref new Platform::InvalidArgumentException();
                }
                m_lastName = value;
        }
}

property String^ EmailAddress
{
        String^ get()
        {
                return m_emailAddress;
        }

        void set(String^ value)
        {
                if (value->IsEmpty())
                {
                        throw ref new Platform::InvalidArgumentException();
                }
                m_emailAddress = value;
        }
}

property String^ FullName
{
        String^ get()
        {
                m_fullName = m_firstName + " " + m_lastName;
                return m_fullName;
        }
}
    };
}
```

We want to display a list of contacts in a XAML ListBox and show more details when an item in the ListBox is selected. Follow these steps to create the app.

1. Using Visual Studio, under the C++ language, create a new Blank XAML Application.

2. Save your project with a name such as **DatabindingApp**.

3. In the MainPage.xaml.cpp after the call to InitializeComponent in the MainPage constructor, add a event handler for the **Loaded** event.

```
this->Loaded += ref new Windows::UI::Xaml::RoutedEventHandler(this, &MainPage::OnLoaded);
```

4. In the MainPage.xaml.h add the call back declaration for the OnLoaded event handler and declare a Vector collection of Person types.

```
virtual void OnLoaded(Platform::Object^ sender, Windows::UI::Xaml::RoutedEventArgs^ e);
Vector<Person^>^ contacts_;
```

5. In the MainPage.xaml.cpp, add the implementation for the OnLoaded event handler. We will setup an unhandled exception handler and then proceed to add the person details to our ListBox.

LISTING 3-20 Listing for the OnLoaded function

```
App::Current->UnhandledException += ref new UnhandledExceptionEventHandler(this,
&MainPage::UnhandledError);
//Always use standard C++ types
const std::wstring fName = L"John";
const std::wstring lName = L"Doe";
const std::wstring email = L"John.Doe@somewhere.com";

auto p1 = ref new Person();
//Use Platform and other WinRT types only when interfacing with WinRT
p1->FirstName = ref new String(fName.c_str());
p1->LastName = ref new String(lName.c_str());
p1->EmailAddress = ref new String(email.c_str());
m_contacts = ref new Vector<Person^>;
m_contacts->Append(p1);
EmployeeListing->ItemsSource = m_contacts;
```

6. The last line in the above code snippet is where we are assigning our collection of persons to the ListBox object. In our case, we have chosen to populate the collection with only one instance of a person. In the MainPage.xaml.h add the call back declaration for the Unhandled event handler

```
virtual void UnhandledError(Platform::Object^ sender, Windows::UI::Xaml::UnhandledExceptionEventArgs^
e);
```

7. In the MainPage.xaml.cpp, add the implementation for the UnhandledError function.

```
void MainPage::UnhandledError(Platform::Object^ sender,
Windows::UI::Xaml::UnhandledExceptionEventArgs^ e)
{
        String^ error = e->Message;
}
```

8. Now, we have all our data setup and assigned to the ListBox. We now need to style the UI appropriately and get our app running.

9. Our UI is pretty simple. It contains a ListBox to hold the list of contacts, a DataTemplate for the ListBox items and finally a StackPanel to show more details for each ListBox item selected.

10. Our ListBox has a x:Name, ContactListing which will be used as a variable name in our cpp

source files.

11. In the ListBox data template, we use the {Binding..} syntax which instructs the XAML runtime that this item receives its value from the data context that is bound either to it or its parent.

12. In our simple scenario, all items in the ListBox are of the same type (Person) and we will bind our list of contacts directly to the ListBox itself.

13. The final thing we want to enable is displaying more data when an item in the ListBox is selected. What we can do is take the data context from the ListBox item and set it to the data context of the StackPanel.

14. Once we set the data context of the StackPanel, we can then display more properties from the selected item inside the StackPanel.

15. That's it. Build and run the sample and you should see the app in all its glory!

Data Binding with existing C++ code

The previous example was all about writing code from scratch using C++ /CX to support data binding with XAML elements. C++ has been around for a long time and there are millions of existing implementations of different kinds of software written in C++. So, how do we make simple code changes to existing code bases and bring them to the XAML and Windows Store world?

What follows next is a very simple example of a C++ Person class. This is not C++ /CX but a plain standard C++ class. For the purpose of our discussion, let us give this class the name, **Person**. Our Person class has a default constructor and destructor. The class has three attributes defining a person: First Name, Last Name and email address. Our **ISO-C++ Person** class is similar in all respects to the **Person** class we created in the preceding example. The class is declared inside a namespace called 'x'.

We want to use this **x::Person** class to support data binding to XAML elements. If we set the **BindableAttribute** on the **x::Person** class, we run into issues right away. XAML cannot bind to non-C++ /CX classes and the **BindableAttribute** cannot be set on standard C++ classes. What we can do however is embed the **x::Person** class inside our **Person** runtime class and make all calls forward to the **x::Person** instance. Our **Person** class can be used to data binding, setting BindableAttributes etc.

All calls on the **Person** object to store the various attributes are forwarded to the embedded **x::Person** instance. Similarly when the binding engine attempts to fetch data from the **Person** object, the data is instead returned from the **x::Person** instance.

A modified view of our Person class looks like below. You can get the full sample from the **DataBindingCpp** project.

```
[BindableAttribute]

public ref class Person sealed

{

public:

        Person();

        virtual ~Person();

private:

        x::Person person;

    ....

};
```

Obviously this is a very trivial example that shows how existing C++ code can be used in conjunction with C++ /CX code to take advantage of XAML concepts. Existing C++ code continues to be a strong intellectual property asset for most customers and it makes maximum sense to reuse as much as possible while building Windows Store apps.

Binding to a Data Model

In order to bind to a data model, you should implement the INotifyPropertyChanged interface on our model class. Implementing this interface enables you to raise events whenever properties are changed.

INotifyPropertyChanged interface contains one event: PropertyChanged. This event is fired whenever a property value changes and listeners are notified. The **DataModel** sample contains an implementation of INotifyPropertyChanged that is used to pass notification events between the UI and the model class.

Building a XAML custom control

In our discussion on XAML until now, we focused on the built-in controls. XAML also allows you as a developer to build your own custom controls. In this section, we will focus on developing custom controls for your projects.

Technically speaking, user-defined controls can be categorized into two types: user controls and custom controls. The distinction between these two types is kind of blurry. User controls are a type of custom controls but we will continue to treat them as two distinct type of controls for the purpose of our discussion in this section.

As you begin contemplating creating your own control, you should think about the goal behind building the control. If your control will be used only within a few projects and does not need to expose rich-styling and first-class theming support, then you should build a user control. The appearance of a user control is defined by a logical tree and the control logic interacts directly with the elements in the tree.

If, on the other hand, you want to build a control whose appearance is defined by a visual tree that is defined in its own control template, and whose functionality continues to work even if re-themed or re-styled, then you should build a custom control.

Creating a User Control

In this section, we will create a user control that combines a TextBox and a Button. The goal is to enable a user to type a string in the TextBox and click the Button to have the same text displayed back. When we are done with building this control, we would have what is called a composite control.

But now, for the basics. A user control is a class that is derived from UserControl. The UserControl class in the XAML framework provides the base class for defining new controls which encapsulate existing controls and then provides its own logic. So let's get started.

You can choose to have your user control either in a separate component or as a separate xaml file within the app itself. In this scenario, we will build an app containing the user control within the main app itself to keep things simple.

The user interface for our user control is very simple. The input TextBox is docked towards the right of the control and provides a way for the user to input their name. A Button is defined below the TextBox and provides a click event handler. Upon clicking the button, the control displays the input string entered back to the user.

The BasicUserControl.xaml is listed below.

LISTING 3-22 BasicUserControl markup listing

```
<UserControl
    x:Class="CxxUserControl.BasicUserControl"
    xmlns="http://schemas.microsoft.com/winfx/2006/xaml/presentation"
    xmlns:x="http://schemas.microsoft.com/winfx/2006/xaml"
    xmlns:local="using:CxxUserControl"
    xmlns:d="http://schemas.microsoft.com/expression/blend/2008"
    xmlns:mc="http://schemas.openxmlformats.org/markup-compatibility/2006"
    mc:Ignorable="d"
    d:DesignHeight="300"
    d:DesignWidth="400">

    <Grid>
        <StackPanel>
```

```
        <StackPanel Orientation="Horizontal">
            <TextBlock Text="Your Name: " FontSize="26.667" Margin="0,0,20,0" />
            <TextBox x:Name="NameInput" Width="300" />
        </StackPanel>
        <Button Content="Click Me" Click="ClickMeButtonClicked"/>
        <TextBlock FontSize="53" x:Name="OutputText" />
    </StackPanel>
  </Grid>
</UserControl>
```

Next, we need to handle the Click event handler for the Button in BasicUserControl.xam.cpp as shown.

```
void BasicUserControl::ClickMeButtonClicked(Platform::Object^ sender, Windows::UI::Xaml::RoutedEventArgs^
e)
{
    OutputText->Text = "Hello " + NameInput->Text;
}
```

Finally, replace the markup in the <Grid> section of the MainPage.xaml with the following markup.

LISTING 3-23 Consuming the user control in MainPage.xaml

```
<Grid Background="{StaticResource ApplicationPageBackgroundThemeBrush}">
    <Grid.RowDefinitions>
        <RowDefinition Height="Auto"/>
        <RowDefinition Height="*"/>
    </Grid.RowDefinitions>
    <Grid x:Name="Output" HorizontalAlignment="Left" VerticalAlignment="Top" Grid.Row="1">
        <!-- observe the xmlns:local scope declaration in the root node of this view -->
        <local:BasicUserControl x:Name="MyHelloWorldUserControl" />

    </Grid>
</Grid>
```

Now build the solution, launch the app. Input a string in the TextBox and then click on the "Click Me" button. The control will relay the string back on the screen as shown below!

FIGURE 3-11 Basic user control

Creating a Basic Custom Control

Just as in the previous section, we will create a very basic custom control in this section. A custom control can be used in multiple projects, can be re-styled and completely re-templated, if needed. Normally custom controls are derived from core controls such as a Button or ListView or from primitive controls such as a Panel but with a different visual style and appearance.

Adding a Custom Control using Visual Studio 2012 is very easy. In any XAML app, you can add a custom control to your project by using the Templated Control item template in the Add New Item dialog box. Doing so will create the two required elements for the custom control: a generic.xaml file under the themes folder and the corresponding code-behind source files.

The generic.xaml file contains the default styles and template for your custom control and you can change them as needed by your project. Do not change either the location of generic.xaml or the name of file. Doing so will cause a failure when the XAML framework attempts to load the control.

The code-behind file contains the logic for your custom control. In the class constructor, you should set the default style key to the type of your control. Setting the default style key informs the XAML framework which style and template to apply to this Type whenever it is used.

Using a Custom control is exactly similar to using a user control. You declare a namespace and place it in XAML wherever you need it. In our case, we place it in MainPage.xaml

LISTING 3-24 Consuming a custom control in MainPage.xaml

```
<Grid Background="{StaticResource ApplicationPageBackgroundThemeBrush}">
    <Grid.RowDefinitions>
        <RowDefinition Height="Auto"/>
        <RowDefinition Height="*"/>
    </Grid.RowDefinitions>
    <Grid x:Name="Output" HorizontalAlignment="Left" VerticalAlignment="Top" Grid.Row="1">
        <StackPanel HorizontalAlignment="Center">
            <TextBlock Text="Below is the result of using our custom control" />
            <!-- observe the xmlns:local scope declaration in the root node of this view -->
            <local:BasicCustomControl Width="300" Height="150" Background="Red" BorderBrush="Black" />
        </StackPanel>
    </Grid>
</Grid>
```

The BasicCustomControl.h is listed below

```
#pragma once

namespace CxxCustomControl
{
    public ref class BasicCustomControl sealed : public Windows::UI::Xaml::Controls::Control
    {
    public:
            BasicCustomControl();
    };
}
```

And finally, the BasicCustomControl.cpp is listed below.

```cpp
#include "pch.h"
#include "BasicCustomControl.h"

using namespace CxxCustomControl;

using namespace Platform;
using namespace Windows::Foundation;
using namespace Windows::Foundation::Collections;
using namespace Windows::UI::Xaml;
using namespace Windows::UI::Xaml::Controls;
using namespace Windows::UI::Xaml::Data;
using namespace Windows::UI::Xaml::Documents;
using namespace Windows::UI::Xaml::Input;
using namespace Windows::UI::Xaml::Interop;
using namespace Windows::UI::Xaml::Media;

// The Templated Control item template is documented at http://go.microsoft.com/fwlink/?LinkId=234235

BasicCustomControl::BasicCustomControl()
{
    DefaultStyleKey = "CxxCustomControl.BasicCustomControl";
}
```

Build the CxxCustomControl solution, launch the app and you should see our custom control rendered on screen. Before we move on further customizing this control, we must explore Dependency Properties in XAML.

Dependency Property Overview

Before we move further down the road customizing the custom control we built above, let us explore Dependency Properties in XAML.

Dependency properties are a special set of properties that have a corresponding backing representation in the Windows Runtime. All dependency properties should derive from a single base class named the *DependencyObject*. Most types in XAML are a subclass of the DependencyObject and hence will support dependency properties. Some of the common usage scenarios for dependency properties include: Data binding, XAM UI styling, animations, fetching default value through metadata etc.

The MobileServicesApp in Chapter 10 that communicates with Windows Azure Mobile Services, relies on dependency properties to change the title and header numbers ☺

Dependency properties are greatly used to change the value of already defined properties when input change events occur. Typical examples of input change events include:

- User changes the input manually.

- Property value is determined through a combination of either data binding or story boards.

- When you bind the property to a template class etc.

The following example defines three new dependency properties: Number, Title and Description.

LISTING 3-25 Defining dependency properties in C++ /CX

```
Windows::UI::Xaml::DependencyProperty^ MobileServicesApp::Task::NumberProperty_ =

    DependencyProperty::Register(ref new String(L"Number"),

    TypeName(int::typeid), TypeName(Task::typeid),

    ref new PropertyMetadata(nullptr) );

Windows::UI::Xaml::DependencyProperty^ MobileServicesApp::Task::TitleProperty_ =

    DependencyProperty::Register(ref new String(L"Title"),

    TypeName(String::typeid), TypeName(Task::typeid),

    ref new PropertyMetadata(nullptr) );

Windows::UI::Xaml::DependencyProperty^ MobileServicesApp::Task::DescriptionProperty_ =

    DependencyProperty::Register(ref new String(L"Description"),

    TypeName(String::typeid), TypeName(Task::typeid),

    ref new PropertyMetadata(nullptr) );
```

In order to setup data binding using dependency properties, the target property must be a dependency property. This is because the computation of the final value of the property is deferred until runtime. At runtime, the value is obtained typically from a data source.

For the dependency properties we defined above, we can also create a simple XAML markup that sets up data binding as shown below.

LISTING 3-26 Dependency properties and binding to properties in XAML markup

```
<Grid VerticalAlignment="Top">
        <StackPanel Orientation="Horizontal">
            <Border BorderThickness="0,0,1,0" BorderBrush="DarkGray" Margin="0,10" MinWidth="70">
                <TextBlock Text="{Binding Number}" FontSize="45" Foreground="DarkGray" Margin="20,0"/>
            </Border>
            <StackPanel>
                <TextBlock Text="{Binding Title}" Margin="10,10,0,0" FontSize="16" FontWeight="Bold"/>
                <TextBlock Text="{Binding Description}" Margin="10,0,0,0" />
            </StackPanel>
        </StackPanel>
    </Grid>
```

Customizing the control templates

If you need to further customize the look and feel of your controls, you can do that too. XAML allows you to have your cake and eat it too. If you want to change the appearance of a checkbox control, you can do that by creating a new control template for the checkbox control.

Defining a control template in XAML

Suppose you want to create a control template for a Button control. XAML allows you to specify a control template in many ways. You can choose any one of the following methods:

1. Set the Template property of the Button control to the definition of a ControlTemplate defined inline as follows.

```
<Button Content="Button1">
  <Button.Template>
    <ControlTemplate TargetType="Button">

      <!--Define the ControlTemplate here.-->

    </ControlTemplate>
  </Button.Template>
</Button>
```

2. Set the Template property of the Button control to the definition of a ControlTemplate defined in the resources section.

```
<StackPanel>
  <StackPanel.Resources>
    <ControlTemplate TargetType="Button" x:Key="newTemplate">

      <!--Define the ControlTemplate here.-->

    </ControlTemplate>
  </StackPanel.Resources>

  <Button Template="{StaticResource newTemplate}" Content="Button1"/>
</StackPanel>
```

3. The most commonly used method however, is to use a Style and set the template and then define the ControlTemplate.

```
  <StackPanel>
  <StackPanel.Resources>
    <Style TargetType="Button" x:Key="newTemplate">
      <Setter Property="Template">
        <Setter.Value>
          <ControlTemplate TargetType="Button">

            <!--Define the ControlTemplate here.-->
```

```
      </ControlTemplate>
    </Setter.Value>
  </Setter>
 </Style>
</StackPanel.Resources>
<Button Style="{StaticResource newTemplate}" Content="Button1"/>
</StackPanel>
```

Changing the visual state of a control

In addition to changing appearance of a control, you can customize the visual state of the control too. XAML allows you to combine multiple FrameworkElement objects and compose them as a single control. A XAML control is usually a composition of multiple FrameworkElement objects. If you intend to customize the visual state of a control, you should begin with a control template for that control.

A ControlTemplate, however, can contain only one FrameworkElement at its root node. Within the root node, you can embed multiple FrameworkElements. All the FrameworkElements are composed together to make up for the visual structure of a XAML control.

The following example shows a very simple control template for a Button control. Our control template defines a Border and a ContentPresenter in the control template. The Border draws a border and having a content presenter allows us to place any kind of XAML object and render on the control.

```
<ControlTemplate TargetType="Button">
    <Border x:Name="RootElement">

        <!--Create the SolidColorBrush for the Background
            as an object elemment and give it a name so
            it can be referred to elsewhere in the control template.-->
        <Border.Background>
          <SolidColorBrush x:Name="BorderBrush" Color="Black"/>
        </Border.Background>

        <!--Use a ContentPresenter to display the Content of
                the Button.-->
          <ContentPresenter
            HorizontalAlignment="{TemplateBinding HorizontalContentAlignment}"
            VerticalAlignment="{TemplateBinding VerticalContentAlignment}"
            Margin="4,5,4,4" />

      </Border>
  </ControlTemplate>
```

Once you create a custom template for your control, you can then use the TemplateBinding markup extension to bind the property of any element that is defined within the ControlTemplate to any public property that is defined by your control. You can use the TemplateBinding markup extension to bind not just visual states but the DataContext too.

Using Animations in XAML Controls

Until now, our focus has been on developing XAM controls and consuming them in various client applications. One of the premises of Windows 8 is fluid interactions. The notion of fluidity encompasses smooth UI animations without blocking the UI. Your UI should flow in and out smoothly with good animations without either consuming too much time or block the user from performing their normal activities in the application. In this section, we will focus on the animation support provided by XAML and how you can incorporate some of the built in animation support within your apps.

The XAML framework contains a dedicated thread to handle all requests related to the composition and animation of controls. This thread is called the "composition thread" and is a thread that is separate from the main UI thread. The main thread handles all the execution of the framework and developer written code whereas the "composition thread" handles all the composition related activities. This decoupling of the main execution thread from the "composition thread" enables the smooth panning and a consistent 60fps panning performance in XAML apps.

XAML animations can be categorized into two types: independent animations and dependent animations.

- Independent animations – If animating a UI element does not change the overall scene of the UI, then such an animation is called as an independent animation. All such animations are run on the composition thread. The composition thread is guaranteed to be scheduled at a regular interval which ensures smooth rendering and animating of UI elements that use independent animations.

- Dependent animations – Animations that affect layout and depend on extra input from the UI thread are called dependent animations. These animations are not run and require an explicit opt-in from you as an app developer. Enabling such animations is still a double edged sword: they work seamlessly when the UI thread is idle but begin to stutter when the UI or the XAML framework is doing a lot of work.

Some of the XAML controls are built with stock animations readily available. Examples of such controls include FlipView, ProgressRing and the Tooltip. If you are using a control that does not contain built-in animations, you can either use transition animations or theme animations when setting various properties on the controls.

Transition animations

Transition animations are a great way to capture user attention when a UI element is either being shown on screen or is being removed from the display. Such animations allow the UI to be faded in or out of view rather than just appear or disappear abruptly. You can combine multiple transition animations to a single UI element or a container that holds UI elements.

A simple example to apply a transition animation for a Button is as below. When you define a Button control is XAML, you can use the transitions property of the Button control, or any XAML UI control, to specify transition animations that will be applied to the said control. In the example below, we apply the **EntranceThemeTransition** to the Button control. Applying the **EntranceThemeTransition** causes the button to animate when displayed for the first time versus abruptly appearing on screen, thus providing a smooth visual cue to the user.

```
<Button Content="Transitioning Button">
    <Button.Transitions>
        <TransitionCollection>
            <EntranceThemeTransition/>
        </TransitionCollection>
    </Button.Transitions>
 </Button>
```

Tip Transition animation APIs can easily be identified by the phrase "**ThemeTransition**" in the API.

Theme animations

For very simple animations, you can use transition animations. If however, you prefer to retain control over the animation and its timing, you should use theme animations. When you use a theme animation, you should also use a storyboard in conjunction with the animation. In your event handler for the UI element, you can make a call to the Begin method of the Storyboard to begin the animation.

In the animation example below, we will fade a rectangle out of view by using a theme animation in conjunction with a Storyboard.

```
<StackPanel>
    <StackPanel.Resources>
        <Storyboard x:Name="myStoryboard">
            <FadeOutThemeAnimation TargetName="myRectangle"  />
        </Storyboard>
    </StackPanel.Resources>
    <Rectangle PointerPressed="Rectangle_Tapped" x:Name="myRectangle"
            Fill="Blue" Width="200" Height="300" />
</StackPanel>
```

It is important to note that theme animations are not run automatically unlike transition animations. This means that you should trigger the animation to begin at runtime. A Storyboard is used to initiate the animation process at run time by calling the Begin method on the Storyboard object instance. Using a Storyboard means you also have control over the animation process. You can control the animation by using the Stop, Pause and Resume methods of the Storyboard class. In addition, you can also change the default behavior of the animation. For example, increasing the Duration value of a FadeOutThemeAnimation causes a slowdown of the fade-out effect.

Tip All theme animation APIs contain the phrase "**ThemeAnimation**" in the API.

Always use the pre-defined PVL animations from the Windows::UI::Xaml::Media::Animation library as these animations are tuned for high performance and provide smooth animation. Do not attempt to build your own animations or expose custom animations through WinRT components. The XAML team has gone to great lengths to tune animations for maximum performance. Building a custom animation that would provide similar performance guarantees while integrating seamlessly into the Windows 8 Modern personality is a non-trivial task. If you eventually decide to build a custom animation and put in all of the effort needed to pull it off, you might still be surprised to discover that the animation does not work optimally on some machines or all of the machines. It is best to use the system provided animations and have your application gel with the overall Windows Modern personality than stand as the odd man out!

In the DrawIt sample that we develop in the next chapter, we will use Theme animations along with Storyboards to smoothly animate application bar and button display.

While the list of animations supported by XAML are more than the simple examples illustrated above and will continue to increase and get tuned as the platform evolves, you should always refer to the official documentation on MSDN for up to date information. And this holds true for all concepts being discussed in the book!

Where are we and what's next

This chapter provided an overview of the native XAML framework in Windows 8 and how to use XAML in C++ /CX applications. While XAML is a boon for C++ developers and is an improvement over the state of affairs that existed with MFC and other GUI frameworks of the 90s era, it is not the only way to develop UI applications for Windows 8 using C++. Microsoft DirectX is an alternative to developing great Windows 8 applications using C++. Although DirectX is a COM based API, there is an excellent integration story between XAML and DirectX, all served through your favorite programming language, C++. In the next chapter, we will explore the ways and means to develop applications using XAML, DirectX and C++. This ability to mix a high level framework (XAML) with a low level framework (DirectX) to develop power efficient and high performance applications, is in fact, one of the most compelling reasons to use C++. Let's get started!

Chapter 4

C++ /CX, XAML and DirectX – Better together

In this chapter:

Introduction to XAML + DirectX
SurfaceImageSource (SiS) and developing an app using SiS
VirtualSurfaceImageSource (VSiS) and developing apps using VSiS
SwapChainBackgroundPanel
The DrawIt Application – C++, XAML and DirectX

Introduction to XAML + DirectX

Microsoft DirectX is a collection of APIs for handling tasks related to graphics, multimedia and game programming on the Microsoft platforms. Direct3D is the 3D graphics API within DirectX. Direct3D is the software representation of the Graphical Processing Unit (GPU) and is the lowest-level graphics API for controlling a GPU from a user-mode application. Direct3D is an immediate mode API. An immediate mode API provides a very thin layer of abstraction over the hardware (in our case the GPU). The API might also contain API support for capabilities that might be missing from the hardware. Programming using an immediate mode API like Direct3D is not easy. Every time you want to display content on screen, you must first notify the API that you are about to render, then build the complete render pipeline and supply it to Direct3D, and then finally signal that you are done. Once you have informed Direct3D that you are finished, the display will be updated.

Windows 8 has been reimagined from the chipset to the user experience. Needless to say, everything in Windows 8 now relies on DirectX: from platform APIs to the Operating System and to hardware design. This implies that you, as a developer, can create applications relying on DirectX to create Windows Store applications that achieve the highest performance rendering in Windows 8. As noted above, Direct3D applications are difficult to create, with the API being a primarily immediate mode API and such applications are traditionally developed using C++.

XAML is a UI framework for building various types of Windows Store apps in Windows 8. It provides support for Windows Store controls and animations, has a great interaction model, supports data binding, media etc. At its core XAML is a retained mode API. A retained mode API retains a complete model of the objects to be rendered. Usually this retention is in the form of a "scene graph". XAML applications update the scene and the API handles the actual process of updating the scene on the display device. As a general purpose framework, XAML does a great job of providing out of the box support for Windows Store app development. These include support for the new Application Model, support for Process Lifecycle Management, integration with the new immersive shell contracts etc. In addition, Visual Studio and Expression Blend provide great design time support to develop Windows Store apps using XAML.

There are certain scenarios where your application might need the processing power of the immediate mode rendering performance and the hardware access provided by DirectX. For example, your app might be performing image processing and you would like to eke out the maximum performance from the system for your image processing routines. Another scenario is that of document viewers that mix DirectX graphics with XAML UI. Games, also, do fall into the same category. All these apps would like to obtain the best performance for their core scenarios. It is in such scenarios that the combination of XAML and DirectX actually makes developers more productive, apps visually richer and faster. You can now build your XAML UI using C#, Visual Basic or C++ and include C++ DirectX components. You cannot, however, build applications using Javascript and try to reference DirectX C++ components. This is not a supported scenario.

The XAML team spent a great amount of time thinking about the various scenarios that need the extra power boost with DirectX integration. From the beginning, it was clear to the teams working on this problem that the developers integrating DirectX and XAML have special requirements from the integration. These requirements mapped nicely to the design goals that the XAML team had in mind to enable DirectX and XAML integration. These design goals are:

1. **Performance**

    a.   Support for low-latency input and interactivity.

    b.   Allow for incremental re-drawing of XAML and DirectX content.

    c.   Minimize the overhead of using XAML.

2. **Flexibility**

    a.   Enable the complete functionality of both DirectX and XAML.

3. **Integration**

    a.   Smooth integration between XAML and DirectX

Put together, the integration of DirectX and XAML allows developers design and develop a XAML interface in Microsoft Blend 2012 and Visual Studio 2012, and combine it with any DirectX content. There is no additional runtime overhead in using DirectX functionality in a XAML App and you can combine DirectX graphics and XAML UI in the same app using familiar XAML concepts.

During the early stage of development of Windows 8, the XAML framework had a single API to mix DirectX and XAML. This API exposed a "drawing surface" that enabled apps to draw content which was then rendered on the display device. With feedback from multiple teams and external users, the XAML team went back to the drawing board to expand on the APIs that enable mixing DirectX and

XAML. As you can see, the scenarios listed above fall into three different categories of mixing DirectX and XAML and in fact, there exist 3 APIs that meet the needs of each of the categories.

1. Combining very small portions of DirectX with a Windows Store app in which the UI is predominantly XAML based.

2. Combining large scale DirectX graphics with a Windows Store app in which the UI is predominantly XAML based.

3. Overlaying XAML UI onto a DirectX App.

SurfaceImageSource

When what you want to achieve is to combine small portions of DirectX with XAML, the SurfaceImageSource (SiS) type present in the Windows::UI::Xaml::Media::Imaging namespace is a perfect fit. An instance of the SurfaceImageSource provides you with a shared DirectX surface you can draw into. You can use all of DirectX functionality as is needed for your app and this surface is then composed onto the rest of the XAML UI. Using a SiS is appealing if you want to use DirectX to render specific portions of components that are part of a larger XAML UI. For instance, you might want to use SiS when applying complex photo processing effects.

Before we get to the nuances of creating a SiS, it is worth mentioning that a SurfaceImageSource derives from the ImageSource XAML class. ImageSource is frequently used in XAML as a source for an ImageBrush. This ImageSource is then used to paint any XAML element. Since brushes are re-usable, you can paint any number of XAML elements using this approach.

The following code sample demonstrates how to create an instance of SurfaceImageSource and then fill a XAML Rectangle.

LISTING 4-1 Creating a SiS object

```
SurfaceImageSource^ surfaceImageSource = ref newSurfaceImageSource(rectangle1->Width, rectangle1->Height,
true);
ImageBrush^ brush = ref newImageBrush();
brush->ImageSource = surfaceImageSource;
rectangle1->Fill = brush;
```

You can now use DirectX to render portions of the Rectangle and update it as often as it needs to be updated. The goodness does not stop here. Because the DirectX content is now composed along with other XAML UI elements, properties applied to the rectangle also apply to the DirectX content. You can apply render transforms, projections and z-ordering all in XAML and it is seamlessly applied to the DirectX content too!

SurfaceImageSource class contains only two constructors. So how does it work? The actual implementation is provided by a native interface: the ISurfaceImageSourceNative that needs to be queried for. This is because the interface needs to refer the DirectX APIs directly and these are available only in C++. The ISurfaceImageSourceNative interface is defined in the "windows.ui.xaml.media.dxinterop.h".

The ISurfaceImageSourceNative interface defines three methods:

a. **SetDevice**: The SetDevice function enables you to create and set a DXGI device and then start drawing.

b. **BeginDraw**: BeginDraw takes a RECT as an input parameter. This RECT region is used to constrain the region that would be updated. If you only need to update small regions on the display, using the RECT constraint allows you to achieve better performance by only updating the needed RECTs. The method returns a POINT offset and a DXGI surface as out parameters. The POINT specifies the offset where you should begin drawing. It is a good practice to check for this offset before beginning the drawing operation. This is because even if you are updating the entire surface, there is a potential change that your surface might be a small portion of a larger one that XAML maintains internally as part of its optimization strategy.

c. **EndDraw**: The EndDraw function signals the completion of drawing routine and the framework begins the updating the scene on the display device.

Creating a XAML + DX App to display images using Windows Imaging Component (WIC)

Time to put our learning to use! In this exercise, we will create a Xaml application with DirectX support to render a bitmap to screen. In our exercise, our bitmap is actually provided by a JPG file that is included in the project solution.

Do not create a C# application here as these types are exposed only to C++ clients.

1. Start by creating a C++ Windows Store Blank XAML project.

2. Let us call our sample, **SiSSample**. Click OK to let Visual Studio generate the solution.

3. Open MainPage.xaml and add the following section in the default <Grid>

```
<StackPanel>
    <Rectangle Height="400" Width="400" x:Name="rectangle1" />
    <Rectangle Height="400" Width="400" x:Name="rectangle2" />
</StackPanel>
```

4. Add a new header file named XamlSis.h. This is accomplished via the Project->Add New Item.

5. Add a new source file named XamlSiS.cpp by clicking on Project->Add New Item.

6. Create a new class named XamlSiS within the SiSSample namespace. This constructor for this class takes 3 parameters: A SurfaceImageSource object and two integers for the width and height of the SurfaceImageSource object that would be created.

7. Add a new public method to the XamlSiS class, DrawD2DImage. This function accepts a single parameter of type String^. This string parameter is used to pass the name of the image (JPG) file that will be drawn on screen.

8. Add two helper functions with protected scope and returning void:

    a. void CreateDeviceIndependentResources(SurfaceImageSource^ surfaceImageSource);

    b. void CreateDeviceResources();

9. Next, we will add a few D2D and D3D smart pointers to our class. These objects are used to do the actual image decoding and drawing on screen.

Microsoft::WRL::ComPtr<ISurfaceImageSourceNative>   m_sisNative;

Microsoft::WRL::ComPtr<ID3D11Device>   m_d3dDevice;

Microsoft::WRL::ComPtr<ID3D11DeviceContext>   m_d3dContext;

Microsoft::WRL::ComPtr<ID2D1DeviceContext>   m_d2dContext;

Microsoft::WRL::ComPtr<ID2D1LinearGradientBrush>   m_d2dBrush;

Microsoft::WRL::ComPtr<IWICImagingFactory>   m_pIWICFactory;

Microsoft::WRL::ComPtr<ID2D1Bitmap>   m_pD2DBitmap;

Microsoft::WRL::ComPtr<IWICFormatConverter>   m_pConvertedSourceBitmap;

10. In the CreateDeviceIndependentResources function, you should QueryInterface (QI) for the ISurfaceImageSource interface on the SurfaceImageSource^ runtime object instance that is passed. In order to successfully QI, you should first obtain the IInspectable interface pointer from the runtime object. This is achieved by making a call to the **GetInspectable** function.

11. We will now implement our actual drawing routine, in the DrawD2DImage function in the XamlSiS.cpp file.

12. All drawing operations should be enclosed within matching **BeginDraw** and **EndDraw** calls on the SiS object. In our example, we will begin the image decoding after making a call to **BeginDraw**.

13. We obtain a pointer to the WIC decoder by calling the CreateDecoderFromFilename function on the IWICImagingFactory interface pointer, m_pIWICFactory. Upon success, it returns an IWICBitmapDecoder* that will be used to retrieve the first frame of the image from the decoder.

14. Once we successfully obtain a frame, we convert it to a matching pixel format, in our case 32bppPBGRA.

15. Once we convert the frame to a matching pixel format, we convert the WIC Bitmap to a D2D Bitmap. The D2D bitmap is the bitmap we will use to draw the content on screen.

16. The complete code is available in the **SiSSample** sample. The following listing shows the DrawD2DImage function.

LISTING 4-2 Listing for the DrawD2DImage function in the SiSSample solution.

```
void XamlSiS::DrawD2DImage(String^ fileName)
{
    // calculate area of update rect
    RECT updateRect;
    updateRect.left = 0;
    updateRect.top = 0;
    updateRect.right = _width;
    updateRect.bottom = _height;

    POINT offset;
    ComPtr<IDXGISurface> surface;
    // begin drawing
    HRESULT beginDrawHR = m_sisNative->BeginDraw(updateRect, &surface, &offset);
    if (beginDrawHR == DXGI_ERROR_DEVICE_REMOVED || beginDrawHR == DXGI_ERROR_DEVICE_REMOVED)
    {
            //re-create the device here
            CreateDeviceResources();
            return DrawD2DImage(fileName);
    }
    else
    {
            ThrowIfFailed(beginDrawHR);
    }

    ComPtr<ID2D1Bitmap1> bitmap;
    ThrowIfFailed(
     m_d2dContext->CreateBitmapFromDxgiSurface(surface.Get(), nullptr, &bitmap)
    );

    //decode the file here
    //*****************************************************************
    HRESULT hr = S_OK;
    // Step 1: Decode the source image
     // Create a decoder
     IWICBitmapDecoder *pDecoder = nullptr;

     hr = m_pIWICFactory->CreateDecoderFromFilename(
        fileName->Data(),                      // Image to be decoded
        nullptr,                               // Do not prefer a particular vendor
        GENERIC_READ,                          // Desired read access to the file
        WICDecodeMetadataCacheOnDemand,        // Cache metadata when needed
        &pDecoder                              // Pointer to the decoder
        );

    // Retrieve the first frame of the image from the decoder
    IWICBitmapFrameDecode *pFrame = nullptr;

    if (SUCCEEDED(hr))
    {
```

```
            hr = pDecoder->GetFrame(0, &pFrame);
        }

        //Step 2: Format convert the frame to 32bppPBGRA
        if (SUCCEEDED(hr))
        {
            m_pConvertedSourceBitmap = nullptr;
            hr = m_pIWICFactory->CreateFormatConverter(&m_pConvertedSourceBitmap);
        }

        if (SUCCEEDED(hr))
        {
            hr = m_pConvertedSourceBitmap->Initialize(
                pFrame,                         // Input bitmap to convert
                GUID_WICPixelFormat32bppPBGRA,  // Destination pixel format
                WICBitmapDitherTypeNone,        // Specified dither pattern
                nullptr,                            // Specify a particular palette
                0.f,                            // Alpha threshold
                WICBitmapPaletteTypeCustom      // Palette translation type
                );
        }

        if (SUCCEEDED(hr))
        {
            // Need to release the previous D2DBitmap if there is one
            m_pD2DBitmap = nullptr;
            hr = m_d2dContext->CreateBitmapFromWicBitmap(m_pConvertedSourceBitmap.Get(), nullptr,
&m_pD2DBitmap);
        }
        pDecoder->Release();
        pFrame->Release();

        //**************************************************************
        m_d2dContext->BeginDraw();
        m_d2dContext->SetTarget(bitmap.Get());
        // clear with background color. Note this will eventually clip to the update
        //   area when the D3D guard rect is implemented
        m_d2dContext->SetTransform(D2D1::Matrix3x2F::Identity());
        m_d2dContext->Clear(D2D1::ColorF(D2D1::ColorF::White));
        // D2DBitmap may have been released due to device loss.
        // If so, re-create it from the source bitmap
        if (m_pConvertedSourceBitmap && !m_pD2DBitmap)
        {
            m_d2dContext->CreateBitmapFromWicBitmap(m_pConvertedSourceBitmap.Get(), nullptr, &m_pD2DBitmap);
        }
        // Create a rectangle same size of current window
        D2D1_RECT_F rectangle = D2D1::RectF(offset.x,
            offset.y,
            offset.x + (updateRect.right - updateRect.left),
            offset.y + (updateRect.bottom - updateRect.top));

        // Draws an image and scales it to the current window size
        if (m_pD2DBitmap)
        {
                m_d2dContext->DrawBitmap(m_pD2DBitmap.Get(), rectangle);
```

```
    }

    // clear target, end drawing
    m_d2dContext->SetTarget(nullptr);
    ThrowIfFailed(
    m_d2dContext->EndDraw()
    );
    ThrowIfFailed(
    m_sisNative->EndDraw()
    );
}
```

VirtualSurfaceImageSource

The VirtualSurfaceImageSource (VSiS) type extends the SurfaceImageSource by providing support for virtualization. Virtualization enables the framework to draw areas of a surface only when they become visible on the screen.

The VSiS is particularly useful in situations where you want to display complex content that is larger than the screen, especially content that can be zoomed and panned. Examples of such apps include mapping applications, fixed format document viewers, medical imaging applications etc. Applications such as these frequently include content that can be many times larger than the maximum possible resolution available on your average computer monitor. When you use a VSiS, you let the framework do all the hard work of tracking the surface area that is visible on screen at any time. That said there is no loss of control, you can always overlay additional XAML or DirectX rendered content.

The XAML team designed the VSiS with performance as their number one priority. The VSiS uses a tiling and callback architecture to implement virtualization. When you create a VSiS and fill it up with your custom DirectX content, the VSiS is split up into small grids called "tiles" behind the scenes. XAML then proceeds to keep track of which tiles are visible on screen plus a few extra buffer tiles versus the tiles that are not visible on screen and not part of the internal buffer it maintains. The extra buffer tiles are needed to keep panning smooth: Imagine a user panning content and your app being forced to draw content as tiles become visible on screen. In order to enable smooth panning and fluid performance, the framework buffers some tiles so they need not be rendered as they become visible on screen. As more tiles come into view, the framework calls back into your app, via a callback your app has previously registered, to provide the content for these newly visible tiles.

This virtualization approach provides a great boost to the performance of applications. Since the framework caches application content, this content is reused automatically when needed later. What's more, the framework also optimizes memory usage and recycles memory used for stale regions after a certain amount of time. This approach works amazingly well when you place your VSiS content in a XAML ScrollViewer to enable smooth panning. You can create a VSiS in a similar manner to creating a SiS.

XAML + DX Apps using VSiS – The Magazine App

A very good example of developing a XAML-DirectX app is the Direct2D Magazine application that can be downloaded along with the code samples accompanying this book. The sample demonstrates how to build a magazine-style presentation layout using XAML, Direct2D, the Windows Imaging Components (WIC), DirectWrite and written using C++ /CX.

A C++ developer wishing to take advantage of the great synergies between XAML and DirectX (which by the way is one of the advantages of using C++ to develop XAML apps) would use any one of the following combinations thus provided by the platform.

- Render 2D/3D graphics using DirectX

- Integrate XAML with DirectX using VSiS

- Use XAML controls to create layouts conducive to the app scenario.

- If loading of application specific fonts is required, then load fonts using DirectWrite

- Use WIC for encoding/decoding image files.

- Take advantage of the effects APIs provided by Direct2D

- And many more.

Let us begin our exploration of the app with the UI layout.

Using a XML document to layout UI

The XML document that serves as a template to layout UI based on aspect ratios is stored in a file named Sample.story. The story file contains a <story> element that serves as the root of the content. It can host content via the <resource> elements, which can be images or text or brush types and <design> elements that define the UI to layout based on the target device aspect ratio. A <design> element accepts a page-width and page-height attribute making the layouting easy.

The Document class is used to load and parse the story file and create the appropriate class instances. The list of classes that are instantiated include: an Element class, a Story class, a Design class and a Renderer class. Some of these class objects, in turn, instantiate other class objects such as Image-File to load image data and Image class to render the image files using WIC.

The important methods of the Document class are LoadAsync which loads the story file asynchronously and Parse. Parse actually parses the XML document to an element tree and then binds various resources to the element needing resources such as image or text.

LISTING 4-3 The Document class LoadAsync method

```
task<void> Document::LoadAsync()
{
    // Get the document file from the storage location
    return task<StorageFile^>(m_location->GetFileAsync(m_fileName)).then([=](StorageFile^ file)
```

```
    {
        auto xmlDocument = ref new XmlDocument();
        return xmlDocument->LoadFromFileAsync(file);

    }).then([=](XmlDocument^ loadedXml)
    {
        m_rootXml = loadedXml->SelectSingleNode("story");

        // Create a font loader and start loading all the font files in the document location.
        m_fontLoader = new FontLoader(m_location, m_dwriteFactory.Get());
        return m_fontLoader->LoadAsync();

    }).then([=]()
    {
        // Register the font loader to DirectWrite factory
        // The loaders are needed to load custom fonts used within the document.
        DX::ThrowIfFailed(
            m_dwriteFactory->RegisterFontCollectionLoader(m_fontLoader.Get())
            );

        DX::ThrowIfFailed(
            m_dwriteFactory->RegisterFontFileLoader(m_fontLoader.Get())
            );
    });
}
```

LISTING 4-4 The Document class Parse method

```
void Document::Parse()
{
    if (m_rootXml != nullptr)
    {
        Story^ rootElement = Element::Create<Story>(this, m_rootXml);

        if (rootElement != nullptr)
        {
            TreeIterator<Element> it(rootElement);
            do
            {
                if (!(it.GetCurrentNode())->BindResource(rootElement))
                    return;

            } while (++it);

            m_rootElement = rootElement;
        }
    }
}
```

The Resource class represents an instance of a <resource> element. Its main functionality is to identify if the child element is of type image or text and add the child element to the element collection.

LISTING 4-5 The Resource class AcceptChildNode method

```
bool Resource::AcceptChildNode(
    _In_ Document^ document,
    _In_ IXmlNode^ childXmlNode
    )
{
    if (childXmlNode->NodeType == NodeType::ElementNode)
    {
        XmlElement^ xmlElement = dynamic_cast<XmlElement^>(childXmlNode);

        Element^ child = nullptr;
        Platform::String^ elementName = xmlElement->TagName;

        if (elementName != nullptr)
        {
            if (elementName == "image")
            {
                child = Element::Create<::Image>(document, childXmlNode);
            }
            else if (elementName == "text")
            {
                child = Element::Create<Text>(document, childXmlNode);
            }
        }

        if (child == nullptr)
        {
            return false;
        }

        AddChild(child);
    }

    return true;
}
```

The Image class is used to render image files using WIC. The actual work of rendering image file content is performed in the DrawBitmap function of the Image class.

LISTING 4-6 Rendering image files using the DrawBitmap method

```
bool ::Image::DrawBitmap(
    _In_ Renderer^ renderer,
    D2D1::Matrix3x2F const& transform,
    D2D1_RECT_F const& destinationBounds,
    D2D1_RECT_F const& bitmapBounds
    )
{
    ComPtr<ID2D1DeviceContext> d2dDeviceContext;
    ComPtr<IWICImagingFactory2> wicFactory;

    // Obtain Direct2D device context and WIC imaging factory
    renderer->GetD2DDeviceContext(&d2dDeviceContext);
    renderer->GetWICImagingFactory(&wicFactory);
```

```
if (m_bitmap == nullptr)
{
    if (!m_file->Ready())
    {
        // The image file is still be loaded, requesting redraw upon return.
        return true;
    }

    // Use Windows Imaging Component to decode an image file into a
    // WIC bitmap and then make a copy as a Direct2D bitmap in video
    // memory.
    ComPtr<IWICBitmapDecoder> decoder;
    ComPtr<IWICBitmapFrameDecode> frame;
    ComPtr<IWICFormatConverter> wicBitmap;

    DX::ThrowIfFailed(
        wicFactory->CreateDecoderFromStream(
            m_file.Get(),
            nullptr,
            WICDecodeMetadataCacheOnDemand,
            &decoder
            )
        );

    DX::ThrowIfFailed(
        decoder->GetFrame(0, &frame)
        );

    DX::ThrowIfFailed(
        wicFactory->CreateFormatConverter(&wicBitmap)
        );

    DX::ThrowIfFailed(
        wicBitmap->Initialize(
            frame.Get(),
            GUID_WICPixelFormat32bppPBGRA,
            WICBitmapDitherTypeNone,
            nullptr,
            0,
            WICBitmapPaletteTypeCustom
            )
        );

    DX::ThrowIfFailed(
        d2dDeviceContext->CreateBitmapFromWicBitmap(
            wicBitmap.Get(),
            D2D1::BitmapProperties(
                D2D1::PixelFormat(),
                96.0,
                96.0
                ),
            &m_bitmap
            )
        );
```

```
    }

    d2dDeviceContext->SetTransform(transform);

    d2dDeviceContext->DrawBitmap(
        m_bitmap.Get(),
        &destinationBounds,
        1.0f,
        D2D1_INTERPOLATION_MODE_HIGH_QUALITY_CUBIC,
        &bitmapBounds
        );

    return false;
}
```

Using DirectWrite in XAML apps

DirectWrite or DWrite is a Microsoft DirectX API that provides support for high-quality text rendering services, resolution-independent fonts, full Unicode text and layout support. As is the norm with DirectX APIs, it DirectWrite a COM-style API. When DWrite is used in conjunction with Direct2D, the result is hardware-accelerated text.

The FontLoader class implements the necessary DWrite interfaces: IDWriteFontCollectionLoader, IDWriteFontFileEnumerator and IDWriteFontFileLoader. These interfaces enable the DWrite to call/load application specific fonts.

The FontLoader class is defined as below. The most important method in this class is the LoadAsync, which does the actual job of parsing the pre-determined fonts folder and loading all the application specific fonts.

LISTING 4-7 The FontLoader class

```
class FontLoader :  public IDWriteFontCollectionLoader,
                    public IDWriteFontFileEnumerator,
                    public IDWriteFontFileLoader
{
public:
    FontLoader(
        _In_ Windows::Storage::StorageFolder^ location,
        _In_ IDWriteFactory* dwriteFactory
        );

    concurrency::task<void> LoadAsync();

    // IUnknown
    virtual HRESULT STDMETHODCALLTYPE QueryInterface(
        REFIID uuid,
        _Outptr_ void** object
        ) override;

    virtual ULONG STDMETHODCALLTYPE AddRef() override;
```

```
    virtual ULONG STDMETHODCALLTYPE Release() override;

    // IDWriteFontCollectionLoader
    virtual HRESULT STDMETHODCALLTYPE CreateEnumeratorFromKey(
        _In_ IDWriteFactory* factory,
        _In_reads_bytes_(fontCollectionKeySize) void const* fontCollectionKey,
        uint32 fontCollectionKeySize,
        _Outptr_ IDWriteFontFileEnumerator** fontFileEnumerator
        ) override;

    // IDWriteFontFileEnumerator
    virtual HRESULT STDMETHODCALLTYPE MoveNext(OUT BOOL* hasCurrentFile) override;

    virtual HRESULT STDMETHODCALLTYPE GetCurrentFontFile(OUT IDWriteFontFile** currentFontFile) override;

    // IDWriteFontFileLoader
    virtual HRESULT STDMETHODCALLTYPE CreateStreamFromKey(
        _In_reads_bytes_(fontFileReferenceKeySize) void const* fontFileReferenceKey,
        uint32 fontFileReferenceKeySize,
        _Outptr_ IDWriteFontFileStream** fontFileStream
        ) override;

private:
    // Reference counter
    ULONG m_refCount;

    // Storage location of the font file(s) to load
    Windows::Storage::StorageFolder^ m_location;

    // Number of font files in the storage location
    size_t m_fontFileCount;

    // A list of font file streams loaded
    std::vector<Microsoft::WRL::ComPtr<FontFileStream>> m_fontFileStreams;

    // Index to the current font file stream in the loaded list
    size_t m_fontFileStreamIndex;

    // Current DirectWrite font file being indexed
    Microsoft::WRL::ComPtr<IDWriteFontFile> m_currentFontFile;

    // DirectWrite factory
    Microsoft::WRL::ComPtr<IDWriteFactory> m_dwriteFactory;
};
```

Outside of the LoadAsync method, there are the usual methods of the interfaces that the FontLoader class implements plus helper member variables to keep track of the current font being loaded, the font stream corresponding to the font and a variable to store the DWrite factory instance itself. It is important to note here that the lifetime of the font loader is tied to the factory it is registered to.

The LoadAsync method navigates through a folder named "fonts" and loads all the files ending with a .ttf extension. The application is hardcoded to lookup for the "fonts" folder within the ApplicationData folder and will not search for the "fonts" folder anywhere else. Once it obtains the location of the "fonts" folder, it searches for all files ending with a ".ttf" extension and populates a vector with them, represented by the WinRT IVectorView type.

Once the font vector is initialized, each of the fonts are read into a buffer. Finally a FontFileStream instance is created for each font file whose data is stored in the buffer specific to the font.

LISTING 4-8 Loading font files via the FontLoader's LoadAsync method

```
task<void> FontLoader::LoadAsync()
{
    // Locate the "fonts" sub-folder within the document folder
    return task<StorageFolder^>(m_location->GetFolderAsync("fonts")).then([=](StorageFolder^ folder)
    {
        // Enumerate a list of .TTF files in the storage location
        auto filters = ref new Platform::Collections::Vector<Platform::String^>();
        filters->Append(".ttf");

        auto queryOptions = ref new QueryOptions(CommonFileQuery::DefaultQuery, filters);
        auto queryResult = folder->CreateFileQueryWithOptions(queryOptions);

        return queryResult->GetFilesAsync();

    }).then([=](IVectorView<StorageFile^>^ files)
    {
        m_fontFileCount = files->Size;

        std::vector<task<IBuffer^>> tasks;

        for (uint32 i = 0; i < m_fontFileCount; ++i)
        {
            auto file = dynamic_cast<StorageFile^>(files->GetAt(i));

            tasks.push_back(task<IBuffer^>(FileIO::ReadBufferAsync(file)));
        }

        return when_all(tasks.begin(), tasks.end());

    }).then([=](std::vector<IBuffer^> buffers)
    {
        for each (IBuffer^ buffer in buffers)
        {
            auto fileData = ref new Platform::Array<byte>(buffer->Length);
            DataReader::FromBuffer(buffer)->ReadBytes(fileData);

            ComPtr<FontFileStream> fontFileStream(new FontFileStream(fileData));
            m_fontFileStreams.push_back(fontFileStream);
        }
    });
}
```

The FontFileStream class implements the IDwriteFontFileStream interface and is used to read font data in chunks as needed by the application. The ability to read font file data in chunks is provided by the ReadFileFragment method.

LISTING 4-9 Reading font file stream in chunks

```
HRESULT STDMETHODCALLTYPE FontFileStream::ReadFileFragment(
    _Outptr_result_bytebuffer_(fragmentSize) void const** fragmentStart,
    UINT64 fileOffset,
    UINT64 fragmentSize,
    _Out_ void** fragmentContext
    )
{
    // The loader is responsible for doing a bounds check.
    if (    fileOffset <= m_data->Length
        && fragmentSize + fileOffset <= m_data->Length
        )
    {
        *fragmentStart = m_data->Data + static_cast<ULONG>(fileOffset);
        *fragmentContext = nullptr;
        return S_OK;
    }
    else
    {
        *fragmentStart = nullptr;
        *fragmentContext = nullptr;
        return E_FAIL;
    }
}
```

The VSiS implementation class - ContentImageSource

The PageModel class binds content worth of one page to one instance of a VirtualSur-faceImageSource. The VSiS is implemented in the ContentImageSource class. In the Magazine app, the page model assumes a layering of UI elements. Each layer is represented by a <layer> attribute in the story file. The first <layer> content of the <page> is the background and the next <layer> is the foreground. The PageModel also exposes the size of the content it binds. This is extremely important as the VSiS needs to be aware of the size of the content. The size of the content should match the size of the UI element hosting the content, in our case, a FlipViewItem. If the sizes do not match, then the content is stretched to fit.

The ContentImageSource class implements the IVirtualSurfaceUpdatesCallbackNative interface that provides the UpdatesNeeded method. The UpdatesNeeded callback method is called whenever the application needs to populate new content to the source when a repainting event occurs.

LISTING 4-10 ContentImageSource class defintion

```
class ContentImageSource : public IVirtualSurfaceUpdatesCallbackNative
{
public:
    ContentImageSource(
        _In_ Element^ content,
        _In_ Document^ document,
        bool isOpaque
```

```
        );

    virtual HRESULT STDMETHODCALLTYPE UpdatesNeeded() override;
    ….
}
```

The Initialize method of the ContentImageSource class creates a new instance of a VSiS as per the bounds of the UI element it is hosted in. It then obtains a reference to the Renderer class and sets the DXGI device to the image source. Finally, it registers the callback with the image source so that updates can be made.

LISTING 4-11 Initializing the VSiS and the native callback method

```
void ContentImageSource::Initialize()
{
    // Measure the content and store its size.
    Measure(&m_contentSize);

    // Create an image source at the initial pixel size.
    // The last parameter helps improve rendering performance when the image source is known to be opaque.
    m_imageSource = ref new VirtualSurfaceImageSource(m_contentSize.cx, m_contentSize.cy, m_isOpaque);

    ComPtr<IUnknown> unknown(reinterpret_cast<IUnknown*>(m_imageSource));
    unknown.As(&m_imageSourceNative);

    auto renderer = m_document->GetRenderer();

    // Set DXGI device to the image source
    ComPtr<IDXGIDevice> dxgiDevice;
    renderer->GetDXGIDevice(&dxgiDevice);
    m_imageSourceNative->SetDevice(dxgiDevice.Get());

    // Register image source's update callback so update can be made to it.
    m_imageSourceNative->RegisterForUpdatesNeeded(this);
}
```

So what happens when content needs to be drawn or when the UI element needs to be repainted? The ContentImageSource instance gets a callback on the UpdatesNeeded method. In the UpdatesNeeded method, we query the image source for the number of rects (tiles) to be updated and then proceed to draw into the rects one by one.

LISTING 4-12 Handling the updates needed callback

```
HRESULT STDMETHODCALLTYPE ContentImageSource::UpdatesNeeded()
{
    HRESULT hr = S_OK;

    try
    {
        ULONG drawingBoundsCount = 0;

        DX::ThrowIfFailed(
            m_imageSourceNative->GetUpdateRectCount(&drawingBoundsCount)
```

```
                );

            std::unique_ptr<RECT[]> drawingBounds(new RECT[drawingBoundsCount]);

            DX::ThrowIfFailed(
                m_imageSourceNative->GetUpdateRects(drawingBounds.get(), drawingBoundsCount)
                );

            for (ULONG i = 0; i < drawingBoundsCount; ++i)
            {
                if (Draw(drawingBounds[i]))
                {
                    // Drawing isn't complete. This can happen when the content is still being
                    // asynchronously loaded. Inform the image source to invalidate the drawing
                    // bounds so that it calls back to redraw.
                    DX::ThrowIfFailed(
                        m_imageSourceNative->Invalidate(drawingBounds[i])
                        );
                }
            }
        }
    }
    catch (Platform::Exception^ exception)
    {
        hr = exception->HResult;

        if (hr == D2DERR_RECREATE_TARGET ||
            hr == DXGI_ERROR_DEVICE_REMOVED)
        {
            // If a device lost error is encountered, notify the renderer. The renderer will then
            // recreate the device and fire the DeviceLost event so that all listeners can take
            // an appropriate action.
            m_document->GetRenderer()->HandleDeviceLost();

            // Invalidate the image source so that it calls back to redraw
            RECT bounds = { 0, 0, m_contentSize.cx, m_contentSize.cy };
            m_imageSourceNative->Invalidate(bounds);
        }
    }

    return hr;
}
```

LISTING 4-13 Performing the actual drawing operation for updated tiles

```
bool ContentImageSource::Draw(RECT const& drawingBounds)
{
    ComPtr<IDXGISurface> dxgiSurface;
    POINT surfaceOffset = {0};
    bool needRedraw;

    HRESULT hr = S_OK;
    {
        // If the underlying device is lost, the virtual surface image source may return a
        // device lost error from BeginDraw. In this case, the error will be thrown here
        // and caught in UpdatesNeeded
```

```
    ImageSourceDrawHelper imageSourceDrawHelper(
        m_imageSourceNative.Get(),
        drawingBounds,
        &dxgiSurface,
        &surfaceOffset,
        &hr
        );

    auto renderer = m_document->GetRenderer();

    ComPtr<ID2D1DeviceContext> d2dDeviceContext;
    renderer->GetD2DDeviceContext(&d2dDeviceContext);

    ComPtr<ID2D1Bitmap1> bitmap;
    DX::ThrowIfFailed(
        d2dDeviceContext->CreateBitmapFromDxgiSurface(
            dxgiSurface.Get(),
            nullptr,
            &bitmap
            )
        );

    // Begin the drawing batch
    d2dDeviceContext->BeginDraw();

    // Scale content design coordinate to the display coordinate,
    // then translate the drawing to the designated place on the surface.
    D2D1::Matrix3x2F transform =
        D2D1::Matrix3x2F::Scale(
            m_document->DesignToDisplayWidth(1.0f),
            m_document->DesignToDisplayHeight(1.0f)
            ) *
        D2D1::Matrix3x2F::Translation(
            static_cast<float>(surfaceOffset.x - drawingBounds.left),
            static_cast<float>(surfaceOffset.y - drawingBounds.top)
            );

    // Prepare to draw content. This is the appropriate time for content element
    // to draw to an intermediate if there is any. It is important for performance
    // reason that SetTarget isn't called too frequently. Preparing the intermediates
    // upfront reduces the number of times the render target switches back and forth.
    needRedraw = m_content->PrepareToDraw(
        m_document,
        transform
        );

    if (!needRedraw)
    {
        // Set the render target to surface given by the framework
        d2dDeviceContext->SetTarget(bitmap.Get());

        d2dDeviceContext->SetTransform(D2D1::IdentityMatrix());

        // Constrain the drawing only to the designated portion of the surface
        d2dDeviceContext->PushAxisAlignedClip(
```

```
            D2D1::RectF(
                static_cast<float>(surfaceOffset.x),
                static_cast<float>(surfaceOffset.y),
                static_cast<float>(surfaceOffset.x + (drawingBounds.right - drawingBounds.left)),
                static_cast<float>(surfaceOffset.y + (drawingBounds.bottom - drawingBounds.top))
                ),
            D2D1_ANTIALIAS_MODE_ALIASED
            );

        d2dDeviceContext->Clear(D2D1::ColorF(0, 0));

        // Draw the content
        needRedraw = m_content->Draw(
            m_document,
            transform
            );

        d2dDeviceContext->PopAxisAlignedClip();

        d2dDeviceContext->SetTarget(nullptr);
    }

    // End the drawing
    // UpdatesNeeded handles D2DERR_RECREATETARGET, so it is okay to throw this error here.
    DX::ThrowIfFailed(
        d2dDeviceContext->EndDraw()
        );
    }

    DX::ThrowIfFailed(hr);

    return needRedraw;
}
```

Running the sample

Once you have the solution open in Visual Studio 2012, you can build the code and deploy the application. Tapping the Magazine App tile on the Start screen launches the app and displays a UI in a FlipView with two articles. You can pan horizontally across the screen to move between articles and then pan vertically within an article to read content that is overflowing beyond the viewport dimensions.

If you attach a debugger to the application and set a breakpoint on the ContentImageSource::UpdatesNeeded method, you will see that the UpdatesNeeded callback gets called whenever you pan (either horizontally or vertically) and the tiles that need to be updated/rendered are computed and only those tiles are re-painted. Painting only the portions of screen that needs to be updated allows you to save both time and CPU/GPU cycles thereby minimizing power consumption, a good optimization in the mobile device world we live in today!

FIGURE 4-1 Output of the Magazine app using a VSiS

Design considerations when using SiS and VSiS

Using DX Interop types to get maximum performance in your app might sound very tempting. There are, however, a few things to consider before you go down the road of mixing DirectX and XAML.

1. DirectX version differences: Be aware of the feature differences between various versions of DirectX. Consider carefully what version of DirectX you would like to target and make sure you test your app for any issues or dependency on later versions of DirectX.

2. Hardware limitation: If your app allows users to zoom using DirectManipulation, be aware that the underlying hardware might have limits on the maximum dimensions on textures that can be created successfully.

3. Creating SiS and VSiS elements: Do not create too many SiS or VSiS layers as frequent creation and destruction of such elements unnecessarily stresses the GPU.

4. Testing your app: Test your app thoroughly to make sure that video memory consumption remains within limits and your app remains responsive to user input at all times.

SwapChainBackgroundPanel

The SwapChainBackgroundPanel is the third API that enables XAML and DirectX composition. Unlike the SiS and VSiS, the SwapChainBackgroundPanel is a full-fledged XAML type. It inherits from the XAML Grid panel and enables applications to have fine grained control over a DirectX swap chain. All the XAML controls are overlaid on top of this swap chain. It is to be noted that the SwapChainBackgroundPanel is the recommended way for developing Windows Store apps having a primary focus on DirectX content such as games.

Using this API in a game enables you to eke out great performance and have an update model similar to pure DirectX apps. At the same time, you can also use XAML to create UI elements such as AppBars and Heads up Display (HUD). You also get the benefit of using data binding too. There are a few restrictions that are placed on the usage of the SwapChainBackgroundPanel.

1. The **SwapChainBackgroundPanel** must be the root XAML element in your app.

2. There can only be one instance of a **SwapChainBackgroundPanel** per app.

3. The **SwapChainBackgroundPanel** is at the bottom of the z-list for the user interface, below all of the XAML elements. (This means that all XAML elements are drawn over the presented contents of the swap chain.)

4. XAML properties such as **Opacity** and **RenderTransform** will not have any effect over the swap chain.

5. You can however, use DirectX functions to apply desired properties and effects to your swap chain.

The DrawIt Application – C++, XAML and DirectX

We have covered a lot of ground in our journey thus far. We explored the new Application Model, the extensions to the C++ programming language, discussed about XAML and its great integration points with DirectX. It is now time to put all the hard learning to use. We will now go through a step by step approach to creating a drawing application using C++, XAML and DirectX. The goal of this application is to allow our users draw on canvas using either touch, mouse, pen/stylus or keyboard. The application allows them to change colors and the thickness of the brush strokes. Once the users are satisfied with making good use of their creative juices they can save the drawing to disk in one of multiple formats: BMP, JPG or PNG. Finally, users can also share their drawing using the Share charm.

Let us now break down the various user interface requirements we need to build this app.

*   An ApplicationBar with options for changing color, brush size, saving the drawing and sharing with other applications.

- The colors and size options open a flyout with sub menu options. XAML does not ship with a built in flyout control, so we will build one using a UserControl.

- A canvas that can be used to draw content on.

A cautionary note however: The Microsoft SurfaceRT device does not support a stylus type input device. You can use touch to draw in the ARM version but the stylus input is limited to x86/x64 versions of the app. A great example of a machine supporting stylus input is the Microsoft Surface Pro that comes with a stylus.

Creating the Basic Application

Let us begin the development of the application by creating a basic XAML application. We will add the required UI elements to this basic application.

1. Launch Visual Studio 2012.

2. Choose File->New->Project.

3. In the New Project dialog, choose Visual C++->Windows Store apps->Blank App (XAML) as the project template.

4. Provide a name for the project. The sample provided with the book assumes a name DrawIt.

5. Choose a folder to save the solution and click OK.

6. Visual Studio 2012 creates the solution named DrawIt successfully.

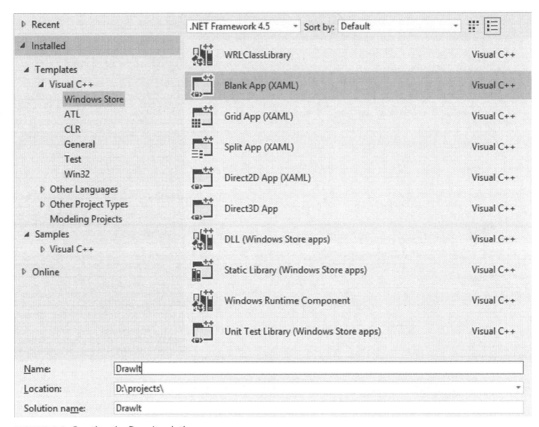

FIGURE 4-2 Creating the DrawIt solution

FIGURE 4-3 The DrawIt solution layout

7. If you build the solution, deploy the app and launch it, you will see a blank screen. Let us now add the various UI elements needed for our app.

8. From the Solution Explorer, locate the MainPage.xaml file.

9. Open the MainPage.xaml file and remove the default generated Grid element. Add a Swap-ChainBackgroundPanel to the Page as below.

```
<SwapChainBackgroundPanel x:Name="DXSwapChainPanel">
</SwapChainBackgroundPanel>
```

10. Add an application bar (AppBar) to the Page as below.

LISTING 4-14 DrawIt Application Bar definition

```
<Page.BottomAppBar>
    <AppBar x:Name="TheAppBar" VerticalAlignment="Bottom" Background="White" Visibility="Collapsed"
IsSticky="true">
        <Grid>
            <StackPanel Grid.Column="0" Orientation="Horizontal" HorizontalAlignment="Left">
                <Border x:Name="AddColorsButtonBorder" Background="White">
                    <Button x:Name="AddColorsButton" Tag="Colors" Click="AddColorsClicked" Style="{StaticResource
ColorsAppBarButtonStyle}" />
                </Border>
                <Border x:Name="ChangeSizeButtonBorder" Background="White">
                    <Button x:Name="ChangeSizeButton" Tag="Size" Click="AddSizeChangeClicked"
Style="{StaticResource ResetAppBarButtonStyle}" />
                </Border>
            </StackPanel>
            <StackPanel Grid.Column="1" Orientation="Horizontal" HorizontalAlignment="Right">
                <Button Tag="Save" Click="SaveClicked" Style="{StaticResource SaveAppBarButtonStyle}" />
                <Button Tag="Share" Click="ShareClicked" Style="{StaticResource ShareAppBarButtonStyle}" />
            </StackPanel>
        </Grid>
    </AppBar>
  </Page.BottomAppBar>
</Page>
```

11. A Page can have an application bar either at the top or bottom. In our example, we have chosen to have a bottom application bar as that is the oft used application bar style in Windows Store apps.

12. With the ApplicationBar, represented by the XAML AppBar class, we have a StackPanel with two buttons, one each for the changing color and changing the brush width.

13. Another StackPanel within the AppBar, contains two buttons, one for saving the drawing and another for Sharing the drawing.

14. We will now define Visual States for the AppBar. Having VisualStates enables us to show/hide the AppBar using smooth animations when the app is running in Full Screen mode or snapped

mode.

15. Add the following VisualState definitions within the SwapChainBackgroundPanel declaration.

LISTING 4-15 Visual State definitions for the XAML SwapChain

```
<VisualStateManager.VisualStateGroups>
  <VisualStateGroup x:Name="DrawItVisualStates">
    <VisualState x:Name="StartingState">
      <Storyboard>
        <ObjectAnimationUsingKeyFrames Storyboard.TargetName="TheAppBar"
Storyboard.TargetProperty="IsOpen">
          <DiscreteObjectKeyFrame KeyTime="00:00:00" Value="False" />
        </ObjectAnimationUsingKeyFrames>
        <ObjectAnimationUsingKeyFrames Storyboard.TargetName="TheAppBar"
Storyboard.TargetProperty="Visibility">
          <DiscreteObjectKeyFrame KeyTime="00:00:01" Value="Visible" />
        </ObjectAnimationUsingKeyFrames>
      </Storyboard>
    </VisualState>
    <VisualState x:Name="ClearState">
      <Storyboard>
        <ObjectAnimationUsingKeyFrames Storyboard.TargetName="TheAppBar"
Storyboard.TargetProperty="IsOpen">
          <DiscreteObjectKeyFrame KeyTime="00:00:00" Value="True" />
        </ObjectAnimationUsingKeyFrames>
        <ObjectAnimationUsingKeyFrames Storyboard.TargetName="TheAppBar"
Storyboard.TargetProperty="Visibility">
          <DiscreteObjectKeyFrame KeyTime="00:00:00" Value="Visible" />
        </ObjectAnimationUsingKeyFrames>
      </Storyboard>
    </VisualState>
    <VisualState x:Name="SnappedState">
      <Storyboard>
        <ObjectAnimationUsingKeyFrames Storyboard.TargetName="TheAppBar"
Storyboard.TargetProperty="IsOpen">
          <DiscreteObjectKeyFrame KeyTime="00:00:00" Value="False" />
        </ObjectAnimationUsingKeyFrames>
        <ObjectAnimationUsingKeyFrames Storyboard.TargetName="TheAppBar"
Storyboard.TargetProperty="Visibility">
          <DiscreteObjectKeyFrame KeyTime="00:00:01" Value="Collapsed" />
        </ObjectAnimationUsingKeyFrames>
      </Storyboard>
    </VisualState>
  </VisualStateGroup>
</VisualStateManager.VisualStateGroups>
```

16. We are more or less complete with our UI elements. All we need now are the Flyouts that represent the submenu options for changing color and brush stroke width.

17. As mentioned above, XAML does not have an in-built flyout control. Let us add a UserControl to our project. This user control will be used to mimic a flyout control.

18. In the Solution Explorer, right click on the DrawIt project and choose Add->New Item.

19. In the Add New Item dialog, choose Visual C++->Windows Store->User Control as the item type.

20. Provide a name for the user control. For our example, we will use ColorsFlyout.

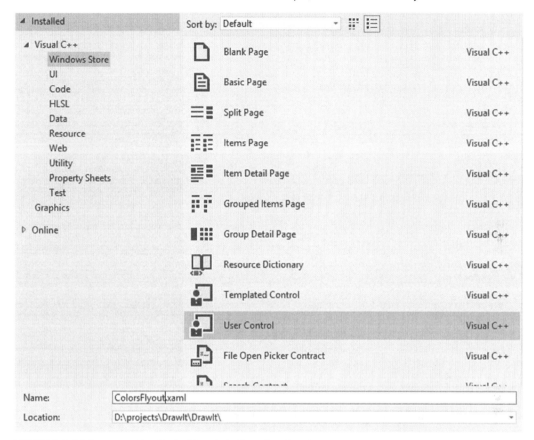

FIGURE 4-4 Adding a new UserControl to mimic the colors flyout

21. In the Solution Explorer, right click on the DrawIt project and choose Add->New Item.

22. In the Add New Item dialog, choose Visual C++->Windows Store->User Control as the item type.

23. Provide a name for the user control. For our example, we will use SizeFlyout.

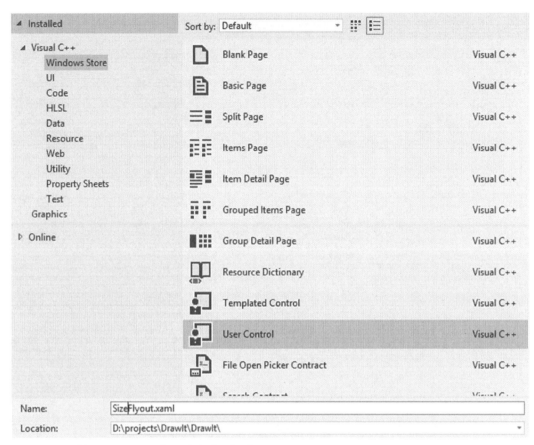

FIGURE 4-5 Adding a user control to mimic the Size flyout

24. The ColorsFlyout displays the colors options: Red and Green.

25. The SizeFlyout displays the size of the brush strokes: 6 point, 8 point and 10 point.

26. Open the ColorsFlyout.xaml file and replace the markup with the markup below. The Colors-Flyout contains a Horizontal-oriented StackPanel with two buttons: Red and Green. Clicking a particular button changes the brush color to the color represented by the button.

LISTING 4-16 The Flyout for the Colors UI

```
<UserControl
    x:Class="DrawIt.ColorsFlyout"
    xmlns="http://schemas.microsoft.com/winfx/2006/xaml/presentation"
    xmlns:x="http://schemas.microsoft.com/winfx/2006/xaml"
    xmlns:local="using:DrawIt"
    xmlns:d="http://schemas.microsoft.com/expression/blend/2008"
    xmlns:mc="http://schemas.openxmlformats.org/markup-compatibility/2006"
    mc:Ignorable="d"
    d:DesignHeight="300"
```

```
    d:DesignWidth="400"
    Height="50">

  <Border BorderThickness="1" BorderBrush="White" Background="Black" Padding="5">
    <StackPanel Orientation="Horizontal">
      <Button Click="RedColorClicked">Red</Button>
      <Button Click="GreenColorClicked">Green</Button>
    </StackPanel>
  </Border>
</UserControl>
```

27. Open the ColorsFlyout.xaml.h file. We will now add events and button click event handlers to the ColorsFlyout class.

28. Declare a delegate of type void that serves as a callback when the color button is clicked in the UI. The delegate should be declared outside the ColorsFlyout class.

```
public delegate void ColorButtonClickedHandler(void);
```

29. Add two ColorButtonClickedHandler events to the ColorsFlyout class: one each for the Red color and Green color buttons. You should add more events if you want to support more colors!

```
event ColorButtonClickedHandler^ RedColorButtonClicked;
event ColorButtonClickedHandler^ GreenColorButtonClicked;
```

30. Add button clicked event handlers for the Red Button and Green button. Finally add a Hide method that hides the buttons.

```
void RedColorClicked(Platform::Object^ sender, Windows::UI::Xaml::RoutedEventArgs^ e);
void GreenColorClicked(Platform::Object^ sender, Windows::UI::Xaml::RoutedEventArgs^ e);
void Hide();
```

31. Open the MainPage.xaml.cpp file and provide an implementation for the button click event handlers as follows:

LISTING 4-17 Handling click event handlers on the Colors Flyout

```
void ColorsFlyout::RedColorClicked(Object^ sender, RoutedEventArgs^ e)
{
    RedColorButtonClicked();
    Hide();
}
void ColorsFlyout::GreenColorClicked(Object^ sender, RoutedEventArgs^ e)
{
    GreenColorButtonClicked();
    Hide();
}
```

32. Finally, implement the Hide method as follows:

LISTING 4-18 Handling the Hide method to mimic soft dismissal

```cpp
void ColorsFlyout::Hide()
{
    Popup^ parent = dynamic_cast<Popup^>(this->Parent);
    if (parent != nullptr)
    {
        parent->IsOpen = false;
    }
}
```

33. Similarly implement delegates and event handlers for the SizeFlyout class. The markup and class implementations are provided below.

LISTING 4-19 The SizeFlyout class

```xml
<UserControl
    x:Class="DrawIt.SizeFlyout"
    xmlns="http://schemas.microsoft.com/winfx/2006/xaml/presentation"
    xmlns:x="http://schemas.microsoft.com/winfx/2006/xaml"
    xmlns:local="using:DrawIt"
    xmlns:d="http://schemas.microsoft.com/expression/blend/2008"
    xmlns:mc="http://schemas.openxmlformats.org/markup-compatibility/2006"
    mc:Ignorable="d"
    d:DesignHeight="300"
    d:DesignWidth="400"
    Height="50">

    <Border BorderThickness="1" BorderBrush="White" Background="Black" Padding="5">
        <StackPanel Orientation="Horizontal">
            <Button Click="SixPointButtonClicked">6Pt</Button>
            <Button Click="EightPointButtonClicked">8Pt</Button>
            <Button Click="TenPointButtonClicked">10Pt</Button>
        </StackPanel>
    </Border>
</UserControl>
```

```cpp
namespace DrawIt
{
    public delegate void SizeButtonClickedHandler(void);

    [Windows::Foundation::Metadata::WebHostHidden]
    public ref class SizeFlyout sealed
    {
    public:
            SizeFlyout();

            event SizeButtonClickedHandler^ SixPtButtonClicked;
            event SizeButtonClickedHandler^ EightPtButtonClicked;
            event SizeButtonClickedHandler^ TenPtButtonClicked;

    private:
            void SixPointButtonClicked(Platform::Object^ sender, Windows::UI::Xaml::RoutedEventArgs^ e);
          void EightPointButtonClicked(Platform::Object^ sender, Windows::UI::Xaml::RoutedEventArgs^ e);
            void TenPointButtonClicked(Platform::Object^ sender, Windows::UI::Xaml::RoutedEventArgs^ e);
```

```
        void Hide();

    };
}



SizeFlyout::SizeFlyout()
{
    InitializeComponent();
}

void SizeFlyout::SixPointButtonClicked(Platform::Object^ sender, Windows::UI::Xaml::RoutedEventArgs^ e)
{
    SixPtButtonClicked();
    Hide();
}

void SizeFlyout::EightPointButtonClicked(Platform::Object^ sender, Windows::UI::Xaml::RoutedEventArgs^ e)
{
    EightPtButtonClicked();
    Hide();
}

void SizeFlyout::TenPointButtonClicked(Platform::Object^ sender, Windows::UI::Xaml::RoutedEventArgs^ e)
{
    TenPtButtonClicked();
    Hide();
}

void SizeFlyout::Hide()
{
    Popup^ parent = dynamic_cast<Popup^>(this->Parent);
    if (parent != nullptr)
    {
        parent->IsOpen = false;
    }
}
```

34. We will now have to wire these flyouts to our main UI. Back to MainPage.xaml

35. In the MainPage.xaml, add two popup elements to the SwapChainBackgroundPanel as shown below.

LISTING 4-20 Hooking up the Flyouts to the main UI

```
<Popup x:Name="ColorsPopup" IsOpen="False" IsLightDismissEnabled="True">
    <Popup.ChildTransitions>
      <TransitionCollection>
        <PopupThemeTransition/>
      </TransitionCollection>
    </Popup.ChildTransitions>
```

```
        <local:ColorsFlyout x:Name="ColorsFlyout" RedColorButtonClicked="RedColorClicked"
GreenColorButtonClicked="GreenColorClicked"/>
    </Popup>

    <Popup x:Name="SizePopup" IsOpen="False" IsLightDismissEnabled="True">
      <Popup.ChildTransitions>
        <TransitionCollection>
          <PopupThemeTransition/>
        </TransitionCollection>
      </Popup.ChildTransitions>
      <local:SizeFlyout x:Name="SizeFlyout" SixPtButtonClicked="SixPointButtonClicked"
EightPtButtonClicked="EightPointButtonClicked" TenPtButtonClicked="TenPointButtonClicked"/>
    </Popup>
```

36. Add event handlers to the MainPage class in MainPage.xaml.h. These event handlers correspond to the various AppBar buttons and flyout buttons in the AppBar.

LISTING 4-21 Declaring event handlers in the MainPage header

```
void AddColorsClicked(Platform::Object^ sender, Windows::UI::Xaml::RoutedEventArgs^ e);
void RedColorClicked();
void GreenColorClicked();
void SaveClicked(Platform::Object^ sender, Windows::UI::Xaml::RoutedEventArgs^ e);
void ShareClicked(Platform::Object^ sender, Windows::UI::Xaml::RoutedEventArgs^ e);

void AddSizeChangeClicked(Platform::Object^ sender, Windows::UI::Xaml::RoutedEventArgs^ e);
void SixPointButtonClicked();
void EightPointButtonClicked();
void TenPointButtonClicked();
```

37. Add the place holders for the event handlers in MainPage.xaml.cpp.

LISTING 4-22 Declaring place holder implementation for event handlers

```
void MainPage::AddColorsClicked(Object^ sender, RoutedEventArgs^ e)
{
}

void MainPage::RedColorClicked()
{
}

void MainPage::GreenColorClicked()
{
}

void MainPage::SaveClicked(Object^ sender, RoutedEventArgs^ e)
{
}

void MainPage::ShareClicked(Object^ sender, RoutedEventArgs^ e)
{
}

void MainPage::AddSizeChangeClicked(Platform::Object^ sender, Windows::UI::Xaml::RoutedEventArgs^ e)
```

```
{
}

void MainPage::SixPointButtonClicked()
{
}

void MainPage::EightPointButtonClicked()
{
}

void MainPage::TenPointButtonClicked()
{
}
```

38. If you compile the solution and launch the app now, you will see a blank screen with the AppBar displayed upon app launch. Clicking the various options in the AppBar do not do anything special as we have not implemented the functionality.

FIGURE 4-6 Default App launch

Adding DirectX support

In order to add DirectX support, either 2D or 3D rendering, we will re-use a helper class from the SDK Samples, DirectXBase. This class will serve as a base class for our rendering class, ShapeRenderer later on. The DirectXBase class contains helper functions for initializing Direct3D, Direct2D and DWrite. We do not need support for DWrite in our sample app, hence we can safely remove code related to DWrite.

The important functions from DirectXBase are given below:

- Initialize: Function to initialize the underlying Direct3D device and save the XAML SwapChainBackgroundPanel instance. The XAML SwapChainBackgroundPanel instance will be used when initializing the Direct3D device and will be associated to the device swap chain.

LISTING 4-23 The DirectXBase Initialize method

```
// Initialize the DirectX resources required to run.
void DirectXBase::Initialize(CoreWindow^ window, SwapChainBackgroundPanel^ swapChainPanel, float dpi)
{
    m_window = window;
    m_swapChainPanel = swapChainPanel;
    CreateDeviceIndependentResources();
    CreateDeviceResources();
    SetDpi(dpi);
}
```

- CreateDeviceIndependentResources: Function to initialize resources that are not dependent on the Direct3D device instance. For our app requirements, this list of resources include the Direct2D library and the Windows Imaging Component (WIC) instance.

LISTING 4-24 The DirectXBase CreateDeviceIndependentResources method

```
// These are the resources required independent of the device.
void DirectXBase::CreateDeviceIndependentResources()
{
    D2D1_FACTORY_OPTIONS options;
    ZeroMemory(&options, sizeof(D2D1_FACTORY_OPTIONS));

#if defined(_DEBUG)
    // If the project is in a debug build, enable Direct2D debugging via SDK Layers.
    options.debugLevel = D2D1_DEBUG_LEVEL_INFORMATION;
#endif

    DX::ThrowIfFailed(
        D2D1CreateFactory(
            D2D1_FACTORY_TYPE_SINGLE_THREADED,
            __uuidof(ID2D1Factory1),
            &options,
            &m_d2dFactory
            )
```

```
        );

    DX::ThrowIfFailed(
        CoCreateInstance(
            CLSID_WICImagingFactory,
            nullptr,
            CLSCTX_INPROC_SERVER,
            IID_PPV_ARGS(&m_wicFactory)
            )
        );
}
```

- • CreateDeviceResources: Function to initialize device specific resources. These resources include the D3D11 device context and the D3D11 device instance itself.

LISTING 4-25 The CreateDeviceResources method

```
// These are the resources that depend on the device.
void DirectXBase::CreateDeviceResources()
{
    // This flag adds support for surfaces with a different color channel ordering
    // than the API default. It is required for compatibility with Direct2D.
    UINT creationFlags = D3D11_CREATE_DEVICE_BGRA_SUPPORT;
    ComPtr<IDXGIDevice> dxgiDevice;

#if defined(_DEBUG)
    // If the project is in a debug build, enable debugging via SDK Layers with this flag.
    creationFlags |= D3D11_CREATE_DEVICE_DEBUG;
#endif

    // This array defines the set of DirectX hardware feature levels this app will support.
    // Note the ordering should be preserved.
    // Don't forget to declare your application's minimum required feature level in its
    // description.  All applications are assumed to support 9.1 unless otherwise stated.
    std::array<D3D_FEATURE_LEVEL, 7> featureLevels =
    {
        D3D_FEATURE_LEVEL_11_1,
        D3D_FEATURE_LEVEL_11_0,
        D3D_FEATURE_LEVEL_10_1,
        D3D_FEATURE_LEVEL_10_0,
        D3D_FEATURE_LEVEL_9_3,
        D3D_FEATURE_LEVEL_9_2,
        D3D_FEATURE_LEVEL_9_1
    };

    // Create the Direct3D 11 API device object and a corresponding context.
    ComPtr<ID3D11Device> device;
    ComPtr<ID3D11DeviceContext> context;
    DX::ThrowIfFailed(
        D3D11CreateDevice(
            nullptr,                    // Specify nullptr to use the default adapter.
            D3D_DRIVER_TYPE_HARDWARE,
            0,
```

```
                creationFlags,              // Set debug and Direct2D compatibility flags.
                featureLevels.data(),       // List of feature levels this app can support.
                UINT(featureLevels.size()),
                D3D11_SDK_VERSION,          // Always set this to D3D11_SDK_VERSION for Windows Store apps.
                &device,                    // Returns the Direct3D device created.
                &m_featureLevel,            // Returns feature level of device created.
                &context                    // Returns the device immediate context.
                )
        );

    // Get the Direct3D 11.1 API device and context interfaces.
    DX::ThrowIfFailed(
        device.As(&m_d3dDevice)
        );

    DX::ThrowIfFailed(
        context.As(&m_d3dContext)
        );

    // Get the underlying DXGI device of the Direct3D device.
    DX::ThrowIfFailed(
        m_d3dDevice.As(&dxgiDevice)
        );

    // Create the Direct2D device object and a corresponding context.
    DX::ThrowIfFailed(
        m_d2dFactory->CreateDevice(dxgiDevice.Get(), &m_d2dDevice)
        );

    DX::ThrowIfFailed(
        m_d2dDevice->CreateDeviceContext(
            D2D1_DEVICE_CONTEXT_OPTIONS_NONE,
            &m_d2dContext
            )
        );
}
```

- CreateWindowSizeDependentResources: Function to allocate all memory resources that change in response to a Window Size changed event. We create a new device swap chain here and associate it with the XAML SwapChainBackgroundPanel instance. It is important to note that using a Swap chain in Windows Store apps imposes certain restrictions. For example, the Scaling property of the DXGI_SWAP_CHAIN_DESC1 structure should always be set to DXGI_SCALING_STRETCH. Similarly, the SwapEffect should always be specified as DXGI_SWAP_EFFECT_FLIP_SEQUENTIAL. Also the Width and Height should be specified and not omitted as 0. Failure to set these values will result in a runtime failure.

LISTING 4-26 The CreateWindowSizeDependentResources method

```
// Allocate all memory resources that change on a window SizeChanged event.
void DirectXBase::CreateWindowSizeDependentResources()
{
```

```cpp
    // Store the window bounds so the next time we get a SizeChanged event we can
    // avoid rebuilding everything if the size is identical.
    m_windowBounds = m_window->Bounds;

    if (m_swapChain != nullptr)
    {
        // If the swap chain already exists, resize it.
        HRESULT hr = m_swapChain->ResizeBuffers(2, 0, 0, DXGI_FORMAT_B8G8R8A8_UNORM, 0);

        if (hr == DXGI_ERROR_DEVICE_REMOVED)
        {
            // If the device was removed for any reason, a new device and swapchain will need to be created.
            HandleDeviceLost();

            // Everything is set up now. Do not continue execution of this method.
            return;
        }
        else
        {
            DX::ThrowIfFailed(hr);
        }
    }
    else
    {
        // Otherwise, create a new one using the same adapter as the existing Direct3D device.
        DXGI_SWAP_CHAIN_DESC1 swapChainDesc = {0};
        swapChainDesc.Width = static_cast<UINT>(m_window->Bounds.Width * m_dpi / 96.0f); // Can not use 0
to get the default on Composition SwapChain.
        swapChainDesc.Height = static_cast<UINT>(m_window->Bounds.Height * m_dpi / 96.0f);
        swapChainDesc.Format = DXGI_FORMAT_B8G8R8A8_UNORM;              // This is the most common swapchain
format.
        swapChainDesc.Stereo = false;
        swapChainDesc.SampleDesc.Count = 1;                            // Don't use multi-sampling.
        swapChainDesc.SampleDesc.Quality = 0;
        swapChainDesc.BufferUsage = DXGI_USAGE_RENDER_TARGET_OUTPUT;
        swapChainDesc.BufferCount = m_numBuffers;                      // Use multiple buffering to enable
flip.
        swapChainDesc.Scaling = DXGI_SCALING_STRETCH;
        swapChainDesc.SwapEffect = DXGI_SWAP_EFFECT_FLIP_SEQUENTIAL; // All Windows Store apps must use this
SwapEffect.
        swapChainDesc.Flags = 0;

        ComPtr<IDXGIDevice1> dxgiDevice;
        DX::ThrowIfFailed(
            m_d3dDevice.As(&dxgiDevice)
            );

        ComPtr<IDXGIAdapter> dxgiAdapter;
        DX::ThrowIfFailed(
            dxgiDevice->GetAdapter(&dxgiAdapter)
            );

        ComPtr<IDXGIFactory2> dxgiFactory;
        DX::ThrowIfFailed(
            dxgiAdapter->GetParent(IID_PPV_ARGS(&dxgiFactory))
```

```
            );

        // Create the swap chain and then associate it with the SwapChainBackgroundPanel.
        DX::ThrowIfFailed(
            dxgiFactory->CreateSwapChainForComposition(
                m_d3dDevice.Get(),
                &swapChainDesc,
                nullptr,
                &m_swapChain
                )
            );

            ComPtr<ISwapChainBackgroundPanelNative> dxRootPanelAsSwapChainBackgroundPanel;

        // Set the swap chain on the SwapChainBackgroundPanel.
        reinterpret_cast<IUnknown*>(m_swapChainPanel)->QueryInterface(
            IID_PPV_ARGS(&dxRootPanelAsSwapChainBackgroundPanel)
            );

        DX::ThrowIfFailed(
            dxRootPanelAsSwapChainBackgroundPanel->SetSwapChain(m_swapChain.Get())
            );


        // Ensure that DXGI does not queue too many frames. This reduces latency and
        // ensures that the application will only render after each VSync, minimizing
        // power consumption.
        DX::ThrowIfFailed(
            dxgiDevice->SetMaximumFrameLatency(m_numBuffers - 1)
            );
}

// Create a Direct3D render target view of the swap chain back buffer.
ComPtr<ID3D11Texture2D> backBuffer;
DX::ThrowIfFailed(
    m_swapChain->GetBuffer(0, IID_PPV_ARGS(&backBuffer))
    );

DX::ThrowIfFailed(
    m_d3dDevice->CreateRenderTargetView(
        backBuffer.Get(),
        nullptr,
        &m_d3dRenderTargetView
        )
    );

// Cache the rendertarget dimensions in our helper class for convenient use.
D3D11_TEXTURE2D_DESC backBufferDesc = {0};
backBuffer->GetDesc(&backBufferDesc);
m_renderTargetSize.Width  = static_cast<float>(backBufferDesc.Width);
m_renderTargetSize.Height = static_cast<float>(backBufferDesc.Height);

D3D11_RENDER_TARGET_VIEW_DESC renderTargetViewDesc = {};
renderTargetViewDesc.Format = DXGI_FORMAT_B8G8R8A8_UNORM;
renderTargetViewDesc.ViewDimension = D3D11_RTV_DIMENSION_TEXTURE2DARRAY;        // Render target view
```

```
is a Texture2D array.
    renderTargetViewDesc.Texture2DArray.MipSlice = 0;                         // Each array element
is one Texture2D.
    renderTargetViewDesc.Texture2DArray.ArraySize = 1;
    renderTargetViewDesc.Texture2DArray.FirstArraySlice = 0;
    DX::ThrowIfFailed(
        m_d3dDevice->CreateRenderTargetView(
            backBuffer.Get(),
            &renderTargetViewDesc,
            &m_d3dRenderTargetView
            )
        );

    D2D1_BITMAP_PROPERTIES1 bitmapProperties = {};
    bitmapProperties.pixelFormat.format = DXGI_FORMAT_B8G8R8A8_UNORM;
    bitmapProperties.pixelFormat.alphaMode = D2D1_ALPHA_MODE_PREMULTIPLIED;
    bitmapProperties.bitmapOptions = D2D1_BITMAP_OPTIONS_TARGET | D2D1_BITMAP_OPTIONS_CANNOT_DRAW;
    bitmapProperties.colorContext = nullptr;
    bitmapProperties.dpiX = m_dpi;
    bitmapProperties.dpiY = m_dpi;

    ComPtr<IDXGIResource1> dxgiBackBuffer;
    DX::ThrowIfFailed(
        m_swapChain->GetBuffer(0, IID_PPV_ARGS(&dxgiBackBuffer))
        );

    ComPtr<IDXGISurface2> dxgiSurface;
    DX::ThrowIfFailed(
        dxgiBackBuffer->CreateSubresourceSurface(0, &dxgiSurface)
        );

    DX::ThrowIfFailed(
        m_d2dContext->CreateBitmapFromDxgiSurface(
            dxgiSurface.Get(),
            &bitmapProperties,
            &m_d2dTargetBitmap
            )
        );

    m_d2dContext->SetTarget(m_d2dTargetBitmap.Get());
}
```

- Present: The method to render the final display on the device. We call the Present1 method on the DXGI Swap chain which causes the rendering to happen on the display device. The first parameter to the Present1 method instructs DXGI to block until the next vertical retrace of VSync and puts the application to sleep in order to save power consumption. It is also a mechanism to not waste any cycles rendering frames that will not be displayed on screen.

LISTING 4-27 The Present method where final rendering presentation occurs

```
// Method to deliver the final image to the display.
void DirectXBase::Present()
```

```
{
    // The application may optionally specify "dirty" or "scroll" rects to improve efficiency
    // in certain scenarios.  In this sample, however, we do not utilize those features.
    DXGI_PRESENT_PARAMETERS parameters = {0};
    parameters.DirtyRectsCount = 0;
    parameters.pDirtyRects = nullptr;
    parameters.pScrollRect = nullptr;
    parameters.pScrollOffset = nullptr;

    // The first argument instructs DXGI to block until VSync, putting the application
    // to sleep until the next VSync. This ensures we don't waste any cycles rendering
    // frames that will never be displayed to the screen.
    HRESULT hr = m_swapChain->Present1(1, 0, &parameters);

    // Discard the contents of the render target.
    // This is a valid operation only when the existing contents will be entirely
    // overwritten. If dirty or scroll rects are used, this call should be removed.
    m_d3dContext->DiscardView(m_d3dRenderTargetView.Get());

    // Discard the contents of the depth stencil.
    m_d3dContext->DiscardView(m_d3dDepthStencilView.Get());

    // If the device was removed either by a disconnect or a driver upgrade, we
    // must recreate all device resources.
    if (hr == DXGI_ERROR_DEVICE_REMOVED)
    {
        HandleDeviceLost();
    }
    else
    {
        DX::ThrowIfFailed(hr);
    }

    if (m_windowSizeChangeInProgress)
    {
        // A window size change has been initiated and the app has just completed presenting
        // the first frame with the new size. Notify the resize manager so we can short
        // circuit any resize animation and prevent unnecessary delays.
        CoreWindowResizeManager::GetForCurrentView()->NotifyLayoutCompleted();
        m_windowSizeChangeInProgress = false;
    }
}
```

As mentioned above, this class serves as a base class for all our rendering needs. For the specific requirements of our app, we will now create a class, ShapeRenderer that derives from DirectXBase and will provide specific implementation for all input event handling, drawing using Ink etc.

A Note on Rendering

We have two rendering modes: live rendering and Bezier (re-)rendering. Live rendering is active from the moment the pointer makes contact to the moment it is released. In order to reduce latencies, in live rendering mode we interpolate inking samples with lines. Bezier rendering improves the quality of the stroke once the pointer is released by re-rendering it with Bezier curves interpolation. Live rendering begins with OnPointerPressed, is updated by OnPointerMoved and ends with OnPointerReleased. BezierRender, called by Render, renders all the strokes contained in the stroke container using Bezier curves.

In the interest of minimizing lagging between the rendered stroke and the position of the inking device, we shall use immediate-mode presentation (Present(0, ...)) while in live rendering. This way we can always present the most up to date inking sample. However immediate mode presentation drains the battery so we shall switch back to non-immediate mode presentation (Present(1, ...)) as soon as we exit live rendering. Did you notice we mentioned battery drain as a technical design constraint there? Such sensitivity to where the app will be used (and how it differs from a desktop app) is what helps separate great touch-first, mobile apps from mere 'desktop ports'.

In order to support the two rendering modes, we will define an enum. The current rendering mode will always be set to one of the values contained in the enum. The current rendering mode value will always be updated when switching between live rendering and Bezier rendering.

```
typedef enum {
    Bezier,
    Live
} RenderingMode;
```

We are now ready to create our ShapeRenderer class.

LISTING 4-28 The ShapeRenderer class definition

```
ref class ShapeRenderer : public DirectXBase
{
internal:
    ShapeRenderer();

    virtual void CreateDeviceIndependentResources() override;
    virtual void CreateDeviceResources() override;
    virtual void CreateWindowSizeDependentResources() override;
    virtual void UpdateForWindowSizeChange() override;
    virtual void Render() override;
    virtual void Present() override;
    void BezierRender();
    // Public saving methods.
    void SaveCanvas(Windows::Storage::Streams::IRandomAccessStream^ randomAccessStream, GUID wicFormat);
private:
    void SaveBitmapToStream(
        _In_ ID2D1Bitmap1* d2dBitmap,
```

```
            _In_  IWICImagingFactory2* wicFactory2,
            _In_  ID2D1DeviceContext* d2dContext,
            _In_  REFGUID wicFormat,
            _In_  IStream* stream
            );

    void CreateBrush(
     _In_  ID2D1DeviceContext* d2dContext,
     _In_  Windows::UI::Color color,
     _Outptr_  ID2D1SolidColorBrush** brush);

    Windows::UI::Xaml::Controls::SwapChainBackgroundPanel^  m_swapChainPanel;
    // D2D data members
    Microsoft::WRL::ComPtr<ID3D11Texture2D>              m_currentBuffer;
    Microsoft::WRL::ComPtr<ID3D11Texture2D>              m_previousBuffer;
    Microsoft::WRL::ComPtr<ID2D1SolidColorBrush>         m_backgroundBrush;
    Microsoft::WRL::ComPtr<ID2D1SolidColorBrush>         m_inkBrush;

    Windows::UI::Color                                   m_backgroundColor;
    RenderingMode                                        m_renderingMode;
};
```

Our ShapeRenderer class defines a BezierRender method that is used in the Bezier render mode to re-render brush strokes using a Bezier curve algorithm, smoothening the brush strokes. The SaveCanvas method is used to save the drawing as an image and relies on the helper function, Save-BitmapToStream to achieve this functionality.

The CreateBrush helper function is used to create an instance of an ID2D1SolidColorBrush. This function accepts a color of the Windows::UI::Color type and creates an ID2D1SolidColorBrush instance.

We now have the rendering class, sans implementation in place. We will now add support for Input events and ink.

Adding Input events

A Pointer is an abstraction of an input device in Windows 8. This is especially true in the context of Windows Store apps. Since our goal is to support all input modalities (touch, stylus and mouse), we will introduce Pointer events in our rendering class, ShapeRenderer. We will add the following Pointer events to our class:

- PointerPressed: The PointerPressed event is fired when a press down event is received by the input subsystem.

- PointerReleased: The PointerReleased event is fired when a press down event is received by the input subsystem.

- PointerMoved: The PointerMoved event is fired when a pointer move occurs without lifting the finger/pen/mouse.

Add the following method declarations to the ShapeRenderer class as intenal methods.

```
void OnPointerPressed(Platform::Object^ sender, Windows::UI::Xaml::Input::PointerRoutedEventArgs^ args);

void OnPointerReleased(Platform::Object^ sender, Windows::UI::Xaml::Input::PointerRoutedEventArgs^ args);

void OnPointerMoved(Platform::Object^ sender, Windows::UI::Xaml::Input::PointerRoutedEventArgs^ args);
```

We also need to handle the type of pointer event: Ink/Draw or Erase. In order to track the pointer event type, we will create an enum that is always updated based on the pointer events being fired. We also create a few helper functions that will enable us to deduce the pointer event type: Erase or Ink.

```
typedef enum
{
    None,
    Ink,
    Erase
} PointerEventType;
PointerEventType GetPointerEventType(_In_ Windows::UI::Xaml::Input::PointerRoutedEventArgs^ e);
bool EventIsErase(_In_ Windows::UI::Xaml::Input::PointerRoutedEventArgs^ e);
bool EventIsInk(_In_ Windows::UI::Xaml::Input::PointerRoutedEventArgs^ e);
```

An erase event occurs when the right mouse button is clicked over a brush stroke. Similarly, an erase event occurs when the barrel of a stylus is pressed over a brush stroke. We will always return a value of true for an Ink event as we want brush strokes to be drawn in all other modes.

Adding Ink support

The Windows 8 platform contains great support for Inking. For the purposes of our app, the following three classes are of great importance.

- InkStrokeBuilder: This class is used to build strokes from raw pointer input.

- InkStrokeContainer: This class contains helper methods to manage input, processing and manipulation of InkStroke objects.

- InkDrawingAttributes: This class provides properties associated with the actual drawing of an InkStroke.

Add the following property to the ShapeRenderer class. This property, DrawingAttributes will be read when the user changes either the stroke color or thickness. The backing instance of Windows::UI::Input::Inking::InkDrawingAttributes, m_drawingAttributes, is a private member variable of the ShapeRenderer class.

LISTING 4-29 The DrawingAttributes property

```
property Windows::UI::Input::Inking::InkDrawingAttributes^ DrawingAttributes
    {
            Windows::UI::Input::Inking::InkDrawingAttributes^ get()
            {
                    return m_drawingAttributes;
            }
```

}

Next, we add a new method, OnChangeDrawingAttributes. This method accepts a Windows::UI::Color and a Windows::Foundation::Size as input. The color and size input values are used to update the InkDrawingAttributes in response to a color changed event or a brush thickness changed event.

LISTING 4-30 Handling the change in drawing attributes

```
void ShapeRenderer::OnChangeDrawingAttributes(Windows::UI::Color newStrokeColor,
Windows::Foundation::Size sz)
{
    m_drawingAttributes->Color = newStrokeColor;

    if (sz != Windows::Foundation::Size(0.0f, 0.0f))
    {
            m_drawingAttributes->Size = sz;
    }
    // update default drawing attributes
    m_strokeBuilder->SetDefaultDrawingAttributes(m_drawingAttributes);

    // update _inkBrush to reflect drawing color change
    CreateBrush(m_d2dContext.Get(), m_drawingAttributes->Color, &m_inkBrush);
}
```

Finally, we add member variables to the ShapeRenderer class. These member variables are used to initialize the various Ink classes, and then capture strokes as the user draws strokes. Once the pointer released event is fired, the strokes from the captured collection are used to re-draw the smooth Bezier curves.

LISTING 4-31 Adding member variables for handling ink

```
// Inking members
Windows::UI::Input::Inking::InkStrokeBuilder^                    m_strokeBuilder;
Windows::UI::Input::Inking::InkStrokeContainer^         m_strokeContainer;
Windows::UI::Input::Inking::InkDrawingAttributes^       m_drawingAttributes;

// Stores the id of the 'active' pointer, -1 if none. We are allowing only
// one 'active' pointer at a time. This variable is set by OnPointerPressed,
// checked by OnPointerMoved, and reset by OnPointerReleased.
int                                     m_pointerId;

Windows::Foundation::Collections::IVector<Windows::Foundation::Point>^    m_manipulationPoints;
Windows::UI::Input::Inking::InkManipulationMode         m_manipulationMode;
```

The BezierRender function renders all strokes as Bezier curves. In order to do this, it relies on the helper function, conveniently named ConvertStrokeToGeometry. ConvertStrokeToGeometry reads one ink stroke at a time and returns an instance of ID2D1PathGeometry of the ink stroke. It converts all Bezier control points in each segment to a Bezier curve in the path geometry.

LISTING 4-32 Converting Bezier control points to Bezier curves

```
// convert bezier control points in each segment to a bezier curve in the path geometry
void ShapeRenderer::ConvertStrokeToGeometry(_In_ Windows::UI::Input::Inking::InkStroke^ stroke, _Outptr_
```

```
ID2D1PathGeometry** geometry)
{
    // create a geometry path
    DX::ThrowIfFailed(m_d2dFactory->CreatePathGeometry(geometry));

    // create and initialize a geometry sink
    Microsoft::WRL::ComPtr<ID2D1GeometrySink> sink;
    DX::ThrowIfFailed((*geometry)->Open(&sink));
    sink->SetSegmentFlags(D2D1_PATH_SEGMENT_FORCE_ROUND_LINE_JOIN);
    sink->SetFillMode(D2D1_FILL_MODE_ALTERNATE);

    // obtain rendering segments for this stroke

Windows::Foundation::Collections::IVectorView<Windows::UI::Input::Inking::InkStrokeRenderingSegment^>^
renderingSegments = stroke->GetRenderingSegments();

    // obtain first rendering segment, set as a starting point
    Windows::UI::Input::Inking::InkStrokeRenderingSegment^ firstSegment = renderingSegments->GetAt(0);
    Windows::Foundation::Point first = firstSegment->Position;
    sink->BeginFigure(D2D1::Point2F(first.X, first.Y), D2D1_FIGURE_BEGIN_FILLED);

    // process all remaining rendering segments, add bezier segment to the geometry path sink
    for (unsigned int j = 1; j < renderingSegments->Size; j++)
    {
        // obtain j-th rendering segment for the given stroke
        Windows::UI::Input::Inking::InkStrokeRenderingSegment^ renderingSegment =
renderingSegments->GetAt(j);

        // add bezier segment to the geometry path sink
        sink->AddBezier(
            D2D1::BezierSegment(
                D2D1::Point2F(renderingSegment->BezierControlPoint1.X,
renderingSegment->BezierControlPoint1.Y),
                D2D1::Point2F(renderingSegment->BezierControlPoint2.X,
renderingSegment->BezierControlPoint2.Y),
                D2D1::Point2F(renderingSegment->Position.X, renderingSegment->Position.Y)
                )
            );
    }

    // done with given stroke, end and close geometry sink
    // sink will be automatically released as it is a smart pointer
    sink->EndFigure(D2D1_FIGURE_END_OPEN);
    DX::ThrowIfFailed(sink->Close());
}
```

The BezierRender function is listed below:

LISTING 4-33 The BezierRender method of the ShapeRenderer class.

```
void ShapeRenderer::BezierRender()
{
    // render all strokes
    Windows::Foundation::Collections::IVectorView<Windows::UI::Input::Inking::InkStroke^>^ inkStrokes =
m_strokeContainer->GetStrokes();
```

```
    for (unsigned int i = 0; i < inkStrokes->Size; i++)
    {
        // obtain the stroke
        Windows::UI::Input::Inking::InkStroke^ stroke = inkStrokes->GetAt(i);

        // convert stroke to geometry
        // geometry is a smart pointer and it is released right after it is used
        // for performance reasons one may consider storing geometry paths instead of auto-releasing them
once they are used
        Microsoft::WRL::ComPtr<ID2D1PathGeometry> strokeGeometry;
        ConvertStrokeToGeometry(stroke, &strokeGeometry);

        // stroke's width and color are retrieved from the stroke's drawing attributes
        float width = stroke->DrawingAttributes->Size.Width;
        // create brush from current stroke
        Microsoft::WRL::ComPtr<ID2D1SolidColorBrush> strokeBrush;
        CreateBrush(m_d2dContext.Get(), stroke->DrawingAttributes->Color, &strokeBrush);

        // render stroke geometry
        m_d2dContext->DrawGeometry(strokeGeometry.Get(), strokeBrush.Get(), width, m_inkStyle.Get());
    }
}
```

Supporting Save

If you think that saving items from a DXGI surface to a file stream is difficult, you are in for a pleasant surprise. Saving the image stream to a file stream is pretty simple and straight forward in the Windows Store apps.

The SaveCanvas method, as mentioned above, relies on the helper method SaveBitmapToStream to save the bitmap to a file stream using WIC. This helper method initializes the WIC bitmap encoder, and proceeds to write the bitmap data to the WIC stream.

The WIC stream itself is created from an IRandomAccessStream instance, which is the stream originally used to write to the StorageFile object.

LISTING 4-34 Saving render target bitmap to a stream

```
// Save render target bitmap to a stream using WIC.
void ShapeRenderer::SaveBitmapToStream(
    _In_ ID2D1Bitmap1* d2dBitmap,
    _In_ IWICImagingFactory2* wicFactory2,
    _In_ ID2D1DeviceContext* d2dContext,
    _In_ REFGUID wicFormat,
    _In_ IStream* stream
    )
{
    // Create and initialize WIC bitmap encoder.
    ComPtr<IWICBitmapEncoder> wicBitmapEncoder;
    DX::ThrowIfFailed(
        wicFactory2->CreateEncoder(
            wicFormat,
            nullptr,
```

```
            &wicBitmapEncoder
            )
        );

DX::ThrowIfFailed(
    wicBitmapEncoder->Initialize(
        stream,
        WICBitmapEncoderNoCache
        )
    );

// Create and initialize WIC frame encoder.
ComPtr<IWICBitmapFrameEncode> wicFrameEncode;
DX::ThrowIfFailed(
    wicBitmapEncoder->CreateNewFrame(
        &wicFrameEncode,
        nullptr     // No encoder options.
        )
    );

DX::ThrowIfFailed(
    wicFrameEncode->Initialize(nullptr)
    );

// Retrieve Direct2D device.
ComPtr<ID2D1Device> d2dDevice;
d2dContext->GetDevice(&d2dDevice);

// Create WIC image encoder.
ComPtr<IWICImageEncoder> imageEncoder;
DX::ThrowIfFailed(
    wicFactory2->CreateImageEncoder(
        d2dDevice.Get(),
        &imageEncoder
        )
    );

DX::ThrowIfFailed(
    imageEncoder->WriteFrame(
        d2dBitmap,
        wicFrameEncode.Get(),
        nullptr     // Use default options.
        )
    );

DX::ThrowIfFailed(
    wicFrameEncode->Commit()
    );

DX::ThrowIfFailed(
    wicBitmapEncoder->Commit()
    );

// Flush all memory buffers to the next-level storage object.
DX::ThrowIfFailed(
```

```
    stream->Commit(STGC_DEFAULT)
        );
}
```

Integration with the Share charm

When a user invokes the Share charm, Windows fires the DataRequested event at our app. In order for Windows to fire the DataRequested app, we must first register for the DataRequested event when our app initializes. This is usually done in the constructor of the MainPage class. Once the registration is successful, we get notified whenever the user invokes the Share charm.

In the DataRequested event callback, we create an instance of a DataPackage. The DataPackage class can be found in the Windows::ApplicationModel::DataTransfer namespace, which is a centralized namespace containing all data sharing and transfer classes and helper methods.

The DataPackage class contains methods and properties that allow us to set the title, description and text, among various things, that will be shared with Share recipient apps. Because we want to share the drawing, in addition to some textual attributes like title, description etc, we will create an in-memory stream and have WIC write the bitmap data to it. Once the stream has been successfully written to, we can then call the SetBitmap method on the DataPackage instance and pass the stream object.

LISTING 4-35 Integrating with the Share charm

```
void ShapeRenderer::OnDataRequested(_In_ DataTransferManager^ sender, _In_ DataRequestedEventArgs^ args)
{
    DataPackage^ package = args->Request->Data;

    // Set the title, description, and text to be shared.
    package->Properties->ApplicationName = "DirectX DrawIt app";
    package->Properties->Title = "A custom drawing for you!";
    package->Properties->Description = "This is a drawing made with the DirectX DrawIt app using C++.";

    // Create an in-memory stream to contain the shared data.
    IRandomAccessStream^ randomAccessStream = ref new InMemoryRandomAccessStream();

    // Create an IStream over that random access stream.
    ComPtr<IStream> stream;
    DX::ThrowIfFailed(
        CreateStreamOverRandomAccessStream(randomAccessStream, IID_PPV_ARGS(&stream))
        );

    Render();

    // Save the bitmap to the stream.
    SaveBitmapToStream(
        m_d2dTargetBitmap.Get(),
        m_wicFactory.Get(),
        m_d2dContext.Get(),
        GUID_ContainerFormatPng,
        stream.Get()
```

```
    );

    // Create a stream reference for the random access stream and give it to the data package.
    RandomAccessStreamReference^ streamReference =
RandomAccessStreamReference::CreateFromStream(randomAccessStream);
    package->SetBitmap(streamReference);
}
```

That is it. We now have our full DrawIt application ready. Build the solution, deploy the application and upon launching you should be able to begin drawing on screen using touch, mouse or a stylus.

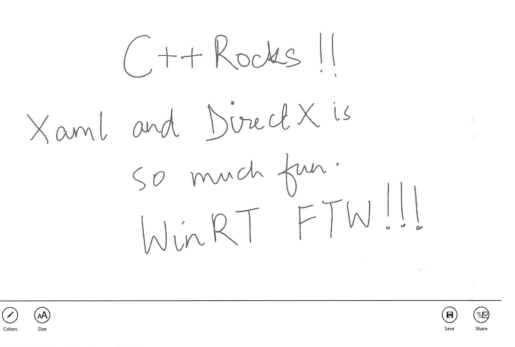

FIGURE 4-7 The DrawIt application screen

I have omitted certain code snippets from the preceding discussion to make the flow easier. You can obtain the full code sample from the Samples download location, along with the rest of the books sample code.

Where are we and what's Next

In this chapter, we explored DirectX integration with XAML. XAML provides three types that allow for seamless integration: SurfaceImageSource, VirtualSurfaceImageSource and the SwapChainBackgroundPanel. Each type is targeted at specific scenarios that you, as a developer, can take advantage of. DirectX is a proven graphics technology on the Windows platform and XAML provides a great way to incorporate DirectX in XAML Store apps using C++. You can have the flexibility of XAML and the power of DirectX and C++, all in your Windows Store app. We will now explore General Purpose Graphics Processing Unit (GPGPU) programming using C++AMP library.

Chapter 5
Advanced GPGPU Programming

In this chapter:

Introduction
The C++ AMP types
Using Tiles in C++ AMP
Debugging C++ AMP apps
Developing Apps using C++ AMP – Case Studies
The ImageEffects application
Where are we and what's Next

Introduction

"The free lunch is over" – Herb Sutter

"Welcome to the Jungle" – Herb Sutter

Ever since the dawn of the Microprocessor age, developers have come to expect that Moore's Law would double the speeds achieved by the processor and new software would be developed to take advantage of all these speed benefits. There were also applications that were written with these potential benefits in mind. If your app ran slowly, it was still fine to ship because advances in hardware meant that newer hardware made up for the loss of performance in the app. Sadly, Moore's Law hit the limits of physics sometime around in 2005 and the performance "free lunch" came to an end. While Moore's Law continues to remain valid in our times today, the increased transistor density does not translate to automatic speedup due to Instruction Level Parallelism (ILP), memory and power walls.

The hardware manufacturers were not so quick to give up and instead began shipping computers with multiple cores. So instead of one processor with a speed of 4 GHz, a customer would get two processors cast into one die with a speed of 2.4 GHz each. This throws up interesting challenges such as the following:

- How do we design software with enough *potential* concurrency such that it can make good use of the number of hardware threads available to it over the lifespan of the software?

- How does one minimize power consumption while getting the maximum performance from each of the processors available?

Unfortunately today users tend not to benefit from faster apps with newer hardware. The primary reason for this is that most, but not all, established applications where not developed during the multi-core era. For example, it is all too common on a quad core machine to see some app peak max out one core, leaving approximately ¾ of the available computing resources utilized. Worse in many ways, there are also apps that simply blocked one CPU and do nothing at all while waiting for some calculation to complete or resource to become available. Those developers who have risen to the challenge of writing parallel apps have once again been able to enjoy the 'free lunch' whereby their software runs approximately twice as fast on a dual core machine, and four times faster on a quad core one etc.

Changes in GPU architectures

At around the same time as CPUs went multi-core, graphics cards were also undergoing a similar transition. GPUs have traditionally been massively parallel. Rather than ship GPUs with two or four cores manufacturers ship GPUs with dozens or even hundreds of simple cores. It wasn't long before developers starting trying to use the phenomenal floating point power of these GPUs for tasks other than just working out what color a particular pixel on the screen should be. As a result of this there has been a shift in recent years to increase the programmability of the GPUs thus making them more amenable for general purpose computing. GPU cores are radically different from the cores on a CPU. Traditionally, GPUs have relied on parallelism to update pixels on display devices. The GPUs were developed to speed up graphically intensive computation such as determining which pixel to update with which particular color and so on. However, as GPUs began shipping with hundreds of cores, utilizing such cores for operations other than just graphical purposes became an inviting possibility. For example, if the GPU cores could be used for numerical computation in addition to just graphical operations, then developers can take advantage of the presence of modern CPUs as well as GPUs to speed up application specific tasks. Such machines are called heterogeneous supercomputers, whether they are hosted in a single PC or a cluster of PCs.

We are effectively transitioning from "putting a computer on every desk and in every home" to "putting a super computer in every desk, in every home and in every pocket".

Just to give a simple example of the differences between a CPU and GPU: My home computer, a desktop, has a dual-core, hyper-threaded CPU clocking 2.4GHz. The GPU on the same machine is an nVidia GeForce GTX 550 Ti capable of performing single-precision calculations. The speeds achieved by the CPU and GPU also vary vastly. This is because a CPU has low memory bandwidth, usually in the range of 10-20 gigabytes per second whereas a modern GPU can handle in the range of 120-160 gigabytes per second. Another factor contributing to low CPU speed is due to the fact that a CPU is a more general purpose utility: A CPU supports multi-tasking, multi-threading, I/O, random access across memory and registers etc. In contrast, a GPU is designed to excel at graphics and data-parallel code. Finally for data parallel operations GPUs tend to consume less power than their CPU counterparts when performing equivalent operations, and efficient power usage is a very big thing when it comes to tablets, smartphones and even ultra-book type form factors which are expected to run on battery for *at least* 8 hours, i.e. more or less a working day.

For applications that will typically be run on battery powered devices, the amount of power consumed can greatly contribute to the perception of the application and whether it is loathed or loved and recommended to others by its users. In other words, efficient power usage is a competitive advantage and something that C++ with its ability to *get down there on the metal* is superbly positioned to deliver. So what tools are available to enable you to eke the maximum benefit from today's hardware?

Programming the GPU

As a developer you are spoiled for choice when it comes to programming the CPU. You can pick and choose from literally hundreds of general-purpose languages or domain specific programming languages. For applications that need power and performance, C++ remains king of the kill as it provides high level programming abstractions, access to low level hardware functionality and powerful libraries. However, when it comes to programming the GPU, the choices historically have been fairly limited. You have to write code in one of the "dialects" of technologies like DirectCompute or OpenCL or CUDA. This restriction meant that General Purpose GPU programming (GPGPU) has remained in the exclusive domain of a few problem spaces and has not gone mainstream. Until now!

C++ AMP

C++ Accelerated Massively Parallelism (C++ AMP) is a library plus a key language extension that unlocks the power of heterogeneous computing within C++ applications. As a developer, you write the code once and the code scales across a wide variety of devices: CPU, GPU, CPU-GPU mix. Thus C++ developers can use the tools and knowledge they have to create applications that employ data parallelism to best exploit the underlying hardware in order to boost acceleration.

C++ AMP accelerates the execution of your C++ code by taking advantage of the data-parallel hardware that's commonly present as a graphics processing unit (GPU) on a discrete graphics card. Graphics cards with GPUs like the nVidia GeForce or ATI/AMD Radeon graphics cards or Intel's IvyBridge are shipped along with a majority of computing devices today.

Within Windows Store apps, you can only use C++ AMP for GPGPU programming as OpenCL or CUDA are not supported.

Hello World with C++ AMP

C++ AMP like STL algorithms and PPL tasks benefits enormously from the introduction of lambda syntax into C++ 11. As we've seen lambda syntax is a compact and elegant means of declaring little snippets of code right at the point where they're needed, rather than having to package the code up in a separate class object. C++ AMP code employing lambdas can not only be screaming fast, but beautiful to read.

Let us now create a simple "Hello World" application using C++ AMP.

LISTING 5-1 Hello World with C++ AMP

```
#include "stdafx.h"

void main()
{
    std::array<int, 11> v = { 'G', 'd', 'k', 'k', 'n', 31, 'V', 'n', 'q', 'k', 'c' };

    concurrency::array_view<int> av(11, v.data());
    concurrency::parallel_for_each(av.extent, [=](concurrency::index<1> idx) restrict(amp)
    {
        av[idx] += 1;
    });

    for(auto i = 0U; i < static_cast<UINT>(v.size()); ++i)
    {
        std::wcout << static_cast<char>(av[i]);
    }
    std::wcout << std::endl;
}
```

1. In order to compile this, create a new project of type Win32 console application and save it as AmpHelloApp.

2. Replace the generated code with the code in Listing 5-1.

3. In the code sample we use an array of characters declared as an array of int because the C++AMP model does not support the use of a char array within a restrict(amp) scope. Attempting to use a char within the restrict(amp) scope generates a compiler error.

4. Build the solution.

5. You now have an executable named "AmpHelloApp.exe" in your project path.

6. Executing AmpHelloApp.exe outputs the string "**Hello World**" at the console window.

7. Congratulations, you have successfully written your first C++ AMP program.

8. Alternatively, you can also download the AmpHelloApp solution along with the book samples, build and execute it from within Visual Studio 2012.

On observing the code closely, a few differences become apparent. There is a new header file we include in our code (amp.h), new types like array_view, and a re-purposed keyword *restrict*. Other than these few differences, the remaining code is the same standard, portable C++ code we are all familiar with. So what are the various types and the new keyword and how do they enable you to take advantage of GPUs present on modern graphic cards?

The C++ AMP programming model includes support for multidimensional arrays, indexing, memory transfer, and tiling. You can use C++ AMP library types to control how data is moved from the CPU to the GPU and back. We will begin by exploring the C++ AMP library.

The C++ AMP Library

The immediate and obvious question that would pop up is how can one use this new C++ AMP library? All mainstream programming languages have rich type systems, provided either as part of the language or through libraries and supporting frameworks, that are geared towards programming a CPU. Writing code the usual way without providing any "hints" for the target hardware is not possible in a seamless manner. Specialized API stacks like DirectCompute, CUDA, OpenCL, all provide a mechanism to target GPUs using their own dialect of the 'C' programming language. These specialized API stacks with their somewhat anachronistic language requirements has meant that GPGPU programming has remained outside the purview of mainstream programming and relevant only within certain domains.

As mentioned above, one of the goals of C++ AMP is to make GPGPU programming mainstream and help developers build on the strengths of the inherent parallelism available on GPUs. Instead of creating a new API stack, the C++ AMP team created a library-only solution with exactly two new keywords: **restrict** and **tile_static**. This enables existing C++ code to be ported over to C++ AMP while also allowing mainstream C++ developers (including developers using C++ inspired languages such as C++ CX) to write applications that harness the power of a GPU using their existing skills. So what are the new types in C++ AMP? Let us briefly explore the C++ AMP library before moving to writing actual programs using the same.

The GPGPU programming support provided by C++ AMP is a C++ API, i.e. a set of classes, STL-like collections and supporting enums that abstract away the developer from having to worry about various types of GPU hardware.

C++ AMP Concepts

The accelerator and accelerator_view classes

A concurrency::accelerator is a high level abstraction for a "target device". This "target device" is where the 'restrict(amp)' decorated code executes and its associated data is stored. If your computer has a GPU with a DirectX 11 driver, C++ AMP uses the concurrency::accelerator to represent the GPU device. All available "target devices", also called accelerators are represented by the accelerator class. These "target machines" could be GPUs, or emulators installed by Visual Studio or WARP or even a Direct3D reference device. The default accelerator is the best accelerator available as determined by the runtime.

In general you will not need to explicitly create an accelerator instance and should instead rely on the C++ AMP runtime to choose the best available accelerator device for executing code. There are certain advanced scenarios, like choosing a particular device for rendering custom DirectX content, which can necessitate the need to query the underlying list of devices and then choose a particular device for executing code or storing data but for regular usage you should rely on the C++ AMP runtime to choose the best available accelerator device.

LISTING 5-2 Querying available accelerators and accelerator properties

```
void PrintAccelerators()
{
    auto accelerators = accelerator::get_all();
    std::for_each(begin(accelerators), end(accelerators), [] (accelerator a)
    {
            std::wcout<< "New Accelerator: " << a.description <<std::endl;
            std::wcout<< "device path = " << a.device_path <<std::endl;
            std::wcout<< "version = " << (a.version >> 16) << '.' << (a.version & 0xFFFF) <<std::endl;
            std::wcout<< "dedicated_memory = " << a.dedicated_memory << "KB" <<std::endl;
            std::wcout<< "doubles = " << ((a.supports_double_precision) ? "true" : "false") <<std::endl;
            std::wcout<< "limited_doubles = " << ((a.supports_limited_double_precision) ? "true" : "false")
<<std::endl;
            std::wcout<< "has_display = " << ((a.has_display) ? "true" : "false") <<std::endl;
            std::wcout<< "is_emulated = " << ((a.is_emulated) ? "true" : "false") <<std::endl;
            std::wcout << "is_debug = " << ((a.is_debug) ? "true" : "false") <<std::endl;
            std::wcout << std::endl;
    });
}
```

The accelerator_view is similar to a Window handle. An accelerator_view represents a logical view of an accelerator. A single physical compute device may have many logical (isolated) accelerator views. Each accelerator has a default accelerator view and additional accelerator views may be optionally created by the user. Physical devices must potentially be shared amongst many client threads. Client threads may choose to use the same accelerator_view of an accelerator or each client may communicate with a compute device via an independent accelerator_view object for isolation from other client threads. Work submitted to an accelerator_view is guaranteed to be executed in the order that it was submitted; there are no such ordering guarantees for work submitted on different accelerator_views. An accelerator_view object can be created by using the *default_view* property of the accelerator class or by calling *create_view* method on the accelerator class object. An accelerator can have multiple view instances. There are, for example, some functions in C++ AMP that accept an accelerator_view object as a parameter. The default accelerator will be used unless you provide a specific accelerator_view to use instead.

The *create_view* method of the accelerator class expects a *queuing_mode* enumeration value. If you omit specifying a value, it uses the default value of queuing_mode_automatic. The *queuing_mode* enum has two members: *queuing_mode_automatic* and *queuing_mode_immediate*. Specifying *queuing_mode_immediate* means that any commands sent to the device like data copy/transfers are submitted immediately whereas *queuing_mode_automatic* means that submission happens when the runtime deems it fit to proceed with the operations. The accelerator_view class also has methods *flush* and *wait* that enable you to send all buffered commands for execution. The only difference is *flush* is a non-blocking function call whereas *wait* is blocking.

> **It is generally good practice, although not absolutely necessary, to create one accelerator_view instance per thread. An accelerator_view is thread-safe and multiple threads can safely submit commands concurrently to an accelerator_view. The accelerator_view class is meant to provide isolation to "consumers" from accelerator devices.**

The extent and index classes

C++ AMP supports the concept of "indexing" in the array. An index represents a unique point in the N dimensional space. This is similar to the concept of using X and Y coordinates to represent a unique point in 2-dimensional spaces. The index in C++ AMP, however, can be used to uniquely represent a point in arbitrary N-dimensional space. Each index object has a field named *Rank* that returns the value N of the N-dimensional space. You can construct an index object in multiple ways:

- By using the default parameterless constructor.

  o index<2> idx; represents a point (0,0)

- Copy an existing index by using the copy constructor or assignment operator.

  o index<2> idx2(idx); or index<2> idx2 = idx;

You can access components in the index using the [] operator.

The extent class is used to define the N-dimensional space in C++ AMP. An extent object is similar to an index object, and is a coordinate vector of N integers ordered from most- to least- significant. Each integer in an extent object represents the size for that dimension. Each extent object has a field *Rank* that returns the value N of the N-dimensional space. You can construct an extent object from an existing object either using the copy constructor or assignment operator. An extent object component can be accessed using the [] operator.

An extent object instance can be created as follows:

```
extent<2> e(3, 4);
```

The restrict (amp) specifier

In the Visual C++ compiler shipping with Visual Studio 2012, the *restrict(cpu)* modifier implicitly applies to functions (including C++ 11 lambdas of course) in the way described below. All functions include the restrict modifier by default and in an invisible manner.

LISTING 5-3 restrict(cpu) snippet

```
void DoSomething(int a, int b) restrict(cpu)
{
    cout << a + b <<endl;
}
```

For all your existing code that you recompile with Visual Studio 2012, you can think of that as a no-op. You can even add the *restrict* modifier with the *cpu* specifier and recompile - you'll see no difference.

In addition to the *cpu* contextual specifier, there is another specifier in Visual Studio 2012, this is the *amp* specifier.

LISTING 5-4 restrict(amp) snippet

```
void DoSomething(int a, int b) restrict(amp)
{
    // Code that can execute on a amp accelerator
    // This function cannot be called from restrict(cpu) functions.
}
```

You can also combine both the *cpu* and *amp* modifiers too. So what does it mean that a function is decorated with restrict(amp) modifier?

The restrict(amp) modifier exists to enable you to declare your intent to the compiler that any code so decorated should be restricted to a subset of the C++ language. It is this restricted subset that is allowed to be used within the C++ AMP kernel, this is necessary since currently GPGPU hardware cannot support the full C++ 11 feature set. By explicitly declaring, with restrict(amp) decorations, those bits of code we want accelerated we are able to further enlist the compilers help to:

- enforce the correct subset of the language

- enforce any limitations of the underlying implementation (e.g. Direct3D aka DirectX 11)

- perform special code generation as appropriate

- perform optimizations as appropriate

- provide compile time checking/reporting of the above

It is important here to note that a function decorated with restrict(amp) cannot be called from a function that is not decorated with restrict(amp). This begs the obvious question, if you author a function decorated with restrict(amp), how does it ever get called? In the current release of C++ AMP, there exists a single exception to this rule: the entry point to C++ AMP: the new parallel_for_each function which can accept and execute a restrict(amp) lambda.

The array and array_view classes

The array class is used to represent a container of data of type T in N dimensions which resides on a specific accelerator or cpu. If the dimensions is not specified, N defaults to 1 which means the array is just a vector of items of type T.

An array_view is a wrapper over the underlying native CPU data that any container represents. An array_view can be used over a concurrency_array, std::array, std::vector or pointer etc. It can be thought of as a multi-dimensional random access iterator.

LISTING 5-5 using array

```
//create an array of 5 integers
std::vector<int> data(5);
for (int count = 0; count < 5; count++)
{
    data[count] = count;
}

//now create and initialize an AMP array with data from the array 'data' created above
//specify the begin and end of the integer array
array<int, 1> arr(5, std::begin(data), std::end(data));

// we will multiply each element in the array by 10 and then copy data back from GPU to CPU.
parallel_for_each(
    arr.extent,
    [=, &arr](index<1> idx) restrict(amp)
    {
        arr[idx] = arr[idx] * 10;
    }
);
data = arr;

// accessing elements in the array
for (UINT i = 0; i < data.size(); ++i)
{
    int x = data[i];
    std::cout << x<<std::endl;
}
```

The parallel_for_each function

The parallel_for_each function is the gateway to the C++ AMP kernel and the means by which restrict(amp) decorated code is executed by (implicitly) restrict(cpu) decorated code. This function enables parallelization of work. In order to parallelize work, you create an *array* and/or *array_view*. An array_view does not have an "attached" accelerator. It can seamlessly be used on multiple accelerators; the data will be copied for you automatically. These data structures can then be used in conjunction with parallel_for_each to iterate over each item in the data structure and work performed on each such item.

The execution of the parallel_for_each lambda function, also called the "kernel" function, takes place on the accelerator that is chosen based on many factors such as location of the array containers, caching state of array_view objects and so on. It runs on the default accelerator if none is specified. Every element in the extent, corresponds to a thread that will execute the kernel, and every index in the extent can be thought of as the thread ID. In our simple example below, it launches 5 threads to perform the computation. Normally, if your array_view has an extent a times b times c (a * b * c) to represent a 3-dimensional array, then the accelerator launches threads equal to the product of a, b and c. In our simple example, we do not see major performance boosts because the overhead of copying data to and from the accelerator outweighs the savings.

LISTING 5-6 Example for parallel_for_each

```
const std::array<int, 5> a = { 1, 3, 5, 7, 11 };
const std::array<int, 5> b = { 2, 4, 6, 8, 10 };

if (static_cast<UINT>( (a.size()) ) != static_cast<UINT>( (b.size()) ))
{
    std::wcout<<"a and b arrays must be of the same size"<<std::endl;
    return;
}
const auto size = 5;
int result[size] = {};

// Begin process in parallel
concurrency::array_view<const int> aView(size, a.data());
concurrency::array_view<const int> bView(size, b.data());
concurrency::array_view<int> resultView(size, result);

concurrency::parallel_for_each(resultView.extent, [=](concurrency::index<1> idx) restrict(amp)
{
    resultView[idx] = aView[idx] + bView[idx];
});

resultView.synchronize();

// End process in parallel
for(auto i = 0U; i < size; ++i)
    std::wcout << result[i] << std::endl;
```

In the above code sample, the C++ AMP array_view arr1 wraps the C-style array a, which contains the first five odd numbers. Similarly array_view arr2 wraps the array b, which contains the first five even numbers. The first parameter that is passed to the parallel_for_each function is the extent of the array_view sum variable. The array_view holds the final result of the computation that happens inside the parallel_for_each block.

The exception classes

As software developers, you know that there are times when errors occur either in your code or code interfacing with underlying sub-systems. When such errors or exceptions do occur, there should be a good mechanism to capture the same. Capturing exceptions ensures that the program can log the exception and try to recover from the situation if possible, or pass the exception as unhandled in which case the application is terminated.

C++AMP supports a programming model based on exceptions. This means that exceptions are thrown as code executes. You should wrap your parallel_for_each call with a try/catch block and catch exceptions of type *concurrency::runtime_exception*. This is a new exception introduced in the C++AMP library and inherits from std::exception. You should also wrap all calls involving a data transfer within a try/catch block and catch the *concurrency::runtime_exception* that might occur.

The serial and accelerated samples

Before we move on to more advanced usage of the C++ AMP library, let us take a quick look at how to obtain a performance boosts by accelerating parallelizable data operations, we'll take as our example the classic matrix multiplication operation. We will consider the serial version of the example before discussing the accelerated version.

A naïve version of a Matrix Multiplication operation is listed below. The function MatrixMultiplySerial takes three vectors, vA, vB and vC. vA and vB are the vectors containing the matrix data that would be multiplied and the result stored in the vector vC. On closer examination of the code, it can be noticed that each iteration in the two outer loops are independent from each other and therefore can be parallelized.

LISTING 5-7 Simple Matrix Multiplication without using C++ AMP

```
void DoMatrixMulWithoutAmp(std::vector<int>& vC, const std::vector<int>& vA, const std::vector<int>& vB,
int M, int N, int W)
{
    // computes result serially
    for(int i = 0; i< M; ++i)
    {
            for(int j = 0; j < N; ++j)
            {
                    int sum = 0;
                    for (int k = 0; k < W; ++k)
                            sum += vA[i * W + k] * vB[k * N + j];
                    vC[i * N + j] = sum;
            }
    }
}
```

The same example with the data offloaded to an accelerator looks like this:

LISTING 5-8 Simple Matrix Multiplication using C++ AMP Simple Model

```
void DoMatrixMulWithAmp(std::vector<int>& vC, const std::vector<int>& vA, const std::vector<int>& vB, int
M, int N, int W)
{
    array_view<const int, 2> a(M, W, vA), b(W, N, vB);
    array_view<int, 2> c(M, N, vC);
    c.discard_data();
```

```
parallel_for_each(c.extent, [=](index<2> idx) restrict(amp)
{
    int row = idx[0]; int col = idx[1];
    int sum = 0;
    for(int i = 0; i < b.extent[0]; i++)
        sum += a(row, i) * b(i, col);
    c[idx] = sum;
});
c.synchronize();
}
```

In order to convert the function to run on an accelerator, you cannot use the std::vector objects in the restrict (amp) function. So we have to copy data over to the accelerator either by using the array<T, N> object or by wrapping the vector container (and hence the underlying data) with an array_view <T,N> object from amp.h. Now we can access the same data through the array_view objects (a and b) instead of the vector objects (vA and vB), and the added benefit is that we can capture the array_view objects in the lambda that we pass to the parallel_for_each call and the data will get copied on demand to the accelerator. As an obvious performance improvement, you should call discard_data on the array_view "c" to ensure that the contents of "c" are not copied to the GPU unnecessarily.

Note that the const before the int when creating vA and vB, will result in the underlying data only being copied to the accelerator and not be copied back – a good optimization for this particular sample. The actual computation happens when we make the call to the C++ AMP entry point (parallel_for_each) to invoke our parallel loop or, as some may say, dispatch our kernel.

The first argument we need to pass describes how many threads we want for this computation. For this algorithm we decided that we want exactly the same number of threads as the number of elements in the output matrix, i.e. in array_view c which will eventually update the vector vC. So each thread will compute exactly one result. Since the elements in c are organized in a 2-dimensional manner we can organize our threads in a two-dimensional manner too. We don't have to think too much about how to create the first argument (an extent) since the array_view object helpfully exposes that as a property. Note that instead of c.extent we could have written extent<2>(M, N) – the result is the same in that we have specified M*N threads to execute our lambda.

The second argument is a restrict(amp) lambda that accepts an index object. Since we elected to use a two-dimensional extent as the first argument of parallel_for_each, the index will also be two-dimensional and it represents the thread ID, which in our case maps perfectly to the index of each element in the resulting array_view.

The lambda body or the kernel, is the code that will actually execute on the accelerator. It will be called by M*N threads and we can use those threads to index into the two input array_views (a,b) and write results into the output array_view (c).

Copying data between CPU and GPU

There are different ways to copy data between CPU and GPU. You should also be aware of unnecessary copying and how to minimize unneeded copying.

1. You can copy data to the accelerator (the GPU) by constructing an array on the default accelerator and copy data using a single call such as the statement below.

   array<int, 1> a(5, begin(v), end(v)) where for example, v is a std::vector.

   You can also construct an uninitialized array and then copy over data using the copy function.

2. When you use an array_view class that is associated with a container such as a std::vector, it automatically copies data from CPU to accelerator and vice-versa when it is used in the lambda or when the elements of the array are accessed or when the *synchronize* method is called on the array after the parallel_for_each function call, not at construction time. This is one of the advantages of using the array_view class. The general rule is that if the target *accelerator_view* does not contain the latest copy of data for *array_view*, an implicit copy will take place from *accelerator_view* which contains latest copy of data to the target *accelerator_view*. Calling synchronize copies the latest data from the accelerator_view to the array_view's data source that it is associated with, while blocking the current thread.

3. When your array_view class is associated with a container such as std::vector, data is copied back into the associated container when the array_view class gets destructed. As a best practice, you should always use synchronize method versus relying on the data being copied back when the array_view class gets destructed. Using the synchronize method also means that you would be able to observe and catch any exceptions that might occur.

4. In order to minimize unwanted copying between CPU and accelerator, you can setup an array_view with the const data type specifier. As existing C++ developers, you already know that specifying const on a type means that data contained in the variable does not change.

   For example, array_view<const int, 1> arr(5, v) means that the data contained by array_view will be sent to the accelerator but does not change.

5. If the initial values from an array_view need not be copied over to the accelerator, you can make use of the discard_data member function that provides a hint to the runtime that initial values need not be copied to the accelerator as they will anyways be overwritten by the kernel functions.

Using Tiles in C++ AMP

Another optimization technique available for you is "tiling". "Tiling" can be used to maximize performance of your app. Tiling enables you to take advantage of the programmable GPU cache. Tiling divides threads into equal rectangular subsets or *tiles*. Each *tile* has access to a local programmable cache which is a couple of orders of magnitude faster to access compared to the global memory. If you use an appropriate tile size and tiled algorithm, you can get even more acceleration from your C++ AMP code. There are two steps in the "tiling" process:

- Tile the computation.

- Copy the tile data into tile_static memory for faster access.

Tiling increases the performance gains you would normally obtain from the simpler C++ AMP model and increases the gains by a 2x factor. C++ AMP provides certain classes to support tiling. These include the tiled_index and tiled_extent classes as well as tile_static class, which is a new storage class for local variables and tile_barrier type. We will now explore tiled_extent and tile_static classes. The tile_barrier type will be explored later when discussing synchronization during tiling.

The tiled_extent and the tiled_index classes

An overloaded version of the parallel_for_each function exists that takes a tiled_extent as a parameter instead of the regular extent class. As discussed earlier, the extent describes the N-dimensional space. In other words, the entire compute domain. The compute domain determines how many threads (typically the size) and the shape (dimension) will execute the computation.

For example, extent<1> e(8) describes a compute domain in which 8 threads execute in single dimension. Similarly, extent<2> e(2, 8) describes a compute domain in which 16 threads execute in two-dimensional space. A tiled_extent describes how to break up the original non-tiled extent into equally sized tiles. Here is a single-dimensional example:

extent<1> e(20);   // 20 units in a single dimension with indices from 0-19

tiled_extent<4> te = e.tile<4>();

In the example above, we subdivided the single-dimensional space e into 5 single-dimensional tiles each having 4 elements, and we captured that result in a *concurrency::tiled_extent*.

In this release of C++ AMP, you can obtain a tiled_extent for up to a rank of only three. If you have more dimensions than three, you can either forego tiling or refactor your code. Another restriction in the current release is that the total number of threads in a tile cannot exceed 1024.

In order to use a tiled_extent class in a parallel_for_each call, you should also pass a tiled_index instead of the regular index instance from the simpler model. The tiled_index provides an index into a tiled_extent class. A tiled_index, however, consists of 4 index objects that are accessible via properties: *global*, *local*, *tile_origin*, and *tile*. The *global* index is the same as the global thread ID. The *local* index is the local thread ID within the tile. The *tile_origin* index returns the global index of the thread that is at position 0,0 of this tile, and the *tile* index is the position of the tile in relation to the overall compute domain.

The following example shows the simple Matrix Multiplication example modified to use the tiled_exent and tiled_index classes.

LISTING 5-9 Matrix Multiplication with C++ AMP Tiling support

```
void DoMatrixMulWithAmpTiling(std::vector<int>& vC, const std::vector<int>& vA, const std::vector<int>& vB,
int M, int N, int W)
{
    static const int TS = 16;
    array_view<const int, 2> a(M, W, vA), b(W, N, vB);
    array_view<int, 2> c(M, N, vC);
    c.discard_data();

    parallel_for_each(c.extent.tile<TS, TS>(), [=](tiled_index<TS, TS> t_idx) restrict(amp)
    {
        index<2> idx = t_idx.global;
        int row = idx[0]; int col = idx[1];
        int sum = 0;
        for(int i = 0; i < b.extent[0]; i++)
            sum += a(row, i) * b(i, col);
        c[idx] = sum;
    });
    c.synchronize();
}
```

To turn the simple Matrix Multiplication example into a tiled example, first we need to decide our tile size. Let's say we want each tile to be 16*16 (which assumes that we'll have at least 256 threads to process, and that *c.extent.size()* is divisible by 256, and moreover that *c.extent[0]* and *c.extent[1]* are divisible by 16). So we define the tile size (which must be a compile time constant) at the beginning of our function DoMatrixMulWithAmpTiling.

```
static const int TS = 16;
```

Next, we need to tile the *extent* to have tiles where each one has 16*16 threads, so we change the extent definition to be as follows

```
parallel_for_each(c.extent.tile<TS,TS>(),
```

Since a tiled_index must be used in conjunction with the tiled_extent, we now use a tiled_index instead of just a plain index

```
[=](tiled_index<TS, TS> t_idx) restrict(amp)
```

Finally, without changing our core algorithm, we need to be using the global index that the tiled_index gives us access to, so we add a new line inside the parallel_for_each definition as follows:

```
index<2> idx = t_idx.global;
```

That's it. Now our code is tiled and it just works! However, there is a subtle race condition in our code above and for correctness, we should ensure that access to shared variables is synchronized.

The tile_static and the tile_barrier classes

The second part of tiling involves copying data into tile_static memory for frequent and faster access to data from all the tiles. Data that is stored in array or array_view classes is held in global memory and access to such data is significantly slower when compared to accessing data from tile_static memory. An instance of a **tile_static** variable is created for each tile, and all threads in the tile have access to the variable. In a typical tiled algorithm, data is copied into **tile_static** memory once from global memory and then accessed many times from the **tile_static** memory.

There are a few restrictions that are placed on the usage of tile_static memory.

1. tile_static can only be used within the context of a restrict(amp) function.

2. tile_static can only be used if the parallel_for_each function uses tiles.

3. Only variables declared within the function block can be used along with tile_static.

4. Pointers and reference types cannot be marked as tile_static.

5. Implicit constructors and destructors for tile_static variables are not called.

In most typical cases, your instance of tile_static would be an array proportional to the tile size. The best way to take advantage of tile_static is to identify global memory that would be frequently accessed in your code. You can then copy those areas into tile_static memory thereby paying the price of global memory access only once in your application and then proceed to change your algorithm to access data from tiled memory which is significantly much faster. You also avoid having to copy data multiple times into multiple places in global memory with this approach.

One thing to be aware of though is this: the programmable cache on a GPU is very small. This means you cannot copy all of the data stored in all arrays or array views to tile_static variables. A tiled algorithm is typically more complex because it needs to work around that by copying only a tile-size-worth of data from global memory.

Tile Synchronization

Tiling becomes useful when the tiles are integral to the algorithm and exploit **tile_static** variables. Because all threads in a tile have access to **tile_static** variables, calls to **tile_barrier::wait** are used to synchronize access to the **tile_static** variables. Although all of the threads in a tile have access to the **tile_static** variables, there is no guaranteed order of execution of threads in the tile. You can't construct a tile_barrier object yourself, but you can obtain one through the barrier property from the tiled_index passed to your lambda.

We can now re-write our Matrix Multiplication sample as follows:

LISTING 5-10 Matrix Multiplication with C++ AMP tile_barrier support

```
void DoMatrixMulwithAmpTileBarrier(std::vector<int>& vC, const std::vector<int>& vA, const
std::vector<int>& vB, int M, int N, int W)
{
    static const int TS = 16;
    array_view<const int, 2> a(M, W, vA), b(W, N, vB);
    array_view<int, 2> c(M, N, vC);
    c.discard_data();

    parallel_for_each(c.extent.tile< TS, TS >(),
        [=] (tiled_index< TS, TS> t_idx) restrict(amp)
        {
            int row = t_idx.local[0]; int col = t_idx.local[1];
            float sum = 0.0f;

            for (int i = 0; i < W; i += TS) {
                tile_static float locA[TS][TS], locB[TS][TS];
                locA[row][col] = a(t_idx.global[0], col + i);
                locB[row][col] = b(row + i, t_idx.global[1]);
                //need to synchronize threads in each tile and hence we need a call to wait on the barrier
                t_idx.barrier.wait();

                for (int k = 0; k < TS; k++)
                    sum += locA[row][k] * locB[k][col];
                // need a wait call on the barrier to synchronize the threads
                t_idx.barrier.wait();
            }
            c[t_idx.global] = sum;
        });
    c.synchronize();
}
```

Why should you want to use tile_static memory? Because accessing tile_static memory is around 50-100 times faster than accessing the global memory on an accelerator like the GPU, e.g. in the code above, if you can get 150GB/second accessing data from an array_view, you can get 1500GB/second accessing the tile_static array. And since by definition you are dealing with really large data sets, the savings really pay off.

Now, some algorithms will not have performance benefits from tiling (and in fact may deteriorate), e.g. algorithms that require you to go only once to global memory may not benefit from tiling, since with tiling you already have to fetch the data once from global memory! Other algorithms may benefit, but you may decide that you are happy with your code being 50 times faster than the serial-version you had, and you do not need to invest to make it 100 times faster. Also algorithms with more than 3 dimensions, which C++ AMP supports in the simple model, cannot be tiled.

And here are the numbers from two different runs. The numbers in below are from a dual-core, hyper-threaded, x64 PC with an nVidia GeForce GTx 550 Ti GPU.

1. Simple Matrix Multiplication: 19208 milliseconds to complete

2. Matrix Multiplication with C++ AMP Basic model: 795 milliseconds to complete

3. Matrix Multiplication with C++ AMP tiling model with race condition: 93 milliseconds to complete

4. Matrix Multiplication with C++ AMP tiling model with tile barriers: 78 milliseconds to complete

Running the same tests on an Intel Core i7 quad-core CPU based PC with an Intel HD Graphics GPU gave the following numbers. Please note that the Intel HD Graphics card does not support DirectX 11 and hence the C++ AMP runtime uses the Microsoft Basic Renderer device.

1. Simple Matrix Multiplication: 8764 milliseconds to complete

2. Matrix Multiplication with C++ AMP Basic model: 3516 milliseconds to complete

3. Matrix Multiplication with C++ AMP tiling model with race condition: 3308 milliseconds to complete

4. Matrix Multiplication with C++ AMP tiling model with tile barriers: 2149 milliseconds to complete

As you can see from the numbers above, having a DirectX 11 capable GPU allows you to offload computational workload to the GPU and C++ AMP makes it very easy to achieve performance boosts that your computationally intensive apps need!

Debugging C++ AMP applications

We shall now explore how to debug an application that C++ AMP to take advantage of the graphics processing unit (GPU). It uses the Matrix Multiplication sample we have developed earlier. You can download the Matrix Multiplication sample (MatrixMul) from the book sample download location.

This walkthrough illustrates the following tasks:

- Launching the GPU debugger.

- Inspecting GPU threads in the GPU Threads window.

- Using the Parallel Stacks window to simultaneously observe the call stacks of multiple GPU threads.

- Using the Parallel Watch window to inspect values of a single expression across multiple threads at the same time.

- Flagging, freezing, thawing, and grouping GPU threads.

- Executing all the threads of a tile to a specific location in code.

Debugging the GPU code

C++AMP programs contain code that executes on the CPU as well on the GPU. In certain cases, you want to debug the code that executes on the GPU. In this section, we will explore how to debug the GPU code, which is the code contained in the parallel_for_each function. The GPU code performs the matrix multiplication across each tile in parallel.

To debug the GPU code

1. In **Solution Explorer**, open the shortcut menu for **MatrixMul.sln**, and then choose **Properties**.

2. In the **Property Pages** dialog box, under **Configuration Properties**, choose **Debugging**.

3. In the **Debugger to launch** list, select **Local Windows Debugger**.

4. In the **Debugger Type** list, select **GPU Only**.

5. Choose the **OK** button.

6. Set a breakpoint at line 83, as shown in the following illustration.

```
75        parallel_for_each(c.extent.tile< TS, TS >(),
76        [=] (tiled_index< TS, TS> t_idx) restrict(amp)
77        {
78            int row = t_idx.local[0]; int col = t_idx.local[1];
79            float sum = 0.0f;
80
81            for (int i = 0; i < result; i += TS) {
82                tile_static float locA[TS][TS], locB[TS][TS];
83                locA[row][col] = a(t_idx.global[0], col + i);
84                locB[row][col] = b(row + i, t_idx.global[1]);
85                t_idx.barrier.wait();
86
87                for (int k = 0; k < TS; k++)
88                    sum += locA[row][k] * locB[k][col];
89
90                t_idx.barrier.wait();
91            }
92            c[t_idx.global] = sum;
93        });
```

FIGURE 5-1 Setting breakpoints in GPU code

7. On the menu bar, choose **Debug**, **Start Debugging**.

Using the GPU Threads Window

GPU threads are different from CPU threads. Visual Studio 2012 debugger includes support to display the GPU threads and associated call stacks in addition to the CPU threads and call stacks that we have all come to know and depend upon. Follow these steps to open the GPU Threads Window (hidden by default).

1. To open the GPU Threads window, on the menu bar, choose **Debug**, **Windows**, **GPU Threads**. You can inspect the state the GPU threads in the GPU Threads window that appears.

2. Dock the GPU Threads window at the bottom of Visual Studio. Choose the **Expand Thread Switch** button to display the tile and thread text boxes. The GPU Threads window shows the total number of active and blocked GPU threads, as shown in the following illustration.

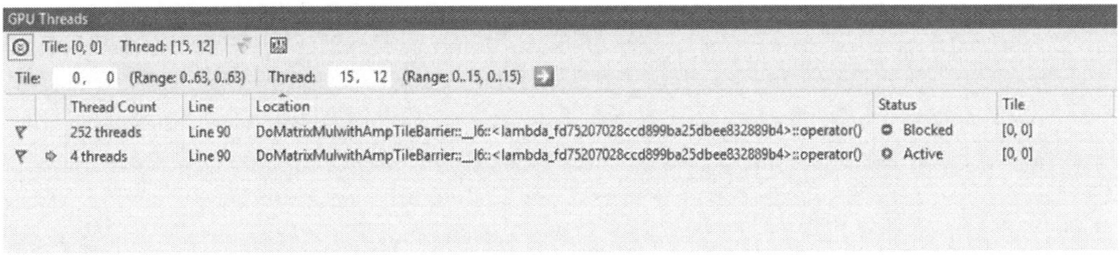

FIGURE 5-2 GPU Threads Window

There are 64x64 tiles allocated for this computation. Each tile contains 16 threads. Because local GPU debugging occurs on a software emulator, there are four active GPU threads. The four threads execute the instructions simultaneously and then move on together to the next instruction.

1. In the GPU threads window, there are four GPU threads active and 252 GPU threads blocked at the tile_barrier::wait statement defined at about line 90 (t_idx.barrier.wait();). All 4 active GPU threads belong to the first tile, tile[0]. An arrow points to the row that includes the current thread. To switch to a different thread, use one of the following methods:

   - In the row for the thread to switch to in the GPU Threads window, open the shortcut menu and choose **Switch To Thread**. If the row represents more than one thread, you will switch to the first thread according to the thread coordinates.

   - Enter the tile and thread values of the thread in the corresponding text boxes and then choose the **Switch Thread** button.

The Call Stack window displays the call stack of the current GPU thread.

Using the Parallel Stacks Window

1. To open the Parallel Stacks window, on the menu bar, choose **Debug**, **Windows**, **Parallel Stacks**. You can use the Parallel Stacks window to simultaneously inspect the stack frames of multiple

GPU threads.

2. Dock the Parallel Stacks window at the bottom of Visual Studio.

3. Make sure that **Threads** is selected in the list in the upper-left corner. In the following illustration, the Parallel Stacks window shows a call-stack focused view of the GPU threads that you saw in the GPU Threads window.

FIGURE 5-3 The Parallel Stacks Window

256 threads went from _kernel_stub to the lambda statement in the parallel_for_each function where the matrix multiplication computation occurs in parallel. You can inspect the properties of a GPU thread that are available in the GPU Threads window in the rich DataTip of the Parallel Stacks window. To do this, rest the mouse pointer on the stack frame of the lamda. The following illustration shows the DataTip.

		Thread Count	Status	Address	Stack Frame
▼	⇨	4 GPU Threads	◉ Active	0x00005768	matrixmul.cpp_line_93!DoMatrixMulwithAmpTileBarrier::_l6::<lambda_b026ed503f8b5aac3bbfc04520e74284>::operator()(Conc...
▼		252 GPU Threads	◉ Active	0x00005684	matrixmul.cpp_line_93!DoMatrixMulwithAmpTileBarrier::_l6::<lambda_b026ed503f8b5aac3bbfc04520e74284>::operator()(Conc...

FIGURE 5-4 Using DataTips in the GPU Threads Window

Using the Parallel Watch Window

1. To open the Parallel Watch window, on the menu bar, choose **Debug**, **Windows**, **Parallel Watch**, **Parallel Watch 1**. You can use the Parallel Watch window to inspect the values of an expression across multiple threads.

2. Dock the Parallel Watch 1 window to the bottom of Visual Studio. There are 256 rows in the table of the Parallel Watch window. Each corresponds to a GPU thread that appeared in both the GPU Threads window and the Parallel Stacks window. Now, you can enter expressions whose values you want to inspect across all 256 GPU threads.

3. Select the **Add Watch** column header, enter **t_idx.local**, and then choose the Enter key.

4. Select the **Add Watch** column header again, type **t_idx.global**, and then choose the Enter key.

5. Select the **Add Watch** column header again, type **locA[t_idx.local[0]]**, and then choose the Enter key.

6. You can sort by a specified expression by selecting its corresponding column header.

7. Select the **locA[t_idx.local[0]]** column header to sort the column. The following illustration shows the results of sorting by **locA[t_idx.local[0]]**.

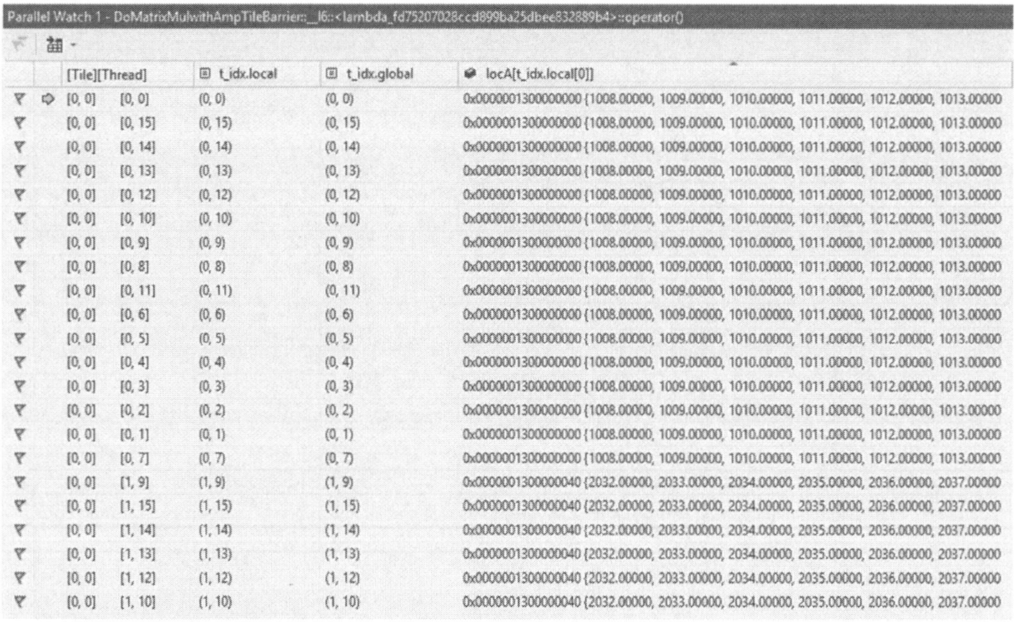

	[Tile][Thread]		⊞ t_idx.local	⊞ t_idx.global	🔗 locA[t_idx.local[0]]
▼ ⇨	[0, 0]	[0, 0]	(0, 0)	(0, 0)	0x0000001300000000 {1008.00000, 1009.00000, 1010.00000, 1011.00000, 1012.00000, 1013.00000
▼	[0, 0]	[0, 15]	(0, 15)	(0, 15)	0x0000001300000000 {1008.00000, 1009.00000, 1010.00000, 1011.00000, 1012.00000, 1013.00000
▼	[0, 0]	[0, 14]	(0, 14)	(0, 14)	0x0000001300000000 {1008.00000, 1009.00000, 1010.00000, 1011.00000, 1012.00000, 1013.00000
▼	[0, 0]	[0, 13]	(0, 13)	(0, 13)	0x0000001300000000 {1008.00000, 1009.00000, 1010.00000, 1011.00000, 1012.00000, 1013.00000
▼	[0, 0]	[0, 12]	(0, 12)	(0, 12)	0x0000001300000000 {1008.00000, 1009.00000, 1010.00000, 1011.00000, 1012.00000, 1013.00000
▼	[0, 0]	[0, 10]	(0, 10)	(0, 10)	0x0000001300000000 {1008.00000, 1009.00000, 1010.00000, 1011.00000, 1012.00000, 1013.00000
▼	[0, 0]	[0, 9]	(0, 9)	(0, 9)	0x0000001300000000 {1008.00000, 1009.00000, 1010.00000, 1011.00000, 1012.00000, 1013.00000
▼	[0, 0]	[0, 8]	(0, 8)	(0, 8)	0x0000001300000000 {1008.00000, 1009.00000, 1010.00000, 1011.00000, 1012.00000, 1013.00000
▼	[0, 0]	[0, 11]	(0, 11)	(0, 11)	0x0000001300000000 {1008.00000, 1009.00000, 1010.00000, 1011.00000, 1012.00000, 1013.00000
▼	[0, 0]	[0, 6]	(0, 6)	(0, 6)	0x0000001300000000 {1008.00000, 1009.00000, 1010.00000, 1011.00000, 1012.00000, 1013.00000
▼	[0, 0]	[0, 5]	(0, 5)	(0, 5)	0x0000001300000000 {1008.00000, 1009.00000, 1010.00000, 1011.00000, 1012.00000, 1013.00000
▼	[0, 0]	[0, 4]	(0, 4)	(0, 4)	0x0000001300000000 {1008.00000, 1009.00000, 1010.00000, 1011.00000, 1012.00000, 1013.00000
▼	[0, 0]	[0, 3]	(0, 3)	(0, 3)	0x0000001300000000 {1008.00000, 1009.00000, 1010.00000, 1011.00000, 1012.00000, 1013.00000
▼	[0, 0]	[0, 2]	(0, 2)	(0, 2)	0x0000001300000000 {1008.00000, 1009.00000, 1010.00000, 1011.00000, 1012.00000, 1013.00000
▼	[0, 0]	[0, 1]	(0, 1)	(0, 1)	0x0000001300000000 {1008.00000, 1009.00000, 1010.00000, 1011.00000, 1012.00000, 1013.00000
▼	[0, 0]	[0, 7]	(0, 7)	(0, 7)	0x0000001300000000 {1008.00000, 1009.00000, 1010.00000, 1011.00000, 1012.00000, 1013.00000
▼	[0, 0]	[1, 9]	(1, 9)	(1, 9)	0x0000001300000040 {2032.00000, 2033.00000, 2034.00000, 2035.00000, 2036.00000, 2037.00000
▼	[0, 0]	[1, 15]	(1, 15)	(1, 15)	0x0000001300000040 {2032.00000, 2033.00000, 2034.00000, 2035.00000, 2036.00000, 2037.00000
▼	[0, 0]	[1, 14]	(1, 14)	(1, 14)	0x0000001300000040 {2032.00000, 2033.00000, 2034.00000, 2035.00000, 2036.00000, 2037.00000
▼	[0, 0]	[1, 13]	(1, 13)	(1, 13)	0x0000001300000040 {2032.00000, 2033.00000, 2034.00000, 2035.00000, 2036.00000, 2037.00000
▼	[0, 0]	[1, 12]	(1, 12)	(1, 12)	0x0000001300000040 {2032.00000, 2033.00000, 2034.00000, 2035.00000, 2036.00000, 2037.00000
▼	[0, 0]	[1, 10]	(1, 10)	(1, 10)	0x0000001300000040 {2032.00000, 2033.00000, 2034.00000, 2035.00000, 2036.00000, 2037.00000

FIGURE 5-5 The Parallel Watch Window

8. You can export the content in the Parallel Watch window to Excel by choosing the Excel button and then choosing **Open in Excel**. If you have Excel installed on your development computer, this opens an Excel worksheet that contains the content.

9. In the upper-right corner of the Parallel Watch window, there's a filter control that you can use to filter the content by using Boolean expressions. The content is still sorted by the lo-calA[localIdx[0]] column, which is the sorting action you performed earlier.

Freezing and Thawing GPU threads

You can freeze (suspend) and thaw (resume) GPU threads from either the GPU Threads window or the Parallel Watch window. You can freeze and thaw CPU threads the same way. Follow the steps below to freeze GPU threads.

1. Select the **[Thread]** column header in the GPU Threads window to sort by tile index and thread index.

2. On the menu bar, choose **Debug**, **Continue**, which causes the four threads that were active to progress to the next barrier at line 90.

3. Click the flag symbol on the left side of the row that contains the four threads that are now active.

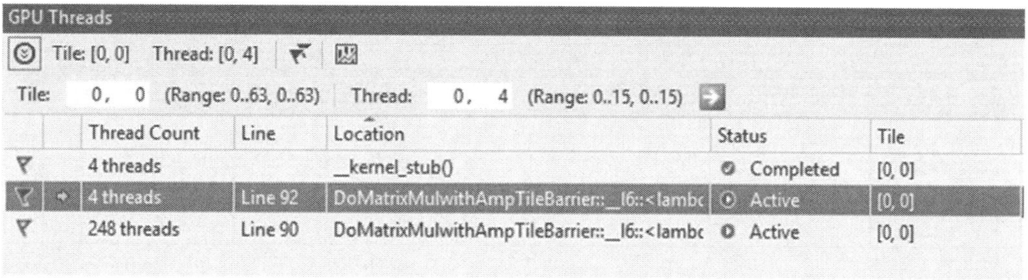

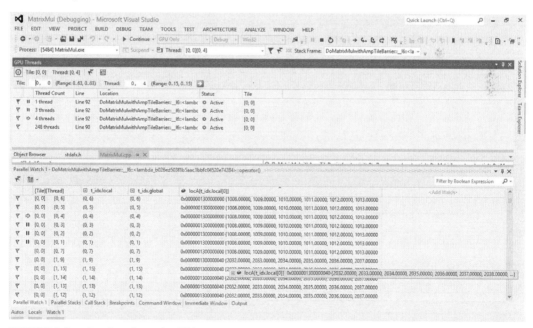

FIGURE 5-6 Active threads on the GPU

4. Choose the **Show Flagged Only** button to display all the threads.

5. On the menu bar, choose **Debug**, **Continue**.

6. Open the shortcut menu for the active row and then choose **Freeze**.

The following illustration of the GPU Threads window shows the frozen threads.

FIGURE 5-7 Freezing threads on the GPU

7. Similarly, the Parallel Watch window shows that all four threads are frozen.

8. On the menu bar, choose **Debug**, **Continue** to allow the next four GPU threads to progress past the barrier at line 90 and to reach the breakpoint at line 92. The GPU Threads window shows that the four previously frozen threads remain frozen and in the active state.

9. On the menu bar, choose **Debug**, **Continue**.

10. From the Parallel Watch window, you can also thaw multiple GPU threads. Note that the GPU debugger will only freeze a group of threads. This group is known as a "warp" and is set to a value of 4 in the software emulator that is used for debugging purposes.

Developing Windows Store apps using C++ AMP and XAML

C++ AMP is supported in Windows Store apps too! As a developer, you can create a Windows Store app and create specific workloads to be executed on the accelerator using C++ AMP. In this section, we will take a look at three case studies.

1. A Windows Store app implementing the Bitonic Sort

2. A Windows Store app implementing 2D triangle rotation.

These two cases are only meant to illustrate how to incorporate C++ AMP in Windows Store apps.

Bitonic Sort case study

Bitonic sort is a simple algorithm that works by sorting the data set into alternating ascending and descending sorted sequences. These sequences can then be combined and sorted to produce larger sequences. This is repeated until you produce one final ascending sequence for the sorted data.

Our input is randomly generated and then sorted using the BitonicSort algorithm. We will also verify if the sorting operation has succeeded and compute the time taken to sort and display the time taken for the sorting operation to complete.

In the XAMLBitonicSort sample, we have a default MainPage.xaml page that displays a TextBlock with updates on the sort progress and a Button that starts the Sorting operation on its Click event. In this example, we do not process the sort operation asynchronously. Asynchronous operations are used in the next example demonstrating the 2D Triangle Rotation.

bitonic_sort_amp is the C++ AMP tiled implementation of the sort algorithm. This function is called from the Button Click event handler with input and output buffers. These buffers are encapsulated in **concurrency::array** objects and passed to kernels for computation. Initially the data is sorted in chunks of *BITONIC_TILE_SIZE*. The bitonic sort shader we have created works great when the data set is small enough to run with one tile. Unfortunately, for ComputeShader 5.0, which C++ AMP supports, this means a maximum of 1024 elements, which is the largest power of 2 number of threads in

245

a tile. To solve this, we can add two additional steps to the algorithm. When we need to sort a section that is too large to be processed by a single group of threads, we transpose the entire data set. With the data transposed, larger sort steps can be performed entirely in shared memory without changing the bitonic sort algorithm. Once the large steps are completed, the data can be transposed back to complete the smaller steps of the sort.

Thus, in our case, if the data size is larger than *BITONIC_TILE_SIZE*, the algorithm breaks the data into multiples of *BITONIC_TILE_SIZE* – this is implemented inside the second *for* loop. This takes data sorted along rows, interprets the data subset as a 2D matrix and transposes to sort the column data, and then sorts column data. It does a transpose again, now to sort the row data and then sorts. This continues until all the data is sorted.

LISTING 5-12 Listing for the bitonic_sort_amp functon

```
template <typename _type>
void bitonic_sort_amp(std::vector<_type>& data_in, std::vector<_type>& data_out)
{
    // Verify assumptions
    assert(NUM_ELEMENTS/MATRIX_WIDTH == MATRIX_WIDTH);
    assert(((MATRIX_WIDTH%TRANSPOSE_BLOCK_SIZE) == 0) && ((MATRIX_HEIGHT%TRANSPOSE_BLOCK_SIZE) == 0));
    assert(data_out.size() == NUM_ELEMENTS);

    array<_type, 1> temp(data_out.size());
    array<_type, 1> data(data_out.size(), data_in.begin());

    // Sort the data
    // First sort the rows for the levels <= to the block size
    extent<1> compute_domain(NUM_ELEMENTS);

    for (unsigned level = 2; level <= BITONIC_BLOCK_SIZE ; level = level * 2 )
    {
        parallel_for_each(compute_domain.tile<BITONIC_BLOCK_SIZE>(), [=, &data]
(tiled_index<BITONIC_BLOCK_SIZE> tidx) restrict(amp)
        {
            bitonic_sort_kernel<_type>(data, level, level, tidx);
        });
    }

    unsigned ulevel;
    unsigned ulevelMask;
    unsigned width;
    unsigned height;

    // Then sort the rows and columns for the levels > than the block size
    // Transpose. Sort the Columns. Transpose. Sort the Rows.
    for( unsigned level = (BITONIC_BLOCK_SIZE * 2) ; level <= NUM_ELEMENTS ; level = level * 2 )
    {
        ulevel = (level / BITONIC_BLOCK_SIZE);
        ulevelMask = (level & ~NUM_ELEMENTS) / BITONIC_BLOCK_SIZE;
        width = MATRIX_WIDTH;
        height = MATRIX_HEIGHT;
```

```
        // Transpose the data from buffer 1 into buffer 2
        extent<2> cdomain_transpose(MATRIX_WIDTH, MATRIX_HEIGHT);
        parallel_for_each (cdomain_transpose.tile<TRANSPOSE_BLOCK_SIZE, TRANSPOSE_BLOCK_SIZE>(),
            [=, &data, &temp] (tiled_index<TRANSPOSE_BLOCK_SIZE, TRANSPOSE_BLOCK_SIZE> tidx)
restrict(amp)
            {
                transpose_kernel<_type>(data, temp, width, height, tidx);
            });

        // Sort the transposed column data
        extent<1> cdomain_num_elements(NUM_ELEMENTS);
        parallel_for_each(cdomain_num_elements.tile<BITONIC_BLOCK_SIZE>(), [=, &temp]
(tiled_index<BITONIC_BLOCK_SIZE> tidx) restrict(amp)
        {
            bitonic_sort_kernel<_type>(temp, ulevel, ulevelMask, tidx);
        });

        ulevel = BITONIC_BLOCK_SIZE;
        ulevelMask = level;
        width = MATRIX_HEIGHT;
        height = MATRIX_WIDTH;

        // Transpose the data from buffer 2 back into buffer 1
        parallel_for_each (cdomain_transpose.tile<TRANSPOSE_BLOCK_SIZE, TRANSPOSE_BLOCK_SIZE>(),
            [=, &data, &temp] (tiled_index<TRANSPOSE_BLOCK_SIZE, TRANSPOSE_BLOCK_SIZE> tidx)
restrict(amp)
            {
                transpose_kernel<_type>(temp, data, width, height, tidx);
            });

        // Sort the row data
        parallel_for_each(cdomain_num_elements.tile<BITONIC_BLOCK_SIZE>(), [=, &data]
(tiled_index<BITONIC_BLOCK_SIZE> tidx) restrict(amp)
        {
            bitonic_sort_kernel<_type>(data, ulevel, ulevelMask, tidx);
        });
    }

    copy(data, data_out.begin());
}
```

bitonic_sort_kernel, called from the **bitonic_sort_amp** is sorting a row of size *BITONIC_TILE_SIZE* number of elements at a time. All *BITONIC_TILE_SIZE* thread will read one element from GPU global memory into tile_static memory to avoid redundant reads. Then sorting is done in tile_static memory, here each thread will pick min or max, and then synchronizes before writing the result to tile_static memory. Eventually each thread will copy out the result from tile_static memory (indexed using the tile local id) to global memory (indexed using the global thread id).

LISTING 5-13 Listing for the bitonic_sort_kernel function

```
//-------------------------------------------------------------------------
// Kernel implements partial sorting on accelerator, BITONIC_BLOCK_SIZE at a time
//-------------------------------------------------------------------------
```

```
template <typename _type>
void bitonic_sort_kernel(array<_type, 1>& data, unsigned ulevel, unsigned ulevelmask,
tiled_index<BITONIC_BLOCK_SIZE> tidx) restrict (amp)
{
    tile_static _type sh_data[BITONIC_BLOCK_SIZE];

    int local_idx = tidx.local[0];
    int global_idx = tidx.global[0];

    // Cooperatively load data - each thread will load data from global memory
    // into tile_static
    sh_data[local_idx] = data[global_idx];

    // Wait till all threads have loaded their portion of data
    tidx.barrier.wait();

    // Sort data in tile_static memory
    for (unsigned j = ulevel >> 1 ; j > 0 ; j >>= 1)
    {
        _type result = ((sh_data[local_idx & ~j] <= sh_data[local_idx | j]) == (bool)(ulevelmask &
global_idx)) ? sh_data[local_idx ^ j] : sh_data[local_idx];
        tidx.barrier.wait();
        sh_data[local_idx] = result;
        tidx.barrier.wait();
    }

    // Store shared data
    data[global_idx] = sh_data[local_idx];
}
```

transpose_kernel, called from *bitonic_sort_amp,* transposes a 2D square matrix of size *TRANS-POSE_TILE_SIZE * TRANSPOSE_TILE_SIZE*. Given the input data as 1D vector, we could have used math to calculate linear address based on thread index and tile index to transpose. Another solution is to use *view_as* member function to view a 1D vector as a 2D matrix and then transform like a regular 2D matrix.

LISTING 5-14 Listing for the transpose_kernel function

```
//---------------------------------------------------------------------------
// Kernel implements 2D matrix transpose
//---------------------------------------------------------------------------
template <typename _type>
void transpose_kernel(array<_type, 1>& data_in, array<_type, 1>& data_out, unsigned width, unsigned height,
tiled_index<TRANSPOSE_BLOCK_SIZE, TRANSPOSE_BLOCK_SIZE> tidx) restrict (amp)
{
    tile_static _type transpose_shared_data[TRANSPOSE_BLOCK_SIZE][TRANSPOSE_BLOCK_SIZE];
    extent<2> e_mat_dim(width, height);

    array_view<_type, 2> transpose_matrix_a = data_in.view_as(e_mat_dim);
    transpose_shared_data[tidx.local[0]][tidx.local[1]] =
transpose_matrix_a[tidx.global[0]][tidx.global[1]];

    tidx.barrier.wait();
```

```
    array_view<_type, 2> transpose_matrix_b = data_out.view_as(e_mat_dim);
    transpose_matrix_b[tidx.global[1]][tidx.global[0]] =
transpose_shared_data[tidx.local[0]][tidx.local[1]];
}
```

Running the XamlBitonicSort sample on an nVidia GeForce Gtx 550Ti produces an output similar to the following screenshot.

FIGURE 5-8 Bitonic Sort verification

Sample 2D Triangle Rotation as a XAML App

Our next sample, AmpXamlD3D, available along with the book samples, displays the rotation animation of a 2D triangle object.

The sample uses two interop APIs that bridge Direct3D and C++ AMP. It uses the *direct3d::ceate_accelerator_view()* and *direct3d::get_buffer()* to share the updated vertex positions computed in the C++ AMP code with the vertex shader in the D3D code. In *ComputeEngine.h* file, the C++ AMP code is encapsulated in an *AMP_compute_engine* class. The TriangleRenderer.h, TriangleRenderer.cpp. Writing shader code is not a strict requirement for using C++AMP.

LISTING 5-15 Listing for the ComputeEngine class

```
class AMP_compute_engine
{
public:
    AMP_compute_engine(ID3D11Device* d3ddevice) : m_accl_view(create_accelerator_view(d3ddevice))
    {
    }

    void initialize_data(int num_elements, const Vertex2D* data)
    {
        m_data = std::unique_ptr<array<Vertex2D,1>>(new array<Vertex2D, 1>(num_elements, data,
```

```
m_accl_view));
    }

    HRESULT get_data_d3dbuffer(void** d3dbuffer) const
    {
        return get_buffer(*m_data)->QueryInterface(__uuidof(ID3D11Buffer), reinterpret_cast<LPVOID*>(
d3dbuffer) );
    }

    void run()
    {
        array<Vertex2D, 1>& data_ref = *m_data;

        // Transform the vertex data on the accelerator which is associated with the array data_ref.
        //
        // If in some cases, you need to use array_view instead of array, you need to explicitily
        // specify the accelerator_view in the parallel_for_each to avoid implicit copy of the array_view
        // data from the acclerator_view m_accl_view to the default accelerator_view of the
        // parallel_for_each
        parallel_for_each(m_data->extent, [=, &data_ref] (index<1> idx) restrict(amp)
        {
            // Rotate the vertex by angle THETA
            DirectX::XMFLOAT2 pos = data_ref[idx].Pos;
            data_ref[idx].Pos.y = pos.y * cos(THETA) - pos.x * sin(THETA);
            data_ref[idx].Pos.x = pos.y * sin(THETA) + pos.x * cos(THETA);
        });
    }

private:
    accelerator_view                                    m_accl_view;
    std::unique_ptr<array<Vertex2D, 1>> m_data;
};
```

The C++ AMP code computes the rotation transformation to get the updated vertex positions using C++ AMP parallel_for_each(). This is stored in a C++ AMP array. The AmpXamlD3D class initializes the main application instance. In our case, the AmpXamlD3D is the name of our application class and this is derived from the Windows::ApplicationModel::Core::IFrameworkView interface.

The program entry point, *main*, creates an instance of the Direct3DapplicationSource class which implements the Windows::ApplicationModel::Core::IFrameworkViewSource interface. It then calls the static method **Run** of the CoreApplication class. This begins the application activation process and creates an instance of the TriangleRenderer class. The Run method dispatches calls to the Render function of the TriangleRenderer class.

LISTING 5-16 Listing of the Run method

```
void AmpXamlD3D::Run()
{
    BasicTimer^ timer = ref new BasicTimer();

    while (!m_windowClosed)
    {
            if (m_windowVisible)
```

```
            {
                    timer->Update();

    CoreWindow::GetForCurrentThread()->Dispatcher->ProcessEvents(CoreProcessEventsOption::ProcessAllIfPr
esent);
                    m_renderer->ComputeRenderData();
                    m_renderer->Render();  // render internally calls Present()

            }
            else
            {

    CoreWindow::GetForCurrentThread()->Dispatcher->ProcessEvents(CoreProcessEventsOption::ProcessOneAndA
llPending);
            }
    }
}
```

The TriangleRenderer class initializes device specific and device independent resources, creates and renders the vertex and pixel shaders.

LISTING 5-17 Listing of the ComputeRenderData method of TriangleRenderer

```
//-------------------------------------------------------------------------------
// Run compute shader to acquire data
//-------------------------------------------------------------------------------
void TriangleRenderer::ComputeRenderData()
{
    // Only draw the triangle once it is loaded (loading is asynchronous).
    if (!m_loadingComplete)
    {
            return;
    }
     m_AmpComputeEngine->run();
}
```

To use the updated vertex position data in the vertex shader, the D3D code creates a shader resource view on the returned D3D buffer. In Visual Studio 2012, the D3D buffer underling C++ AMP array is implemented as (RW) ByteAddressBuffer. This is important to know when creating the shader resource view. It also requires adjustments in the vertex shader when accessing the corresponding buffer.

Here is the code snippet to create the shader resource view.

```
            // Bind a resource view to the CS buffer
            D3D11_BUFFER_DESC descBuf;
            ZeroMemory( &descBuf, sizeof(descBuf) );
            m_vertexPosBuffer->GetDesc(&descBuf);

            D3D11_SHADER_RESOURCE_VIEW_DESC DescRV;
            ZeroMemory( &DescRV, sizeof( DescRV ) );
            DescRV.Format = DXGI_FORMAT_R32_TYPELESS;
            DescRV.ViewDimension = D3D11_SRV_DIMENSION_BUFFEREX;
            DescRV.BufferEx.Flags = D3D11_BUFFEREX_SRV_FLAG_RAW;
```

```
          DescRV.Buffer.FirstElement = 0;
          DescRV.Buffer.NumElements = descBuf.ByteWidth / sizeof(int);
          ID3D11Resource* pRes = m_vertexPosBuffer.Get();
          m_d3dDevice->CreateShaderResourceView(pRes, &DescRV, &m_VertexPosBufferRV);
          pRes = NULL;
```

On every frame, the vertex position of the rotated triangle is computed in the C++ AMP code. The vertex shader and the pixel shader use the shared data to render the triangle. The actual draw operation happens when you finally call the *Present* method on the underlying SwapChain.

LISTING 5-18 Listing of the Render method of TriangleRenderer

```
void TriangleRenderer::Render()
{
    // Only draw the triangle once it is loaded (loading is asynchronous).
    if (!m_loadingComplete)
    {
            return;
    }

    // Bind the vertex shader data though the compute shader result buffer view
    UINT stride = sizeof( Vertex2D );
    UINT offset = 0;
    m_d3dContext->IASetVertexBuffers(0, 1, m_vertexBuffer.GetAddressOf(), &stride, &offset);
    m_d3dContext->IASetPrimitiveTopology( D3D11_PRIMITIVE_TOPOLOGY_TRIANGLELIST );

    ID3D11ShaderResourceView* aRViews[ 1 ] = { m_VertexPosBufferRV.Get() };
    m_d3dContext->VSSetShaderResources( 0, 1, aRViews );

    // Clear the back buffer
    const float ClearColor[] = { 0.0f, 0.125f, 0.3f, 1.0f };
    m_d3dContext->ClearRenderTargetView(
            m_renderTargetView.Get(),
            ClearColor
            );

    m_d3dContext->OMSetRenderTargets(1, m_renderTargetView.GetAddressOf(), NULL);

    // Render the triangle
    m_d3dContext->VSSetShader( m_vertexShader.Get(), NULL, 0 );
    m_d3dContext->PSSetShader( m_pixelShader.Get(), NULL, 0 );
    m_d3dContext->Draw( m_numVertices, 0 );

    ID3D11ShaderResourceView* ppSRVNULL[1] = { NULL };
    m_d3dContext->VSSetShaderResources( 0, 1, ppSRVNULL );

    // Present the information rendered to the back buffer to the front buffer (the screen)
    Present();
}
```

Replacing the compute shader in a DirectX 3D Windows Store application with C++ AMP features can simplify your effort, and with the C++ AMP interoperability you can integrate C++ AMP code and DirectX 3D code seamlessly without sacrificing the benefits of resource sharing. Obviously, without the interoperability APIs, you would have had to copy-back-and-forth through CPU memory to communicate the data between the compute and rendering shaders.

Running the app produces output similar to the following.

FIGURE 5-8 AMP Triangle Renderer output

The ImageEffects application

In this section, we will develop a Windows Store app using XAML, Direct3D and C++. Our goal is to implement "image effects" on a picture that is rendered on screen. This sample is a port from the original Win32 application developed by the C++AMP team and hosted on their blog at http://blogs.msdn.com/b/nativeconcurrency/archive/2012/07/13/image-effects-sample-in-c-amp.aspx.

> **Tip** We do not discuss C++AMP and DirectX interop in great detail here. A great reference option is the companion Microsoft Press book "C++AMP" authored by Ade Miller and Kate Gregory.

Prerequisites

Before we get started, make sure you download the ImageEffects sample from the samples download location.

1. In order to run this sample, you will need a graphics card that is DirectX 11 certified and

supports DirectX Feature level 11.0

2. Microsoft Windows 8

3. Microsoft Visual Studio 2012

If your machine does not have a DirectX 11 certified graphics card with DirectX 11 feature level support, you can re-compile the code to run under Windows Advanced Rasterization Platform (WARP). WARP is a high speed, fully conformant software rasterizer that is a part of the DirectX runtime. You can get more details on WARP at http://msdn.microsoft.com/en-us/library/gg615082(v=VS.85).aspx.

Follow the instructions located in the DirectXBase::CreateDeviceResources function in order to build the sample to run under WARP.

Running the sample

The sample will run on any machine with atleast one DirectX 11 GPU with DirectX Feature 11 support. The sample makes extensive use of asynchronous tasks to load an image file and then render it on screen using Direct3D textures. A complete description of DirectX textures is outside the scope of this book.

To run the sample, build the ImageEffects solution and deploy it to your Windows 8 machine. Tap the tile on the Start screen to launch the app. When the app starts, it displays an Application bar with two buttons: Effects and Open. Tap the Open button to launch the File Picker that displays your Pictures Library. Select any picture from the Pictures Library and click on the Open button in the File Picker. The app displays the selected picture on screen with a black border around the picture.

FIGURE 5-10 ImageEffects start screen

FIGURE 5-11 After loading a sample image

Once the picture is displayed, swipe from the bottom of the screen to launch the application bar (Or if you are using a non-touch machine, you can launch the application bar by using either the shortcut key Win + Z or by right clicking the mouse). Tap on the Effects menu option to launch a flyout containing various image effect options.

You can apply various effects to the rendered image and observe the changes.

FIGURE 5-12 The "Image Effects" menu options

Load image to a texture

For the purposes of loading an image to a texture, we make use of the WICTextureLoader from the DirectX Toolkit, available at http://directxtk.codeplex.com/. WICTextureLoader is a Windows Imaging Component (WIC)-based image file texture loader.

Windows Store apps cannot directly load files based on the file name or path. In order for us to load a file, we use the file picker to get the path of the file and then use the StorageFile APIs to get the entire data of the file into a buffer. Our method to get the file data as an array is listed below:

LISTING 5-19 Reading image file data asynchronously

```
inline Concurrency::task<Platform::Array<byte>^> ReadPictureDataAsync(Windows::Storage::StorageFile^
file)
{
    using namespace Windows::Storage;
    using namespace Concurrency;

    return create_task(FileIO::ReadBufferAsync(file)).then([] (Streams::IBuffer^ fileBuffer) ->
Platform::Array<byte>^
    {
        auto fileData = ref new Platform::Array<byte>(fileBuffer->Length);
        Streams::DataReader::FromBuffer(fileBuffer)->ReadBytes(fileData);
        return fileData;
    });
}
```

Once we have the file loaded into a buffer, we proceed to use the WICTextureLoader to load the buffer into memory and create an ID3D11Texture2D object and its corresponding ID3D11ShaderResource object. This code is very simple and is listed below.

LISTING 5-20 Creating a texture using WICTextureLoader

```
ComPtr<ID3D11ShaderResourceView> sptextureView;
ComPtr<ID3D11Resource> sptexture;
DX::ThrowIfFailed(CreateWICTextureFromMemory(m_d3dDevice.Get(), m_d3dContext.Get(), &fileData[0],
(size_t)fileData->Length, &sptexture, &sptextureView, NULL));
```

We now have an ID3D11Texture2D object from the physical image file. In our sample, we assume that the image file has a format as DXGI_FORMAT_R8G8B8A8_UNORM. We now have a texture on the GPU containing the pixels of the source image along with a corresponding ID3D11ShaderResourceView object. This will be bound to the graphics pipeline when we need to render them on screen.

Creating an accelerator_view from an ID3D11Device object

In order to support seamless interop between C++AMP for computational needs and DirectX for rich graphical rendering, C++AMP provides 4 APIs in the concurrency::direct3d namespace. They are:

- accelerator_view create_accelerator_view(IUnknown* _D3d_device_interface) which returns a newly created instance of an accelerator_view from an existing Direct3D device interface pointer.

- template<typename T, int N>

  array<T,N> make_array(const extent &_Extent, const accelerator_view &_Rv, IUnknown *_D3d_buffer_interface) which creates an array with the specified extents on the specified accelerator_view from an existing Direct3D buffer interface pointer.

- IUnknown* get_device(const accelerator_view &_Rv) which returns an IUnknown interface pointer corresponding to the D3D device underlying the passed accelerator_view.

- template<size_t RANK, typename _Elem_type>

  IUnknown* get_buffer(const array<_Elem_type, RANK> &_F) which returns an IUnknown interface pointer corresponding to the D3D buffer underlying the passed array.

In our sample, we will use the first API, create_accelerator_view to interop between DirectX device interface and C++AMP. For the purposes of our sample, we will create a class that encapsulates C++AMP functionality: this includes the DirectX interop APIs as well as the image filters that are applied.

The C++AMP Compute Engine class

The C++AMP Compute Engine class, AMP_compute_engine, has a constructor that accepts an ID3D11Device instance and creates an accelerator_view using the create_accelerator_view interop API. A helper method getView, is used to fetch this instance whenever we need it in code.

The class also contains various helper methods that implement a few convolution based image effects, namely ApplyEdgeDetection and ApplyOneConvolutionFilter. This code is a direct port from the corresponding Win32 sample mentioned above without any changes whatsoever. The algorithms themselves are a translation from the algorithms in any image processing textbook to the corresponding C++AMP code.

LISTING 5-21 The AMP_compute_engine class

```
class AMP_compute_engine
{
public:
    AMP_compute_engine(ID3D11Device* d3ddevice) : m_accl_view(create_accelerator_view(d3ddevice))
    {
    }

    accelerator_view getView()
    {
            return m_accl_view;
    }
```

```
// filter traits
template<filter_kind kind>
struct filter_trait;
template<>
struct filter_trait<sobel_kind>
{
        static const int size = 3;
        static void create_filter(filter<3> &GX, filter<3> &GY) restrict(cpu, amp)
        {
                GX(0, 0) = -1.0f; GX(0, 1) = 0.0f; GX(0, 2) = 1.0f;
                GX(1, 0) = -2.0f; GX(1, 1) = 0.0f; GX(1, 2) = 2.0f;
                GX(2, 0) = -1.0f; GX(2, 1) = 0.0f; GX(2, 2) = 1.0f;

                GY(0, 0) =  1.0f; GY(0, 1) =  2.0f; GY(0, 2) =  1.0f;
                GY(1, 0) =  0.0f; GY(1, 1) =  0.0f; GY(1, 2) =  0.0f;
                GY(2, 0) = -1.0f; GY(2, 1) = -2.0f; GY(2, 2) = -1.0f;
        }
};

template<>
struct filter_trait<prewitt_kind>
{
        static const int size = 3;
        static void create_filter(filter<3> &GX, filter<3> &GY) restrict(cpu, amp)
        {
                GX(0, 0) = -1.0f; GX(0, 1) = 0.0f; GX(0, 2) = 1.0f;
                GX(1, 0) = -1.0f; GX(1, 1) = 0.0f; GX(1, 2) = 1.0f;
                GX(2, 0) = -1.0f; GX(2, 1) = 0.0f; GX(2, 2) = 1.0f;

                GY(0, 0) =  1.0f; GY(0, 1) =  1.0f; GY(0, 2) =  1.0f;
                GY(1, 0) =  0.0f; GY(1, 1) =  0.0f; GY(1, 2) =  0.0f;
                GY(2, 0) = -1.0f; GY(2, 1) = -1.0f; GY(2, 2) = -1.0f;
        }
};

template<>
struct filter_trait<scharr_kind>
{
        static const int size = 3;
        static void create_filter(filter<3> &GX, filter<3> &GY) restrict(cpu, amp)
        {
                GX(0, 0) =  3.0f; GX(0, 1) =  10.0f; GX(0, 2) =  3.0f;
                GX(1, 0) =  0.0f; GX(1, 1) =   0.0f; GX(1, 2) =  0.0f;
                GX(2, 0) = -3.0f; GX(2, 1) = -10.0f; GX(2, 2) = -3.0f;

                GY(0, 0) =  3.0f; GY(0, 1) =  0.0f; GY(0, 2) =  -3.0f;
                GY(1, 0) = 10.0f; GY(1, 1) =  0.0f; GY(1, 2) = -10.0f;
                GY(2, 0) =  3.0f; GY(2, 1) =  0.0f; GY(2, 2) =  -3.0f;
        }
};

template<>
struct filter_trait<emboss_kind>
{
```

```
            static const int size = 3;
            static const int factor = 1;
            static const int offset = 127;
            static void create_filter(filter<3> &GX) restrict(cpu, amp)
            {
                    GX(0, 0) = -1.0f; GX(0, 1) = 0.0f; GX(0, 2) =  0.0f;
                    GX(1, 0) =  0.0f; GX(1, 1) = 0.0f; GX(1, 2) =  0.0f;
                    GX(2, 0) =  0.0f; GX(2, 1) = 0.0f; GX(2, 2) =  1.0f;
            }
    };


    template<>
    struct filter_trait<gaussian_kind>
    {
            static const int size = 5;
            static const int factor = 577;
            static const int offset = 1;
            static void create_filter(filter<5> &GX) restrict(cpu, amp)
            {
                    GX(0, 0) =  2.0f; GX(0, 1) =  7.0f; GX(0, 2) =  12.0f; GX(0, 3) =  7.0f; GX(0, 4) =
2.0f;
                    GX(1, 0) =  7.0f; GX(1, 1) = 31.0f; GX(1, 2) =  52.0f; GX(1, 3) = 31.0f; GX(1, 4) =
7.0f;
                    GX(2, 0) = 15.0f; GX(2, 1) = 52.0f; GX(2, 2) = 127.0f; GX(2, 3) = 52.0f; GX(2, 4) =
15.0f;
                    GX(3, 0) =  3.0f; GX(3, 1) = 31.0f; GX(3, 2) =  52.0f; GX(3, 3) = 31.0f; GX(3, 4) =
7.0f;
                    GX(4, 0) =  2.0f; GX(4, 1) =  7.0f; GX(4, 2) =  12.0f; GX(4, 3) =  7.0f; GX(4, 4) =
2.0f;
            }
    };


    template<>
    struct filter_trait<sharpen_kind>
    {
            static const int size = 3;
            static const int factor = 3;
            static const int offset = 1;
            static void create_filter(filter<3> &GX) restrict(cpu, amp)
            {
                    GX(0, 0) =  0.0f; GX(0, 1) = -2.0f; GX(0, 2) =  0.0f;
                    GX(1, 0) = -2.0f; GX(1, 1) = 11.0f; GX(1, 2) = -2.0f;
                    GX(2, 0) =  0.0f; GX(2, 1) = -2.0f; GX(2, 2) =  0.0f;
            }
    };


    template<>
    struct filter_trait<mean_removal_kind>
    {
            static const int size = 3;
            static const int factor = 1;
            static const int offset = 1;
            static void create_filter(filter<3> &GX) restrict(cpu, amp)
            {
```

```
                        GX(0, 0) = -1.0f; GX(0, 1) = -1.0f; GX(0, 2) = -1.0f;
                        GX(1, 0) = -1.0f; GX(1, 1) =  9.0f; GX(1, 2) = -1.0f;
                        GX(2, 0) = -1.0f; GX(2, 1) = -1.0f; GX(2, 2) = -1.0f;

                }
    };


    // ==================================================================================================
    // C++ AMP algorithm layer
    //==================================================================================================


    // Apply edge detection with two filters
    template<filter_kind kind>
    void ApplyEdgeDetection(const texture<unorm4, 2> & input_tex,  const writeonly_texture_view<unorm4, 2>
output_tex_view)
    {
            parallel_for_each(input_tex.accelerator_view, output_tex_view.extent, [=, &input_tex]
(index<2> idx) restrict(amp) {
                        int y = idx[0];
                        int x = idx[1];

                        const int N = filter_trait<kind>::size; // filter size
                        static_assert(N % 2 == 1, "N has to be a odd number"); // odd number
                        static const int W = N/2;

                        if( idx[0] < W || idx[0] >= output_tex_view.extent[0] - W || idx[1] < W || idx[1] >=
output_tex_view.extent[1] - W) // edge
                        {
                                output_tex_view.set(idx, unorm4());
                        }
                        else
                        {
                                static const int LB = -(W), UB = W; // loop bound

                                filter<N> GX, GY;
                                filter_trait<kind>::create_filter(GX, GY);

                                float sumX = 0.0f;
                                float sumY = 0.0f;
                                float sum = 0.0f;

                                auto f = [=, &input_tex] (int offset_y, int offset_x) restrict(amp) -> float
{
                                        index<2> id(offset_y + y, offset_x + x);
                                        float3 pixel = static_cast<float3>(input_tex[id].rgb);
                                        return (pixel.r + pixel.g + pixel.b)/3.0f;
                                };

                                // apply the filter
    #ifdef _DEBUG // for easier debugging
                                for(int i = LB; i <= UB; i++)
                                {
                                        for (int j = LB; j <= UB; j++)
                                        {
                                                float val = f(i, j);
                                                sumX += val * GX(i+1, j+1);
```

```
                                                sumY += val * GY(i+1, j+1);
                                        }
                                }
                        }
    #else // !_DEBUG
                                array_view<float> sumX_view(1, &sumX);
                                array_view<float> sumY_view(1, &sumY);
                                loop_unroller<LB, UB>::func([=](int i) restrict(amp) {
                                        loop_unroller<LB, UB>::func([=](int j) restrict(amp) {
                                                float val = f(i, j);
                                                sumX_view(0) += val * GX(i+W, j+W);
                                                sumY_view(0) += val * GY(i+W, j+W);
                                        });
                                });
    #endif // _DEBUG
                                sum = fabs(sumX);
                                sum += fabs(sumY);

                                sum = 1.0f  - fmin(sum, 1.0f);
                                output_tex_view.set(idx, unorm4(sum, sum, sum, 1.0f));
                        }
                });
        }

    // Apply a filter via convolution
    template<filter_kind kind>
    void ApplyOneConvolutionFilter(const texture<unorm4, 2> & input_tex,  const
writeonly_texture_view<unorm4, 2> output_tex_view)
    {
                parallel_for_each(input_tex.accelerator_view, output_tex_view.extent, [=, &input_tex]
(index<2> idx) restrict(amp) {
                        int y = idx[0];
                        int x = idx[1];

                        const int N = filter_trait<kind>::size;
                        static_assert(N % 2 == 1, "N has to be a odd number"); // odd number
                        static const int W = N/2;

                        if( idx[0] < W || idx[0] >= output_tex_view.extent[0] - W || idx[1] < W || idx[1] >=
output_tex_view.extent[1] - W) // edge
                        {
                                output_tex_view.set(idx, unorm4());
                        }
                        else
                        {
                                static const int LB = -(W), UB = W; // loop bound

                                filter<N> GX;
                                filter_trait<kind>::create_filter(GX);

                                auto f = [=, &input_tex] (int offset_y, int offset_x) restrict(amp) -> float3
{
                                        index<2> id(offset_y + y, offset_x + x);
                                        float3 pixel = static_cast<float4>(input_tex[id]).rgb;
                                        return pixel * GX(offset_y + W, offset_x + W);
                                };
```

```
                                  float3 result(0.0f);
        #ifdef _DEBUG // for easier debugging
                                  for(int i = LB; i <= UB; i++)
                                  {
                                          for (int j = LB; j <= UB; j++)
                                          {
                                                  result += f(i, j);
                                          }
                                  }
        #else // !_DEBUG
                                  array_view<float3> result_view(1, &result);
                                  loop_unroller<LB, UB>::func([=](int i) restrict(amp) {
                                          loop_unroller<LB, UB>::func([=](int j) restrict(amp) {
                                                  result_view(0) += f(i, j);
                                          });
                                  });
        #endif // _DEBUG

                                  result /= static_cast<float>(filter_trait<kind>::factor);
                                  result += (static_cast<float>(filter_trait<kind>::offset) / 255.0f);

                                  output_tex_view.set(idx, unorm4(result.r, result.g, result.b,
        input_tex[idx].a));
                          }
                  });
          }

private:
    accelerator_view                                    m_accl_view;

};
```

So where do we instantiate this class? When we create device resources, we create a DirectX SwapChain and then load the pixel and vertex shaders. Once we are done loading the compiled shader objects (or cso files) we will instantiate the AMP class. As you are probably aware by now, loading files is an asynchronous task in WinRT. We create the tasks needed for loading the cso files and "await" on their completion before proceeding to instantiate the AMP class. C++ does not support the "await" keyword as C# does but what we can do via the PPL is to combine tasks and then run our code in the completion handlers as shown below.

LISTING 5-22 Instantiating the compute engine class

```
auto loadVSTask = DX::ReadDataAsync("vs.cso");
auto loadPSTask = DX::ReadDataAsync("ps.cso");

// load vshader
auto createVSTask = loadVSTask.then([this](Platform::Array<byte>^ fileData) {
DX::ThrowIfFailed(m_d3dDevice->CreateVertexShader(fileData->Data, fileData->Length, nullptr,
&m_vertexShader));
    const D3D11_INPUT_ELEMENT_DESC basicVertexLayoutDesc[] =
    {
        { "POSITION", 0, DXGI_FORMAT_R32G32_FLOAT, 0,  0, D3D11_INPUT_PER_VERTEX_DATA, 0 },
        { "TEXCOORD", 0, DXGI_FORMAT_R32G32_FLOAT, 0, 12, D3D11_INPUT_PER_VERTEX_DATA, 0 },
```

```
    };

    DX::ThrowIfFailed(m_d3dDevice->CreateInputLayout(basicVertexLayoutDesc, ARRAYSIZE(basicVertexLayoutDesc),
fileData->Data, fileData->Length, &m_inputLayout));
                m_d3dContext->IASetInputLayout(m_inputLayout.Get());
    });

    auto createPSTask = loadPSTask.then([this](Platform::Array<byte>^ fileData){
    m_d3dDevice->CreatePixelShader( fileData->Data, fileData->Length, nullptr, &m_pixelShader );
    });

    auto createAmpTask = (createPSTask && createVSTask).then([this] ()
    {
        //associate the DXGI Device to the C++AMP Accelerator
        m_AmpComputeEngine = new AMP_compute_engine(m_d3dDevice.Get());


        …
    }
```

Interop between C++AMP and DirectX textures

In our sample, the C++AMP code deals with two textures: One containing the original image created via the call to WICTextureLoader and another texture containing the image after an effect has been applied. The modified image is as the same size as the source image.

We create the second texture in C++AMP directly, specifically in the LoadImage function.

// Create a texture the same size as m_inputTexture, it's used to store the effect applied texture

m_ampProcessedTexture = new texture<unorm4, 2>(static_cast<int>(imageHeight), static_cast<int>(imageWidth), 8U, m_AmpComputeEngine->getView());

In order to author the computational code that applies the effect using C++AMP, we want to use the C++AMP textures for both input as well as output. We will use the make_texture interop API to get a C++AMP texture from the DirectX input texture as below.

// input texture, original picture

const texture<unorm4, 2> input_tex = make_texture<unorm4, 2>(m_AmpComputeEngine->getView(), reinterpret_cast<IUnknown *>(m_inputTexture.Get()));

Now, we can use the input_tex for the computation using C++AMP.

Finally, when we want to render the processed texture, m_ampProcessedTexture, to screen using the graphics pipeline, we need to read it from the pixel shader. This can be done by obtaining an ID3D11Texture2D object and then create an ID3D11ShaderResourceView which can be bound to the graphics pipeline as shown below.

// Get the D3D texture from interop, and create the corresponding SRV that could be later bound to graphics pipeline

ID3D11Texture2D * processedTexture = reinterpret_cast<ID3D11Texture2D *>(get_texture<unorm4, 2>(*m_ampProcessedTexture));

m_d3dDevice->CreateShaderResourceView(processedTexture, nullptr, m_processedTextureSRV.GetAddressOf());

Once we have this setup, we can simply bind the processed texture shader resource view to the graphics pipeline. This can be done as shown in the ShowProcessedImage function of the PictureEffects class.

LISTING 5-23 The ShowProcessedImage method

```
void PictureEffects::ShowProcessedImage()
{
    if (m_inputTexture == nullptr)
    {
            return;
    }

    D3D11_TEXTURE2D_DESC input_tex_desc;
    m_inputTexture->GetDesc(&input_tex_desc);

    size_t imageWidth = input_tex_desc.Width;
    size_t imageHeight = input_tex_desc.Height;

    float ratio = static_cast<float>( imageWidth ) / static_cast<float>( imageHeight );

    size_t windowWidth = static_cast<size_t>(m_window->Bounds.Width);
    size_t windowHeight = static_cast<size_t>(m_window->Bounds.Height);

    // resize the image to fit into the window without changing the ratio
    // will only scale-down
    if (imageHeight > windowHeight)
    {
            imageHeight = min(imageHeight, windowHeight);
            imageWidth = static_cast<size_t>(static_cast<float>(imageHeight) * ratio);
    }

    if (imageWidth > windowWidth)
    {
            imageWidth =  min(imageWidth, windowWidth);
            imageHeight = static_cast<size_t>(static_cast<float>(imageWidth) / ratio);
    }

    DXGI_SWAP_CHAIN_DESC1 sd;
    m_swapChain->GetDesc1(&sd);
    if (sd.Width != imageWidth || sd.Height != imageHeight)
    {
        DX::ThrowIfFailed(m_swapChain->ResizeBuffers(sd.BufferCount, static_cast<UINT>(windowWidth),
static_cast<UINT>(windowHeight), DXGI_FORMAT_B8G8R8A8_UNORM, 0));
    }

    // Create a render target view using the back buffer
```

```
ComPtr<ID3D11Texture2D> pBackBuffer = nullptr;
DX::ThrowIfFailed(m_swapChain->GetBuffer( 0, __uuidof( ID3D11Texture2D ), &pBackBuffer ));


ComPtr<ID3D11RenderTargetView>  pRenderTargetView = nullptr;
DX::ThrowIfFailed(m_d3dDevice->CreateRenderTargetView(pBackBuffer, nullptr, &pRenderTargetView));
pBackBuffer.Reset();


std::array<ID3D11RenderTargetView*, 1> rgRViews = { pRenderTargetView.Get() };

m_d3dContext->OMSetRenderTargets( static_cast<UINT>( (rgRViews.size() )), rgRViews.data(). Nullptr );
// Setup the viewport
D3D11_VIEWPORT vp;
vp.Width = static_cast<FLOAT>(windowWidth);
vp.Height = static_cast<FLOAT>(windowHeight);
vp.MinDepth = 0.0f;
vp.MaxDepth = 1.0f;
vp.TopLeftX = 0;
vp.TopLeftY = 0;

m_d3dContext->RSSetViewports( 1, &vp );

// set the vertex buffer with four vetices that describe the shape of the
// resized image (without changing the aspect ratio)
float h_offset = static_cast<float>(imageHeight) / static_cast<float>(windowHeight);
float w_offset = static_cast<float>(imageWidth) / static_cast<float>(windowWidth);
float d_offset = 0.1f;
simple_vertex vertices[] =
{
        { float3( w_offset,  h_offset, d_offset), float2(1.0f, 0.0f) },
        { float3( w_offset, -h_offset, d_offset), float2(1.0f, 1.0f) },
        { float3(-w_offset,  h_offset, d_offset), float2(0.0f, 0.0f) },
        { float3(-w_offset, -h_offset, d_offset), float2(0.0f, 1.0f) },

};

m_d3dContext->UpdateSubresource(m_vertexBuffer.Get(), 0, nullptr, vertices, 0, 0);

// Clear the back buffer
float ClearColor[4] = { 0.0f, 0.0f, 0.0f, 0.0f }; // clear with black
m_d3dContext->ClearRenderTargetView(pRenderTargetView, ClearColor);

// Render
m_d3dContext->VSSetShader( m_vertexShader.Get(), nullptr, 0 );
m_d3dContext->PSSetShader( m_pixelShader.Get(), nullptr, 0 );
// use the m_processedTextureSRV
{
        ID3D11ShaderResourceView* rgSRVs[1];
        rgSRVs[0] = m_processedTextureSRV.Get();
        m_d3dContext->PSSetShaderResources( 0, 1, rgSRVs );
}
ID3D11SamplerState* aRState[1] = { m_samplerState.Get() };
m_d3dContext->PSSetSamplers( 0, 1, aRState );
m_d3dContext->Draw(4, 0); // draw the four vertices
```

```
    // Present our back buffer to our front buffer
    m_swapChain->Present(0, 0);

    // Clean the pipeline
    ID3D11ShaderResourceView * emptySRV = nullptr;
    m_d3dContext->PSSetShaderResources(0, 1, &emptySRV);
    if (pRenderTargetView) pRenderTargetView->Release();
}
```

The Output

On a C++AMP capable GPU, the image effects are applied without barely a spike in CPU processing power. A screenshot of the processed image is shown below, after applying the "Emboss" effect.

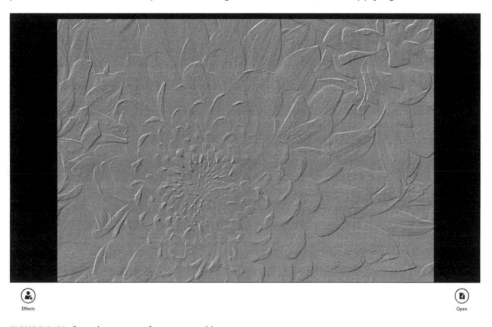

FIGURE 5-13 Sample output of a processed image

Where are we and what's Next

In this chapter, we discussed the C++ AMP technology stack. We explored the C++ AMP Library and how to use the various types provided by C++ AMP enabling GPGPU programming. We also took a look at the various techniques of C++ AMP programming, including using the Basic Model and using Tiles. Next we explored how to debug C++ AMP applications and the first class debugging support provided by Visual Studio 2012. Finally, we also studied the case of two Windows Store apps and how they integrated C++ AMP into Windows Store apps. For a more detailed discussion and exploration of C++ AMP, please refer to the authoritative title, "C++ AMP Accelerated Massive Parallelism with Microsoft® Visual C++® by Ade Miller and Kate Gregory" and published by Microsoft Press.

Thus far we have spent our time exploring various aspects of the so-called C++ renaissance, we've looked at some of the improvements that C++11 brings, then we covered C++ /CX and Windows 8 app development using XAML and DirectX. Now we've seen C++ AMP we have all the ingredients we need to create compelling Windows Store apps that differentiate themselves from their C# and HTML5 / JavaScript counterparts by being able to make full use of all the available hardware while still delivering on that 'frugal power usage' message that underpins the untethered, wires-free, device centric computing that is now on the rise.

That said we're not done yet, as C++ developers we are always curious as to how things work 'under the hood'. Let us now explore what is the Windows Runtime and take a detailed look at what enables this asynchronous, touch-centric, hardware accelerated, graphically rich and responsive platform. As part of this exploration, we will also learn how to build a simple Hello World app using C++ and the Windows Runtime Library (WRL), a low level alternative to using C++ CX.

Chapter 6
Under the covers

In this chapter:
Playing by the rules of the Windows Runtime
Introduction to the Windows Runtime Library
Hello World XAML App using the Windows Runtime Library
Working with the Windows Runtime Library
Using the Windows Runtime Library in Windows Store apps
Where are we and what's Next

Playing by the rules of the Windows Runtime

The Windows Runtime platform supports Windows Store applications that only execute within a trustworthy system environment, named the AppContainer. Windows Store applications are also to use only authorized functions (APIs), data types, devices and should be distributed via the Windows Store.

The Windows Runtime platform defines a programming model that enables writing object oriented code in the supporting languages, which in turn, can be shared across programming languages. The key to enabling such support lies in metadata. Native code cannot contain metadata; hence the Windows Runtime metadata is stored in platform agnostic WINMD files. The metadata contained in these WINMD files is based on the .NET metadata format. Hence .NET programmers can use the code written in native programming languages. Similarity with the .NET metadata also allows reflection-like functionality for the Windows Runtime metadata.

- A Windows metadata file supports only publicly declared (public) classes, class methods, class properties, structures, structure data members, enumerations, interfaces, parameterized interfaces, interface member functions, delegates, fully instantiated templates, and generics.

- A well-formed .winmd file has the same name as the root namespace that is defined in the code. For example, a class that's named A.B.C.MyClass can be instantiated only if it's defined in a metadata file that's named A.winmd or A.B.winmd or A.B.C.winmd.

The Windows Runtime type system defines how types are declared and used in the runtime. The type system is also an important part of the runtime's support for language projections. The type system performs the following functions:

- Establishes a robust framework enabling for language projections and type safety.

- Provides an object oriented programming model.

- Defines rules that languages must follow which helps ensure that objects written in different programming languages can interact with each other.

Versioning Support in the Windows Runtime

Except for the primitive types, all other types in WinRT support versioning. All types included in the Windows and nested namespace include a version attribute. Since this is the first version of Windows that supports WinRT, the version attribute is a forward thinking attribute for future versions of WinRT that will offer new and enhanced capabilities. As WinRT becomes more prevalent and popular, language projections, including C++ /CX, C# and JS use the version attribute to enable compatibility with previous systems and enable APIs for the right platform.

The version attribute includes a 32-bit integer. For WinRT types, this value is the value for version of Windows for which the type was initially defined in. For third party components, it is up to the author to define whatever value they deem fit for their component.

It must be noted here that third party WinRT components can have the version attribute, however these would be ignored by the language projections. This is because all third party WinRT components are packaged along with the app and can never be updated independent of the app itself.

Type System Overview

The Windows Runtime supports a rich variety of types ranging from fundamental types like integers, double etc to user-defined types such as classes and interfaces. All types, except for the fundamental types, are contained in namespaces. No types, other than fundamental types are allowed in the global namespace.

All of the types provided by Windows, other than fundamental types, are contained in the **Windows** namespace or one of its nested namespaces. Types that are provided by teams other than Windows are contained in specific namespaces and not in the Windows namespace. For example, the C++ projection namespaces are contained in the **Platform** namespace. The CLR has a similar namespace for types projected for the managed languages.

Types in WinRT can be broadly classified into two categories:

- Value Types: Value types directly contain their data, and instances of value types are either allocated on the stack or allocated inline in a structure.

- Reference Types: Reference types store a reference to the value's memory address, and are allocated on the heap. Reference types can be self-describing types, pointer types, or interface types. The type of a reference type can be determined from values of self-describing types. Self-describing types are further split into arrays and class types.

Fundamental Types

The Windows Runtime type system includes a core set of fundamental or primitive types. The following table lists the set of primitive types supported in WinRT.

TABLE 6-1   List of WinRT fundamental types.

WinRT Type	Type Description
Int16	A 16 bit signed integer
Int32	A 32 bit signed integer
Int64	A 64 bit signed integer
UInt8	An 8 bit unsigned integer
UInt16	A 16 bit unsigned integer
UInt32	A 32 bit unsigned integer
UInt64	A 64 bit unsigned integer
Single	A 32-bit IEEE 754 floating point number
Double	A 64-bit IEEE 754 floating point number
Char16	a 16-bit non-numeric value representing a UTF-16 code unit
Boolean	an 8-bit Boolean value
String	an immutable sequence of Char16s used to represent text
Guid	A 128-bit standard Guid

Enums

An enum type is a distinct value type with a set of named constants. The enum type itself is backed by an integral type representation. This integral type is also known as the underlying enum type. WinRT allows only Int32 and UInt32 as underlying enum types. You might pause to think what the difference is between using an Int32 versus using UInt32 as the underlying enum type. Well, enums with a UInt32 backing type must specify the FlagsAttribute whereas enums with an Int32 backing type must not specify the FlagsAttribute. The FlagsAttribute indicates that the enum values can be treated as a bit flag. Consider the following two code samples:

LISTING 6-1   Declaring enums in WinRT

```
public:
[FlagsAttribute]
    enum class Season
    {
            Summer,
            Fall,
            Winter,
            Autumn,
            All = Summer | Fall | Winter | Autumn
    };
public:
    enum class SeasonNoFlags
    {
            Summer,
            Fall,
```

```
        Winter,
        Autumn
};
```

The enum, SeasonWithFlags, has an enumeration value of All, which could carry one of the values of Summer, Fall, Winter or Autumn. Hence this enumeration must carry the [FlagsAttribute].

The second enum, SeasonNoFlags, has no enumeration which combines the values of any of its enum values. Hence it should not carry the [FlagsAttribute] attribute.

All enums must have public accessibility. Enums are also versionable. Additions to an enum may add values. However, values already added must not be removed or changed. Enum values also have the option of carrying the [VersionAttribute] to distinguish between when specific values were added to the enum type. If, however, the [VersionAttribute] is not specified, then it is considered that the enum value has the same version value of the enclosing type.

Structures in WinRT

Structures or Structs are record types with at least one or more fields. Structs in WinRT are always passed and returned by value. Structs in WinRT are value types and hence the fields contained in Structs can only be enums, other structs and WinRT primitive types including Strings.

Like enums, structs must also have public visibility and all its fields must be public. In addition, structs cannot be generic or parameterized.

The following example shows how to declare structs

LISTING 6-2 Structs in WinRT

```
value struct Employee
{
   int          Age_;
   String^      FirstName_;
   String^      LastName_;
   String^      Address_;
   int          EmpID_;
};
```

Parameterized Types in the Windows Runtime

A parameterized type defines a family of related types. In addition to supporting parameterization of primitive types, WinRT allows parameterization of interfaces and delegate types too. The parameterized types permit a family of interfaces to be defined that may be processed polymorphically in programming languages that support parametric polymorphism.

WinRT interfaces are assigned GUIDs to uniquely identify the interface from all other interfaces on the same object. The GUIDs are also used to marshal the correct interface and its methods. A parameterized type instantiation occurs when a parameterized type is specified with an argument list of types in a type context, such as a method parameter position. For example, "HRESULT foo(IVector<int> myVector)" instantiates the parameterized type named by "IVector" with the type "int" as its first and only type argument.

Each parameterized interface (eg IVector<T>) and parameterized delegate (eg EventHandler<T>) is assigned a parameterized interface ID (PIID) - a GUID uniquely identifying this parameterized type. This is not an IID. This GUID is used in generating IIDs for parameterized type instances (eg IVector<int>).

Parameterized Type Arguments

The following WinRT types are permitted to appear in a parameterized argument list.

- WinRT primitive types. The primitive types are listed in Table 1-1.

- WinRT enums

- WinRT structs

- WinRT interfaces

- WinRT delegates

- WinRT Runtime classes

- Other parameterized types like IVector<IVector<int>> etc.

Other than the types listed above, it is forbidden to use any other type as a parameterized type argument.

Parameterized Type Instances

A parameterized type instance can appear in any context that a non-parameterized type can appear. Parameterized interface instances may be used anywhere an interface may be used, such as in the list of interfaces implemented by a runtime class. Parameterized delegate instances may be used anywhere a delegate may be used, such as in the definition of an event.

Parameterized type parameters can appear, in the parameterized interface or delegate definition, any place that a normal type can normally appear. If a parameter appears where only an interface can appear, that parameter is restricted to be an interface; if a parameter appears in a context where any type can appear, that parameter is not restricted; and so forth. Arguments to parameterized type instances must meet all such restrictions.

Interfaces in WinRT

An *interface* defines a set of methods that an object can support, without dictating anything about the implementation. The interface marks a clear boundary between code that calls a method and the code that implements the method. Interfaces must have a unique interface identifier (IID) specified using the GuidAttribute.

Interfaces may have public or private visibility. This reflects the fact that some interfaces represent shared contracts implemented by multiple WinRT classes while other interfaces represent members implemented by a single WinRT class. Private visibility interfaces must specify the WinRT class they are exclusive to via the ExclusiveToAttribute. Private interfaces may only be implemented by the WinRT class specified in the ExclusiveToAttribute.

IUnknown and IInspectable

If you have programmed COM, you would know that **IUnknown** is the base interface in COM. All other COM interfaces derive from **IUnknown**. COM classes, or co-classes, implement all the methods in **IUnknown** plus any other derived interfaces too. For the Windows Runtime, the base interface is no longer **IUnknown** but a brand new interface called **IInspectable**. **IInspectable** derives from **IUnknown** but also adds three new methods in addition to the **AddRef**, **QueryInterface** and **Release** methods from **IUnknown**. The three new methods added by **IInspectable** are

- **GetIids**: fetches the interface IDs implemented by the current Windows Runtime component

- **GetRuntimeClassName**: returns the fully qualified name of the current Windows Runtime object.

- **GetTrustLevel**: returns the trust level of the current Windows Runtime object. This function is used during component activation.

These three methods, in addition to IUnknown's three methods, allow a client to retrieve information about the WinRT object. For example, classic COM uses GUIDs to uniquely identify interfaces and classes. WinRT, however, uses normal Strings. The **GetRuntimeClassName**, for example, returns the complete String that is used to identify the object. This value is particularly used to resolve WinRT type names the Windows Runtime Metadata thus allowing for language projection.

An interface may also specify that it requires one or more interfaces that must be implemented on any object that also implements the current interface. For example, if **IFoo** requires **IMust** then any class implementing **IFoo** must also implement **IMust**.

There is however a deviation from traditional COM with respect to adding new features by deriving from an existing interface. The usual practice of creating a new interface **IFoo2** by inheriting from **IFoo** and adding new features is not allowed.

Interface Members

WinRT interfaces support three types of members: methods, properties and events. WinRT interfaces cannot contain data fields.

Interface Methods

WinRT interfaces support methods that take zero or more parameters and return a HRESULT indicating success or failure of the method call. Methods cannot have default values.

Interface Methods may optionally include a single [out] parameter. The [out] parameter is used by exception based languages to be projected as the return type. Note that C++ /CX follow this pattern v/s exposing HRESULTs. All interface methods must have public accessibility. It is also prohibited to have variable number of arguments in interface methods.

Interface Methods may not be parameterized. Parameterized delegates and methods of parameterized interfaces may use type parameters of the containing type in the method signature.

Method Parameters

All method parameters except array length parameters must have a name and a type. Return values must specify a name just like parameters do. Method name parameters including the return type must be unique within the scope of the method. As mentioned above, methods may not be individually parameterized; however parameters for parameterized delegates and methods of parameterized interfaces may specify parameterized type for the parameter type. Parameterized property types must specify a type parameter from the containing type as the parameter type.

All method parameters must be exclusively in or out parameters, in/out parameters are not supported.

Methods may optionally indicate that their final out parameter is intended to be used as the return value when the method is projected into exception based languages. When a return value out parameter is specified, it must be the last parameter in the method signature. Other than return value position, there are no other ordering requirements for out parameters.

Array Parameters

WinRT only supports array parameters of most WinRT types including fundamental types (including string and guid), structs, enums, delegates, interfaces and runtime classes. Arrays of other arrays are not allowed. Because they are conformant, arrays parameters must always be immediately preceded in the parameter list by a parameter for the array length. The array length parameter must be a UInt32. The array length parameter does not have a name.

WinRT supports three different array passing styles:

- PassArray – this style is used when the caller is providing an array to the method. In this style, both the array length parameter and array parameter are both in parameters

- FillArray – this style is used when the caller is providing an array for the method to fill, up to a maximum array length. In this style, the array length parameter is an in parameter while the array parameter is an out parameter.

- ReceiveArray – this style is used when the caller is receiving an array that was allocated by the method. In this style, the array length parameter and the array parameter are both out parameters.

- The combination of out array length parameter and in array parameter is not valid in WinRT.

When an array parameter is used as an [out,retval] parameter, the array length parameter must be an [out] parameter – that is, only the RecevieArray style is legal for retval arrays.

Method Overloading

Within the scope of a single interface, more than one method may have the same name. Methods with the same name on an interface must have unique signatures. Properties and Events cannot be overloaded. When an interface has multiple methods of the same name and number of input parameters, exactly one of those methods must be marked as the default. Of all the overloaded methods with the same name and number of input parameters, only the method marked as the default will be projected by a dynamic, weakly typed language. If there is only a single overloaded method of a given name and number of input parameters, marking it as the default is supported, but not required.

WinRT supports overloading on parameter types but favors overloading on the number of input parameters – aka the method's arity. This is done in order to support dynamic, weakly typed languages (aka JavaScript).

Properties

Properties are a paired get/set methods with matching name and type that appear in language projections as fields rather than method. Properties and their get/set methods must have public visibility.

Properties must have a get method. A property getter method has no parameters and returns a value of the property type. Properties with only a get method are called read only properties.

Properties may optionally have a set method. A property setter method has a single parameter of the property type and returns void. Properties with both a get and set method are called read/write.

Properties may not be parameterized. Properties from parameterized interfaces may use type parameters of the containing type as the property type.

Events

Events are paired add/remove listener methods with matching name and delegate type. They are a mechanism for the interface to notify interested parties when something of interest happens.

Events and their add/remove listener methods must have public visibility.

An add listener method has a single parameter of the event delegate type and returns a Windows.Foundation.EventRegistrationToken. An event remove listener method has a single parameter of the Windows.Foundation.EventRegistrationToken type and returns void.

Events may not be parameterized. Events from parameterized interfaces may use type parameters of the containing type as the event delegate type.

Parameterized Interfaces in WinRT

WinRT interfaces support type parameterization. The parameterized interface definition specifies a type parameter list in addition to interface members. The parameterized interface definition might also specify the required interfaces. A required interface of a parameterized interface may share the same type argument list, such that a single type argument is used to specify the parameterized instance of both the interface and the interface it requires. For example, if **IFoo<T>** supports iteration over the collection, it might specify **IFoo<T>** requires **IIterable<T>**. The signature of any member (aka method, property or event) of a parameterized interface may reference a type from the parameterized interface's type arguments list.

In Windows 8, third parties cannot define parameterized types. Only the parameterized interfaces defined by the system are supported.

Delegates in WinRT

Delegates in WinRT are type-safe function pointers and have public visibility. They are a simple WinRT object and expose an **Invoke** method. Invoking a delegate in turn invokes the method it references. WinRT delegates are named types and define a method signature. The signature and parameter names of the Invoke method must match the definition of the delegate. Like interfaces, delegates must have a unique interface ID (aka IID) specified via a GuidAttribute.

Unlike other WinRT objects, delegates do not implement the **IInspectable** interface. Delegates in WinRT only implement **IUnknown**. This means that delegates cannot be inspected for run time type information.

Parameterized Delegates

WinRT delegates support type parameterization. A parameterized delegate definition specifies a type parameter list in addition to the traditional method signature as specified above. In the method signature, any parameter may be specified as one of the types from the parameterized delegates' type arguments list.

In Windows 8, 3rd parties cannot define parameterized delegates. Only the parameterized delegates defined by the system are supported.

Runtime classes in WinRT

You can define classes in WinRT. These classes are called **Runtime Classes**. A class cannot, however, implement type members like methods, properties and events, directly. Instead, a class must implement one or more interfaces and all the methods from the interfaces. Runtime classes should always have public visibility.

The rules for parameterized types in runtime classes are no different from the rules governing their use in WinRT interfaces. Runtime classes cannot be parameterized. A runtime class may implement a parameterized interface instance (aka a parameterized interface with all its type parameters specified) anywhere it would typically accept a non-parameterized interface.

Runtime classes should not implement interfaces that are exclusive to another runtime class. An exclusive interface is specified via the [ExclusiveTo] attribute. A runtime class should only implement an interface if it is declared exclusive to itself or an interface that does not carry the [ExclusiveTo] attribute.

Runtime class Member Interfaces

Runtime classes may implement zero or more member interfaces. Member interfaces enable classes to expose functionality that is associated with instances of the class. Runtime classes specify a list of the member interfaces they implement. Runtime classes that implement one or more member interfaces must specify one of the member interfaces to be the default interface. Runtime classes that implement zero member interfaces do not specify a default interface.

Static Interfaces

WinRT classes may implement zero or more static interfaces. Static interfaces enable classes to expose functionality that is associated with the class itself rather than with specific instances of the class.

A runtime class must specify at least one member interface or a static interface. A class with no member and no static interfaces is invalid. Static interfaces are specified via the [StaticAttribute] associated with the runtime class. While static interfaces are declared as part of the runtime class, they are actually not implemented on class instances themselves. Rather, they are implemented on the class's activation factory.

Runtime Class Activation

Runtime classes support activation – the ability to create instances of the specified class. In order for activation to succeed, a runtime class must implement at least one member interface. WinRT supports activation via three different mechanisms. They are:

- Direct Activation with no constructor parameters
- Factory Activation with one or more constructor parameters
- Composition Activation

Direct Activation with no constructor parameters
A runtime class that supports direct activation may be activated by calling the **IActivationFactory::ActivateInstance** method on the activation factory of the runtime class. This method accepts zero parameters and returns a new instance of the runtime class.

Factory Activation with one or more constructor parameters
A runtime class that supports factory activation defines one or more factory interfaces. These factory interfaces are implemented on the activation factory of the runtime class. Such factory methods accept one or more [in] parameters and return a new instance of the runtime class. [out] parameters are strictly not allowed on such factory methods.

Factory activation needs at least one parameter. Should you need activation without parameters, instead use direct activation.

Classes that support either direct or factory activation are marked with the ActivatableAttribute. This attribute carries version information as well as an optional reference to the activation factory interface. Classes marked with the activatableAttribute must not be marked with the ComposableAttribute.

Composition
A runtime class may optionally composition – the ability to support combining multiple class instances into what appears to be a single object from outside. Composition is used to describe *has-a* relationship between multiple classes.

At runtime, a composable class is an aggregation of WinRT objects, one for each object in the composition chain. The aggregated objects delegate identity and lifetime to the controlling object. The controlling object is the object that has the activation method call on. Each object in the composition chain holds an **IInspectable*** to the class it composes. This **IInspectable*** is used to make method calls on composed base class interfaces.

Composable classes must be marked with one or more ComposableAttributes. The ComposableAttribute carries a reference to the composition factory interface, whether the factory methods on the composition factory interface can be used for controlling object activation or not as well as version information.

Composable Activation
Composable classes must define one or more composition factory interfaces, which in turn implement one or more composition factory methods. Composition factory interfaces are implemented on the class's activation factory. Composition factory interfaces are used to create composable instances of the class. Composable factory interfaces declare zero or more composable factory methods that can be used to activate instances of the class for composition purposes. Composable classes declare if the factory methods on a given composition factory interface can be used to activate the class directly as a controlling object or not. Composable factory interfaces marked as public may be used to directly activate a class as a controlling object as well as indirectly to activate a class as a composed object. Composable factory interfaces marked protected may only be used to indirectly activate a class as a composed object. Composable classes can always be activated as composed objects. Composition factory interfaces must be [ExclusiveTo] the runtime class they are implemented by.

Activation Factories

A runtime class must have an activation factory if the class is activatable, composable or has static interfaces. Activation Factories must implement the **IActivationFactory** interface. However, only classes that support direct activation provide an implementation of **IActivationFactory**'s single method **ActivateInstance**. Classes that don't support direct activation will return **E_NOTIMPL** from **IActivationFactory::ActivateInstance**.

Some Standard Patterns in WinRT

Boxing

Boxing is the ability to wrap a plain data object, such as a fundamental type, an enum or a struct, in a WinRT object that implements **IInspectable***. Parameters that accept boxed values are defined as taking an **IInspectable*** value.

Three interfaces in WinRT participate in the boxing process: **IPropertyValue**, **IReference<T>** and **IReferenceArray<T>.** Boxed value objects must implement **IPropertyValue** and may optionally implement either **IReference<T>** or **IReferenceArray<T>**, but not both.

IPropertyValue implements 37 "GetType" methods which return an unboxed value of the specific underlying type. This list covers all the fundamental types, arrays of the fundamental types, several system-defined structs, arrays of the system-defined structs as well as an array of **IInspectable** objects. There is also a Type property, which returns an enum indicating the type of the boxed value. The **IPropertyValue::Type** enum includes **OtherType** and **OtherTypeArray** values for non-system defined boxed objects.

Nullable Parameters

Nullable is the ability to support null parameter values for value types (fundamental types, enums, arrays and structs) that don't support nullability.

Interfaces, runtime classes and delegates are inherently nullable and are never used with IReference<T> as parameter types.

Async

Asynchronous APIs are present all over the Windows Runtime APIs. The Foundation namespace contains the basic classes and interfaces from which specific async-type APIs are derived. An Async pattern is as follows:

- Obtain an async operation object

- Configure that object with properties that affect the operation

- Assign a Completed handler, along with an optional Progress handler. The Async operation does not need an explicit "Start" operation.

Inside the Completed handler, check the status via the AsyncStatus object and take action as appropriate. Usually this involves calling the operation's GetResults method, which supplies an object through which you can work with those results. In order to address the vast majority of scenarios, which might cause the UI to not respond, "async" is designed into most APIs at a very low level.

Collections

The Windows.Foundation.Collections namespace defines a number of interfaces for collection types: iterators, key-value pairs, maps, map views, observable maps, observable vectors, vectors, and vector views. For example, if you get the settings container for your app's LocalSettings, you get an IApplicationSettingsContainer interface. This has a method GetChildren that returns an IMapView<string, Windows.Storage.ApplicationDataItem>, which is derived from IIterable and IIterator. So you then iterate over the collection using methods like First and MoveNext that are present in those interfaces.

Introduction to the Windows Runtime Library

The Windows Runtime C++ Template Library (WRL) is a COM-based template library that provides a low-level way to use Windows Runtime components.

As we have seen in the preceding section on the Windows Runtime, WinRT is implemented using Component Object Model (COM) technology. WinRT depends on reference-counting to manage the lifetime of objects, and other housekeeping techniques, and on testing HRESULT values to determine whether an operation succeeded or not. To successfully write a WinRT app or library, you must carefully follow WinRT rules and techniques detailed in the above section.

As a C++ developer, you are spoiled for options when you want to develop Windows Store apps. There are three ways of developing Windows Store apps using C++:

- Use a tool like ildasm to discover WinRT classes, interfaces etc and code using plain C++.

- Use a template library like the Windows Runtime C++ Template Library (WRL)

- Use the high level Visual C++ projections, C++ /CX

In this section, we explore the WRL and look at how WRL helps in developing Windows Store apps. The next section will discuss a few examples of developing Windows Store apps using WRL.

There are a few reasons why, as a developer, you might want to use WRL. Consider each of the following scenarios. If a majority of these scenarios are applicable to you, choose WRL. Else for all practical purposes of authoring and consuming WinRT components, you should choose C++ /CX.

- **Using a non-Microsoft toolset**: The WRL is a compiler-agnostic way to create and consume Windows Runtime APIs. Even if you don't use the Microsoft compiler, linker, and other development tools, you can use WRL to write apps that use Windows Runtime components, or write custom Windows Runtime components that can be used by others.

- **Performance**: By using the WRL, you can optimize your code for performance or for specific scenarios. C++/CX doesn't expose the underlying COM technology in the Windows Runtime. However, your app or component might require control of the underlying COM code to better create or consume Windows Runtime APIs. When you use the WRL, you can control critical COM directly, but also allow the WRL to control the remaining COM on your behalf. You have complete command. A good example is when working with DirectX which is not a "pure" WinRT API. You use WRL to encapsulate DirectX types and use C++ /CX to represent XAML/WinRT types.

- **Exception-free code**: C++/CX represents COM HRESULT values as exceptions. If you've inherited a code base that uses COM, or one that doesn't use exceptions, you might find that the WRL is a more natural way to work with the Windows Runtime because you don't have to use exceptions.

- **You don't like the ^**: Although C++/CX is easy to use, you might prefer not to use "handle to object (^)", **ref new**, **ref class**, and its other language features to write your code. WRL provides an alternative for developers who want to use a template library and standard C++ to write Windows Runtime code.

- **Similarity with ATL**: The purpose and design of the WRL is inspired by the Active Template Library (ATL), which is a set of template-based C++ classes that simplify the programming of COM objects. If you already know ATL, you might find that WRL programming is easier.

Exploring the Windows Runtime Library

In this section, we will explore some of the important helper classes in the Windows Runtime Library.

The RuntimeClass

If at all there is one class, other than the **ComPtr** class, which is predominantly used across WRL programming, it would be the RuntimeClass. This is a template helper class that is used to initialize any runtime class. Consider the following code sample. The RuntimeClass is used to instantiate a Windows Runtime object that inherits a specified number of interfaces. It provides automatic facility of implementing the specified interfaces and also Weak Reference support. This sample demonstrates how to declare a C++ class that implements the IFrameworkView interface. The IFrameworkView interface is defined in the ABI::Windows::ApplicationModel::Core namespace.

LISTING 6-3 Using the RuntimeClass template helper class

```
class MyAppView:public
Microsoft::WRL::RuntimeClass<ABI::Windows::ApplicationModel::Core::IFrameworkView>
{
// regular class member functions plus IFrameworkView member functions.
…..
};
```

The RuntimeClass can be used to instantiate the runtime classes with the following member interfaces:

- Runtime class with the **IWeakReference** member interface

- Runtime class with the **IWeakReferenceSource** member interface

- Runtime class that inhibit weak references.

The WeakRef Class

WinRT uses a reference counting mechanism to manage object lifetimes. In order to avoid cyclic references, it is recommended that WinRT objects implement the **IWeakReference** and **IWeakRefer-**

enceSource interfaces. The WRL WeakRef helper class helps in implementing the **IWeakReference** interface. This class can only be used by the Windows Runtime and not for classic COM classes.

A WeakRef object maintains a strong reference, which is associated with an object, and can be valid or invalid. You should call the As() or AsIID() method to obtain a strong reference. When the strong reference is valid, it can access the associated object. When the strong reference is invalid, the calls to As() or AsIID() return a nullptr implying the associated object is inaccessible.

A WeakRef object is typically used to represent an object whose existence is controlled by an external thread or application. For example, construct a WeakRef object from a reference to a file object. While the file is open, the strong reference is valid. But if the file is closed, the strong reference becomes invalid.

The ActivationFactory class

The ActivationFactory implementation in WRL provides registration methods and basic functionality for the **IActivationFactory** interface. This helper class also enables developers to provide custom factory implementation.

The ActivationFactory is used in conjunction with the SimpleActivationFactory class for instantiating runtime classes with default factory. For example, the following code instantiates a hypothetical WinRT class named MyWinRTClass using the default factory.

```
ActivableClassWithFactory(MyWinRTClass, SimpleActivationFactory<MyWinRTClass>);
```

If however you want to provide a custom factory implementation, you would override the **ActivateInstance** function and provide the implementation yourself.

LISTING 6-4 Providing a custom activation factory implementation

```
class MyWinRTClass : public ActivationFactory<IMyAdditionalWinRTInterfaceonFactory>
{
    STDMETHOD(ActivateInstance)(_Outptr_result_nullonfailure_ IInspectable **ppvObject)
{
    // custom implementation
}
};
```

When more than 3 interfaces are required to be implemented (unusual but nevertheless) on an Activation factory,

LISTING 6-5 Implementing more than 3 interfaces on an Activation Factory

```
class MyWinRTClass : public ActivationFactory<Implements<Interface1, Interface2, Interface3>, Interface4,
Interface5 etc>
{
    STDMETHOD(ActivateInstance)(_Outptr_result_nullonfailure_ IInspectable **ppvObject)
{
    // custom implementation
}
```

};

Hello World XAML App using Windows Runtime Library

Visual Studio 2012 has great support for developing Windows Store apps using C++ /CX. What it does not have is support for developing Windows Store apps using C++ and WRL. Instead, what you will have to do is write code in Visual Studio using the Code Editor and then use a makefile for compiling and building your executable. Once the executable is built, you can then package the app and sign the package using command line tools.

In this walkthrough, we will first build a XAML App using WRL that displays a Hello World on screen. We will then proceed to build and package the app, deploy the package using Powershell scripts and then launch the App from the Start screen.

Creating the XAML UI

The most frequently used method for creating XAML apps is to have an App.xaml file that declares application level resources and a MainPage.xaml that contains the various UI elements that make up the UI. This pattern is followed by all the project templates that ship along with Visual Studio 2012 and is an accepted pattern for creating XAML apps.

Another option, although not used frequently, is to create the application instance and have your markup in code itself. For the Hello World app, we will take this approach to keep things simple. The goal here to explain how things are tied together between various components in the Windows Runtime and how they work together.

Our task is very simple: Upon launch by clicking/tapping the app tile, our app should display the words "Hello World" on screen. In order to define such a UI in XAML, we will write the markup in our code. Follow these steps to get started.

- Launch Visual Studio 2012.

- Select File->New File.

- From the New File Dialog, choose Visual C++ from the Installed templates on the left pane and then select C++ File (.cpp) from the middle pane as shown in Figure 6-1.

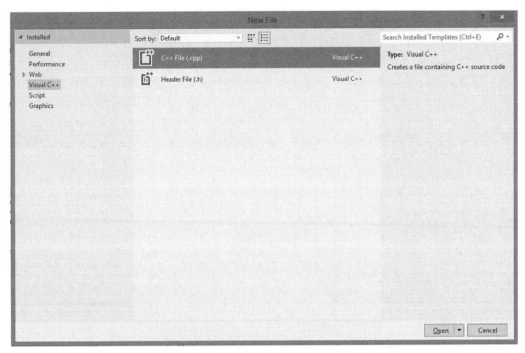

FIGURE 6-1 Creating empty C++ source file

- Click the Open button.

- Save the file with the name main.cpp. For this sample, I created a folder named Hel-loWorld and saved the file as main.cpp. My folder hierarchy looks as follows: C:\build\HelloWorld which contains main.cpp

- In the main.cpp file, add a function named CreateXamlUI. This function does not ac-cept any parameters but returns a HRESULT that indicates success or failure of the UI creation or associated steps.

- In the CreateXamlUI function, declare the markup as follows

```
    wchar_t* pszXaml =
            L"<StackPanel
xmlns='http://schemas.microsoft.com/winfx/2006/xaml/presentation' x:Name='root' "
            L"xmlns:x='http://schemas.microsoft.com/winfx/2006/xaml'> "
            L"<TextBlock Text='Hello World!' x:Name='myTextBlock' FontSize='65' /> "

            L"</StackPanel>";
```

- There are some APIs in the Windows Runtime that takes parameters of type HSTRING. A HSTRING is like any normal string except that once it is declared, it is immutable. WRL includes some handy wrappers for most of the common WinRT-types in the corewrappers.h header. We will use the HString and HStringReference wrapper classes for consuming HSTRINGs in our sample. You should use these wrappers as much as possible too.

- We need to read these series of characters, which is essentially our markup. In order to do so, we will make use of the IXamlReaderStatics interface. The XAML framework includes this interface that enables you to load and parse xaml markup. In order to obtain an instance of the IXamlReaderStatics interface pointer, you should call GetActivationFactory.

- The GetActivationFactory, present in the Windows::Foundation namespace accepts a HSTRING parameter and returns an instance of the activatable class whose name is passed as the HSTRING. You can create a HSTRING to the activatable class that contains the Xaml Reader component.

```
HStringReference xamlAc-
id(RuntimeClass_Windows_UI_Xaml_Markup_XamlReader);
```

- In the above declaration, we declare the variable xamlAcid as of type HStringReference. The HStringReference is the WRL provided wrapper for consuming HSTRING types. It contains a helpful method Set that can be used to pass WCHAR type characters to the underlying HSTRING.

- The Runtime class name for the Xaml Reader component is declared in the windows.ui.xaml.markup.h header file and this header must be included in main.cpp

- Next, we create a HStringReference to the XAML Window.

```
HStringReference windowAcid(RuntimeClass_Windows_UI_Xaml_Window);
```

- The Runtime class name for the XAML Window component is declared in windows.ui.xaml.h, along with other commonly used xaml components.

- With these declarations available, we are now ready to load and parse the markup and create our main window.

- Bare bones WinRT programming resembles COM-style programming. In order to facilitate such a style, WRL includes a handy ComPtr<T> class that helps you consume WinRT interfaces.

- You can now write the code below for parsing xaml and then create the window.

LISTING 6-6 Parsing XAML using WinRT APIs

```
ComPtr<IXamlReaderStatics> spXamlReader;
HString xaml;
ComPtr<IDependencyObject> spVisualRoot;
ComPtr<IUIElement> spRootElementasUIElement;
ComPtr<IWindowStatics> spWindowStatics;
ComPtr<IWindow> spWindow;
//Activate the Markup XAML Reader component
```

```
IFC(GetActivationFactory(xamlAcid.Get(), &spXamlReader));
IFC(xaml.Set(pszXaml, (UINT32) wcslen(pszXaml)));
IFC(spXamlReader->Load(xaml.Get(), &spVisualRoot));
IFC(spVisualRoot.As(&spRootElementasUIElement));

IFC(GetActivationFactory(windowAcid.Get(), &spWindowStatics));
IFC(spWindowStatics->get_Current(&spWindow));
IFC(spWindow->put_Content(spRootElementasUIElement.Get()));
IFC(spWindow->Activate());
```

- In the above code block, you are essentially activating the Xaml Reader component, loading the markup we declared at the beginning of the section. You then create an instance of the Xaml Window component, obtain a reference to the current window and put its content as the visual element that was obtained when you parsed the markup successfully.

- Finally calling the Activate method on the IWindow instance causes the window and its contents as defined by the markup, to be rendered on screen.

- The complete code for the CreateXamlUI method is listed below.

LISTING 6-7 Creating the XAML UI through code-behind

```
HRESULT CreateXamlUI()
{
    HRESULT hr = S_OK;
    wchar_t* pszXaml =
            L"<StackPanel xmlns='http://schemas.microsoft.com/winfx/2006/xaml/presentation'
x:Name='root' "
            L"xmlns:x='http://schemas.microsoft.com/winfx/2006/xaml'> "
            L"<TextBlock Text='Hello World!' x:Name='myTextBlock' FontSize='65' /> "
            L"</StackPanel>";

    HStringReference xamlAcid(RuntimeClass_Windows_UI_Xaml_Markup_XamlReader);
    HStringReference windowAcid(RuntimeClass_Windows_UI_Xaml_Window);


    ComPtr<IXamlReaderStatics> spXamlReader;
    HString xaml;
    ComPtr<IDependencyObject> spVisualRoot;
    ComPtr<IUIElement> spRootElementasUIElement;
    ComPtr<IWindowStatics> spWindowStatics;
    ComPtr<IWindow> spWindow;

    //Activate the Markup XAML Reader component
    IFC(GetActivationFactory(xamlAcid.Get(), &spXamlReader));
    IFC(xaml.Set(pszXaml, (UINT32) wcslen(pszXaml)));
    IFC(spXamlReader->Load(xaml.Get(), &spVisualRoot));
    IFC(spVisualRoot.As(&spRootElementasUIElement));

    IFC(GetActivationFactory(windowAcid.Get(), &spWindowStatics));
    IFC(spWindowStatics->get_Current(&spWindow));
```

```
    IFC(spWindow->put_Content(spRootElementasUIElement.Get()));
    IFC(spWindow->Activate());


Cleanup:
    return hr;
}
```

Creating the Application class

In the previous section, we were able to successfully load and parse a simple markup and activate the window on screen. But before this is usable in any manner, it needs to be more fully functional! It needs an application class. For WinRT Xaml apps, this means that apps must implement the IApplicationOverrides interface.

> **Tip** If you are writing code in WRL, all WinRT namespaces are nested inside the top-level ABI namespace. For example, Windows::UI::Xaml becomes ABI::Windows::UI::Xaml etc. This is to prevent ODR violations with C++ /CX code.

The IApplicationOverrides interface derives from IInspectable, the base interface for all WinRT interfaces. It also provides 9 methods that should be implemented in the class implementing IApplicationOverrides. These 9 methods are in addition to the 3 methods provided by IInspectable and the 3 methods provided by IUnknown making for a grand total of 15 methods to be implemented by our application class.

A simple class implementing the IApplicationOverrides interface is given below. In the OnLaunched method implementation, we call the CreateXamlUI function we created in the previous section. All other methods of IApplicationOverrides either return S_OK or E_NOTIMPL. Add the code below in main.cpp.

LISTING 6-8 The HelloWorld Application class

```
namespace Demo
{
    class HelloWorldApp : public ABI::Windows::UI::Xaml::IApplicationOverrides
    {
    private:
            ULONG m_cRef;
            IInspectable* m_pInner;

    protected:
            HelloWorldApp() :
                    m_cRef(1),
                    m_pInner(nullptr)
            {
            }

            ~HelloWorldApp()
            {
```

```
                    ReleaseInterface(m_pInner);
            }

            void SetInnerInspectable(__in IInspectable* pInner)
            {
                    AddRefInterface(pInner);
                    ReleaseInterface(m_pInner);
                    m_pInner = pInner;
            }

    public:
            //IUnknown
            IFACEMETHODIMP_(ULONG) AddRef()
            {
                    return ++m_cRef;
            }

            IFACEMETHODIMP_(ULONG) Release()
            {
                    ULONG cRef = --m_cRef;
                    if (0 == cRef)
                    {
                            delete this;
                    }
                    return cRef;
            }

            IFACEMETHODIMP QueryInterface(__in REFIID riid, __deref_out void** ppvObject)
            {
                    *ppvObject = NULL;
                    if (IID_IInspectable == riid)
                    {
                            *ppvObject = static_cast<IInspectable*>(this);
                    }
                    else if (IID_IUnknown == riid)
                    {
                            *ppvObject = static_cast<IUnknown*>(this);
                    }
                    else if (__uuidof(ABI::Windows::UI::Xaml::IApplicationOverrides) == riid)
                    {
                            *ppvObject =
static_cast<ABI::Windows::UI::Xaml::IApplicationOverrides*>(this);
                    }
                    else
                    {
                            if(m_pInner)
                                return m_pInner->QueryInterface(riid, ppvObject);
                            else
                                    return E_NOINTERFACE;
                    }

                    AddRef();
                    return S_OK;
            }
```

```
        //IInspectable
        IFACEMETHODIMP GetRuntimeClassName(__out HSTRING* pRuntimeClassName)
        {
                return E_NOTIMPL;
        }


        IFACEMETHODIMP GetTrustLevel(__out TrustLevel* trustLevel)
        {
                return E_NOTIMPL;
        }


        IFACEMETHODIMP GetIids(__out ULONG* iidCount, __deref_out IID** iids)
        {
                return E_NOTIMPL;
        }


        //HelloWorldApp methods
        static HRESULT Create(__deref_out HelloWorldApp** ppApp)
        {
                HRESULT hr = S_OK;
                ComPtr<HelloWorldApp> spApp;
                HStringReference applicationAcid(RuntimeClass_Windows_UI_Xaml_Application);
                ComPtr<IApplicationFactory> spAppFactory;
                ComPtr<IInspectable> spAppInner;
                ComPtr<IApplication> spAppInnerInstance;

                spApp.Attach(new HelloWorldApp());
                IFCOOM(spApp.Get());

                IFC(GetActivationFactory(applicationAcid.Get(), &spAppFactory));
                IFC(spAppFactory->CreateInstance(spApp.Get(), &spAppInner, &spAppInnerInstance));
                spApp->SetInnerInspectable(spAppInner.Get());

                *ppApp = spApp.Detach();

Cleanup:
                return hr;
        }

         virtual HRESULT STDMETHODCALLTYPE OnInitialize( void)
        {
                return S_OK;
        }


        virtual HRESULT STDMETHODCALLTYPE OnActivated(
                /* [in] */ __RPC__in_opt
ABI::Windows::ApplicationModel::Activation::IActivatedEventArgs *args)
        {
                return S_OK;
        }


        virtual HRESULT STDMETHODCALLTYPE OnLaunched(
                /* [in] */ __RPC__in_opt
ABI::Windows::ApplicationModel::Activation::ILaunchActivatedEventArgs *args)
        {
```

```
                    HRESULT hr = S_OK;
                    IFC(CreateXamlUI());
            Cleanup:
                    return hr;
            }

            virtual HRESULT STDMETHODCALLTYPE OnFileActivated(
                    /* [in] */ __RPC__in_opt
ABI::Windows::ApplicationModel::Activation::IFileActivatedEventArgs *args)
            {
                    return E_NOTIMPL;
            }

            virtual HRESULT STDMETHODCALLTYPE OnSearchActivated(
                    /* [in] */ __RPC__in_opt
ABI::Windows::ApplicationModel::Activation::ISearchActivatedEventArgs *args)
            {
                    return E_NOTIMPL;
            }

            virtual HRESULT STDMETHODCALLTYPE OnShareTargetActivated(
                    /* [in] */ __RPC__in_opt
ABI::Windows::ApplicationModel::Activation::IShareTargetActivatedEventArgs *args)
            {
                    return E_NOTIMPL;
            }

            virtual HRESULT STDMETHODCALLTYPE OnFileOpenPickerActivated(
                    /* [in] */ __RPC__in_opt
ABI::Windows::ApplicationModel::Activation::IFileOpenPickerActivatedEventArgs *args)
            {
                    return E_NOTIMPL;
            }

            virtual HRESULT STDMETHODCALLTYPE OnFileSavePickerActivated(
                    /* [in] */ __RPC__in_opt
ABI::Windows::ApplicationModel::Activation::IFileSavePickerActivatedEventArgs *args)
            {
                    return E_NOTIMPL;
            }

            virtual HRESULT STDMETHODCALLTYPE OnCachedFileUpdaterActivated(
                    /* [in] */ __RPC__in_opt
ABI::Windows::ApplicationModel::Activation::ICachedFileUpdaterActivatedEventArgs *args)
            {
                    return E_NOTIMPL;
            }

            virtual HRESULT STDMETHODCALLTYPE OnWindowCreated(
                    /* [in] */ __RPC__in_opt ABI::Windows::UI::Xaml::IWindowCreatedEventArgs *args)
            {
                    return S_OK;
            }

    };
```

}

We now have a fully contained application class and a function that creates the UI. What is needed now is the main function that drives the application object creation. Let's code the WinMain program entry point function.

```
// Application entry point
int APIENTRY WinMain(
    HINSTANCE hInstance,
    HINSTANCE hPrevInstance,
    LPTSTR lpCmdLine,
    int nCmdShow)
{

}
```

Our Application class has a protected constructor and hence cannot be initialized as regular C++ classes are. We need a few more helper classes to aid in instantiating our application class and also perform plumbing work like instantiating the Windows Runtime, setting up callbacks for system level events etc.

In our sample, I have created a header file named AppHelper.h that contains a method named StartApplication. This method accepts a parameter of type IApplicationInitializationCallback* and returns a HRESULT indicating success or failure of application initialization.

StartApplication also initializes the Windows Runtime using the WRL handy wrapper, aptly named as RoInitializeWrapper. After initializing WinRT, it creates an instance of the Xaml Application object and calls the Start method of the application object. The StartApplication method is listed below.

LISTING 6-9 The helper StartApplication method to initialize an application

```
HRESULT StartApplication(ABI::Windows::UI::Xaml::IApplicationInitializationCallback* pCallback)
{
    HRESULT hr = S_OK;
    Microsoft::WRL::Wrappers::RoInitializeWrapper initWinrt(RO_INIT_MULTITHREADED);          {

        HStringReference applicationAcid(RuntimeClass_Windows_UI_Xaml_Application);
        Microsoft::WRL::ComPtr<ABI::Windows::UI::Xaml::IApplicationStatics> spAppStatics;
    IFC(Windows::Foundation::GetActivationFactory(applicationAcid.Get(), &spAppStatics));
    IFC(spAppStatics->Start(pCallback));
}

Cleanup:

    return hr;

}
```

StartApplication accepts an IApplicationInitializationCallback interface pointer. How do you get one for your app? By now, you must be familiar with the exercise. Implement the IApplicationInitializationCallback interface!

Here is the implementation and some helper functions to instantiate or create interface pointers of the IApplicationInitializationCallback interface.

LISTING 6-10 The BaseApplicationInitializationCallback class

```
class BaseApplicationInitializationCallback :
        public ABI::Windows::UI::Xaml::IApplicationInitializationCallback
{
public:
        IFACEMETHODIMP_(ULONG) AddRef()
        {
                return InterlockedIncrement(&m_cRef);
        }

        IFACEMETHODIMP_(ULONG) Release()
        {
                LONG cRef = InterlockedDecrement(&m_cRef);

                if (0 == cRef)
                {
                        delete this;
                }

                return cRef;
        }

        IFACEMETHODIMP QueryInterface(__in REFIID riid, __deref_out void** ppvObject)
        {
                *ppvObject = NULL;

                if (IID_IUnknown == riid)
                {
                        *ppvObject = static_cast<IUnknown*>(this);
                }
                else if (__uuidof(ABI::Windows::UI::Xaml::IApplicationInitializationCallback) ==
riid)
                {
                        *ppvObject =
static_cast<ABI::Windows::UI::Xaml::IApplicationInitializationCallback*>(this);
                }
                else if (IID_IMarshal == riid)
                {
                        return m_pUnkFTM->QueryInterface(riid, ppvObject);
                }
                else
                {
                        return E_NOINTERFACE;
                }

                AddRef();
                return S_OK;
        }

        IFACEMETHODIMP Invoke(__in ABI::Windows::UI::Xaml::IApplicationInitializationCallbackParams*
```

```
p) = 0;

    protected:
            BaseApplicationInitializationCallback() :
                    m_cRef(1),
                    m_pUnkFTM(NULL)
            {
                    CoCreateFreeThreadedMarshaler(this, &m_pUnkFTM);
            }

            virtual ~BaseApplicationInitializationCallback()
            {
                    ReleaseInterface(m_pUnkFTM);
            }

    private:
            ULONG m_cRef;
            IUnknown* m_pUnkFTM;
    };

    template <class T>
    class ApplicationInitializationCallback_Instantiate : public BaseApplicationInitializationCallback
    {
    public:
            static Microsoft::WRL::ComPtr<ApplicationInitializationCallback_Instantiate<T>> New()
            {
                    ComPtr<ApplicationInitializationCallback_Instantiate<T>>
spApplicationInitializationCallback;
                    spApplicationInitializationCallback.Attach(new
ApplicationInitializationCallback_Instantiate<T>());
                    return spApplicationInitializationCallback;
            }

            IFACEMETHODIMP Invoke(__in ABI::Windows::UI::Xaml::IApplicationInitializationCallbackParams*
p)
            {
                    HRESULT hr = S_OK;

                    T* pApp = new T();
                    IFCOOM(pApp);
                    pApp->Release();

            Cleanup:
                    RRETURN(hr);
            }
    };

    template <class T>
    class ApplicationInitializationCallback_Create : public BaseApplicationInitializationCallback
    {
    public:
            static Microsoft::WRL::ComPtr<ApplicationInitializationCallback_Create<T>> New()
            {
                    ComPtr<ApplicationInitializationCallback_Create<T>>
spApplicationInitializationCallback;
```

```
                    spApplicationInitializationCallback.Attach(new
ApplicationInitializationCallback_Create<T>());
                    return spApplicationInitializationCallback;
        }

        IFACEMETHODIMP Invoke(__in ABI::Windows::UI::Xaml::IApplicationInitializationCallbackParams*
p)
        {
                HRESULT hr = S_OK;

                Microsoft::WRL::ComPtr<T> spApp;
                IFC(T::Create(&spApp));

        Cleanup:
                RRETURN(hr);
        }
    };

    template <class T>
    class ApplicationInitializationCallback_Make : public BaseApplicationInitializationCallback
    {
    public:
        static Microsoft::WRL::ComPtr<ApplicationInitializationCallback_Make<T>> New()
        {
                ComPtr<ApplicationInitializationCallback_Make<T>>
spApplicationInitializationCallback;
                spApplicationInitializationCallback.Attach(new
ApplicationInitializationCallback_Make<T>());
                return spApplicationInitializationCallback;
        }

        IFACEMETHODIMP Invoke(__in ABI::Windows::UI::Xaml::IApplicationInitializationCallbackParams*
p)
        {
                Microsoft::WRL::ComPtr<T> spApp = Make<T>();
                return S_OK;
        }
    };
```

Armed with all this boiler plate code, you can now add the two needed lines of code to your Win-Main method!

```
// Application entry point
int APIENTRY WinMain(
    HINSTANCE hInstance,
    HINSTANCE hPrevInstance,
    LPTSTR lpCmdLine,
    int nCmdShow)
{

    HRESULT hr = StartApplication(
            ApplicationInitializationCallback_Create<HelloWorldApp>::New().Get());
    return SUCCEEDED(hr) ? 0 : -1;
```

```
}
```

That's it. Our app is essentially now code complete! This is only the first step towards our goal. We now have to build our application package and then deploy it on the local machine.

Building the package

We have written code to create a simple Xaml app and now need to build it. We will make use of a makefile to build the code and create the executable. One of the new additions to WinRT Store apps is that they need to be appContainer executables i.e these apps run within a sandboxed environment named as the AppContainer. The native linker, link.exe accepts a parameter APPCONTAINER which can be specified while creating Store executables. Along with the code, I have created a simple makefile script which will compile the source code and then create the executable file.

The makefile script is listed below. You can also get it along with the complete list of samples from the book sample downloads.

```
# makefile for building a WRL + Xaml Win8 Store App

HOME = C:\build\HelloWorld
OUTPATH = C:\build\HelloWorld\appx\HelloWorld.exe
INCLUDES = $(WindowsSDK_IncludePath);$(HOME)
LIBS = $(WindowsSDK_LibraryPath_x86);
SOURCE = $(HOME)

wrlbuild : main.obj
 cl /MD main.obj /link /APPCONTAINER /LIBPATH:$(LIBS) runtimeobject.lib /SUBSYSTEM:Windows /OUT:$(OUTPATH)

main.obj : main.cpp
cl /c /EHsc /Zc:wchar_t main.cpp -I $(INCLUDES)

all : wrlbuild

clean:
  del *.exe *.obj
```

In order to build the app, open the Developer Command Prompt for VS2012 and navigate to the folder where you saved your app source file. In our case, it is located under C:\build\HelloWorld. Then execute the following command:

    nmake makefile.mak

This command triggers the build process by compiling the main.cpp and then proceeding to create the executable named HelloWorld.exe. As you can see from the parameters passed to the link command, we specify /APPCONTAINER.

Creating the application manifest file

An application manifest contains important information about your application package. This information, among other things, includes application metadata, the executable to launch, the application capabilities and permissions. If you were creating an app using Visual Studio 2012 templates, it creates one for you automatically. In our case, however, you should create one manually.

Here is the simple appxmanifest.xml for our hello world app. Do not worry about the details. The most important details to remember are the following:

- The Package Identity Name: This is a GUID and should be unique.

- The Package Publisher.

- The Application Executable

- The Application entry point and

- The Dependencies on any external frameworks, if any. In our case, we need to specify a dependency on the Visual C++ runtime package and specify the RTM version.

LISTING 6-11 The Application Manifest for our Hello World app

```xml
<?xml version="1.0" encoding="utf-8"?>
<Package xmlns="http://schemas.microsoft.com/appx/2010/manifest">

  <Identity Name="65ab3801-5e81-4723-8df4-fea1ff0f2d31"
            Publisher="CN=sridharpoduri.com"
            Version="1.0.0.0" />

  <Properties>
    <DisplayName>HelloWorld</DisplayName>
    <PublisherDisplayName>Sridhar Poduri</PublisherDisplayName>
    <Logo>Assets\StoreLogo.png</Logo>
  </Properties>

  <Prerequisites>
    <OSMinVersion>6.2.1</OSMinVersion>
    <OSMaxVersionTested>6.2.1</OSMaxVersionTested>
  </Prerequisites>

  <Resources>
    <Resource Language="en-us"/>
  </Resources>

  <Applications>
    <Application Id="App"
        Executable="HelloWorld.exe"
        EntryPoint="HelloWorldApp">
        <VisualElements
            DisplayName="HelloWorldApp"
            Logo="Assets\Logo.png"
            SmallLogo="Assets\SmallLogo.png"
            Description="HelloWorld"
            ForegroundText="light"
            BackgroundColor="#464646">
            <DefaultTile ShowName="allLogos" />
            <SplashScreen Image="Assets\SplashScreen.png" />
```

```
        </VisualElements>
      </Application>
    </Applications>
<Dependencies>
    <PackageDependency Name="Microsoft.VCLibs.110.00" MinVersion="11.0.0.0"/>
</Dependencies>
</Package>
```

The Publisher attribute should match the root certificate that will be generate in the next section. If these do not match, you cannot sign the app package. The Application name and entry point values must be updated if you change them in the code.

Before creating the appx package, your directory structure should look as follows:

FIGURE 6-2 Directory layout for the scripts

The Appx folder contains the Appxmanifest.xml file, the HelloWorld.exe file and an assets folder. The Assets folder contains 4 images and these are copied from the Visual Studio 2012 project assets folder.

From the Developer Command Prompt for VS2012, run the following command to build the application package

    makeappx pack /d c:\build\HelloWorld\appx /p c:\build\helloworld\HelloWorld.appx

This command creates an application package from the files present in the c:\build\HelloWorld\appx folder and places the package named HelloWorld.appx at c:\build\HelloWorld.

We need to sign the created appx package with a certificate before deploying the package.

Creating a signing certificate

Before you can sign the package, you should generate a trusted certificate. Execute the following command to generate the public and private components of a root certificate.

makecert.exe –n "CN=sridharpoduri.com" –r –a sha1 –sv sridharpoduri.com.pvk sridharpoduri.com.cer –ss root

These components are stored in the sridharpoduri.com.cer and sridharpoduri.com.pvk files respectively. Replace the sridharpoduri.com part in the file names as well as the certificate name indicated by CN= to any string you are comfortable with and make sure the certificate name matches the Identify attribute specified in the appxmanifest file.

> **Warning** The command above installs the certificate into the root store. Make sure to keep the private key (the file with pvk extension) and remove the certificate after you are done with it.

Execute the following command to create the client certificate that will be used to sign your appx package.

> **makecert.exe –a sha1 –sk "sridharpoduri.com" –iv sridharpoduri.com.pvk –n "CN=sridharpoduri.com" –ic sridharpoduri.com.cer –sr currentuser –ss My**

This command creates the client certificate and installs into the personal store.

Signing the app package

In order to sign the app package, we need to obtain the thumbprint of the certificate created in the above section. Luckily for us, Powershell contains utilities that allow us to query for this information in a hassle free manner.

Launch Powershell as an Administrator and then execute the following command.

> **dir cert:\CurrentUser\My**

This command prints the thumbprints for various certificates installed on your machine. Copy the thumbprint associated with the certificate created above. With this information, you are now ready to sign the package. Switch back to the Developer Command Prompt for VS2012 and execute the following command to sign your package.

> **signtool sign /fd sha256 /sha1 8B1181908FEB8E13CA2AA36B73897C04C44ADD02 c:\build\helloworld\HelloWorld.appx**

This command signs your appx package with the client certificate. After successful signing of the package, you can install it using PowerShell. Navigate to the folder where the appx file is located and run the following command as admin.

> **Add-AppxPackage .\HelloWorld.appx**

After the application is successfully deployed, you can launch it by clicking/tapping on the tile from the Start screen and our app launches in all its glory as shown below.

FIGURE 6-3 The Hello World App using WRL and XAML

Before you deploy the app to another machine, you should install the client certificate on the target machine using the following command. After the command completes successfully, you can use Powershell to deploy the app.

certutil.exe –addstore root sridharpoduri.com.cer

Using the Windows Runtime Library in Windows Store apps

Authoring a Simple WinRT component using WRL

In this section, we will create a simple WinRT component using WRL.

1. Launch Visual Studio 2012.

2. Choose New Project.

3. Under the Visual C++ Language, select Windows Store->WRL Class Library.

4. Type in a name for the solution, such as, WRLClassLibrary1.

5. Choose a destination to Save the solution. The Project Solution and initial source files are created and saved to this location.

    At this point, your screen should look similar to the following figure.

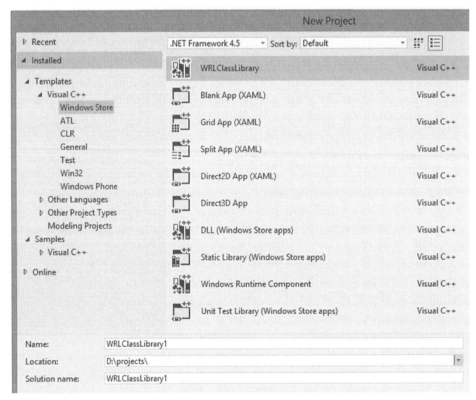

FIGURE 6-4 Creating a new WRL component using Visual Studio

6. Click OK.

7. Visual Studio generates creates the default solution and initial files.

8. From the Solution Viewer, double click the WRLClassLibrary1.idl file.

9. Add the following method inside the IWinRTClass interface declaration.

```
HRESULT Calculate([in] int a, [in] int b, [out, retval] int *result);
```

10. The complete idl file should resemble the following figure.

```
import "inspectable.idl";
import "Windows.Foundation.idl";

#define COMPONENT_VERSION 1.0

namespace WRLClassLibrary1
{
    interface IWinRTClass;
    runtimeclass WinRTClass;

    [uuid(d7c1c987-09e3-4919-8420-008aead9f9ba), version(COMPONENT_VERSION), exclusiveto(WinRTClass)]
    interface IWinRTClass : IInspectable
    {
        HRESULT Calculate([in] int a, [in] int b, [out, retval] int *result);
    }

    [version(COMPONENT_VERSION), activatable(COMPONENT_VERSION)]
    runtimeclass WinRTClass
    {
        [default] interface IWinRTClass;
    }
}
```

FIGURE 6-5 Simple WRL Component IDL file

11. At a quick glance, you will notice some familiar WinRT concepts that we covered in the earlier part of this chapter.

    a. The interface is contained within a namespace named WRLClassLibrary1.

    b. An exclusiveto attribute has been added to the IWinRTClass interface. You might recollect that using the exclusiveto attribute means that this interface can only be used within the interface in which it has been declared.

    c. The interface IWinRTClass is inherited from IInspectable v/s IUnknown for normal COM.

12. Now let us add the implementation for the Calculate method.

13. In the WRLClassLibrary1.cpp, add the following code inside the WinRTClass.

LISTING 6-12 A Simple Calculate method

```
HRESULT __stdcall Calculate (int a, int b, _Out_ int* result)
{
    *result = a + b;
    return S_OK;
}
```

14. Now build the solution to generate the winmd and the WinRT component (dll).

15. The full source is reproduced below for your reference.

LISTING 6-13 The Complete Listing For The Wrlclasslibrary1.Idl

```
import "inspectable.idl";
import "Windows.Foundation.idl";

#define COMPONENT_VERSION 1.0

namespace WRLClassLibrary1
{
    interface IWinRTClass;
    runtimeclass WinRTClass;

    [uuid(d7c1c987-09e3-4919-8420-008aead9f9ba), version(COMPONENT_VERSION), exclusiveto(WinRTClass)]
    interface IWinRTClass : IInspectable
    {
            HRESULT Calculate([in] int a, [in] int b, [out, retval] int *result);
    }

    [version(COMPONENT_VERSION), activatable(COMPONENT_VERSION)]
    runtimeclass WinRTClass
    {
        [default] interface IWinRTClass;
    }
}
```

LISTING 6-14 The complete listing for the WRLClassLibrary1.cpp

```
#include "pch.h"

#include "WRLClassLibrary1_h.h"
#include <wrl.h>

using namespace Microsoft::WRL;
using namespace Windows::Foundation;

namespace ABI
{
    namespace WRLClassLibrary1
    {
            class WinRTClass: public RuntimeClass<IWinRTClass>
            {
                    InspectableClass(L"WRLClassLibrary1.WinRTClass", BaseTrust)

                    public:
                    WinRTClass()
                    {
                    }

                    HRESULT __stdcall Calculate (int a, int b, _Out_ int* result)
```

```
        {
            *result = a + b;
            return S_OK;
        }
    };

    ActivatableClass(WinRTClass);
  }
}
```

Creating a C# client application to call into the WRL component

1. Launch Visual Studio 2011.

2. Choose New Project.

3. Under the Visual C# Language, select Blank Windows Store App

4. Type in a name for the solution, such as, TestApp.

5. Choose a destination to Save the solution. The Project Solution and initial source files are created and saved to this location.

6. Modify the MainPage.xaml file by copying the following markup. Be sure to paste the markup between the <Grid> </Grid> sections only.

LISTING 6-15 MainPage.xaml

```
<TextBox x:Name="One" HorizontalAlignment="Left" Height="23" Margin="241,159,0,0" TextWrapping="Wrap"
VerticalAlignment="Top" Width="110"/>
<TextBox x:Name="Two" HorizontalAlignment="Left" Height="23" Margin="402,159,0,0" TextWrapping="Wrap"
VerticalAlignment="Top" Width="110"/>
<TextBlock HorizontalAlignment="Left" Height="21" Margin="230,95,0,0" TextWrapping="Wrap" Text="Input two
numbers in the Text boxes below" VerticalAlignment="Top" Width="300" FontSize="15.5"/>
<TextBlock x:Name="Result"  HorizontalAlignment="Left" Height="31" Margin="230,226,0,0"
TextWrapping="Wrap" VerticalAlignment="Top" Width="363" FontSize="15.5" Text="And the Result is "/>
<Button Content="Add" HorizontalAlignment="Left" Height="42" Margin="560,149,0,0" VerticalAlignment="Top"
Width="110" Click="Button_Click_1"/>
```

7. In the Solution Explorer, right click on the Project and choose Add Reference.

8. In the Add Reference Window, navigate to the Recent column on the left and choose WRLClassLibrary1 and click OK.

9. In the MainPage.xaml.cs, add **using WRLClassLibrary1;** directive at the top of the file.

10. Navigate to the Button_Click_1 method in MainPage.xaml.cs and add the following code

LISTING 6-16 Button_Click_1 method implementation in MainPage.xaml.cs
```
int result = 0;
WRLClassLibrary1.WinRTClass obj = new WRLClassLibrary1.WinRTClass();
try
{
```

```
    result = obj.Calculate(Convert.ToInt32(One.Text) , Convert.ToInt32(Two.Text));
}
catch (Exception ex)
{
    Result.Text = ex.Message;
}
Result.Text += result.ToString();
```

11. Build the solution.

12. Press F5 to launch the App. Input two numbers into the text boxes and click on the Add button. You should see the result updated in the test block below. The full source listing is given below.

LISTING 6-17 The full listing for the MainPage.xaml

```xml
<Page
    x:Class="TestApp.MainPage"
    IsTabStop="false"
    xmlns="http://schemas.microsoft.com/winfx/2006/xaml/presentation"
    xmlns:x="http://schemas.microsoft.com/winfx/2006/xaml"
    xmlns:local="using:TestApp"
    xmlns:d="http://schemas.microsoft.com/expression/blend/2008"
    xmlns:mc="http://schemas.openxmlformats.org/markup-compatibility/2006"
    mc:Ignorable="d">

    <Grid Background="{StaticResource ApplicationPageBackgroundThemeBrush}">
        <TextBox x:Name="One" HorizontalAlignment="Left" Height="23" Margin="241,159,0,0"
TextWrapping="Wrap" VerticalAlignment="Top" Width="110"/>
        <TextBox x:Name="Two" HorizontalAlignment="Left" Height="23" Margin="402,159,0,0"
TextWrapping="Wrap" VerticalAlignment="Top" Width="110"/>
        <TextBlock HorizontalAlignment="Left" Height="21" Margin="230,95,0,0" TextWrapping="Wrap"
Text="Input two numbers in the Text boxes below" VerticalAlignment="Top" Width="300" FontSize="15.5"/>
        <TextBlock x:Name="Result"  HorizontalAlignment="Left" Height="31" Margin="230,226,0,0"
TextWrapping="Wrap" VerticalAlignment="Top" Width="363" FontSize="15.5" Text="And the Result is "/>
        <Button Content="Add" HorizontalAlignment="Left" Height="42" Margin="560,149,0,0"
VerticalAlignment="Top" Width="110" Click="Button_Click_1"/>

    </Grid>
</Page>
```

LISTING 6-18 The full listing for the MainPage.xaml.cs file

```csharp
using System;
using System.Collections.Generic;
using System.IO;
using System.Linq;
using Windows.Foundation;
using Windows.Foundation.Collections;
using Windows.UI.Xaml;
using Windows.UI.Xaml.Controls;
using Windows.UI.Xaml.Controls.Primitives;
using Windows.UI.Xaml.Data;
using Windows.UI.Xaml.Input;
```

```
using Windows.UI.Xaml.Media;
using Windows.UI.Xaml.Navigation;

using WRLClassLibrary1;
// The Blank Page item template is documented at http://go.microsoft.com/fwlink/?LinkId=234238

namespace TestApp
{
    /// <summary>
    /// An empty page that can be used on its own or navigated to within a Frame.
    /// </summary>
    public sealed partial class MainPage : Page
    {
        public MainPage()
        {
            this.InitializeComponent();
        }

        /// <summary>
        /// Invoked when this page is about to be displayed in a Frame.
        /// </summary>
        /// <param name="e">Event data that describes how this page was reached.  The Parameter
        /// property is typically used to configure the page.</param>
        protected override void OnNavigatedTo(NavigationEventArgs e)
        {
        }

        private void Button_Click_1(object sender, RoutedEventArgs e)
        {
            int result = 0;
            WRLClassLibrary1.WinRTClass obj = new WRLClassLibrary1.WinRTClass();
            try
            {
                result = obj.Calculate(Convert.ToInt32(One.Text) , Convert.ToInt32(Two.Text));
            }
            catch (Exception ex)
            {
                Result.Text = ex.Message;
            }
            Result.Text += result.ToString();
        }
    }
}
```

Where are we and what's Next

So far we have covered salient features of Modern C++ and the component extensions that enable C++ developers bring forth existing skills to the WinRT platform. We have explored the many different "native" options that are the exclusive domain of C++ developers and how Microsoft is investing heavily and is fully committed to the "native" stack. In the next few sections, we will briefly cover native unit testing, learn how to develop Windows Azure connected apps using C++ and take a sneak preview of sharing native code between Windows 8 and Windows Phone 8. This brings to full circle a major native C++ renaissance at Microsoft.

Chapter 7
Unit testing Windows 8 C++ Apps

In this chapter:

Introduction

Unit testing native code

Adding unit tests to existing C++ apps

Unit tests for Windows Store apps

Where are we and what's Next

Introduction

In the preceding chapters we have explored different technologies that enable you, as a C++ developer, design and build Windows Store apps. While design and developing an app are important, an equally important paradigm of software development is testing. Testing early and frequently helps you and your teams catch bugs early and avoid nasty surprises later on. One of the strategies to catch bugs early is to write unit tests based on the design of your application. Writing good unit tests helps you be more productive in writing shipping code for your application. This is because unit tests are by definition, designed to catch errors that deviate from desired functionality.

Visual Studio 2012 includes support for developing unit tests for your C++ applications. We will begin our exploration of the support for unit testing by creating a simple Win32 DLL and then discuss approaches to test native code, including how to unit test Windows Store apps.

Unit testing native code

Before we begin the unit testing our code, we need some code. We will create a very basic Win32 Dynamic Link Library (DLL) and base our exploration of unit testing on this DLL.

Create a Win32 DLL

Follow the steps below to create a basic Win32 DLL.

1. Launch Visual Studio 2012.

2. From the File menu, select New and then Project.

3. On the Project types pane, under Visual C++, select Win32.

4. On the Templates pane, select Win32 Project.

5. Choose a name for the project, such as CppAddDll.

6. Click OK to start the Win32 application wizard. On the Overview page of the Win32 Application Wizard dialog box, click Next.

7. On the Application Settings page of the Win32 Application Wizard, under Application type, select DLL.

8. On the Application Settings page of the Win32 Application Wizard, under Additional options, select Empty project.

9. Click Finish to create the project.

The DLL we created does not export any functions that can be re-used across modules. Let us add a C++ class and some functions to the class and export them.

Adding a class to the DLL

Follow these steps to add a class and some methods to the DLL.

1. To create a header file for a new class, from the Project menu, select Add New Item. The Add New Item dialog box will be displayed. On the Categories pane, under Visual C++, select Code. On the Templates pane, select Header File (.h). Choose a name for the header file, such as CppAddDll.h, and click Add.

2. Add a simple class named CppMath to support addition of two numbers. The code should resemble the following:

LISTING 7-1 CppMath class

```
//CppAdd.h

namespace CppMathDll
{
    class CppMath
    {
    public:
        //returns the result of x + y
        static __declspec(dllexport) int Add(int x, int y);
    };
}
```

3. Note the __declspec(dllexport) modifier in the method declarations in this code. These modifiers enable the method to be exported by the DLL so that it can be used by other applications.

4. To create a source file for a new class, from the Project menu, select Add New Item. The Add New Item dialog box will be displayed. On the Categories pane, under Visual C++, select Code. On the Templates pane, select C++ File (.cpp). Choose a name for the source file, such as CppAddDll.cpp, and click Add.

5. Implement the functionality for Add method in the source file. The code should resemble the

following:

LISTING 7-2 Add method implementation

```
#include "CppAddDll.h"
using namespace CppMathDll;

int CppMath::Add(int x, int y)
{
    return x + y;
}
```

6. Compile the dynamic link library by selecting Build Solution from the Build menu. This creates a DLL that can be used by other programs.

We now have a basic Win32 DLL with a class and one exported method. We are now ready to begin unit testing these methods.

Adding unit tests for a Win32 DLL

Follow these steps to get started with adding unit tests for the DLL we just created above.

1. Use the Native Test Project template to create a separate Visual Studio project for your tests. The project contains some sample test code.

2. Make the DLL accessible to the test project:

   - #include the header file that contains declarations of the DLL's externally-accessible functions. In our case it is the CppAddDll.h

   - The header file should contain function declarations marked with _declspec(dllimport). Alternatively, you can export the methods using a DEF file.

   - The unit tests you author can only access functions that are exported from the DLL under test.

   - Add the DLL project to the References of the test project:

   - In the Properties of the test project, expand Common Properties, Framework and References, and choose Add Reference.

3. In the test project, create test classes and test methods by using the TEST macros and ASSERT class in the following way:

LISTING 7-3 Test code for the Add Method

```
#include "stdafx.h"
#include "CppUnitTest.h"
#include "..\CppAddDll\CppAddDll.h"

using namespace Microsoft::VisualStudio::CppUnitTestFramework;
```

```
namespace UnitTestCppAdd
{
    TEST_CLASS(UnitTest1)
    {
    public:
        TEST_METHOD(TestMethod1)
        {
            // TODO: Your test code here
            CppMathDll::CppMath mathObj;
            Assert::AreEqual(45, mathObj.Add(25, 20), 0.1, L"message", LINE_INFO());
        }
    };
}
```

- The Assert class contains static functions that you can use to verify the result of a test.

- The LINE_INFO parameter is optional. In cases where there is no PDB file, it allows the test runner to identify the location of a failure.

4. Use Test Explorer to run the tests:

- On the View menu, choose Other Windows, Test Explorer.

- Build the Visual Studio solution.

- In Test Explorer, choose Run All.

That's it. Your unit tests are now ready and you can use the Test Explorer to verify your code. This process can be streamlined a little more. What we will outline now is a process to enable Test Driven Development (TDD) wherein you write your unit tests first and then code the functionality of the application.

Test driven development with Test Explorer

The TDD approach follows a very simple blue print for software development. The basic steps are:

- Create a native test project.

- Create a DLL project that contains your code.

- Export DLL functions to the test project.

- Add new test functions to the test project in an iterative fashion.

- Debug your failing tests.

- Modify your code while keeping your tests unchanged.

Create a native test project

The first step in the process of TDD is to create a native test project as follows.

- On the **File** menu, choose **New**, **Project**.

- Choose **Visual C++**, **Test**. Choose the **Native Test Project** template. In this walkthrough, the test project is named **NativeStringTest**.

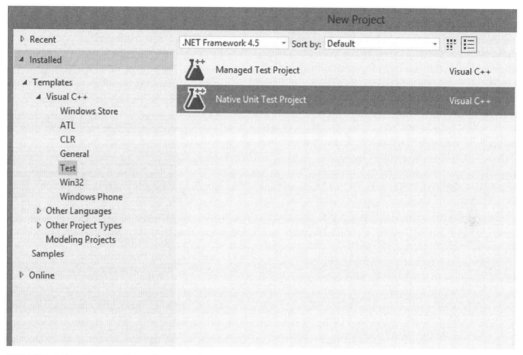

FIGURE 7-1 Creating a native unit test project

- In the new project, inspect unittest1.cpp. In the generated code you will notice the following pre-defined helper macros.

  o Each test is defined by using TEST_METHOD (TestMethod1).

  o You do not have to write a conventional function signature. The signature is created by the macro TEST_METHOD.

  o The TEST_METHOD macro generates an instance of the function with a void return type. It also generates a static function that returns information about the method to be tested. This information allows the test explorer to find the method.

  o Test methods are grouped into classes by using TEST_CLASS (Unittest1), for example.

  o When the tests are run, an instance of each test class is created. The test methods are called in an unspecified order. You can define special methods that are invoked before and after each module, class, or method.

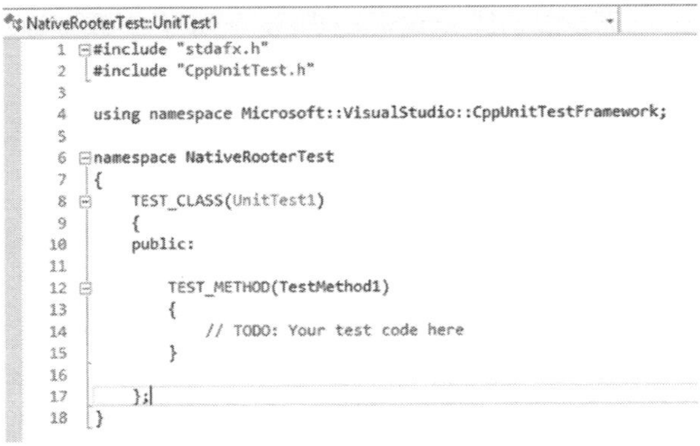

```
NativeRooterTest::UnitTest1
1  #include "stdafx.h"
2  #include "CppUnitTest.h"
3
4  using namespace Microsoft::VisualStudio::CppUnitTestFramework;
5
6  namespace NativeRooterTest
7  {
8      TEST_CLASS(UnitTest1)
9      {
10     public:
11
12         TEST_METHOD(TestMethod1)
13         {
14             // TODO: Your test code here
15         }
16
17     };
18 }
```

FIGURE 7-2 Generated code for a native test project

- Verify that the tests run in Test Explorer.

  o Insert some test code.

  ```
  TEST_METHOD(TestMethod1)
  {
      Assert::AreEqual(1,1);
  }
  ```

  The Assert class provides several static methods that you can use to verify results in test methods.

  o On the Test menu, choose Run-> All Tests. The test builds and runs. Test Explorer appears. The test appears under Passed Tests.

Create a native DLL

The next step in TDD is to create the DLL that contains the code to be tested.

1. Create a **Visual C++** project by using the **Win32 Project** template. In this walkthrough, the project is named **ClassNameFinder**.

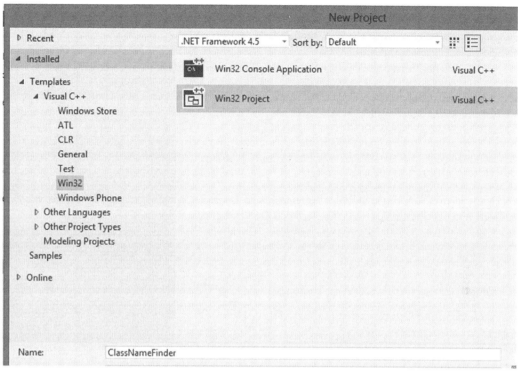

FIGURE 7-3 Creating the ClassNameFinder project

2. Select DLL and Export Symbols in the Win32 Application Wizard.

3. The Export Symbols option generates a convenient macro that you can use to declare exported methods.

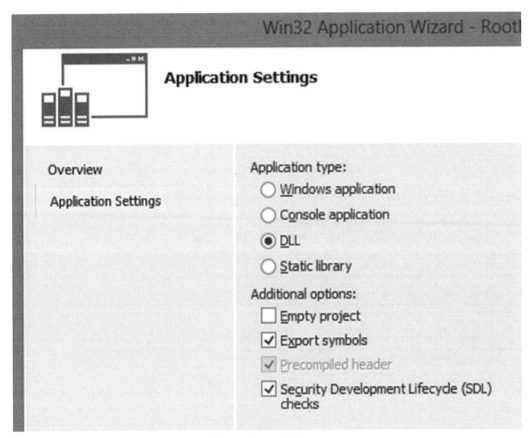

FIGURE 7-4 Selecting project type as DLL and exporting symbols

4. Declare an exported function in the header file.

```
1  // The following ifdef block is the standard way of creating ma
2  // from a DLL simpler. All files within this DLL are compiled w
3  // symbol defined on the command line. This symbol should not b
4  // that uses this DLL. This way any other project whose source
5  // CLASSNAMEFINDER_API functions as being imported from a DLL,
6  // defined with this macro as being exported.
7  #ifdef CLASSNAMEFINDER_EXPORTS
8  #define CLASSNAMEFINDER_API __declspec(dllexport)
9  #else
10 #define CLASSNAMEFINDER_API __declspec(dllimport)
11 #endif
12
13 // This class is exported from the ClassNameFinder.dll
14 class CLASSNAMEFINDER_API CClassNameFinder {
15 public:
16     CClassNameFinder(void);
17     // TODO: add your methods here.
18     const char* GetNameOfClass();
19 };
```

FIGURE 7-5 Adding the new exported function GetNameOfClass

5. The declarator __declspec(dllexport) enables the public and protected members of the class to be visible and callable outside the DLL.

6. In the main .cpp file, add a minimal body for the function

```
23
24    //return the name of the class
25  ⊟const char* CClassNameFinder::GetNameOfClass()
26    {
27        return typeid(*this).name();
28    }
```

FIGURE 7-6 Implementation of the GetNameOfClass method

Reference the native DLL with the test project

Before you can successfully test code, you should wire-up the native DLL with the native test project.

1. Add the DLL project to the project references of the test project.

   • Open the properties of the test project and choose Common Properties, Framework and References.

   • Choose **Add New Reference**. In the **Add Reference** dialog box, select the DLL project and choose **Add**.

2. In the unittest1.cpp file, include the .h file of the DLL code

   #include "..\ClassNameFinder\ClassNameFinder.h"

3. Add a basic test that uses the exported function

   LISTING 7-4 Test code for the Class Name finder class

```
namespace NativeStringTest
{
    TEST_CLASS(UnitTest1)
    {
    public:

        TEST_METHOD(TestMethod1)
        {
            // TODO: Your test code here
            CClassNameFinder clName;
            const char* strName = clName.GetNameOfClass();
            Assert::AreEqual("class CClassNameFinder", strName);
        }

    };
}
```

4. Build the solution. The new test appears in Test Explorer.

5. In Test Explorer, choose Run All.

You have set up the test and the code projects, and verified that you can run tests that run functions in the code project. Now you can begin to write real tests and code.

Improve tests iteratively

Once you have the basic framework for writing tests ready, you can begin adding new unit tests in an iterative fashion. You can add a new test, validate the test and then add the code so that the tests pass.

In this example, we will add new tests to the **NativeRooterTest** sample.

> **Tip** Do not change existing tests. Instead add a new test and update your code so that the tests pass. As the functionality in your app changes, disable tests that are no longer needed. Write new tests for the new functionality and test them iteratively.

- Add a new test

LISTING 7-5 Adding a new test

```
TEST_METHOD(RangeChecker)
        {
          CRootFinder finder;
          for (double v = 1e-6; v < 1e6; v *= 3.2)
          {
              double value = finder.SquareRoot(v*v);
              Assert::AreEqual(v, value, v/1000);
          }
    }
```

- Build the solution, and then in Test Explorer, choose Run All. The new test fails.

> **Tip** Verify that newly created tests always fail. This helps you avoid falling into the trap of creating tests that will always pass!

- Add new methods to the code under test so that the new test passes

LISTING 7-6 Code for determining the square root

```
#include <math.h>
double CRootFinder::SquareRoot(double input)
{
    double value = input;
    double diff = input;

    while (diff > value/1000)
    {
        double oldValue = value;
        value = value - (value * value - input)/(2*value);
```

```
        diff = abs(oldValue - value);
    }
    return value;
}
```

- Build the solution and then in Test Explorer, choose Run All. Both tests pass.

Debugging failed tests

If for any reason, your tests fail, you can easily debug the failed tests.

- Add another test

LISTING 7-7 Code for a failing test

```
#include <stdexcept>
TEST_METHOD(NegativeRangeChecker)
{
    CRootFinder finder;
    for (double v = -0.1; v > -3.0; v -= 0.5)
    {
        try
        {
            double value = finder.SquareRoot(v);
            Assert::Fail(L"No exception for input", LINE_INFO());
        }
        catch(const std::out_of_range&)
        {
            continue;
        }
        catch(...)
        {
            Assert::Fail(L"Incorrect exception for input value", LINE_INFO());
        }
    }
}
```

Build the solution and choose Run All.

- Open (or double-click) the failed test.

- The failed assertion is highlighted. The failure message is visible in the detail pane of Test Explorer.

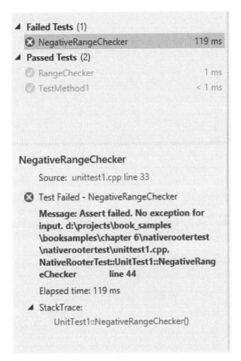

FIGURE 7-7 Test Explorer status Window

- To see why the test fails, step through the function

  o Set a breakpoint at the start of the SquareRoot function.

  o On the shortcut menu of the failed test, choose Debug Selected Tests.

  o When the run stops at the breakpoint, step through the code.

- Insert validation code in the function as shown in italicized below.

LISTING 7-8 Complete code listing for the Square root method

```cpp
#include <stdexcept>
// Find the square root of a number.
double CRootFinder::SquareRoot(double input)
{
    if (input < 0.0)
    {
        throw std::out_of_range("Cannot determine square root of negative numbers");
    }
    double value = input;
    double diff = input;

    while (diff > value/1000)
    {
        double oldValue = value;
```

```
                    value = value - (value * value - input)/(2*value);
                    diff = abs(oldValue - value);
                }
                return value;
            }
```

- All tests now pass

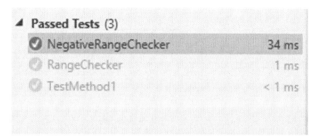

FIGURE 7-8 Test Explorer showing list of Passed Tests.

Refactoring code without changing tests

With TDD, you can refactor your existing code without changing your tests.

- Simplify the central calculation in the SquareRoot function

  // old code:

  //   result = result - (result*result - v)/(2*result);

  // new code:

  result = (result + v/result)/2.0;

- Build the solution and choose **Run All**, to make sure that you have not introduced an error.

Note A good set of unit tests gives confidence that you have not introduced bugs when you change the code. Keep refactoring separate from other changes.

Adding unit tests for existing C++ applications

If your existing app does not already have tests, you can add tests using Test Explorer. Before adding tests, however, you should inspect your code and decide how you want to add unit tests.

You should separate your changes into small tasks. Before each small change, write unit tests for aspects of the behavior that will remain the same. These tests will continue to pass after you have made the change. For example, if you plan to change a file reading function, then you can write a unit test that verifies output being in the proper format.

You should always test functions that are exported from your library. If however, you want to add unit tests only for new functionality, you can do that too. At times the new functionality being added might be internal only for your product or may not be part of code that is being exported. In such cases, you can create a static library and write tests to verify such internal functions.

Testing a static library

If your tests must use members that are not exported by a project under test, and the project under test is built as a dynamic library, you should consider converting it to a static library.

- In Solution Explorer, on the shortcut menu of the project under test, choose **Properties**. The project properties window opens.

- Choose **Configuration Properties, General**.

- Set **Configuration Type** to **Static Library (.lib)**.

Refer exported functions from test project

- If a project under test exports the functions that you want to test, then you can add a reference to the code project from the test project.

    o Create a C++ test project.

    o On the File menu, choose New, Project, Visual C++, Test, C++ Unit Test Project.

- In Solution Explorer, on the shortcut menu of the test project, choose References. The project properties window opens.

- Select Common Properties, Framework and References, and then choose the Add New Reference button.

- Select Projects, and then the project to be tested.

- Choose the Add button.

- In the properties for the test project, add the location of the project under test to the Include Directories.

- Choose Configuration Properties, VC++ Directories, Include Directories.

- Choose Edit, and then add the header directory of the project under test.

Linking tests to object files

- If the code under test does not export the functions that you want to test, you can add the output .obj or .lib file to the dependencies of the test project.

- ○ Create a C++ test project.

  - ▪ On the File menu, choose New, Project, Visual C++, Test, C++ Unit Test Project.

- ○ In Solution Explorer, on the shortcut menu of the test project, choose Properties. The project properties window opens.

- ○ Choose Configuration Properties, Linker, Input, Additional Dependencies.

- ○ Choose Edit, and add the names of the .obj or .lib files. Do not use the full path names.

- ○ Choose Configuration Properties, Linker, General, Additional Library Directories.

- ○ Choose Edit, and add the directory path of the .obj or .lib files. The path is typically within the build folder of the project under test.

- ○ Choose Configuration Properties, VC++ Directories, Include Directories.

- ○ Choose Edit, and then add the header directory of the project under test.

Add unit tests to an existing project

Modify the product code project properties to include the headers and library files that are required for unit testing.

a. In Solution Explorer, in the shortcut menu of the project under test, choose Properties. The project properties window opens.

b. Choose **Configuration Properties**, **VC++ Directories**.

c. Edit the Include and Library directories

  - Include Directories: $(VCInstallDir)UnitTest\include;$(IncludePath)

  - Library Directories: $(VCInstallDir)UnitTest\lib;$(LibraryPath)

Add a C++ Unit Test file. In Solution Explorer, in the shortcut menu of the project, choose **Add**, **New Item**, and then choose **C++ Unit Test**.

You can now write your tests and run them.

Unit tests for Windows Store apps

In this section, we will explore how to write unit tests for Windows Store apps. There are two scenarios we will walkthrough.

- Writing unit tests for a WinRT component developed using the Windows Runtime Library (WRL)

- Writing unit tests for a C++ /CX component.

Developing a WinRT component using WRL

We have developed a simple WinRT component using WRL in the first chapter. The steps to create the component are reproduced below. We will be using the same component and add tests to it.

1. Launch Visual Studio 2012.

2. Choose New Project.

3. Under the Visual C++ Language, select WRL Class Library.

4. Type in a name for the solution, such as, WRLAddComponent.

5. Choose a destination to Save the solution. The Project Solution and initial source files are created and saved to this location.

   At this point, your screen should look similar to the following figure.

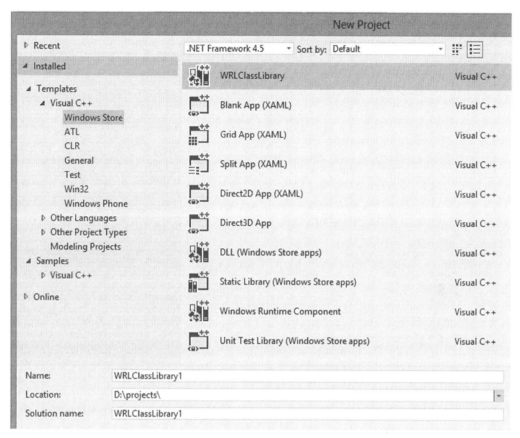

FIGURE 7-9 Creating a new WRL component using Visual Studio

6. Click OK.

7. Visual Studio generates creates the default solution and initial files.

8. From the Solution Viewer, double click the WRLClassLibrary1.idl file.

9. Add the following method inside the IWinRTClass interface declaration.

```
HRESULT Calculate([in] int a, [in] int b, [out, retval] int *result);
```

10. The complete idl file should resemble the following figure.

```
import "inspectable.idl";
import "Windows.Foundation.idl";

#define COMPONENT_VERSION 1.0

namespace WRLClassLibrary1
{
    interface IWinRTClass;
    runtimeclass WinRTClass;

    [uuid(d7c1c987-09e3-4919-8420-008aead9f9ba), version(COMPONENT_VERSION), exclusiveto(WinRTClass)]
    interface IWinRTClass : IInspectable
    {
        HRESULT Calculate([in] int a, [in] int b, [out, retval] int *result);
    }

    [version(COMPONENT_VERSION), activatable(COMPONENT_VERSION)]
    runtimeclass WinRTClass
    {
        [default] interface IWinRTClass;
    }
}
```

FIGURE 7-10 Simple WRL Component IDL file

11. At a quick glance, you will notice some familiar WinRT concepts that we covered back in chapter 6.

   a. The interface is contained within a namespace named WRLClassLibrary1.

   b. An exclusiveto attribute has been added to the IWinRTClass interface. You might recollect that using the exclusiveto attribute means that this interface can only be used within the interface in which it has been declared.

   c. The interface IWinRTClass inherits from IInspectable rather than IUnknown, which it would where this a 'classic COM' interface rather than a WinRT interface.

12. Now let us add the implementation for the Calculate method.

13. In the WRLClassLibrary1.cpp, add the following code inside the WinRTClass.

LISTING 7-9 A Simple Calculate method

```
HRESULT __stdcall Calculate (int a, int b, _Out_ int* result)
{
    if(result == nullptr)
        return E_POINTER;

    *result = a + b;
    return S_OK;
}
```

14. Now build the solution to generate the winmd and the WinRT component (dll).

15. The full source is reproduced below for your reference.

LISTING 7-10 The Complete Listing For The Wrlclasslibrary1.ldl

```
import "inspectable.idl";
import "Windows.Foundation.idl";

#define COMPONENT_VERSION 1.0

namespace WRLClassLibrary1
{
    interface IWinRTClass;
    runtimeclass WinRTClass;

    [uuid(d7c1c987-09e3-4919-8420-008aead9f9ba),

    version(COMPONENT_VERSION),

    exclusiveto(WinRTClass)]
    interface IWinRTClass : IInspectable
    {
        HRESULT Calculate([in] int a, [in] int b, [out, retval] int *result);
    }

    [version(COMPONENT_VERSION), activatable(COMPONENT_VERSION)]
    runtimeclass WinRTClass
    {
        [default] interface IWinRTClass;
    }
}
```

LISTING 7-11 The complete listing for the WRLClassLibrary1.cpp

```
#include "pch.h"

#include "WRLClassLibrary1_h.h"
#include <wrl.h>

using namespace Microsoft::WRL;
using namespace Windows::Foundation;

namespace ABI
{
    namespace WRLClassLibrary1
    {
        class WinRTClass: public RuntimeClass<IWinRTClass>
        {
            InspectableClass(L"WRLClassLibrary1.WinRTClass", BaseTrust)

            public:
            WinRTClass()
            {
            }

            HRESULT __stdcall Calculate (int a, int b, _Out_ int* result)
            {
                if(result == nullptr)
```

```
            return E_POINTER;

        *result = a + b;
        return S_OK;
    }
};

ActivatableClass(WinRTClass);
    }
}
```

Unit testing the WinRT component

Our WRLAddComponent is ready. Now let us create the test project and code up the test methods.

1. In the Solution Explorer, right click on the WRLAddComponent solution and choose Add->Add New Project.

2. Under the Visual C++ node, choose Windows Store->Unit Test Library (Windows Store apps).

3. Save the project with a name, such as, AddComponentTest as shown below.

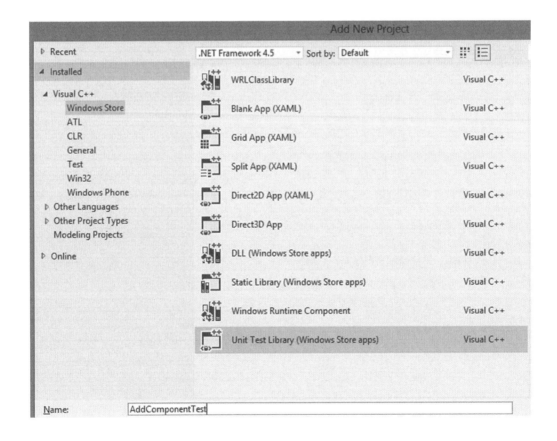

FIGURE 7-11 Creating a new Unit Test Library for a Windows Store app

4.   After the test project is created successfully, right click on the AddComponentTest project and choose References.

5.   In the AddComponentTest Property Pages dialog, click on Add New Reference.

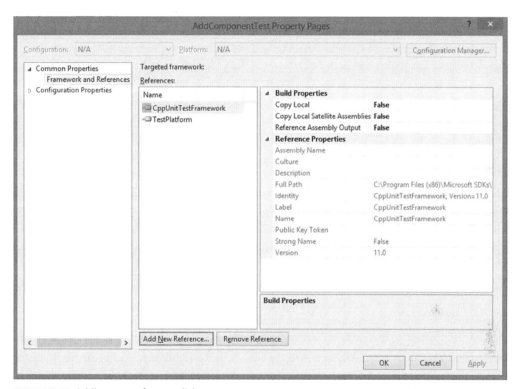

FIGURE 7-12 Adding new reference dialog

6.   In the Add Reference dialog, choose the Solution->Projects node in the left pane.

7.   Choose the WRLAddComponent as the reference project from the right pane. Click OK.

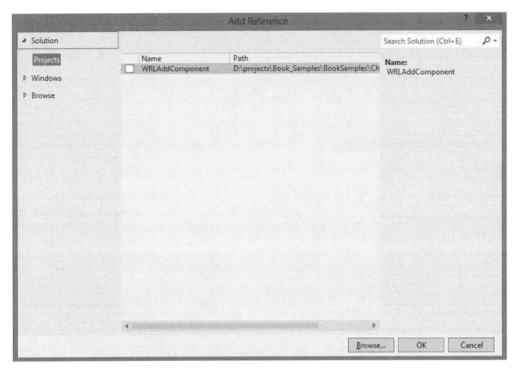

FIGURE 7-13 Selecting the WRL Component to add as a refernce

8. Once the reference to the WRL component is added, you are now ready to code the test method.

9. Add a reference to the header file where the WinRTClass definition can be found.

```
#include "..\WRLAddComponent\WRLAddComponent_h.h"
```

10. Before you write your actual test method, there are a few things to keep in mind. Since you have authored your WinRT component using WRL and not C++ /CX, the runtime class and other metadata is generated inside the ABI::WRLAddComponent namespace.

11. Since the component is dependent on WRL, you cannot use the ^ syntax for activating the runtimeclass. What you should be doing is the classical COM way of instantiating COM interface and make the method call, albeit updated for the WinRT.

12. Add include header files for wrl\client.h, roapi.h and winstring.h

```
#include <wrl\client.h>
#include <roapi.h>
#include <winstring.h>
```

13. In the TEST_METHOD(TestMethod1), you should make a call to RoInitialize. RoInitialize initializes the Windows Runtime and in order to do so, it needs a parameter of type RO_INIT_TYPE. Since this is a Windows Store app, pass a value of RO_INIT_MULTITHREADED, to RoInitialize. RO_INIT_MULTITHREADED initializes the Windows Runtime and allows COM calls on any thread.

14. RoInitialize returns a HRESULT indicating either success or any error condition. You should always check the HRESULT value before proceeding to make calls on any WinRT object.

15. The next step is to create an instance of the WinRT class. In order to do so, you should call the ActivateInstance method from the Windows::Foundation namespace. Since your WinRT component does not define an ActivationFactory, calling ActivateInstance should suffice.

16. If your component defines a custom activation factory, you should call GetActivationFactory instead of ActivateInstance.

17. The ActivationFactory takes a parameter of HSTRING that represents the runtime class name and returns the activated instance pointer as an out param. Add the code below in your test method to activate the runtime class.

LISTING 7-12 Activation code for the WRL component

```
std::wstring strCompName(RuntimeClass_WRLAddComponent_WinRTClass);
HSTRING comphString;
WindowsCreateString(strCompName.data(), wcslen(strCompName.data()), &comphString);
ComPtr<ABI::WRLAddComponent::IWinRTClass> spAddClass;
Windows::Foundation::ActivateInstance(comphString, &spAddClass);
```

18. All that remains now is to make the method call and then verify the result.

LISTING 6-13 Test code for the Calculate method

```
int result = 0;
spAddClass->Calculate(2, 3, &result);
Assert::AreEqual(5, result, 0.0);
WindowsDeleteString(comphString);
```

19. That's it. Our test is now ready. Build the solution now.

20. Navigate to Test Explorer and Click on Run All to begin test method execution.

21. The test passes and the status is updated in Test Explorer.

22. The complete code for the test class is listed below.

LISTING 7-14 Complete listing for the Calculate test method

```cpp
#include "pch.h"
#include "CppUnitTest.h"
#include <wrl\client.h>
#include <roapi.h>
#include <winstring.h>
#include <string>

#include "..\WRLAddComponent\WRLAddComponent_h.h"

using namespace Microsoft::VisualStudio::CppUnitTestFramework;
using namespace Microsoft::WRL;
using namespace ABI::WRLAddComponent;

namespace AddComponentTest
{
    TEST_CLASS(UnitTest1)
    {
    public:
        TEST_METHOD(TestMethod1)
        {
            // TODO: Your test code here
            HRESULT hr = RoInitialize(RO_INIT_MULTITHREADED);
            std::wstring strCompName(RuntimeClass_WRLAddComponent_WinRTClass);
            HSTRING comphString;
            WindowsCreateString(strCompName.data(), wcslen(strCompName.data()), &comphString);
            ComPtr<ABI::WRLAddComponent::IWinRTClass> spAddClass;
            Windows::Foundation::ActivateInstance(comphString, &spAddClass);
            int result = 0;
            spAddClass->Calculate(2, 3, &result);
            Assert::AreEqual(5, result, 0.0);
            WindowsDeleteString(comphString);
        }
    };
}
```

Developing a WinRT component using C++ /CX

In this walkthrough, you will first build a WinRT component using C++ /CX. The steps below will help you develop a simple component that exports a single method Add. Add takes two parameters of type int and returns their sum as an int.

1. Launch Visual Studio 2012.

2. Choose New Project.

3. Under the Visual C++ Language, select Windows Store->Windows Runtime Component.

4. Type in a name for the solution, such as, CxxAdd.

5. Choose a destination to Save the solution. The Project Solution and initial source files are created and saved to this location.

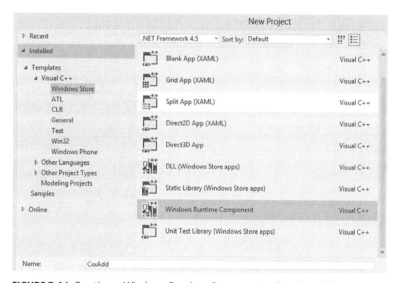

FIGURE 7-14 Creating a Windows Runtime Component using C++ /CX

6. Click OK.

7. Visual Studio generates creates the default solution and initial files.

8. From the Solution Viewer, double click the Class1.h file.

9. Rename the generated class name from Class1 to AddClass.

10. Add a new public method named Add. Add takes two parameters of type integer and returns an integer type.

11. The code for the AddClass is shown below.

LISTING 7-15 AddClass listing

```
namespace CxxAdd
{
    public ref class AddClass sealed
    {
    public:
        AddClass();
        int Add(int x, int y);
    };
}
```

12. Implement the Add member function in the Class1.cpp file as shown below.

```
// adds two numbers and returns the sum
int AddClass::Add(int x, int y)
{
    return x + y;
}
```

13. Build the solution. The component is now ready.

Unit testing the C++ /CX based WinRT component

We will now build a test project and write a test for the component developed in the preceding section.

1. In the Solution Explorer, right click on the CxxAdd solution and choose Add->Add New Project.

2. Under the Visual C++ node, choose Windows Store->Unit Test Library (Windows Store apps).

3. Save the project with a name, such as, AddTest as shown below.

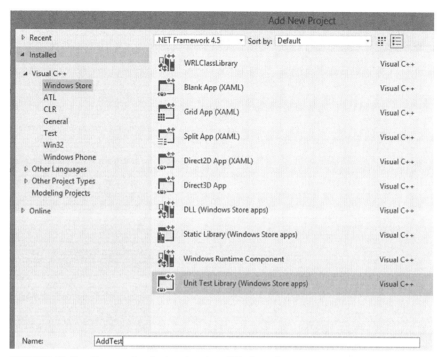

FIGURE 7-15 Creating a native test project for a Windows Store app.

4. After the test project is created successfully, right click on the AddTest project and choose References.

5. In the AddTest Property Pages dialog, click on Add New Reference.

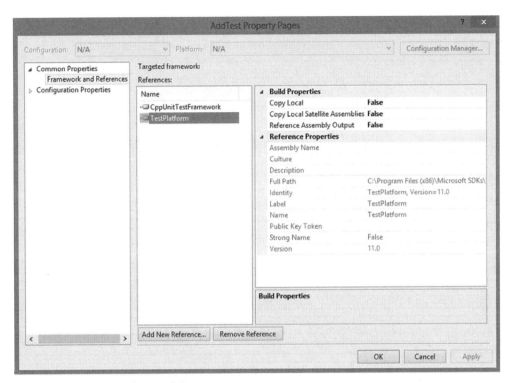

FIGURE 7-16 Add New Reference dialog

6. In the Add Reference dialog, choose the Solution->Projects node in the left pane.

7. Choose the CxxAdd as the reference project from the right pane. Click OK.

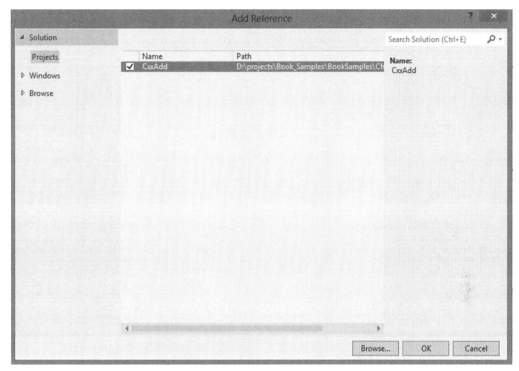

FIGURE 7-17 Adding reference to the CxxAdd component

8. Once the reference to the CxxAdd component is added, you are now ready to code the test method.

9. In the AddTest project, open the unittest1.cpp file.

10. Add a reference to the namespace CxxAdd.

    using namespace CxxAdd;

11. Change the name of the test from the default generated TestMethod1 to AddTestMethod.

12. Write your test code as shown below.

LISTING 7-16 Test code for the Add method

```
namespace AddTest
{
    TEST_CLASS(UnitTest1)
    {
    public:
        TEST_METHOD(AddTestMethod)
        {
            // TODO: Your test code here
            AddClass addObj;
            const auto result = addObj.Add(2, 3);
```

```
        Assert::AreEqual(5, 5);
    }
};
}
```

13. Save your code and build the Solution.

14. The test method, AddTestMethod appears in Test Explorer.

15. Right click on the AddTestMethod in Test Explorer and choose Run Selected Tests.

16. The test method is executed and passes. The status is reflected in Test Explorer.

FIGURE 7-18 Test Explorer with list of passed tests

Where are we and what's Next

Visual Studio 2012 includes great support for testing your native C++ apps and Windows Store apps. Whether you work as an independent developer or as part of a team of developers in an Organization, you should take advantage of this support for unit testing C++ code. Testing code early in the development lifecycle allows you to catch a good number of bugs early on and helps raise the quality bar as the project progresses and more code is added. Furthermore unit testing gives you the confidence to revisit existing code and refactor it safely, minimizing the chance of introducing regression bugs. Shipping with good quality and shipping frequently helps you listen to customer needs and respond faster. This is especially true with the Windows Store and Windows Store apps and helps you/your teams iterate faster, add new features to your app and push out updates to your app on the Store as quickly as the updates are ready to go. Windows 8 and Windows Store are a great opportunity to design good looking Windows Store apps and release your code to the world. Visual Studio 2012 has great tools to help you get there quickly and you should make the best use of it!

Chapter 8
Debugging Windows Store apps

Introduction
Local debugging
Debugging in the Simulator
Debugging PLM events
Where are we and what's Next

Introduction

Debugging is a vital and necessary part of the development cycle, and with Visual Studio 2012 Microsoft has brought their powerful visual debugging experience to the new world of Windows Store Apps.

When you want to begin debugging your Windows Store apps, you can choose the target location where your code will execute. These could either be your local machine, or a Simulator or a remote machine. Debugging on the local machine is exactly what it sounds like: your appx package is deployed and executed in the actual WinRT environment on the same machine that Visual Studio is running on.

When you choose to debug using the Simulator, Visual Studio launches an instance of the WinRT desktop simulator application and deploys and loads your app package into this rather than into actual WinRT environment. The simulator allows you to test your apps support for multi-touch gestures, orientation and resolution changes even if you happen to be using a development hardware that does not inherently have these capabilities.

On choosing remote debugging, your app will be deployed over the network onto another machine. This is the route you'd take if you wanted to debug on an actual Surface RT device (Surface RT cannot itself run Visual Studio 2012)

Let us now explore each of these debugging techniques in more detail.

Local debugging

Visual Studio enables you to debug and test your classic desktop apps on the local machine. The great news is this support has been added for Windows Store apps too. You can run your Windows Store app on the same local machine which hosts Visual Studio. There is one small limitation though: If your monitor is not touch-enabled, you will be restricted to keyboard and mouse interaction only.

If you have multiple monitors, you can choose to choose to take advantage of the additional monitor. You can designate one monitor for your Windows Store app and another for Visual Studio. Splitting the monitors allows you to look at your app and the debugger side-by-side and saves you from having to switch between the app and the debugger.

Launch the debugger on the local machine

In order to debug your app on the local machine, you should follow these steps.

1. From the debugger Standard toolbar, select Local Machine.

2. Click on the Start Debugging button.

3. If you do not see the Standard toolbar, click View->Toolbars and then the Standard menu option.

4. Your preference to debug on the local machine is saved along with the project settings file.

5. For C++ and JavaScript apps, you can also choose the local debugger by right clicking on the project in the Solution Explorer and then choose Debugging from the project options.

6. In the Debugging options pane, choose Local Debugger from the Debugger to launch list on the right pane.

7. If you are using a single monitor for debugging and running your Windows Store app, you can switch between the debugger and your app at any time by pressing the **ALT + TAB** key combination.

Both the approaches of choosing the local debugger are illustrated below.

FIGURE 8-1 Choosing the Local Machine as the target for debugging

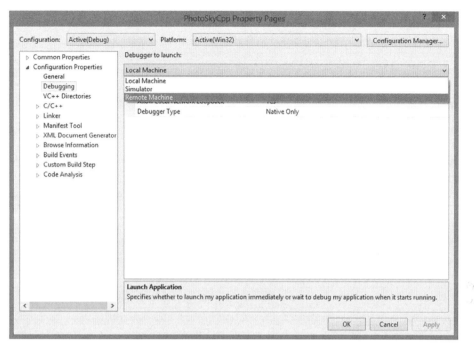

FIGURE 8-2 Choosing the Local Machine as the target for debugging from the Project Property page dialog

Debugging in the Simulator

The Visual Studio Simulator is a desktop app that simulates the environment of a Windows Store app. This enables you to test not just your code but also how well your app responds to touch events, orientation changes etc.

> **Tip** While the Simulator is a great tool to debug and test your apps, you should always test and verify your app on a physical device before uploading to the Store. This is particularly true if your application makes significant use of DirectX.

Launch the Simulator

In order to debug your app on the Simulator, you should follow these steps.

1. From the debugger Standard toolbar, select Simulator.

2. Click on the Start Debugging button.

3. If you do not see the Standard toolbar, click View->Toolbars and then the Standard menu option.

4. Your preference to debug on the Simulator is saved along with the project settings file.

5. For C++ and JavaScript apps, you can also choose the Simulator by right clicking on the project in the Solution Explorer and then choose Debugging from the project options.

6. In the Debugging options pane, choose Simulator from the Debugger to launch list on the right pane.

Both the approaches of choosing the Simulator are illustrated below.

FIGURE 8-3 Choosing the Simulator for debugging apps

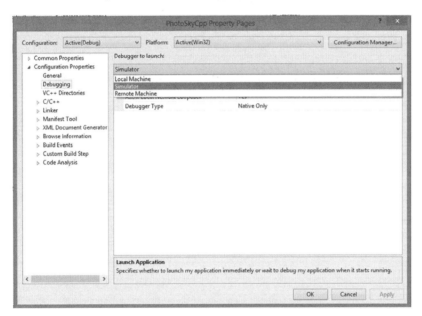

FIGURE 8-4 Choosing the Simulator launching the debugger using the Project Property pages

When you select the debugger as the Simulator and launch your app, the Simulator screen looks like the figure 8-5

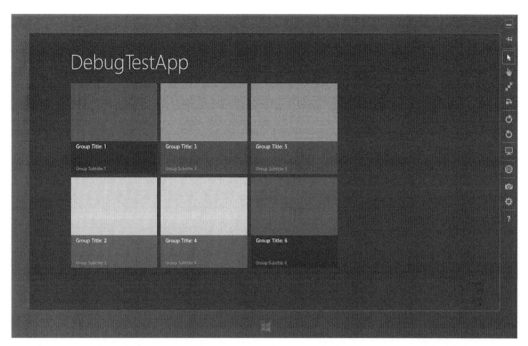

FIGURE 8-5 Simulator screen after your app launches

The various Simulator options are available along the right edge of the Simulator desktop application. Each of the options allow you to test different aspects of Windows Store app environment. Some of the debugging options include testing your app for touch mode (especially useful if you do not have a touch enabled device), testing the pinch-zoom gesture, orientation change testing etc.

The Simulator also includes the option to test your app against a variety of display resolutions. This is especially useful considering that Windows 8 is targeted at devices that support monitors from 10" to 72" in size. You can also use the Simulator to test location-aware apps and obtain screenshots from your app and submit them to the Store. The screenshots are used as part of the Store landing page to describe the functionality supported by your app.

Remote debugging Windows Store apps

If debugging on the local machine or using the Simulator are such a great additions, what purpose does remote debugging serve? One good answer is: Windows RT apps. Windows RT, as you may already know, is the version of Windows that runs on the ARM architecture. If you have a Windows RT device, such as the Microsoft Surface RT, you can use the remote debugging capabilities available in Visual Studio 2012 to test and debug your app on the ARM device.

In order to remote debug your app, you should connect the host machine and the remote machine using either a local Wi-Fi network connection or an Ethernet cable. Debugging over the internet is not supported however. You should also install a Developer License on the remote device as a pre-requisite for debugging on the device.

Visual Studio 2012 comes with support for remote debugging components that you should install on the remote device. These components enable you to send commands to the remote device and receive output back on the host machine.

Note You should be running as an administrator on the remote device for remote debugging to work properly.

You can install the remote tools by running the setup program either from the Visual Studio installation media or from the Microsoft Download Center at http://go.microsoft.com/fwlink/?linkid=219549. Be sure to download and install the right tools for the correct architecture (x86, x64 or ARM). Once you complete the installation, you can proceed with starting the remote debugger.

From the Start screen, choose the Remote Debugger to start the remote debugger. The first time configuration screen appears and will prompt you to install mandatory components and configure your firewall for traffic to pass through between your host machine and the remote machine. You will also be able to grant needed permissions for users to the remote tools and set advanced options.

Once you have completed installing and configuring remote tools, you can choose to deploy and debug your project over the remote machine. You can set the remote debugger using the Project configuration properties as shown in figure.

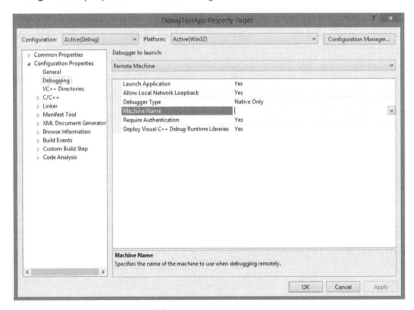

FIGURE 8-6 Opting to remote debug your app

You can start debugging using the same set of commands as you would on a local machine. You can set breakpoints and navigate the debugging session too. However, you should make sure that you are logged in using the same user credentials on both the host machine as well as the remote machine.

Remote debugging is especially useful to profile, test and debug ARM versions of your Windows Store apps. Should you choose to profile your app directly on the device, you should start the Performance Analysis (ALT + F2) to start your app. Your app starts with profiling suspended. Before you begin the scenario that you intend to profile, you should resume profiling. Once you work through your scenario, you can pause profiling and collect profiling data. You should repeat profiling over all your key scenarios to gather as much accurate data as possible. Once you stop profiling, the profiler analyses the data and displays the results in a window.

Debugging PLM events

During the normal process of execution of your app, Windows PLM controls the apps lifecycle – start, suspend, resume – all in response to user interaction. Termination of the app usually happens in response to the state of the machine (usually low resource or app not being used for a long time). When your app is in debug mode, Windows suspends all PLM events. You can use the Visual Studio debugger to fire PLM events and test how your app responds to such events.

Your app could be suspended when a user switches away from your app for instance. You should always subscribe to the **Suspending** event and save all pertinent app state and user data. When the app is resumed, either due to user switching to the app or a re-launch using the tile on the Start screen, your app enters into the **Running** state. Before entering into this state, you should reload saved app and user data. You can do this by subscribing to the **Resuming** event and perform the necessary restore activity.

It is important to note here that Windows can also choose to just terminate your app. Termination does not fire any events that your app can subscribe to. Think of it as a good, old Win32 equivalent of TerminateProcess API call! For this reason, you should not rely on save during exit and should handle all persist activities during Suspend event.

Test Suspend and Resume events

You should follow these steps to manually suspend or resume your app to debug PLM related events.

1. Set a breakpoint in your event handler (either the Suspending or Resuming events)

2. Start debugging. This is usually achieved by pressing F5 key.

3. On the debug location toolbar, you can then choose the fire the appropriate event. The supported events are shown in figure.

FIGURE 8-7 Support for PLM events in the Visual Studio 2012 debugger

Debugging background tasks

Your app can contain code that initiates background tasks. These tasks can include, but are not limited to, toast notifications, tile updates or badge updates. These tasks cannot update the main UI of your app. Any background task that does not contain data or does not need user input can be triggered from the debugger.

In order to debug a background task from a normal debug session, follow these steps.

1. Set breakpoints in the background tasks you intend to debug.
2. Start the debug session by pressing the F5 key.
3. From the debug location toolbar, choose the background task to start as shown in figure.

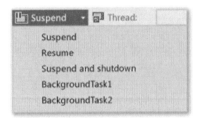

FIGURE 8-8 Suspending Background tasks

To debug a background task when your app is not running, follow these steps

1. Set breakpoints in the background tasks you intend to debug.
2. Navigate to the Debugging property page by right clicking on your project and choosing Properties.
3. Choose **No** from the Launch Application list.
4. Begin debugging by pressing the F5 key.
5. The Process list on the Debug location toolbar is updated to display the app package name.
6. From the debug location toolbar, choose the background task to start as shown in figure.

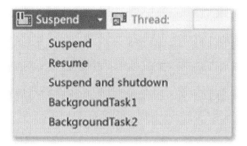

FIGURE 8-9   Suspending Background tasks when your app is not in running state

Where are we and what's Next

In this section we have explored the various debugger options and the first class support for Windows Store application debugging in Visual Studio 2012. With the in-built debugger, you can choose to deploy your Windows Store apps to the local machine or a remote machine like the Surface RT or launch the in-built Simulator to test/debug your application for debugging application failures. The Simulator in particular, is an excellent deploy target for your Windows Store applications and provides various test options: Testing your app UI for various resolutions, touch input, sensor input etc. As a recommendation, you should always test/validate your apps before publishing them to the Windows Store.

Chapter 9
Performance Tips for XAML apps

Introduction
Remaining responsive
Ensuring fast and fluid animations
Fast app activation
Application lifetimes
Optimizing data
Media packaging into resources

Introduction

Thus far we have seen how to build Windows Store Apps using a combination of modern C++ 11, C++ CX, XAML and DirectX. These are powerful technologies and when used in conjunction they are untouchable, however building an app that looks great and is loved by users requires more than just lush graphics, eye candy and animations that delight the first time you see them, great apps are the ones that provide meaningful functionality to users while simultaneously providing fast and fluid interactions. These days business, social and entertainment titles typically involve significant computation, often this involves the mathematical modelling of different entities and the interactions between them, if the developer wishes to also present high fidelity interaction then the performance of the code will need to be carefully monitored. This should be familiar territory for the C++ developer for whom performance has always been part of their value statement.

One way to think about performance is in terms of a feature. Within Windows, performance is always treated as a "tenet". Planning any feature or a feature enhancement always has to take into consideration how the said feature performs. In fact, it goes beyond metrics and ties into the quality of user experience the performance results in. While there is no "one way" of measuring performance and its impact, I strongly believe planning for performance as a feature is a nice mechanism to stay on track to provide a delightful experience to the users' of your app.

In this chapter, we will explore a few design concepts that would result in a satisfying end user experience.

Remaining responsive

Users today expect apps to remain responsive while handling all kinds of computational tasks. If your app is even perceived to not respond to user demands and expectations, then you should be prepared to hear quite vocally from your users. An app that does not remain responsive will certainly get negative feedback in the "store driven" world we are in and can definitely expect to be down rated over similar apps.

Remaining responsive means different things to different users. For some, it might mean opening files from disk a lot faster, rendering content or changing UI states quickly or number crunching fast enough. Irrespective of the actual scenario, users demand that the app respond to their input and do not show "ghost windows" wherein the app appears hung or frozen. In this section, we will highlight facilities built into WinRT that allow you to build responsive apps.

Never block the UI thread

The XAML framework is an event driven framework, just like the rest of Windows is. This means, that events are processed in the order they arrive. Your application code is run only in response to events. If no events are fired, then your app sits idling by waiting for events to occur. The XAML UI framework code and your application code are run on the same thread, conveniently named the UI thread. While the XAML UI framework code has been optimized and tuned enough, if your code takes too long to complete execution on the UI thread, then the XAML framework code either cannot run or notify UI changes that have taken place while your code is executing. A lost-lose situation indeed!

One way to ensure your code does not interfere with the XAML framework code is to return control as quickly as possible to the framework. However, this is easier said than done. Reading from a file, for example, takes time. If you are sure that your code will take a long time to complete execution, consider moving it to a background thread. Background threads do not interfere with the work being performed by the UI thread and run independent of the UI thread.

Async, async and async

One of the facilities provided by the WinRT platform to keep your apps responsive is the asynchrony built into the APIs. An asynchronous API executes in the background and upon completion, returns the result to the calling thread. Always prefer to use the async version of an API especially when making the call from the UI thread. The Parallel Patterns Library (PPL) provides a task based library that allows C++ developers code async APIs seamless and easy. Please refer to chapter 2 for more information on PPL.

Another frequently overseen aspect is performing disk access multiple times. If your app needs to access the disk and query for file properties, you should consider using the Windows::Storage::BulkAccess APIs v/s repeatedly calling the StorageFile APIs and query for file properties.

Do not invalidate UI

XAML is different from traditional Win32-based UI frameworks. Do not call Invalidate frequently as it interferes with XAML framework's invalidation operation. This means:

- Do not modify parts of the visual tree other than the current control in MeasureOverride

- Changing dimensions in ArrangeOverride

- Calling UpdateLayout when a layout pass is in progress

- Changing a property that affects a layout such as Height, Width etc from a layout event such as FrameworkElement.SizeChanged etc.

Checking the Frame rate counter

The XAML framework ships with a frame rate counter. The counter can be enabled using the DebugSettings::EnableFrameRateCounter property. The frame rate numbers produced by this property are accurate only when the UI thread is creating the frames. Sadly, what this means is you cannot use this property when developing mixed-mode applications such as XAML-DirectX or pure DirectX applications. , that said this counter is a good tool for pure XAML applications.

Ensuring fluid animations

The Windows 8 user experience makes extensive use of fast and fluid animations. In order to deliver these XAML has a dedicated thread whose sole task is to process the composition and animation of an application's visuals. This thread is called the composition thread. The composition thread is separated from the UI thread thus allowing XAML apps to achieve a consistent frame rate and smooth animations regardless of the complexity of the layout passes. For more information on animations and using the built-in animations, please refer to chapter 3. Building your own animation might sound compelling but you should stay away from doing so. XAML is tuned and optimized to provide the best performance for the built-in animations, called PVL animations, and you should endeavor to use these as much as possible.

Fast app activation

The activation period is the time when a user chooses to start an app and the moment when the app is functional to the user. This time period is super critical as a user's initial impressions are formed based on how long they need to wait before your app is fully functional. This ties back to our initial discussion around having quickly launching and responsive apps. When apps do not launch fast enough, the apps or at times the system gets blamed. With Windows 8 PLM, if an app does not start quickly enough, the app might get suspended or worse, terminated by the PLM manager.

Improving an app's startup performance

- Utilize the app constructor to initialize data structures that are only critical to the app. The app constructor is called only once. If your app is suspended and then resumes, the app constructor is not called.

- Design your app to handle the various activation types that exist in Windows 8. Activation types include OnActivated, OnSearchActivated etc. You should create the necessary UI for these activations in the method, assign it to Window::Content property and then call Window::Activate.

- If your app has an extended initialization phase, you should show a loading page.

- If Window::Activate is not called within 15 seconds of the start of the activation process, your application is terminated.

- Show UI while data is loaded asynchronously in the background.

- Only load the XAML needed to get past the app startup process. Parsing XAML and creating the corresponding objects can be time consuming for complex layouts. Make sure you read through your XAML markup and ensure that the first page contains all of the stuff you need to display the visual. If you refer a control or a style that is not in your initial page, the framework will load and parse the other files too thereby increasing startup time.

- Move application specific resources to the app object thus avoiding duplication. Any resources that are specific to a particular page should be moved to the resource dictionary of that page. This reduces the amount of XAML parsed when the app starts and incur the cost of parsing that XAML only when the specific page is navigated to.

- Remove unwanted and unused elements from designer generated XAML markup.

- Avoid setting properties of elements to their default values. The parser already does this on creation of the object. Explicitly setting the property induces an unnecessary property assignment. If something else happens to be bound to that property, the change notification then bubbles through the property system.

- While the XAML framework is designed to display thousands of objects, having a finite number of objects makes your app layout and scene render faster. Thus, avoid unnecessary elements.

- Remove elements that are not visible because they are hidden / transparent, or collapse them if they are needed for other visual states.

- If you reuse the same vector based element multiple times, make it an image. Vector-based elements are potentially more expensive because the CPU needs to create each individual element separately. The image needs to be decoded only once.

- Minimize or if possible, avoid managed assemblies or controls especially in the startup path.

- Package resources along with your app. Loading from disk is faster than fetching stuff over a network.

Application lifetimes

The Windows 8 process lifetime system can suspend or terminate an app for a variety of reasons. The system is designed to quickly return an app to the state it was in before it was suspended or terminated. When done optimally the user won't be aware that the app ever stopped running. This section discusses a few tricks that your app can use to help the system streamline transitions in an app's lifetime.

- Your app can be suspended when the user moves it to the background or when the system enters a low power state. When the app is being suspended, it raises the suspending event and has up to 5 seconds to save its data. If the app's suspending event handler doesn't complete within 5 seconds, the system assumes the app has stopped responding and terminates it. A terminated app has to go through the long startup process again instead of being immediately loaded into memory when a user switches to it.

- The app should determine if its state has actually changed, and if so, only serialize and deserialize the data that changed. A good way to ensure that this happens in to serialize data as it changes. When you use this technique everything that needs to be serialized at suspension has already been saved so there is no work to be done and an app suspends quickly.

- The system tries to keep as many suspended apps in memory as possible so that users can quickly and reliably switch between them. When an app is suspended and stays in the system's memory, it can quickly be brought to the foreground for the user to interact with, without having to display a splash screen or perform a lengthy load operation. If there aren't enough resources to keep an app in memory, the app is terminated. This makes memory management important for two reasons:

  o Freeing as much memory as possible at suspension minimizes the chances that your app is terminated because of lack of resources while it's suspended.

  o Reducing the overall amount of memory your app uses reduces the chances that other apps are terminated while they are suspended.

- Certain objects, such as files and devices, occupy a large amount of memory. We recommend that during suspension, an app release handles to these objects and recreate the handle when needed. This is also a good time to purge any caches that won't be valid when the app is resumed.

- The XAML framework tries to cache commonly used objects so that they can be efficiently reused with as little overhead as possible. One action that prevents XAML from doing this is declaring the same brush in multiple templates. Instead, create commonly used brushes as root ResourceDictionary elements and then refer to that object in templates.

A very good example of implementing suspend and restore operations is the DXBouncingBall sample from Chapter 1. The only data that is saved during suspension is the ball color and that is restored when the app is resumed. I cannot stress enough: only save the data that needs to be saved, do not try to implement a virtual memory manager and save your entire app state to disk during suspension.

Optimizing data

Manipulating lists and other collections of information are primary scenarios for almost all apps. Collections are ubiquitous and there are two key performance factors that you must think of when using them. The first is the amount of time spent on the UI thread creating items. The quicker items can be instantiated; data bound, and laid out, the faster a user can pan a collection while instantaneously seeing items appear on screen.

The second performance consideration is the amount of memory the rendered items in the collection use and the space it takes to store the data set displayed. The likelihood that a suspended app will be terminated rises with the amount of memory used by the active app. This is also true for the chances of the active app getting terminated when it is suspended. In general, high memory use degrades the experience for all apps on the system.

UI Virtualization

UI virtualization is the most important improvement you can make to the performance of collections. UI virtualization creates the UI elements that represent each item in a collection on demand. Imagine an app that displays 1000 items in a list control.   There's no reason to create the UI for each item and hold it in memory.

The standard ItemsControls preform UI virtualization on your behalf. As items are close to being visible (a few items before and after the visible items are cached to improve performance), XAML generates the UI for the item and holds it in memory. When it's no longer likely that the item will be shown, XAML reuses the memory that was used to display the item for another item that is close to being displayed. Sometimes app designs require that the default panel an ItemsControl uses to organize items be switched with a different one. As long as the new panel supports UI virtualization, the control continues to perform this optimization for free. Standard virtualizing panels include WrapGrid and VirtualizingStackPanel. Replacing the default panel in an ItemsControl with non-virtualizing panels (VariableSizedWrapGrid and StackPanel) disables UI virtualization for that control.

Data Virtualization

Sometimes the data set an app must work with is so large that it cannot or should not be stored in memory. In these cases you must implement some form of data virtualization. In this type of virtualization an initial portion of the full data set is loaded into memory (read off a disk or pulled from the web) and UI virtualization is applied to this partial data set. You can later download data incrementally or from random points in the master data set on demand.

Incremental data virtualization sequentially downloads data. For example, a ListView that uses incremental data virtualization and contains 1,000,000 items may only down the first 20. Then the next 20 items are downloaded as user pans towards the end of the list. Each time more items are downloaded the scroll bar for the list becomes a little smaller. For this type of data virtualization you must use a data source that implements ISupportIncrementalLoading.

Random access data virtualization allows a control to download data from any point in the data set. For example, a ListView that uses random access data virtualization may download the items 100,000 – 100,020. If the user then jumps to the top of the list, the control downloads items 1 – 20. The whole time the scroll bars are sized to a collection of 1,000,000 and only move the thumb relative to where the items in the view port are located in the collection's data set. To enable this type of data virtualization you need to use a data source that implements INotifyCollectionChanged and IObservableVector.

Item templates

In addition to only creating the objects that are near to the viewport (ie. UI virtualization), make sure that the objects that are actually created are not unnecessarily complex. Reducing XAML complexity was stressed in the section on startup and it applies to scrolling and panning too. As items are panned into view, the framework must update the fields in cached item templates with the data of the items being panned onto the screen. Reducing the complexity of these XAML trees can pay off both in the amount of memory needed to store the elements and the amount of time it takes to data bind and propagate the individual properties within the template. This reduces the amount of work the UI thread must do, which helps ensure that items appear immediately in a collection that a user quickly pans.

Item template Selectors

Item template selectors introduce two extra steps in the process of rendering of items. First, XAML framework instantiates only enough item templates to display the items that are close to being displayed. The individual elements that make up these templates are cached and updated with the data of other items as they get close to being displayed. This saves the time of instantiating an item template. When you use an item template selectors, the framework can no longer cache item templates because it doesn't know what type of template is needed until the item template selector is run.

This brings us to the second step, actually determining which item template to use. The code in your item template selector must be run for each item that is close to being displayed. This is helpful when the data being displayed is intrinsically different; but when the data is very similar this extra step is not needed. Make sure that data template selectors are actually necessary to provide a meaningful visual for each element instead of having a uniform data template applied to all items in the collection.

Media packaging into resources

Media files are some of the most common and expensive resources apps typically use. Because media file resources can greatly increase the size of your app's memory footprint, you must remember to release the handle to media as soon as the app is finished using it.

For example, if your app is working with a RandomAccessStream or IInputStream object, be sure to **delete** the object when your app has finished using it, to release the underlying object.

Beyond this, here are some valuable performance tips for resource frugal use of media within apps:

- Use full screen video playback whenever possible.

- Do not overlay embedded video.

- Try delaying setting the Source property of the MediaElement as long as possible.

- If the same video is encoded at different resolutions and is available, use an encoding that is a close match to the target device resolution.

- Decode images only once.

Where are we and what's Next

Windows 8 is designed to provide a fast and fluid experience to users. As application developers, writing apps for the Windows Store, you should pay attention to the end user experience. While it is very easy to design and develop XAML applications, you should also be mindful of the costs you pay for using functionality in the framework that your app either no longer needs or is particularly costly. The tips suggested above would help you get started and will enable you to build well behaving XAML applications for Windows 8 and beyond.

In the next chapter, we will learn how to build connected applications using Windows Azure Mobile Services and C++ /CX.

Chapter 10

Introduction to Windows Azure Mobile Services

Introduction
Getting Started with Windows Store apps and Windows Azure Mobile Services
Creating a simple Windows Store app with Windows Azure Mobile Services
Supporting Push Notifications using Windows Azure Mobile Services
Where are we and what's Next

Introduction

With connected applications being the norm today, developers have the additional responsibility of creating middle-tier data access layers that can communicate with the back-end services. In addition to providing simple data access, they also need to code for authentication, structuring their queries and also include the possibility of sending push notifications etc. This is very complex, time consuming and non-trivial. Enter Windows Azure Mobile Services. The Windows Azure Mobile Services SDK allows you to connect your apps to Windows Azure services and lets you focus on the code to be written for your app. You need to write simple logic on the server to ensure security and input validation (as is the case with any database), add the capability to call http services and send push notifications to your app.

Getting Started with Windows Store apps and Windows Azure Mobile Services

Before you begin

1. In order to successfully build Windows Store apps that communicate with Windows Azure Mobile Services, you should obtain the Mobile Services SDK from http://www.windowsazure.com/en-us/develop/mobile/tutorials/create-a-windows-azure-account.

2. Setup your app for Windows Live authentication and Windows Live push notification support by configuring your app. The configuration steps can be found at https://manage.dev.live.com/build

Creating a simple Windows Store app with Windows Azure Mobile Services

This section walks through the process of creating a C++ /CX Windows Store app and connects your app with Windows Azure Mobile Services.

1. Open Microsoft Visual Studio 2012. Select File->New Project->Templates->Visual C++->Windows Store and pick a Blank App (XAML) project template. Save the project with a name, such as, MobileServicesApp.

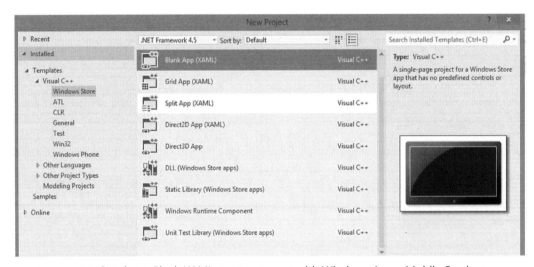

FIGURE 10-1 Creating a Blank XAML app to connect with Windows Azure Mobile Services

2. Add a reference to the Windows Azure Mobile Services by right clicking on the project file and choosing References.
3. In the References dialog, click on Add New Reference. In the Add Reference dialog, choose Windows Azure Mobile Services Native Client from the Windows->Extensions node.

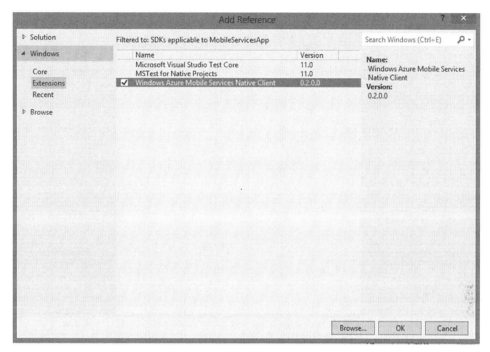

FIGURE 10-2 Adding references to the Windows Azure Mobile Services SDK

4. Replace the xaml markup in the MainPage.xaml with the one shown below. When you replace the markup, make sure to do so only the section in the Grid and not the complete Page markup.

```xml
<Grid Background="{StaticResource ApplicationPageBackgroundThemeBrush}">
        <Grid Margin="50,50,10,10">
            <Grid.ColumnDefinitions>
                <ColumnDefinition Width="*" />
                <ColumnDefinition Width="*" />
            </Grid.ColumnDefinitions>
            <Grid.RowDefinitions>
                <RowDefinition Height="Auto" />
                <RowDefinition Height="*" />
            </Grid.RowDefinitions>

            <Grid Grid.Row="0" Grid.ColumnSpan="2" Margin="0,0,0,20">
                <StackPanel>
                    <TextBlock Foreground="#0094ff" FontFamily="Segoe UI Light"
Margin="0,0,0,6">WINDOWS AZURE MOBILE SERVICES</TextBlock>
                    <TextBlock Foreground="Gray" FontFamily="Segoe UI Light" FontSize="45" >Windows
Azure Mobile Services App</TextBlock>
                </StackPanel>
            </Grid>


            <Grid Grid.Row="1">
                <StackPanel>
```

```xml
            <local:Task Number="1" Title="Create a Todo Item" Description="Enter some text below
and click Save to insert a new todo item into your database" />

                        <StackPanel Orientation="Horizontal" Margin="72,0,0,0">
                            <TextBox Name="TextInput" Margin="5" MinWidth="300"></TextBox>
                            <Button Name="ButtonSave" Click="ButtonSave_Click">Save</Button>
                        </StackPanel>

                </StackPanel>
            </Grid>

            <Grid Grid.Row="1" Grid.Column="1">
                <Grid.RowDefinitions>
                    <RowDefinition Height="Auto" />
                    <RowDefinition />
                </Grid.RowDefinitions>
                <StackPanel>
                    <local:Task Number="2" Title="Refresh List" Description="Click refresh below to
load the unfinished todo items from your database." />
                        <Button Margin="72,0,0,0" Name="ButtonRefresh"
Click="ButtonRefresh_Click">Refresh</Button>
                </StackPanel>

                <ListView Name="ListItems" Margin="62,10,0,0" Grid.Row="1">
                    <ListView.ItemTemplate>
                        <DataTemplate>
                            <StackPanel Orientation="Horizontal">
                                <CheckBox IsChecked="{Binding Complete, Mode=TwoWay}"
Checked="CheckBox_Checked_1" Content="{Binding Text}" Margin="10,5" VerticalAlignment="Center"/>
                            </StackPanel>
                        </DataTemplate>
                    </ListView.ItemTemplate>
                </ListView>

            </Grid>

        </Grid>
    </Grid>
```

5. Right click on the project file and choose Add->New Item. From the Add New Item dialog, choose User Control. Save it as Task.xaml

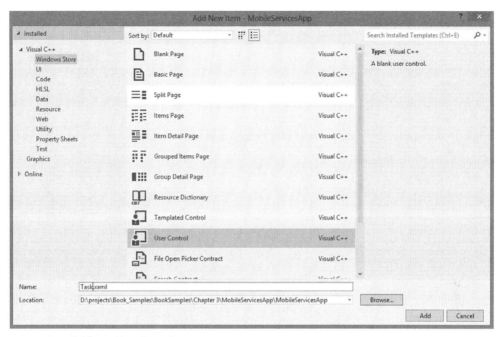

FIGURE 10-3 Adding a User Control

6. Replace the xaml markup in Task.xaml with the one below.

```xml
<UserControl
    x:Class="MobileServicesApp.Task"
    xmlns="http://schemas.microsoft.com/winfx/2006/xaml/presentation"
    xmlns:x="http://schemas.microsoft.com/winfx/2006/xaml"
    xmlns:local="using:MobileServicesApp"
    xmlns:d="http://schemas.microsoft.com/expression/blend/2008"
    xmlns:mc="http://schemas.openxmlformats.org/markup-compatibility/2006"
    mc:Ignorable="d">


    <Grid VerticalAlignment="Top">
        <StackPanel Orientation="Horizontal">
            <Border BorderThickness="0,0,1,0" BorderBrush="DarkGray" Margin="0,10" MinWidth="70">
                <TextBlock Text="{Binding Number}" FontSize="45" Foreground="DarkGray" Margin="20,0"/>
            </Border>
            <StackPanel>
                <TextBlock Text="{Binding Title}" Margin="10,10,0,0" FontSize="16" FontWeight="Bold"/>
                <TextBlock Text="{Binding Description}" Margin="10,0,0,0" />
            </StackPanel>
        </StackPanel>
    </Grid>
</UserControl>
```

7. We will use a Number, Title and Description for each of our tasks. All of these, Number, Title and Description are dependency properties and their values will be set through the backing logic in the code-behind.

8. Replace the contents of the Task.xaml.h with the following code.

```cpp
//
// Task.xaml.h
// Declaration of the Task class
//

#pragma once

#include "Task.g.h"

namespace MobileServicesApp
{
    [Windows::Foundation::Metadata::WebHostHidden]
    public ref class Task sealed
    {
    public:
        Task();
        virtual ~Task(){};

    public:
        property int Number
        {
            int get()
            {
                return static_cast<int>(GetValue(NumberProperty_));
            }
            void set(int number)
            {
                SetValue(NumberProperty_, number);
            }
        }

        property Platform::String^ Title
        {
            Platform::String^ get()
            {
                return static_cast<Platform::String^>(GetValue(TitleProperty_));
            }
            void set(Platform::String^ s)
            {
                SetValue(TitleProperty_, s);
            }
        }

        property Platform::String^ Description
        {
            Platform::String^ get()
            {
                return static_cast<Platform::String^>(GetValue(DescriptionProperty_));
            }
            void set(Platform::String^ description)
            {
                SetValue(DescriptionProperty_, description);
            }
        }
```

```
        }

    private:
            static Windows::UI::Xaml::DependencyProperty^ NumberProperty_;
            static Windows::UI::Xaml::DependencyProperty^ TitleProperty_;
            static Windows::UI::Xaml::DependencyProperty^ DescriptionProperty_;
    };
}
```

9. Replace the contents of Tasks.xaml.cpp with the following code.

```
//
// Task.xaml.cpp
// Implementation of the Task class
//

#include "pch.h"
#include "Task.xaml.h"

using namespace MobileServicesApp;

using namespace Platform;
using namespace Windows::UI::Xaml;
using namespace Windows::UI::Xaml::Interop;

Windows::UI::Xaml::DependencyProperty^ MobileServicesApp::Task::NumberProperty_ =

    DependencyProperty::Register(ref new String(L"Number"),

    TypeName(int::typeid), TypeName(Task::typeid),

    ref new PropertyMetadata(nullptr) );

Windows::UI::Xaml::DependencyProperty^ MobileServicesApp::Task::TitleProperty_ =

    DependencyProperty::Register(ref new String(L"Title"),

    TypeName(String::typeid), TypeName(Task::typeid),

    ref new PropertyMetadata(nullptr) );

Windows::UI::Xaml::DependencyProperty^ MobileServicesApp::Task::DescriptionProperty_ =

    DependencyProperty::Register(ref new String(L"Description"),

    TypeName(String::typeid), TypeName(Task::typeid),

    ref new PropertyMetadata(nullptr) );


Task::Task()
{
    InitializeComponent();
    this->DataContext = this;
```

}

10. We are now ready to connect our app with the Windows Azure Mobile Services.

11. Add four methods to the MainPage.xaml.h in the MainPage class as shown below.

```
virtual void CheckBox_Checked_1(Platform::Object^ sender, Windows::UI::Xaml::RoutedEventArgs^
args);
virtual void ButtonRefresh_Click(Platform::Object^ sender, Windows::UI::Xaml::RoutedEventArgs^
args);
virtual void ButtonSave_Click(Platform::Object^ sender, Windows::UI::Xaml::RoutedEventArgs^ args);
void RefreshData();
```

12. Add a new class named "ToDoItems" as shown below. This can be added in the Main-Page.xaml.h class. This class will have the BindableAttribute set. We will use data binding to set values to the right XAML elements from the properties exposed by this class. This class and its properties also correspond to the table we create on the Windows Azure Mobile Services backend.

```
[BindableAttribute]
public ref class ToDoItems sealed
{
public:
        ToDoItems()
        {
                text_ = L"";
                complete_ = false;
        }
        property int ID
        {
                int get()
                {
                        return ID_;
                }
                void set(int value)
                {
                        ID_ = value;
                }
        }

        property Platform::String^ Text
        {
                Platform::String^ get()
                {
                        return text_;
                }
                void set(Platform::String^ value)
                {
                        text_ = value;
                }
        }

        property bool Complete
        {
```

```
                bool get()
                {
                        return complete_;
                }
                void set(bool value)
                {
                        complete_ = value;
                }
        }
private:
        int ID_;
        Platform::String^ text_;
        bool complete_;
};
```

13. Also add a Vector of ToDoItems in the MainPage class.

```
private:
        Vector<ToDoItems^>^ items_;
```

14. Connect your app to the Windows Azure Mobile Services. In the App constructor, create an instance of the Mobile Service client.

```
client_ = ref new MobileServiceClient(ref new Uri(Your App Uri"),
        ref new String(The Secret Key));
```

15. Inserting data into the table in easy. You create an instance of a "ToDoItem", create a JSON object from the item and call the InsertAsync method of the corresponding table in the Windows Azure Mobile Service.

```
void MainPage::ButtonSave_Click(Platform::Object^ sender, Windows::UI::Xaml::RoutedEventArgs^ args)
{
    auto item = ref new ToDoItems();
    item->Text = TextInput->Text;
    item->Complete = false;
    //save data to AzureMobile
    auto client = App::MobileClient;
    auto jsonObject = ref new JsonObject();
    jsonObject->Insert(L"text", JsonValue::CreateStringValue(item->Text));
    jsonObject->Insert(L"complete", JsonValue::CreateBooleanValue(item->Complete));

    auto table = client->GetTable("TodoItem");
    task<IJsonValue^> insertTask(table->InsertAsync(jsonObject));
    insertTask.then([this, item](IJsonValue^ V)
    {
            auto results = V->Stringify();
            JsonObject^ savedItem = ref new JsonObject();
            if (JsonObject::TryParse(results, &savedItem))
            {
                    item->ID = savedItem->GetNamedNumber("id");
                    items_->Append(item);
                    ListItems->ItemsSource = items_;
            }
    });
}
```

```
}
```

16. Updating the items follows a similar process as inserting items. You create a JSON object of the "ToDoItem" to be updated and call the UpdateAsync method on the table.

```cpp
void MainPage::CheckBox_Checked_1(Platform::Object^ sender, Windows::UI::Xaml::RoutedEventArgs^ args)
{
    auto cb = dynamic_cast<CheckBox^>(sender);
    ToDoItems^ item = dynamic_cast<ToDoItems^>(cb->DataContext);
    auto client = App::MobileClient;
    auto jsonObject = ref new JsonObject();
    int ID = item->ID;
    bool Status = item->Complete;
    jsonObject->Insert(L"id", JsonValue::CreateNumberValue(item->ID));
    jsonObject->Insert(L"complete", JsonValue::CreateBooleanValue(item->Complete));


    auto table = client->GetTable("TodoItem");
    task<IJsonValue^> updateTask(table->UpdateAsync(jsonObject));
    updateTask.then([this, item](IJsonValue^ V)
    {
            int x = items_->Size;
            for (int i = 0; i < x; ++i)
            {
                    if (items_->GetAt(i) == item)
                    {
                            items_->RemoveAt(i);
                    }
            }
    });
}
```

17. Querying the table for all records is also simple. You create a simple "SQL" query and call the ReadAsync method on the table. The response is a JSONValue that can be parsed and populated as per your needs. In our case, we update the list of items for our sample.

```cpp
void MainPage::RefreshData()
{
    String^ query = "Select * from TodoItem";
    auto client = App::MobileClient;
    auto table = client->GetTable("TodoItem");
    task<IJsonValue^> readTask(table->ReadAsync(query));
    readTask.then([this](IJsonValue^ V)
    {
            auto list = V->Stringify();
            JsonArray^ mapValue = ref new JsonArray();
            if(JsonArray::TryParse(list, &mapValue))
            {
                    auto vec = mapValue->GetView();
                    std::for_each(begin(vec), end(vec), [this](IJsonValue^ M)
                    {
                            if (M->GetObject()->GetNamedBoolean("complete") == false)
                            {
                                    String^ str = M->Stringify();
```

```
                            ToDoItems^ item = ref new ToDoItems();
                            item->Text = M->GetObject()->GetNamedString("text");
                            item->ID = M->GetObject()->GetNamedNumber("id");
                            item->Complete = M->GetObject()->GetNamedBoolean("complete");
                            items_->Append(item);


                    }
                });
                ListItems->ItemsSource = items_;
            }
        });
    }
```

18. Now you can go to the portal and verify that insertion and updating of records work.

Supporting Push Notifications using Windows Azure Mobile Services

In this section, you will learn to add push notification support in your Windows Store App using Windows Azure Mobile Services. We will begin with re-using the MobileServicesApp we developed in the previous section and add support for Push Notifications to the same.

This section assumes you have a Windows Azure account and have configured the account for Mobile Services Support. You can sign up for a trial account at http://azure.windows.com

This walkthrough demonstrates a basic mechanism of sending push notifications. This is accomplished by attaching a push notification channel to each inserted record in the Mobile Service database. The process of adding push notifications is simple and straight forward. To begin with, you should register your app for push notifications and configure Mobile Services, then add push notifications to your app. On the server side, you should also update scripts to send notifications and then finally insert data to receive notifications.

Register your app

To be able to send push notifications to Windows Store apps from Mobile Services, you must register your app at the Live Connect Developer Center. You must then configure your mobile service to integrate with Windows Push Notification Services (WNS).

1. If you have not already registered your app, navigate to the Submit an app page (http://go.microsoft.com/fwlink/p/?LinkID=266582&clcid=0x409) at the Dev Center for Windows Store apps, log on with your Microsoft account, and then click **App name**.

Submit an app

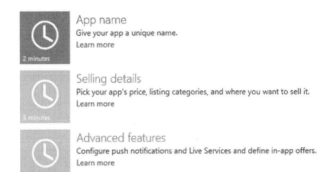

App name
Selling details
Advanced features
Age rating
Cryptography
Packages
Description
Notes to testers

App name
Give your app a unique name.
Learn more

Selling details
Pick your app's price, listing categories, and where you want to sell it.
Learn more

Advanced features
Configure push notifications and Live Services and define in-app offers.
Learn more

FIGURE 10-4 Registering your app

2. Type a name for your app in **App name**, click **Reserve app name**, and then click **Save**. This creates a new Windows Store registration for your app.

Submit an app

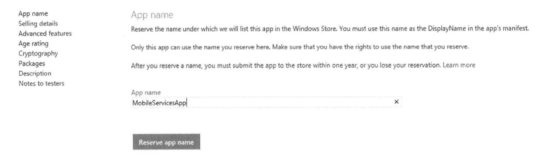

App name
Selling details
Advanced features
Age rating
Cryptography
Packages
Description
Notes to testers

App name
Reserve the name under which we will list this app in the Windows Store. You must use this name as the DisplayName in the app's manifest.

Only this app can use the name you reserve here. Make sure that you have the rights to use the name that you reserve.

After you reserve a name, you must submit the app to the store within one year, or you lose your reservation. Learn more

App name
MobileServicesApp   ×

Reserve app name

FIGURE 10-5 Reserving an app name

3. In Visual Studio 2012, open the MobileServicesApp project that you created in the preceding section. You can also get the sample app along with the rest of the samples.

4. In solution explorer, right-click the project, click **Store**, and then click **Associate App with the Store...** This displays the Associate Your App with the Windows Store Wizard.

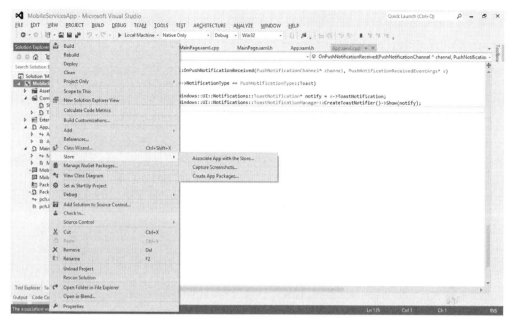

FIGURE 10-6 Associating app with the Store

5. In the wizard, click **Sign in** and then login with your Microsoft account.

6. Select the app that you registered in step 2, click **Next**, and then click **Associate**.

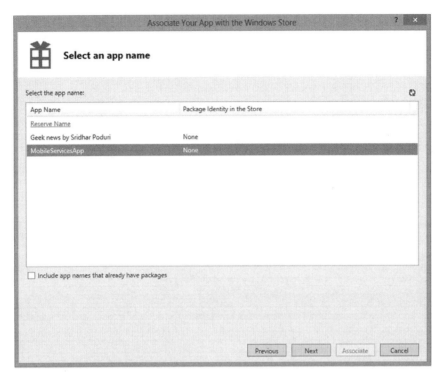

FIGURE 10-7 Selecting an app name

7. This adds the required Windows Store registration information to the application manifest.

8. Log on to the Windows Azure Management Portal (https://manage.windowsazure.com/), click **Mobile Services**, and then click your Mobile Service.

FIGURE 10-8 Windows Azure Management Portal

9. Click the **Dashboard** tab and make a note of the **Site URL** value. You will use this value to de-

fine the redirect domain.

10. Navigate to the My Applications (http://go.microsoft.com/fwlink/p/?LinkId=262039&clcid=0x409) page in the Live Connect Developer Center and click on your app in the **My applications** list.

My applications

My applications

Create application

If you want to register a Windows Store app, this is not the site you need. Go to the Windows Store Dashboard.

View Live Connect services status

		Daily users	Monthly users
MobileServicesApp 00000000400D8AC2		0	0

FIGURE 10-9 Managing connected applications

11. Click Edit settings, then API Settings and make a note of the value of Client secret.

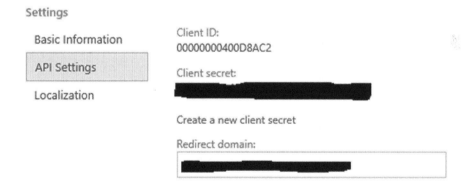

MobileServicesApp

My applications > MobileServicesApp > API Settings

Settings

Basic Information

API Settings

Localization

Client ID:
00000000400D8AC2

Client secret:
▮▮▮▮▮▮▮▮▮▮▮▮▮

Create a new client secret

Redirect domain:
▮▮▮▮▮▮▮▮▮▮

FIGURE 10-10 Accessing the Client Secret

Tip The client secret is an important security credential. Do not share the client secret with anyone or distribute it with your app.

12. In **Redirect domain**, enter the URL of your mobile service from Step 8, and then click **Save**.

13. Back in the Management Portal, click the Identity tab, enter the Client secret obtained from Windows Store, and click **Save**.

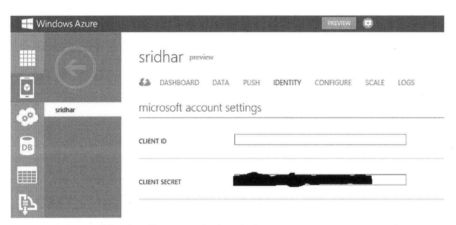

FIGURE 10-11 Specifying the Client Secret in the Windows Azure Management Portal

14. Both your mobile service and your app are now configured to work with Live Connect.

Add push notifications

Follow these steps to add push notifications in your app.

1. Open the App.xaml.cpp file and add the following namespace reference.

```
using namespace Windows::Networking::PushNotifications;
```

2. Add the following property declarations to the App.xaml.h file. These properties should be added inside your App class declaration.

```
static property Windows::Networking::PushNotifications::PushNotificationChannel^ CurrentChannel
            {
                    Windows::Networking::PushNotifications::PushNotificationChannel^ get()
                    {
                            return channel_;
                    }
                    void set(Windows::Networking::PushNotifications::PushNotificationChannel^
notificationChannel)
                    {
                            channel_ = notificationChannel;
                    }
            }
```

3. Add a new private function named AcquirePushChannel to your App class. Its implementation is given below

```
void App::AcquirePushChannel()
{
        task<PushNotificationChannel^>
channelTask(PushNotificationChannelManager::CreatePushNotificationChannelForApplicationAsync());
        channelTask.then([this](PushNotificationChannel^ ch){
                CurrentChannel = ch;
                CurrentChannel->PushNotificationReceived += ref new
TypedEventHandler<PushNotificationChannel^, PushNotificationReceivedEventArgs^>(this,
&App::OnPushNotificationReceived);
        });
}
```

4. The code inside the AcquirePushChannel acquires and stores a push channel. After it acquires the channel, it also subscribes to the PushNotificationReceived event handler. This event handler will be used to display the toast notification when the push notification is received from the Mobile Services.

5. At the top of the **OnLaunched** event handler in App.xaml.cpp, add the following call to the new **AcquirePushChannel** method:

AcquirePushChannel();

6. This guarantees that the **CurrentChannel** property is initialized each time the application is launched.

7. Open the project file MainPage.xaml.h and add the following new attributed property to the **TodoItem** class:

```
property Platform::String^ Channel
  {
        Platform::String^ get()
        {
                return channelUri_;
        }
        void set(Platform::String^ value)
        {
                channelUri_ = value;
        }
  }
```

8. When dynamic schema is enabled on your mobile service, a new 'channel' column is automatically added to the TodoItem table when a new item that contains this property is inserted.

9. Replace the **ButtonSave_Click** event handler method with the following code:

```
void MainPage::ButtonSave_Click(Platform::Object^ sender, Windows::UI::Xaml::RoutedEventArgs^ args)
{
        auto item = ref new ToDoItems();
        item->Text = TextInput->Text;
        item->Complete = false;
```

```
item->Channel = App::CurrentChannel->Uri;
//save data to AzureMobile
auto client = App::MobileClient;
auto jsonObject = ref new JsonObject();
jsonObject->Insert(L"text", JsonValue::CreateStringValue(item->Text));
jsonObject->Insert(L"complete", JsonValue::CreateBooleanValue(item->Complete));
jsonObject->Insert(L"channel", JsonValue::CreateStringValue(item->Channel));

auto table = client->GetTable("TodoItem");
task<IJsonValue^> insertTask(table->InsertAsync(jsonObject));
insertTask.then([this, item](IJsonValue^ V)
{
        auto results = V->Stringify();
        JsonObject^ savedItem = ref new JsonObject();
        if (JsonObject::TryParse(results, &savedItem))
        {
                item->ID = savedItem->GetNamedNumber("id");
                items_->Append(item);
                ListItems->ItemsSource = items_;
        }
});
}
```

10. This sets the client's current channel value on the item before it is sent to the mobile service.

11. Add the implementation for the OnPushNotificationReceived event handler in the App.xaml.cpp file as follows:

```
void App::OnPushNotificationReceived(PushNotificationChannel^ channel,
PushNotificationReceivedEventArgs^ e)
{
        if (e->NotificationType == PushNotificationType::Toast)
        {
                Windows::UI::Notifications::ToastNotification^ notify = e->ToastNotification;

                Windows::UI::Notifications::ToastNotificationManager::CreateToastNotifier()->Show(notify);
        }
}
```

12. One last action you need to perform is to declare the push notification capability in your application's manifest. Open the **Package.appxmanifest** file in the Solution Explorer. Under the **Application UI** tab, navigate to the **Notifications** section and modify the value of **Toast Capable** from Not Set to **Yes**. Save the settings and you are good to go.

13. This is all that needs to be done on the client side in your app.

Update the insert script

Follow these steps to update the insert script in the Mobile Services Management portal.

1. In the Management Portal, click the **Data** tab and then click the **TodoItem** table.

FIGURE 10-12 Updating the insert script for sending push notifications

2.   In **Todoitem**, click the **Script** tab and select **Insert**.

3.   This displays the function that is invoked when an insert occurs in the **TodoItem** table.

4.   Replace the insert function with the following code, and then click **Save**:

```
function insert(item, user, request) {
    request.execute({
        success: function() {
            // Write to the response and then send the notification in the background
            request.respond();
            push.wns.sendToastText04(item.channel, {
                text1: item.text,
                text2: "Hello World"
            }, {
                success: function(pushResponse) {
                    console.log("Sent push:", pushResponse);
                }
            });
        }
    });
}
```

5.   This registers a new insert script, which sends a push notification (the inserted text) to the channel provided in the insert request.

Testing your app

Your app is now ready to be tested with Mobile Services and push notifications. In Visual Studio 2012, press the F5 key to run the app. In the app, type text in **Insert a TodoItem**, and then click **Save**. Note that after the insert completes, the app receives a push notification from WNS.

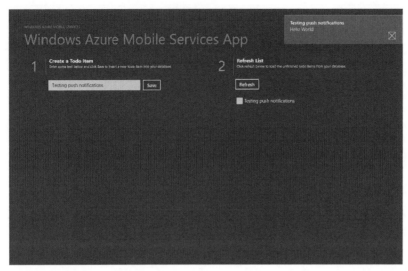

FIGURE 10-13 Testing the app

Where are we and what's Next

In this chapter, we briefly discussed how to build connected applications using Windows Azure Mobile Services and C++ /CX. With Windows Azure Mobile Services, you can create applications that need on-demand storage and can be accessed by any device that has your application installed. The APIs provided to push data to the Azure database, fetch data or query data are all really simple to use from C++ /CX and provide a lightweight solution to meeting your data storage needs.

In the last chapter of our journey, we will now focus on how to share native code between Windows 8 and Windows Phone 8.

Chapter 11

A sneak preview of Windows Phone 8.0 Shared code

Introduction
The various API sets in Windows Phone 8
Modifying the TriangleRenderer app for Windows Phone 8

Introduction

With all the goodness of the modern app development discussion covered so far, wouldn't it be great if there exists a way to share code between Windows 8 and Windows Phone 8? If you are thinking of sharing code between the two platforms, I have some good news for you. Yes, it is possible to share code and we will explore the process using a XAML+ DX application. But first, a high level introduction to Windows Phone 8 application development.

Windows 8 allows you as a developer to develop your app using a variety of programming languages and technologies. Windows Phone 8 follows a similar model. I say similar because there are a few differences between what's allowed in Windows 8 v/s Windows Phone 8. For starters,

- You can build your Phone 8 app using XAML and a choice of managed programming language such as VB.net or C#.

- For better performance and flexibility, you can use C++ components within your XAML app. The app itself needs to be developed using either C# or VB.net.

- You can go the whole hog and develop DirectX games using Direct3D and C++.

- You cannot use Javascript to develop apps for Phone 8.

The various API sets in Windows Phone 8

The Windows Phone 8 encompasses different API sets that allow you to develop apps based on your specific scenarios and requirements. The API sets can be categorized as follows:

- .NET APIs allowing apps written using managed languages

- Windows Phone Runtime that allows apps written using both native C++ and managed languages.

- Win32 and COM which is completely native only.

The .Net API for Windows Phone 8

The APIs in this set represent the managed API on Windows Phone 8. If you have developed apps for Windows Phone 7 or 7.5, this API set will be very familiar to you. In addition to existing functionality in the System and Microsoft.Phone namespace, it also contains newly added functionality tailored for Windows Phone 8.

The Windows Phone Runtime API

The Windows Phone Runtime is a new, native API built into the Windows Phone 8 core operating system. This API set contains a subset of the entire native API in Windows Phone 8. Similar to how the Windows Runtime is implemented in Windows 8, this API set is implemented in C++ and is projected into C#, VB.net and C++ /CX.

If you are familiar with the Windows Runtime and C++ /CX (you should be if you have come this far!), then consuming the Windows Phone Runtime appears very familiar and extremely easy to learn as the frameworks are very similar.

There are three distinct aspects to consider between the Windows Runtime and the Windows Phone Runtime.

1. There is a large set of APIs in the Windows Runtime that do not have corresponding APIs in the Windows Phone Runtime. Specifically, the APIs available in the Windows Phone Runtime are focused on helping you as a developer, build compelling experiences for tailored the phone.

2. There is a set of APIs in the Windows Runtime that has been adopted for Windows Phone 8.0. These APIs might have a few members/types removed and some new members added which are specific for the phone scenarios.

3. There are new APIs that are available only in Windows Phone Runtime and not in the Windows Runtime. These include, but are not limited to, speech recognition, VOIP support etc.

It is the API sets in items 2 and 3 above that make up the new Windows Phone Runtime API.

Win32 and COM API

In addition to the managed API set and WinPRT, you can also use a variety of APIs from the native Win32 and COM API. These APIs are available for native code only and give you access to low-level features of the phone platform. An example of such an API is the WinSock API that enables you to develop apps using sockets.

Modifying the TriangleRenderer app for Windows Phone 8

In the "XAML DirectX and C++ /CX" samples, we have packaged a TriangleRenderer app that renders a triangle on screen. Let us now create the same app for Windows Phone 8. The primary goal of this exercise is to learn how much code can be "shared" between a DirectX based app written for Windows 8 and Windows Phone 8.

Before you begin

There are a few prerequisites for completing this exercise. Make sure

1. You have downloaded the Windows Phone 8 SDK and developer tools.

2. If you have a Windows Phone 8 device, make sure it is unlocked.

3. Download the TriangleRenderer sample from the samples download location.

4. Do not worry if you do not have a physical device. The developer tools come with excellent simulators and you can use them to debug/test your apps.

Creating the Windows Phone 8.0 app using Direct3D and C++

Let us now create the Windows Phone 8.0 project. Follow these steps to create the initial project.

1. Launch Visual Studio 2012.

2. Click File->New Project.

3. From the Installed Templates, choose Visual C++ and then Windows Phone.

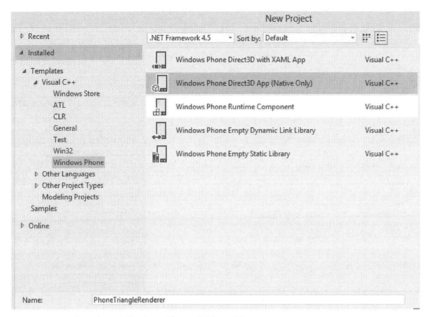

FIGURE 11-1 Creating a Windows Phone 8 Direct3D app

4. Provide a name for your project. I have given the name PhoneTriangleRenderer. Click OK.

5. Visual Studio 2012 will create the initial project. This project will have a cube renderer already written for you.

6. If you compile the solution as-is and deploy it to a Windows Phone 8 device or emulator, it will display a rotating cube.

7. Let us now begin the process of sharing code from our earlier Windows 8 project.

8. Remove the CubeRenderer.cpp and CubeRenderer.h files from the solution as we do not need them.

9. Open Solution Explorer and double click the SimplePixelShader.hlsl file to open it. Replace the contents of the file with the hlsl code below and save the file. This portion of code is exactly same as the one we used in our earlier TriangleRenderer sample.

```
struct PixelShaderInput
{
    float4 pos : SV_POSITION;
};

float4 SimplePixelShader(PixelShaderInput input) : SV_TARGET
{
    // shade it yellow
    return float4(1.0f, 1.0f, 0.0f, 1.0f);
}
```

10. Right click the SimplePixelShader.hlsl file and choose Properties. In the Properties Window, make changes to the HLSL entry points as shown in the figure. Click OK to save and apply your changes.

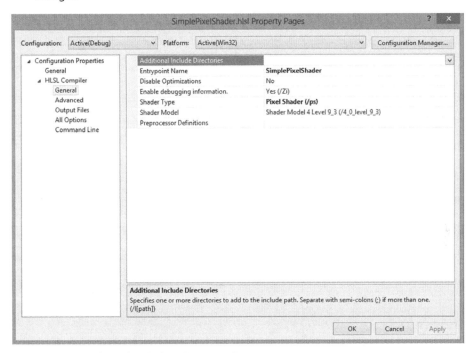

FIGURE 11-2 Modifying the Pixel Shader properties

11. Open the SimpleVertexShader.hlsl file and replace the contents with the hlsl code below. This code also is shared from the earlier TriangleRenderer sample.

```
struct VertexShaderInput
{
    float2 pos : POSITION;
};

struct PixelShaderInput
{
    float4 pos : SV_POSITION;
};

PixelShaderInput SimpleVertexShader(VertexShaderInput input)
{
    PixelShaderInput vertexShaderOutput;

    //set vertex depth = 0.5
    vertexShaderOutput.pos = float4(input.pos, 0.5f, 1.0f);

    return vertexShaderOutput;
```

}

12. Right click the SimpleVertexShader.hlsl file and choose Properties. In the Properties Window, make changes to the HLSL entry points as shown in the figure. Click OK to save and apply your changes.

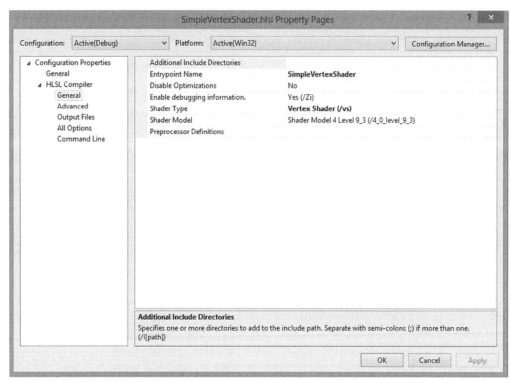

FIGURE 11-3 Modifying the vertex shader properties

13. At this point, you might observe a difference if you look closely. Our Windows 8 sample supported the Shader Model 4.0 whereas the Windows Phone 8 only supports Shader Model 4 Level 9. Minor detail but still significant!

14. Add a new header file to the project named TriangleRenderer.h and add the code below to the file.

```
#pragma once

#include "Direct3DBase.h"
#include "BasicMath.h"
#include "DirectXHelpers.h"

// This class renders a simple triangle.
ref class TriangleRenderer sealed : public Direct3DBase
```

```
{
public:
    TriangleRenderer();

    // Direct3DBase methods.
    virtual void CreateDeviceResources() override;
    virtual void CreateWindowSizeDependentResources() override;
    virtual void Render() override;

private:
    bool m_loadingComplete;

    Microsoft::WRL::ComPtr<ID3D11InputLayout> m_inputLayout;
    Microsoft::WRL::ComPtr<ID3D11Buffer> m_vertexBuffer;
    Microsoft::WRL::ComPtr<ID3D11Buffer> m_indexBuffer;
    Microsoft::WRL::ComPtr<ID3D11VertexShader> m_vertexShader;
    Microsoft::WRL::ComPtr<ID3D11PixelShader> m_pixelShader;
    Microsoft::WRL::ComPtr<ID3D11Buffer> m_constantBuffer;

    uint32 m_indexCount;
};
```

15. Add a new source file to the solution, named TriangleRenderer.cpp and add the following code.

```cpp
#include "pch.h"
#include "TriangleRenderer.h"

using namespace DirectX;
using namespace Microsoft::WRL;
using namespace Windows::Foundation;
using namespace Windows::UI::Core;
using namespace DXHelpers;

// set up a triangle
float2 m_triangleVertices[] =
    {
        float2(-0.5f, -0.5f),
        float2( 0.0f,  0.5f),
        float2( 0.5f, -0.5f)
    };

unsigned short m_triangleIndices[] = {0, 1, 2};

TriangleRenderer::TriangleRenderer() :
    m_loadingComplete(false),
    m_indexCount(0)
{
}

void TriangleRenderer::CreateDeviceResources()
{
    Direct3DBase::CreateDeviceResources();

    // load vshader
    DXHelpers::ReadDataAsync("SimpleVertexShader.cso").then([this](Platform::Array<byte>^ fileData) {
```

```
        m_d3dDevice->CreateVertexShader(fileData->Data, fileData->Length, nullptr, &m_vertexShader);
        const D3D11_INPUT_ELEMENT_DESC basicVertexLayoutDesc[] = {{ "POSITION", 0,
DXGI_FORMAT_R32G32_FLOAT, 0,  0, D3D11_INPUT_PER_VERTEX_DATA, 0 }};
        m_d3dDevice->CreateInputLayout(basicVertexLayoutDesc, ARRAYSIZE(basicVertexLayoutDesc),
fileData->Data, fileData->Length, &m_inputLayout);

    });

    // load pshader
    DXHelpers::ReadDataAsync("SimplePixelShader.cso").then([this](Platform::Array<byte>^ fileData){
        m_d3dDevice->CreatePixelShader(fileData->Data, fileData->Length, nullptr, &m_pixelShader);
    });

    // create static vertex buffer
    D3D11_BUFFER_DESC vertexBufferDesc = {0};
    vertexBufferDesc.ByteWidth = sizeof(float2) * ARRAYSIZE(m_triangleVertices);
    vertexBufferDesc.Usage = D3D11_USAGE_DEFAULT;
    vertexBufferDesc.BindFlags = D3D11_BIND_VERTEX_BUFFER;
    vertexBufferDesc.CPUAccessFlags = 0;
    vertexBufferDesc.MiscFlags = 0;
    vertexBufferDesc.StructureByteStride = 0;

    D3D11_SUBRESOURCE_DATA vertexBufferData;
    vertexBufferData.pSysMem = m_triangleVertices;
    vertexBufferData.SysMemPitch = 0;
    vertexBufferData.SysMemSlicePitch = 0;

    m_d3dDevice->CreateBuffer(&vertexBufferDesc, &vertexBufferData, &m_vertexBuffer);

    // create index buffer
    D3D11_BUFFER_DESC indexBufferDesc;
    indexBufferDesc.ByteWidth = sizeof(unsigned short) * ARRAYSIZE(m_triangleIndices); //
sizeof(triangleIndices)
    indexBufferDesc.Usage = D3D11_USAGE_DEFAULT;
    indexBufferDesc.BindFlags = D3D11_BIND_INDEX_BUFFER;
    indexBufferDesc.CPUAccessFlags = 0;
    indexBufferDesc.MiscFlags = 0;
    indexBufferDesc.StructureByteStride = 0;

    D3D11_SUBRESOURCE_DATA indexBufferData;
    indexBufferData.pSysMem = m_triangleIndices;
    indexBufferData.SysMemPitch = 0;
    indexBufferData.SysMemSlicePitch = 0;

    m_d3dDevice->CreateBuffer(&indexBufferDesc, &indexBufferData, &m_indexBuffer);
}

void TriangleRenderer::CreateWindowSizeDependentResources()
{
    Direct3DBase::CreateWindowSizeDependentResources();

}

void TriangleRenderer::Render()
{
```

```
    // set render target
    m_d3dContext->OMSetRenderTargets(1, m_renderTargetView.GetAddressOf(), nullptr); // no depth stencil

    // set vbuffer input layout
    m_d3dContext->IASetInputLayout(m_inputLayout.Get());

    // set vbuffer
    UINT stride = sizeof(float2);
    UINT vBufferOffset = 0;
    m_d3dContext->IASetVertexBuffers(0, 1, m_vertexBuffer.GetAddressOf(), &stride, &vBufferOffset);

    // set index buffer
    m_d3dContext->IASetIndexBuffer(m_indexBuffer.Get(), DXGI_FORMAT_R16_UINT, 0);

    // set topology to triangle list
    m_d3dContext->IASetPrimitiveTopology(D3D11_PRIMITIVE_TOPOLOGY_TRIANGLELIST);

    // set shader stage states
    m_d3dContext->VSSetShader(m_vertexShader.Get(), nullptr, 0);
    m_d3dContext->PSSetShader(m_pixelShader.Get(), nullptr, 0);

    // draw
    m_d3dContext->DrawIndexed(ARRAYSIZE(m_triangleIndices), 0, 0);
}
```

16. If you compare the contents of this file with the sources from the earlier TriangleRenderer sample, you will notice that the functions have not changed at all. We have simply used the code as-is with very minor changes.

17. The first big change or rather omission is the Initialize method of the TriangleRenderer class. We do not need this as there is no XAML SwapChainBackgroundPanel element involved in our phone app. Also our app is a pure Direct3D app and does not contain any XAML UI elements. Hence we no longer need to obtain a pointer to the XAML SwapChainBackgroundPanel control.

18. The CreateDeviceResources function and the Render function are exact copies from our earlier sample with no changes at all.

19. Now, we need to create a few helper functions and our app will be ready to go.

20. Add a new empty header file named BasicMath.h. Add the code from the BasicMath.h header from our earlier example to this newly created header file.

21. Add a new empty header file named DirectXHelpers.h and add the following code. This code is also shared from our earlier example.

```
#pragma once

#include <wrl/client.h>
#include <ppl.h>
#include <ppltasks.h>

namespace DXHelpers
```

```
{
    inline void ThrowIfFailed(HRESULT hr)
    {
            if (FAILED(hr))
            {
                    // Set a breakpoint on this line to catch Win32 API errors.
                    throw Platform::Exception::CreateException(hr);
            }
    }


    // Function that reads from a binary file asynchronously.
    inline Concurrency::task<Platform::Array<byte>^> ReadDataAsync(Platform::String^ filename)
    {
            using namespace Windows::Storage;
            using namespace Concurrency;

            auto folder = Windows::ApplicationModel::Package::Current->InstalledLocation;

            return create_task(folder->GetFileAsync(filename)).then([] (StorageFile^ file)
            {
                    return file->OpenReadAsync();
            }).then([] (Streams::IRandomAccessStreamWithContentType^ stream)
            {
                    unsigned int bufferSize = static_cast<unsigned int>(stream->Size);
                    auto fileBuffer = ref new Streams::Buffer(bufferSize);
                    return stream->ReadAsync(fileBuffer, bufferSize,
Streams::InputStreamOptions::None);
            }).then([] (Streams::IBuffer^ fileBuffer) -> Platform::Array<byte>^
            {
                    auto fileData = ref new Platform::Array<byte>(fileBuffer->Length);
                    Streams::DataReader::FromBuffer(fileBuffer)->ReadBytes(fileData);
                    return fileData;
            });
    }
}
```

22. Open the DirectXBase.cpp file and navigate to the Present method. Replace the Present method with the code below. As is the norm now, even this code is shared with our previous example.

```
// Method to deliver the final image to the display.
void Direct3DBase::Present()
{
    // The first argument instructs DXGI to block until VSync, putting the application
    // to sleep until the next VSync. This ensures we don't waste any cycles rendering
    // frames that will never be displayed to the screen.
    HRESULT hr = m_swapChain->Present(1, 0);

    // If the device was removed either by a disconnect or a driver upgrade, we
    // must recreate all device resources.
    if (hr == DXGI_ERROR_DEVICE_REMOVED)
    {
            HandleDeviceLost();
    }
    else
    {
```

```
                DXHelpers::ThrowIfFailed(hr);
    }
}
```

23. We are mostly done. Now open the PhoneTriangleRenderer.h file and replace the #include "CubeRenderer.h" declaration with #include "TriangleRenderer.h"

24. Change the type of the variable m_renderer from CubeRenderer to TriangleRenderer.

25. Open the PhoneTriangleRenderer.cpp file and in the Initialize method, change the instantiation of the m_renderer object from CubeRenderer to TriangleRenderer, as follows:

```
m_renderer = ref new TriangleRenderer();
```

26. In the same file, navigate to the Run method and delete the BasicTimer objects. We do not have any timer related UI controls to be updated and hence this object and associated code is not needed. The updated Run method is listed below.

```
void PhoneTriangleRenderer::Run()
{
    while (!m_windowClosed)
    {
            if (m_windowVisible)
            {

    CoreWindow::GetForCurrentThread()->Dispatcher->ProcessEvents(CoreProcessEventsOption::ProcessAllIfPr
esent);
                        m_renderer->Render();
                        m_renderer->Present(); // This call is synchronized to the display frame rate.
            }
            else
            {

    CoreWindow::GetForCurrentThread()->Dispatcher->ProcessEvents(CoreProcessEventsOption::ProcessOneAndA
llPending);
            }
    }
}
```

27. Now build the app and launch it in one of the emulators. Our Triangle is rendered on the Phone device screen.

28. The complete sample is also available for download along with the rest of the samples.

FIGURE 11-4 The triangle rendered in the Windows Phone 8 emulator

For a comparison, here is a snapshot of the projects in Visual Studio 2012. On the left is the Windows 8 Solution Explorer View and to the right is the Windows Phone 8 Solution Explorer View.

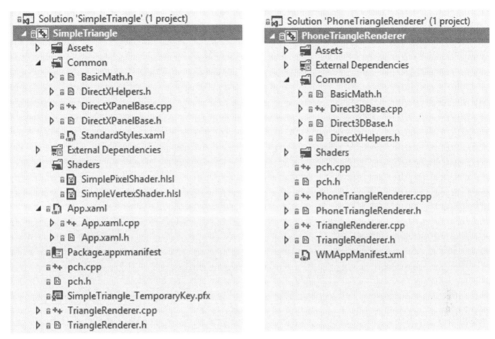

FIGURE 11-5 Solution explorer comparison between Windows 8 and Windows Phone 8

Creating the Windows Phone 8 app using C# and C++ component

In the previous section, we have walked through creating a Windows Phone 8 application using Direct3D and C++. We borrowed and liberally re-used most of the code from the TriangleRenderer sample developed earlier. Windows Phone 8 programming model also allows you to build a backend C++ component and then consume it within an application written in a managed programming language. Our next walkthrough does exactly that.

1. Launch Visual Studio 2012.

2. Click File->New Project.

3. From the Installed Templates, choose Visual C++ and then Windows Phone.

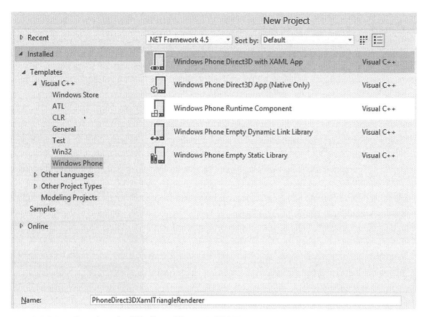

FIGURE 11-6 Creating the Windows Phone 8 XAML app

4. Provide a name for your project. I have given the name PhoneDirect3DXamlTriangleRenderer. Click OK.

5. Visual Studio 2012 will create the initial solution with two projects. One project is the Direct3D component named **PhoneDirect3DXamlAppComponent** and the other project is the actual application project named **PhoneDirect3DXamlAppInterop** which is a C# project.

6. The C# project contains the entry point for the application and if you notice carefully, the MainPage.xaml renders the Direct3D component. This rendering is achieved by the **Drawing-SurfaceBackgroundGrid** control that is available only for Windows Phone 8 apps.

7. The **DrawingSurfaceBackgroundGrid** control allows you to render Direct3D graphics on to the viewport and our application utilizes the same.

8. If you compile the solution as-is and deploy it to a Windows Phone 8 device or emulator, it will display a rotating cube.

9. Let us now begin the process of sharing code from our earlier Windows 8 project.

10. Remove the CubeRenderer.cpp and CubeRenderer.h files from the solution as we do not need them.

11. Open Solution Explorer and double click the SimplePixelShader.hlsl file to open it. Replace the contents of the file with the hlsl code from the PhoneTriangleRenderer walkthrough above and save the file.

12. Right click the SimplePixelShader.hlsl file and choose Properties. In the Properties Window, make changes to the HLSL entry points as performed in the PhoneTriangleRenderer walkthrough. Click OK to save and apply your changes.

13. Open the SimpleVertexShader.hlsl file and replace the contents with the hlsl code from the PhoneTriangleRenderer walkthrough above and save the file.

14. Add the TriangleRenderer.h, TriangleRenderer.cpp, BasicMath.h and DirectXHelpers.h file to the **PhoneDirect3DXamlAppComponent** project.

15. Remove the DirectXHelper.h file from the **PhoneDirect3DXamlAppComponent** project.

16. Replace all instances of the namespace DX with DXHelpers.

17. We are mostly done. Now open the PhoneTriangleRenderer.h file and replace the #include "CubeRenderer.h" declaration with #include "TriangleRenderer.h"

18. Change the type of the variable m_renderer from CubeRenderer to TriangleRenderer.

19. Open the PhoneDirect3DXamlAppComponent.cpp file and in the Connect method, change the instantiation of the m_renderer object from CubeRenderer to TriangleRenderer, as follows:

```
m_renderer = ref new TriangleRenderer();
```

20. In the same file, update the PrepareResources method as follows:

```
void Direct3DBackground::PrepareResources(LARGE_INTEGER presentTargetTime)
{
        m_timer->Update();
}
```

21. That's it. If you build the solution and deploy it to a Windows Phone 8 device, you should see the triangle rendered!

You can get the complete code along with the rest of the code samples.

Where are we and what's Next

Windows 8 and Windows Phone 8 allow you to reuse a good portion of your native code and build common code bases for such shared modules. The platform specific portions can be layered to access these shared code modules thereby giving you the benefit of developing apps near simultaneously for both platforms.

Epilogue

As a first time author, it has been a great learning experience to bring this story of Windows 8, the Modern Application development platform and the resurgence of Modern C++ to life. It has also been a challenging task. Learning on a constantly moving platform which was actively under development and trying to create learning material simultaneously is both exciting and demanding. While I could have taken the route of doing a step-by-step tutorial or talk about what makes your Windows 8 app a good citizen in the eyes of your users, I chose not do so. There are books and enough documentation on MSDN and other sources that provide detailed design guidance on how to format icons, polish your UI to make your apps comply with the Modern UI principles and philosophy. Instead, I wanted this book to tell the story of how Modern C++ is making a strong comeback on the Microsoft platform and how you can put the various pieces of the puzzle together and write apps for Windows 8 and beyond.

I underestimated the time and effort needed to bring this work to closure. Although I was mapping the native renaissance closely due to my association with the Windows Reader team, I must honestly profess I had to connect the dots to understand the story better. This book is born partly out of my desire to share those findings with the broader C++ community. I sincerely hope this book helps developers connect the seemingly varying native technologies being incubated and released by various groups at Microsoft and build amazing apps showcasing the power and flexibility of native code as we move to a devices centric world.

To that end, as I mention above, I had to knowingly omitted topics that would help a budding developer create their first Windows Store app using C++. If there is significant demand for such a title, I might consider writing such a book in the future. Please reach out with your feedback at win8book@sridharpoduri.com. For now, however, revel in the significant native investments made in Windows 8 and bring forth your existing C++ skills to build differentiated application experiences for your users.

C++ FTW!

A

Agile Pointers	79
AppContainer	3, 10, 272, 300
Application Capabilities	8
AppState	3, 11

auto type inference 11, 21, 22, 25, 26, 27, 32, 33, 34, 38, 46, 47, 53, 59, 67, 71, 75, 76, 77, 80, 82, 83, 84, 91, 99, 101, 118, 119, 130, 157, 160, 183, 188, 191, 192, 220, 228, 230, 234, 260, 264, 266, 341, 369, 370, 371, 378, 392

B

Bezier curves	215, 218, 219
Boxing	52

C

C++ /CX inheritance	54, 56, 57
C++ lambdas	11, 26, 27, 29, 38, 228, 231
C++AMP concepts	230, 261, 267
COM	1, 284

Component Extensions3, 4, 5, 7, 11, 12, 4, 23, 24, 39, 40, 41, 42, 43, 44, 45, 46, 47, 51, 52, 53, 54, 55, 58, 59, 60, 61, 65, 66, 67, 68, 69, 72, 73, 75, 76, 79, 80, 81, 82, 85, 86, 89, 97, 98, 99, 103, 104, 110, 111, 112, 117, 120, 121, 122, 123, 127, 144, 155, 157, 158, 161, 162, 167, 173, 174, 182, 271, 273, 278, 285, 287, 292, 327, 334, 337, 338, 360, 362, 381, 383, 384

Contracts	2, 12, 16, 17
CoreApplication	4, 254
CoreWindow	4, 208, 254, 393

D

Data Binding	4, 155, 156
Debugging background tasks	351
Debugging GPU code	242, 244, 245, 246, 247, 248
Debugging PLM events	7, 350
Debugging Windows Store apps	7, 343, 345, 346,

347, 349, 351

Delegates	69, 72, 280
Dependency Properties	167

DirectX 5, 6, 9, 11, 12, 13, 15, 7, 19, 39, 40, 173, 174, 175, 176, 177, 182, 186, 195, 196, 208, 209, 222, 224, 230, 232, 242, 254, 256, 257, 258, 260, 261, 266, 267, 271, 285, 345, 352, 354, 383, 384, 389

E

Enumerations	275
Exceptions	25, 72, 73

G

Generated source code	317
GPU	224
GridView control	4, 141, 142, 143, 144, 145

H

Handled Property	152
Header property	134, 135, 142, 313

Height property 21, 50, 94, 125, 126, 128, 130, 132, 133, 134, 136, 138, 140, 142, 143, 144, 147, 152, 164, 166, 172, 177, 178, 203, 204, 210, 211, 268, 269, 308, 309, 354, 364

Herb Sutter	14, 24, 225

HorizontalAlignment Property 20, 94, 113, 120, 132, 133, 134, 138, 140, 147, 165, 166, 170, 199, 308, 309

I

IClosable	47, 104, 107, 108, 109

IInspectable 1, 46, 51, 103, 104, 179, 277, 280, 282, 283, 287, 292, 306, 307, 329, 330

ImageBrush class	7, 176, 177
IMap interface	66
Ink support	217, 218
INotifyPropertyChanged	156, 163
Input events	4, 2, 5, 151, 152, 153, 172, 216
ItemsControl class	141, 142, 144, 156, 358

ItemsPanel property   144

ItemsSource collection 102, 142, 143, 144, 160, 370,
    371, 379

IUnknown   1, 51, 104, 107, 108, 187, 191, 212, 261,
    267, 277, 280, 292, 293, 297, 306, 329

IValueConverter interface   155

IVector interface   66, 67, 99, 100, 102, 218, 276

M

MainPage.xaml file19, 64, 93, 94, 112, 113, 114, 115,
    117, 118, 121, 124, 154, 156, 158, 160, 161, 164,
    166, 178, 199, 203, 205, 206, 249, 288, 308, 309,
    364, 368, 378, 396

MainPage.xaml.cpp file 112, 113, 114, 118, 160, 161,
    203, 206

MainPage.xaml.h file   112, 113, 114, 115, 117, 118,
    160, 206, 368, 378

Manipulation events   151

Map class   66, 67, 101

Markup extensions   4, 5, 20, 94, 111, 119, 125, 130,
    134, 136, 137, 139, 140, 142, 143, 144, 146, 153,
    154, 155, 156, 157, 161, 163, 164, 166, 168, 169,
    170, 199, 309, 364, 366

Modern C++9, 11, 12, 23, 24, 25, 26, 33, 36, 110, 271

P

Partial Class   62

Performance Tips   7, 352, 353, 355, 356, 358, 360

Pickers   2, 3, 83, 84

PLM   3, 11, 175

PPL tasks   84, 88, 89, 91, 260, 392

Properties 64, 65, 153, 167, 222, 243, 279, 301, 314,
    320, 325, 326, 351, 386, 387, 397

S

ScrollViewer control   6, 134, 144, 151, 153, 182

Signature XAML Controls   4, 5, 131, 133, 134, 141,
    142, 143, 144, 145, 149, 150, 151, 165, 171, 194,
    358, 359, 364

Smart pointers   11, 25, 33, 34, 35, 51, 191, 253

Styling XAML Controls   136, 137, 138, 139, 140, 146,
    154, 169, 170

T

Templates   4, 68, 112, 117, 136, 137, 156, 313, 314,
    362, 385, 396

Transformations   7, 135, 136

U

Unit testing C++ apps   6, 7, 11, 312, 331, 338

User controls   163

V

Vector class   66, 67, 77, 99, 100, 101, 102, 160, 188,
    276, 356, 369

Virtualization   7, 352, 358

Virtualization Support   7, 358

Visual State Manager   139, 199

W

WARP   258

Weak Reference   79, 110

WIC   5, 177, 182, 185, 208, 260

Windows 8 XAML   3, 4, 5, 6, 7, 9, 10, 11, 12, 14, 4, 5,
    18, 19, 20, 22, 39, 40, 41, 42, 55, 62, 63, 93, 103,
    110, 111, 112, 113, 114, 115, 116, 117, 118, 119,
    120, 121, 122, 123, 124, 125, 126, 127, 130, 131,
    132, 134, 135, 136, 137, 141, 142, 143, 144, 151,
    152, 153, 154, 155, 156, 158, 160, 161, 162, 163,
    165, 166, 167, 168, 170, 171, 173, 174, 175, 176,
    177, 178, 182, 186, 195, 196, 197, 199, 200, 208,
    210, 224, 248, 253, 257, 271, 272, 285, 287, 288,
    290, 291, 304, 352, 353, 354, 355, 356, 357, 358,
    359, 360, 362, 363, 368, 382, 383, 384, 391, 396

Windows Application Activation   3

Windows Azure Mobile Services   8, 361, 372

Windows Phone 8 8, 12, 15, 311, 381, 382, 383, 384,
    385, 388, 394, 395, 396, 397, 398

Windows Runtime   3, 4, 6, 7, 10, 11, 16, 1, 2, 11, 12,
    19, 24, 39, 40, 42, 43, 45, 46, 47, 51, 53, 55, 57,
    64, 66, 68, 69, 72, 73, 75, 76, 77, 80, 81, 82, 85,

86, 88, 89, 90, 93, 98, 99, 100, 101, 103, 104, 110,
120, 122, 160, 173, 188, 266, 273, 274, 275, 276,
277, 278, 279, 280, 281, 282, 283, 284, 285, 286,
287, 289, 290, 292, 296, 300, 305, 306, 307, 311,
327, 329, 331, 334, 335, 337, 338, 343, 353, 354

WinRT Arrays   76, 278

WinRT async pattern   88, 89, 90, 91, 96, 101, 102

WinRT Dispatcher   84, 254, 393

WinRT Events   4, 75, 111, 151, 152, 153, 279, 280

WinRT File Objects   83, 84, 91, 183, 189, 220, 260,
354, 392

WinRT interfaces   46, 59, 61, 62, 277, 280, 281, 283

WinRT patterns   7, 52, 283, 284, 354

WinRT Streams   84, 91, 215, 220, 222

WRL   6, 11, 271, 272, 284, 286, 287, 305, 327

WRL classes   286, 287

X

XAML animations   5, 171, 172, 173

XAML Controls   15, 5, 6, 20, 50, 94, 102, 113, 115,
116, 118, 119, 120, 121, 122, 123, 125, 126, 128,
130, 131, 132, 133, 134, 137, 138, 139, 140, 141,
142, 145, 152, 155, 156, 157, 163, 164, 165, 166,
168, 169, 170, 171, 172, 199, 203, 204, 205, 206,
207, 249, 289, 291, 308, 309, 310, 364, 366

XAML Panels   4, 5, 20, 94, 113, 118, 119, 120, 126,
127, 128, 129, 130, 131, 134, 136, 137, 138, 140,
142, 143, 144, 146, 152, 154, 156, 157, 161, 164,
166, 168, 169, 172, 178, 196, 199, 202, 203, 204,
289, 291, 308, 309, 358, 364, 365

XAML Syntax   4, 13, 119, 123, 125

XAML_DirectX+C++AMP sample   6, 225, 257, 258

XAML+DirectX sample   5, 173, 174, 196, 197, 198,
199, 201, 202, 204, 222, 223

XAML-DirectX interop   5, 7, 20, 174, 176, 177, 178,
179, 181, 182, 190, 191, 192, 194, 195, 196, 199,
200, 205, 208, 210, 212, 216, 224, 391

Made in the USA
San Bernardino, CA
31 January 2014